Praise for *To the End of Time*:

"So finely crafted and so amazingly well reported it beats most of the spy novels I've read."

—Detroit News

"A jet stream of juicy anecdotes, sharp perceptions and brilliant character sketches."

—New York magazine

"Intimate . . . sometimes startling and occasionally amusing chronicle of the courtship and union of what was widely perceived to be two disparate American cultures. . . . [A] penetrating and to those who care somewhat jarring account of the nuptials. . . . Critic's Choice."

—Time

"A provocative inside account of who did what to whom during the celebrated and contentious merger. The author captures the ego, the ambition, the greed, quirks and occasionally strengths of his protagonists in a jaunty, confident prose."

—Fortune

"Formidable reporting, intense and lucid."

—San Francisco Chronicle

"A masterful account . . . powerful and riveting. One could not ask for a better, more timely book."

—New York Law Journal

"A thriller, so gifted is [the author] at drawing the attention of the reader and dazzling him with fascination of corporate goings on."

—William F. Buckley (syndicated columnist)

Also by Richard M. Clurman

BEYOND MALICE:
The Media's Years of Reckoning

TO THE END OF
TIME

The Seduction and Conquest of a Media Empire

Richard M. Clurman

A TOUCHSTONE BOOK
Published by Simon & Schuster
New York   London   Toronto   Sydney   Tokyo   Singapore

To Shirley, who cares

TOUCHSTONE
Simon & Schuster Building
Rockefeller Center
1230 Avenue of the Americas
New York, New York 10020

First Touchstone Edition 1993

Designed by Laurie Jewell
Manufactured in the United States of America

1   3   5   7   9   10   8   6   4   2

Library of Congress Cataloging in Publication Data
Clurman, Richard M.
To the end of Time : the seduction and conquest of a media empire
/ Richard M. Clurman.
p.   cm.
1. Time, inc.—History. 2. Publishers and publishing—United
States—Mergers—History—20th century. 3. Consolidation and merger
of corporations—United States—History. 4. Mass media—United States—
Mergers—History—20th century. 5. Warner Communications, inc.—
History.   I. Title.
Z473.T54C58   1992
070.5'0973—dc20   91-41293
CIP
ISBN 0-671-69227-5
ISBN 0-671-86739-3(PBK)

Contents

PART 3

TIME WARNER INC. 259

ANCESTORS

TIME INC. FOUNDER
Henry R. Luce

*"Getting bigger and more profitable
was never the main point about Time Inc.
and is not likely to become so."*

Portrait by Aaron Shikler

Portrait by Aaron Shikler

CHAIRMAN
Andrew Heiskell

*"Yardsticks don't invent
magazines. People do. It's not like
the cereal or soap business."*

EDITOR-IN-CHIEF
Hedley Donovan

*"It didn't look to me as
if the alternatives had been
adequately explored."*

INHERITORS

Steve Fenn

CHAIRMAN
J. Richard Munro

*"Let's make this goddamn
deal happen. . . . Time Inc. is gone.
Long live Time Warner."*

Henry Grossman

PRESIDENT
Nicholas J. Nicholas

*"In 1995 and in the year 2000,
when we have access to every
home in the world, that's when
the big numbers kick in."*

VICE CHAIRMAN
Gerald M. Levin

*"The digital intersection
of print and video is where
this company is headed.
It's just so clear."*

EDITOR-IN-CHIEF
Jason McManus

*"I don't understand the
protocol about how such major
corporate events are conducted.
I can imagine like a Bulgarian
wedding you don't ever see
the bride beforehand."*

DEAL MAKERS

WARNER CHAIRMAN
Steven J. Ross

"When you look at it as a businessman, it was there and we did it. Other people describe it differently."

FINANCIAL ADVISER
Oded Aboodi

"Steve is always searching for a way to improve a deal and make it better."

COUNSELOR
Arthur L. Liman

"I know Steve in a way few people know him."

Whosoever, in writing a modern history, shall follow truth too near the heels, it may haply strike out his teeth.

—Sir Walter Raleigh, *History of the World*

Prologue

"**A** CIRCUS MAXIMUS," one headline writer called it. *Variety*, the slangy bible of show biz, screamed, "NO BIGNESS LIKE SHOW BIGNESS. Ego, hostility, greed, fear and power-lust: Suddenly the war over the singular prize of Time Inc. has all the elements of a silver screen epic."

Robert Lenzner, the experienced and usually restrained financial reporter, wrote that it was "The greatest spectacle in the history of the takeover game. The epic proportions of the drama attracted Wall Street's investment bankers sweeping the world for bidders and big bucks, while the legal eagles invent new offensive and defensive strategies." *USA Today* weighed in with "Henry Luce wouldn't be very happy. Time Inc., Luce's beloved empire, is on the block like a side of beef."

Even the *Times of London* billed it as a "Hollywood takeover epic." On the CBS Evening News, the sums of money involved were described as just about equaling "the total U.S. foreign aid program in 1989." Interest at home in Manhattan's Time & Life Building ran so high that the *Wall Street Journal* sold out in the lobby before 8:30 A.M. day after day.

What was all the shouting about? Only the creation of the biggest media empire ever, the corporate interfaith marriage of sixty-seven-year-old Time Inc., a WASPy blue-chip American institution, for years the largest combined magazine and book publisher on earth, to Steven J. Ross's poker-chip Warner Communications Inc., the swinging pop entertainment conglomerate whose movies and sounds of music ricocheted around the world.

All that was up front—out in the open in newspapers and on TV news programs. But behind the façade of the daily news was a rich, mixed—and often mixed-up—battling cast of stars, feature players

and an anguished cast of extras. Many in the cast were working from
secret scripts.

The answer to the question "What is Steve Ross really like?" was
more complex than those who asked it knew. So were the facts of
the familiar assertion that "Steve really took those Time guys to the
cleaners."

"If you get underneath the deal," says one of the leading deal
makers, "to the cultural consequences, to the human reality, to the
angst, that's the unwritten, real story."

Here is that story.

part 1

DIFFERENT FOLKS

chapter 1

Roots

THE WALLS OF THE forty-eight-story Time & Life Building in Manhattan's Rockefeller Center have been adorned in recent years by only three oil portraits commissioned by Time Inc. One was of Henry R. ("Harry") Luce, who died a long time ago in 1967 at age sixty-eight. Luce was more than the founder and editor-in-chief—"The Proprietor" of the world's largest publishing company. Before television in the 1970s became the country's primary information and entertainment medium, the four magazines Luce created were the most dominant media force in America.

- *Time,* for news, organized and within easy reach for the first time, heavily larded with opinion. For decades, it was the most argumentative nationwide news voice in the U.S. More important, it set the pace for magazine, newspaper and even TV journalism all over the world.

- *Life,* a pictorial window on the world at work, play and in anguish ("To see life; to see the world; to eyewitness great events"). Its new photojournalism and its thirst for cultural change made *Life* the most talked about and popular weekly in the country.

- *Fortune,* the heavyweight of American business journalism, a chronicler (and critic) of the enterprise system, creator of a sobriquet that gained the status of a dictionary entry, the "Fortune 500" company.

- *Sports Illustrated,* which moved sports from the locker room into the living room, a weekly not only for addicted sports fans but for an audience of urban and suburban players.

Each had competition and detractors, but no one doubted their trademark preeminence. Nor did anyone doubt the stylish aura and swagger of those who produced them. Time Inc. radiated a certain élan inside, a reputation for professional self-assurance and clout outside. The biographer Ralph G. Martin remarked that "Politicians and leaders in every segment of society yearned to be on the cover of *Time* as a peak fulfillment, on the cover of *Life* as a celebration, and on the cover of *Fortune* as a special distinction."

The creator and energizer of the magazines, as well as the company that published them, was a journalistic and corporate evangelist. The script Luce worked from when he was alive was written into his will when he died: "Time Incorporated is now, and is expected to be, principally a journalistic enterprise operated in the public interest." Long before, he had said, "What we want to do is not to leave to posterity a great institution but to leave behind us a great tradition of journalism."

His staff was more united by its journalistic zeal and eccentricities than by shared views of the world. Luce gave them close to limitless indulgence in the pursuit of ideas and news. "His success seemed almost to embarrass him," a freewheeling member of his senior staff once said. "It came as a by-product not a goal of his subtle, probing restless mind, so full of surprising facts, questioning everybody and everything, including his own loyalties."

Luce was often maddening with his relentless zigzag curiosity and his staccato musings. Many of his senior editors, as gifted as they were on paper, shared his near incoherence in conversation. One of them was so mute that a writer once said to him, "Damnit, if you spoke English, you'd be bilingual." Luce dominated by his presence as much as his high office. He respected and stimulated the spirited group on his magazines. Their work gave him such vicarious pleasure—so long as they didn't stray too far off his reservation. "Harry's little people," his wife, Clare Boothe Luce, once called them, to her eternal regret and to her husband's dismay.

Luce's ways and his magnetic field for talent led his empire to be dubbed enviously "Paradise Publishing"—a wild exaggeration. Some of his most accomplished staff found Luce's wonderland more hell than heaven—and left never to return. *Time*'s most brilliant managing editor, Tom Matthews, who left in anger in the 1950s, said of him, "Luce was not what you'd call a likable man but there was, believe it or not, something lovable about him." His political views were deplored as often as they were admired. "Luce's place" was a hurly-burly Camelot, with its warring lords and unruly plebeians, talented, diverse and well tended. The heady environment around him and the magazines his messianic near genius created, extended the range and sophistication of journalism beyond that of any press eminence of the century.

The other two oil portraits in the Time & Life Building were of the memorable duo Luce handpicked to carry on his publishing, if not his political, legacy. They did so faithfully, leaving their own stamp, as seamless partners for close to twenty years. Andrew Heiskell served as chairman of the board (from 1960 to 1980); Hedley Donovan, first as editorial director (1959 to 1964) and then editor-in-chief after Luce (1964 to 1979).

Heiskell had the panache; Donovan the gravitas. When rare differences arose between them, they would go into each other's offices and work them out. Together they gracefully and forcefully dominated. They did not have a proprietor's license, but they dominated nonetheless, perpetuating Luce's journalistic ethos, without trying to match his exhilarating zaniness or often skewed political views. As much as Luce, above all they wanted Time Inc. to make a difference, while making money doing it. They were an ensemble, leaving an imprint on their inheritance which defied the homily that powerful creators typically pick unworthy successors.

Then came the third generation of inheritors, different buds, seeded from the same tree. The roots had thinned and mutated. The environment was changing. They redefined Time Inc.'s goals and "mission," expanded its size, reaching for hegemony of a different order.

The corporate leader of this third Time generation was J. Richard ("Dick") Munro, who at fifty became chairman and chief executive officer of Time Inc. in 1980.

ON A GRAY NOVEMBER afternoon in 1987, Dick Munro, the successor Andrew Heiskell himself had chosen seven years earlier to take his place, phoned Heiskell from the thirty-fourth-floor executive power center. He asked if he could come up to see the retired Heiskell "for a minute." Stripped to his trademark shirtsleeves, informal and jolly as always, Munro ascended to the forty-third floor, saying "Hi" to everyone he encountered on the way. He walked down a narrow corridor and closed the door of Heiskell's twelve-by-fourteen-foot office.

They were an odd pair. Heiskell is a towering (six feet five inches) multilingual cosmopolite. Born of American parents in Naples, Italy, Heiskell was educated in Switzerland, France, Germany and at the Harvard Business School. Among his many retirement activities, he presided over the rebirth of the New York Public Library and was one of the seven-member Harvard Corporation, the ultimate governor of the university's affairs.

Munro is a compact (five feet eight inches) sinewy populist born in upstate New York. He started college in Western Kentucky, dropped out to join the Marines and finished at Colgate. As Time's chief executive, Munro was happiest in the company cafeteria at his daily 7:30 A.M. breakfast joking it up with a random bunch of Time Inc. employees, or coaching Little League baseball and hockey near his home in New Canaan, Connecticut. He spurned the trappings of corporate stardom, caring as much for those who worked for him as the work they did. He was the kind of leader who has an army of devoted personal fans—from privates to generals—but no disciples. His guilelessness was authentic and palpable. Like the Marine sergeant he once was, he willingly took the heat for carrying out decisions made "on my watch" that he did not himself initiate.

"Andrew, you can have your portrait back," Munro cheerfully announced.

"I beg your pardon?" said the startled Heiskell. "Oh yeah," Munro continued, "we're redecorating the thirty-fourth floor and we don't have any place for your picture and Hedley's." Heiskell balked. "And Luce's picture goes too?" he asked half facetiously. Munro was flustered and blurted out, "Yeah that will go too. I don't know why I always have these terrible things to say to you."

Could he ever forget at least one of those "terrible things" he had to say to Heiskell two years earlier? "I should have learned from that first go-around," he recalls. "It was a horrible experience. I guess I'm a slow learner. I'm indebted to Andrew. I wouldn't have gotten my job without him. Andrew has been incredibly good as an ex-CEO. He's never gotten into our hair."

Yet in a wave of "lean-and-mean" corporate cost-cutting, Munro in the mid-'80s had been given the task of telling Heiskell he would either have to vacate his out-of-the-way little office or start paying for it, a total cost, with services, of about $50,000 a year. That mission had provoked a letter from Heiskell's wife, Marian Sulzberger, handwritten from the offices of the New York *Times,* where she is both a director and part owner. Savvy in the world of high corporate matters, she has served on the boards of other companies, including Ford and Merck, and prominently chaired a number of charities. Her searing letter said:

Dear Dick,

This is the 100th letter I have written and not sent since I heard the news.

Andrew tells me to be compassionate and that I should feel sorry for you. I do. I feel sorry that you made so many promises and that you then proceeded to make a complete about face. I am deeply disappointed and hurt. How can you ever have told me not to worry and that Andrew was like a father to you? (I sure would not like being your mother, if this is the case.)

Can't you (Time Inc.) remember what Andrew did for the company? Are you all so short-sighted and unfeeling that you'd toss him out after all those years of service and leadership? My god man! Ask your board of directors what they've done with their retired CEOs and don't bother telling me about the ones who were gently eased. I'm talking about a man whose record was good all the way.

I'm afraid you have become so engrossed in what you consider the major problem of the day, "take over," that you've lost sight of what makes a good company. It's *people*. People who enjoy this work. People who will do anything for you because they know they've got the support of their CEO. People are more creative when they are happy and not constantly worried about what the next day will bring and I gather that there is a lot of worry in your shop. Your fears have taken the heart and drive out of a lot of people. The sex appeal of working for Time Inc. is fast disappearing. Now to prove how "lean" you all are, you're about to kick out the former CEO under whose leadership Time Inc. grew to the great heights it reached. Yes, I do feel sorry for you. You've nearly broken Andrew's heart.

Sincerely, Marian.

Munro had earnestly apologized. He called on Marian Heiskell in her New York *Times* office to try to explain and seek forgiveness, without, however, reversing the collective decision. She was polite but standoffish and unrelenting. Munro confessed his pain to colleagues and friends for weeks. The episode was blabbed across the media grapevine. Encounters with outside Time Inc. directors and lower-level members of the staff compounded Munro's misery. But it did not occur to him, a few years later, that this new foray into his mentor's by then rented office to tell Heiskell about the portraits would produce an even stronger reaction. Munro quickly found out.

Right after his awkward attempt to deaccession the pictures, Munro flew to California, where he got another hammering missive:

> From: Andrew Heiskell
> To: Dick Munro
> Date: November 9, 1987
> cc: Time Inc. Board
> You came to my office to tell me you were remodeling the 34th floor reception room and that the Donovan and Heiskell portraits were to be taken down. Furthermore, you said there would be no other place in Time Inc. where they could hang. You added that Henry Luce's picture would also go. I believe you said something like "this is a different world you know."
> Indeed it is, and what management does with today's Time Inc. is obviously its responsibility.
> However Time Inc.'s history belongs to the corporation, not its current management. And rewriting history is not part of *our* company tradition.
> I hope and trust you can find a way of accommodating these elements of Time Inc. history and heritage.

Heiskell never sent the memo to other members of the board. He didn't need to. After getting the message, Munro again rang up Heiskell. "Oh forget it," he said. "I shouldn't have done that."

Munro's successor, Nicholas J. ("Nick") Nicholas, Jr., is less sentimental about the encounter. At work, he is an even more focused and "results-oriented" executive than many others who came out of the Harvard Business School. An admiring colleague says, "Nick can bite a bullet like no one I've ever seen." Nicholas, whose better qualities are not as consistently displayed as he wants them to be, indignantly recalls both of those incidents in which he had been involved. "Here are these two pictures," he explains. "This is not a company that worships deities. Luce's picture will never leave. Who is Andrew Heiskell? Andrew was the latest guy to come along. Hedley Donovan was the number-two editor-in-chief. We're now into number four. Big deal. Give me a break. This really angers me."

The pictures didn't come down. Two years later the company did—in the biggest media merger ever.

A sentimental judgment? Not at all. Munro himself described the event in a prepared speech at a gala in 1989 celebrating the company's transformation. "As jolting as it may sound," Munro announced, "Time Inc. is gone. Long live Time Warner."

Nobody planned it that way, but the date of the formal signing and posting of new marriage vows was March 3, 1989. It happened to be the sixty-sixth birthday of the start-up of Time Inc., the publication date of the first issue in 1923 of *Time,* The Weekly Newsmagazine.

NICHOLAS SUCCEEDED MUNRO EARLY in 1990 and threw a farewell, no-tears lunch for him at New York's '21' Club, once a favorite hangout for Time brass. Some seventy-five company executives gathered in a private room for good fun and the handing off of a few gifts: a Boston Red Sox uniform (Munro's favorite ball club), a gift certificate for two hundred hamburgers (his favorite edible), the cover of a Time-Life book entitled *The Munro Gourmet* (bound around six different jars of peanut butter—his favorite staple on the road).

One of the props for the party was the Heiskell portrait. (Heiskell himself was not invited.) It had been temporarily removed from the wall. Over Heiskell's face was attached a photo of Dick Munro. Most of those present were not aware of the picture incident. "That's an inside joke," Munro said as he shot a glance at Nicholas, slapped his forehead and guffawed.

Very few others in the room understood this reminder of all the executive anguish Munro had suffered during his ten-year stewardship. Why should they? As the likable guy he was, Munro had no personal detractors. And now, after all his travail, he had finally left his own corporate legacy. On the eve of his long-planned retirement, he had unveiled what he considered the most redeeming monument of his thirty-three-year-long Time career. "The crowning achievement of the Munro era," Nicholas called it, "capping nearly ten years of rethinking, restructuring and rebuilding." There it stood, for all to see—Time Warner Inc., emblazoned on the front pages of newspapers, in magazines and on TV news.

The new company's supercharged prose gushed with Churchillian rhetoric: "Now a new era of human history has begun. In spirit, if not in fact, we have already entered the 21st century. The world is our audience." Time Warner was heralded, with its own new emblem, as the largest media and entertainment company in the world.

Time Inc. had always been identified the world over by its journalism. Munro helped push the company beyond the confines of that tradition by a corporate marriage to a high-flying entertainment group known in the listings as Warner Communications Inc. But Warner was even more recognizable by what it was informally and correctly called, Steve Ross's Company.

Warner's full-course international entertainment menu had everything, from hundreds of movies like *Batman* and *Chariots of Fire,* to such popular musical stars at the top of the charts as Madonna, Rod Stewart and Natalie Cole, comic books, hardcover and paperback books, cable TV and a menagerie of Looney Tunes cartoons, including the Bugs Bunny and Daffy Duck families. It was an entertainment colossus.

"1989," said Munro and Nicholas in a year-end memo to the entire worldwide Time staff, "was the most extraordinary year for this company, fraught with more turmoil, change and uncertainty than any comparable period in our 67-year history."

WARNER AND TIME WERE as different from each other—in their people and their products—as the scrappy old Brooklyn Dodgers and the haughty old New York Yankees. Different leagues, different managers, different fans—same hometown. Time's Munro, who never goes to the movies but devours books on American history, pronounces the name of the international film company "Path" not "Pathé"; Warner's Ross, who sees every movie but never reads a book, calls the author of *Madame Bovary* "Flow Bert."

Munro, who is appealingly unguarded, describes his feeling of relief with utter candor. "This will now be a $12 billion company, complicated, demanding. I couldn't be the Dick Munro I was in the '80s. I just couldn't be. I would not survive. I couldn't go down and schmooze with my buddies in the cafeteria. That's another era. I was lucky to get through the '80s without having the company come down around my ears."

Now his burden would be borne on the broad shoulders of engaging Steve Ross. He was Warner's builder, seducer of talent and dealmaking engine—a "communications visionary," many people called him. Others, less enthusiastic, saw him as "the world's best deal-maker," "pitchman" and "baker of pies-in-the-sky."

Ross and many of his cohorts had risen impressively from the mean streets of New York, arriving from all over the career map at what became Warner Communications. Most of the Time crowd had different histories. Their early playing fields were often the campuses of the Ivy League, then up the ladder, rung by rung, on the tidy organization chart of Time Inc. When the two companies and two cultures came together, some considered it a metaphor for the American dream of cultural pluralism annealed in the corporate Melting Pot.

What was really notable about the marriage was that Time's executives, and twelve outside directors who were so full of doubts about Ross when they got engaged, still knew so little about him when they wed. None had known him except distantly before. Of the dozen outside Time directors who agreed to make Ross their new chairman and co-CEO, only one on the new combined Time Warner board had taken the trouble ever to meet with him (at one dinner) before the final deal was completed. But for that single encounter, the outside directors of Time Inc. chose Ross to be their chairman and leader for the next ten years, and co-CEO for at least five, without ever talking to him first.

The three Time executives who negotiated the deal (Munro, Nicholas and Time vice chairman Gerald M. Levin—pronounced like "begin") spent hours with him, but they knew Ross only in the most superficial way. They had volumes of numbers and analysis on the deal itself but only the sketchiest knowledge of Ross. What they knew of his personality, his strengths and weaknesses, they gleaned from his wooing ways in face-to-face observation. They never informed themselves by seriously seeking out the scores of people— many unabashed admirers—who could have filled out the picture of the man who they agreed to take in as their seniormost partner. A writer or reporter from any one of Time's magazines would have been severely chastised or fired for turning in even a short profile of Ross on the scant insight and information Time's board and top executives had. Ross was willing, eager to meet with the Time directors, but they never asked him. The answers to their initial doubts and questions would have been readily available to them had they inquired.

. . .

NOR DID THE TIME board or any of the Time executives know
or inquire about some of the unusual personal and office habits of
Steve Ross.

The essentials of what had bothered them about Ross were entered
into court files in June 1987, the same month Time first started talking
to Ross about a business combination. The case was a by-product
of a front-page bribery, racketeering and fraud criminal action, concluded in 1985, involving Ross and Warner.

The information about Ross was not faded old stuff. It had been
collected afresh after an eight-year investigation and reported to the
Warner board in a secret 663-page document in May 1986. Known
as the "Armstrong Report," it concerned a criminal fraud, for which
one Warner consultant had gone to jail; Ross's top lieutenant and
closest friend had admitted guilt; and Warner's assistant treasurer,
who handled Ross's personal accounts, had been convicted of fraud
and perjury. The report could have been available to Time by just
asking Warner for it.

Key Time executives and board members say they didn't ask for
the report because it might have been "embarrassing" to Ross.
"Steve is such a sensitive soul," one of them said, with another adding
that it might have "killed the deal."

Time board members repeatedly said that their rock-bottom concern was to preserve and protect the "Time culture." From the report
alone, had the Time executives or their establishment outside directors inquired, they would have learned that, apart from Ross's business success, he had a number of un-Timely habits, even though
there was no credible evidence of criminality that would stand up in
court. Ross's own Warner board was required to conduct the independent investigation after the bribery and fraud scandal became
public. The secret report revealed that:

- After denying it three times, Ross finally admitted in 1985 that for
  years, including the period during the '70s when the bribery and
  fraud occurred, he kept a secret briefcase in his office closet stuffed
  with tens of thousands of dollars in cash. Armstrong and his investigators found "implausible" Ross's explanation of the briefcase
  and the source of the cash hoard inside it.

- He often took a Warner Gulfstream jet to transport himself and some of his seniormost executives and friends to Las Vegas, where Ross said he regularly won $60,000 to $90,000 playing blackjack and stashed it in the closet briefcase. Ross's own lawyer said for him to claim such a sum from his gambling was "ridiculous."

- Like some other gamblers, Ross never reported his winnings to the IRS, because, he said, his losses "netted out" at the end of each year, which the investigators said "could not have been true."

- When he finally acknowledged the cash hoard in 1985, Ross claimed he used the money in the briefcase for "various purposes," including having handy "cash and gifts" for a girlfriend.

- Michael F. Armstrong, a respected, well-known criminal lawyer who Warner's board hired as their independent investigator, was unconvinced. He concluded in his 663-page Armstrong Report: "Our concerns about Ross' credibility have prevented us from reaching any definitive conclusions about his possible involvement" in the criminal fraud and bribery activity.

- Ross was listed in the fraud as an unindicted "co-conspirator" by the Justice Department. To avoid what his lawyer called "pre-trial publicity" the designation was kept secret until it was printed in federal court records. Ross says that "on advice of counsel" he availed himself of the Fifth Amendment right against self-incrimination and decided not to testify.

Had the Time executives and outside directors asked and found out these or other easily obtainable facts and insights about Ross and the history of his management, maybe it wouldn't have mattered to them. Nor might it have made any difference to know that Ross's recollection of his World War II service, his college degree, pro-football experiences and other milestones in his autobiography were the products of his own imagination. Perhaps it would have seemed irrelevant. They liked and admired the present Ross and his company for other reasons. Ask Ross what the most important thing is to know about him and he responds proudly with a homily that he repeatedly expressed to the Time executives: "More important than anything else is that my word is my bond."

Dick Munro and the others were happy with the union. Not everyone shared his enthusiasm. In moments of stress, Munro often expressed himself in barracks explosions. "So some people say Warner wins," Munro acknowledges with a shoulder shrug. Then, voice rising, "What the fuck do they mean Warner wins? Time Warner Inc. wins. Everybody wins. There's this mentality out there of the scorekeeper. It always comes out in the press as 'Nick the prick. Dick the dummy. And Steve the hustler'—that Ross is smarter than we are. No. We won—both companies. Don't those assholes out there understand that? We *all* won!" And finally, with resignation, "But nobody's going to buy that. What really bothers me is that it was so difficult to get people to believe us."

Jason McManus, Luce's third successor as Time Inc.'s editor-in-chief, puts the same view in a more worldly frame: "It's the outcome that matters. It's like what Gorbachev said about Eastern Europe. 'Would you do me a favor. Let's not talk about who won the Cold War. Let's get on with it.' "

FIRST A WARNING: NOSTALGIA has its place. But nostalgia often embellishes, even tells tall tales. It is hardly the most important guide to act upon or to make judgments in the present. To remember may be to understand; it can as easily leave you stuck in another era.

From the old Time Inc. there is enough nostalgia to fill libraries of reminiscences, museums of memorabilia, graveyards of unique worthies. The Time-Life Alumni Society alone has close to 2,000 members. The world of journalism, publishing, the arts and public service has been populated with people who once labored in Luce's vineyards. But he had been dead for twenty-two years when Time Inc. took its most radical leap, toward Steve Ross, Hollywood and a variety show of popular entertainment. Many asked the ghost question: "What would Luce have thought?" And many answered, "He would roll over in his grave." Both the question and the answer were irrelevant—and more complicated.

Two episodes from the past that give a clue—and two that contradict:

One day in the 1950s Luce scribbled across a business story scheduled for publication: "I resent the fact that these men are fighting for a huge chunk of the 'national estate' without there seeming to be any point to the fight. None seems to stand for a damn thing. This is the sort of thing that turns one against capitalism. I resent having these great companies owned by pointless men like these. And as for the vast investment trusts, I am inclined to think they should be abolished."

On another occasion, in the spring of 1964, as Luce was talking to an aide, his secretary inched open the sliding glass door of his office and shouted (Luce was losing his hearing), "Mr. Luce, Siegmund Warburg is calling from London." "Who's he?" Luce demanded of the aide, who explained that Sir Siegmund Warburg was an internationally renowned banker representing, among others, the London Daily Mirror Group, then the largest newspaper company in the world. Luce picked up the old-fashioned phone on his modern desk, listened for a moment, and said, "Sell my interest in Time Incorporated? Why would I want to do that? No. No. Absolutely not," and slammed down the phone. Then, without missing a beat resumed his conversation about the war in Vietnam.

But hear the contrary:

In the mid-'60s, James A. Linen, the president of Time Inc., asked Luce whether he might attend Luce's sacrosanct Friday editorial lunch where few Time Inc. businessmen ever trod. He wanted to introduce the president of the first book company that Linen had arranged for Time to acquire. Luce agreed.

Linen began the lunch by introducing the smiling book publisher, who was about to fold his company into the large arms of Time Inc. Linen, always upbeat, exclaimed, "Imagine, Harry, they publish more than 125 textbooks a year." Luce interrupted, bushy gray eyebrows arched. "I can't read 125 textbooks a year! You and I had better talk about this later, Jim." Linen, embarrassed and red-faced alongside the visiting book publisher, suffered the rest of the meal in silence. When lunch was over, Luce walked down the hall with one of his other staffers. "I guess I shouldn't have done that," he said. "Tell Jim I didn't mean it. He can go ahead and buy the company." Then wistfully he added, "Times are changing."

Or consider a memo that Heiskell wrote in 1970 on the blue stationery of the Ritz Hotel in Paris, on the third anniversary of Luce's death: "Luce died in the right year. It was at that point that the principles that had guided us for decades had eroded so much as to be meaningless. Not for all Americans but a sufficient percentage to prove that this was indeed a new watershed. In today's world he would have been miserable."

. . .

MANY GREAT TRADEMARK COMPANIES in America—
IBM, Coca-Cola, Ford, Xerox, General Electric, Disney, RCA, Po-
laroid and Time-Life—rose to fame and fortune under founders who
became legends. In corporate folklore they are as often remembered
for their quirks as for their business statesmanship. Henry Robinson
Luce, known to those who really knew him as "Harry," was most
certainly one of them.

Founding Fathers abound—of nations, institutions and even corporations. But the pace of change in the past half century has been
faster than the more than 2,000 years that preceded it. The good old
days get glorified and sentimentalized. Survivors cling to them like
life rafts in a sea of change.

Elders are too often crabby about those who succeed them. An
office boy named Henry Grunwald, who came to Time young and
wide-eyed in 1944 and later rose to the highest editorial reach of the
magazine company, was told upon his arrival, "You should have
been here in the good old days." Forty-one years later, a corporate
speechwriter, recruited by Time from politics, heard precisely the
same refrain. In the movie *Atlantic City* Burt Lancaster, down on
his luck and up in his age, stands on the boardwalk and laments to
a younger friend, "The Atlantic Ocean used to be something. You
should have seen it then."

It is not surprising that the three most senior executives in Time
Inc. in the late 1980s—all on the edge of or in their fifties—barely
knew Harry Luce, mostly from having met him in an elevator, where
he was always silent. Nor did any member of the company's board
of directors, excluding, of course, his son Henry Luce III. Ask half
a hundred old Timeincers (rhymes with "thinkers" as the old *Time*
magazine would say) how they felt about the merger of "their"
company with Warner Communications and they are almost unanimous, varying mostly in degrees of their distress. "I could weep,"
"a disaster," they say at one extreme. Or more colorfully from an
old magazine hand, "We're now like the tender to a battleship."
And at the most benign, "Maybe it had to happen."

Why not? Haven't the Berlin Wall and Soviet Communism come
down? Don't the Japanese now have a piece of Rockefeller Center?
Disney executives were stagnating for years while they asked, "What
would Walt have done?" until they found their own way of doing
things. CBS and NBC are now controlled by financial rather than

broadcasting interests. Four of the seven biggest Hollywood mov-
iemakers are now owned by foreign investors.

IN THE DECADE OF the 1980s, the American economy and corporate life were transformed by an exploding financial device called
"leverage." Once it was more simply known as going into debt. In
the '80s, through the use of leverage, hundreds of big companies and
the lives of millions of their employees were clutched into new hands.
Some to their benefit, others destroyed or their identities and lines
of business made unrecognizable, like Unisys, Esmark or Allegis.

Many under siege were household American names: graham crackers and Oreo cookies (RJR Nabisco); department stores like Bloom-
ingdale's and Filene's (Campeau); supermarkets (Safeway); Fruit of
the Loom underwear and Pepperell bed sheets (Farley Industries);
Florsheim shoes and furniture (Interco); Samsonite luggage, Wesson
oil and Swift ham (Beatrice); gambling casinos, real estate and an
airline (Trump); lipstick, perfume and cosmetics (Revlon).

Then suddenly as the overheated '80s raced to the finish line, the
debt engine blew out. The financial markets did an abrupt about-
face. Overnight, debt became a different kind of four-letter word.
The last huge high-leveraged deal of the '80s ($11.5 billion of debt)
did not involve underwear, lipsticks or cookies. Nor was it simply
high finance. The *last* such transaction was the joining of Time Inc.
and Warner Communications Inc. They were just under the wire.
Exactly one month later federal bank regulators all but closed down
such highly leveraged transactions. Time Warner and RJR Nabisco
were the biggest offenders. "We beat the rule by about three weeks,"
recalls Steve Ross.

Time Warner is a combination whose creations (magazines, books,
movies, music, cable TV and programming) are now exposed to the
minds and emotions of more people than those of any other commercial enterprise on earth. The new company mattered not just as
an overpowering business venture. At its birth, Time Warner had
the aspiration and potential—more than any single company—to
dominate the information and entertainment markets of America,
and perhaps the rest of the world.

"In 1995 and the year 2000," Nick Nicholas told an interviewer,
"when we have access to every home in the world on a direct-to-
consumer basis, that's when big numbers kick in."

How that became a possibility, how Time and Warner became one, requires a look at each company as it approached and then chugged through the '80s. They came into the decade like two trains starting from different stations, running not only on separate tracks but on rails of a different gauge.

"It was much more dramatic," says Time's leading tactician, "than the usual ragged normal business process."

chapter 2

Succession & Obsession

THE TELEPHONE RANG IN a bedroom of the government's official guest house at 3 A.M. on March 1, 1967, in Canberra, Australia's capital. Hedley Donovan, Time Inc.'s editor-in-chief, was not easy to awaken. Until well after midnight, he had been at a talky and boozy dinner with the prime minister. A familiar voice in New York, a world away, gave him a startling brief message. Luce had suddenly died of a heart attack. Come right back.

Donovan needed no urging. First he checked in by phone with his partner in New York, Time Inc. chairman Andrew Heiskell. For the rest of the night, aides scurried around to make emergency travel arrangements. At breakfast, Donovan was even quieter and more reflective than usual. "I felt good about him. He was obviously thinking ahead—a good man in a clutch," remembers one executive who accompanied him back.

It was not much of a clutch. Three years earlier Donovan was set in place by Luce himself, when Luce surprised everyone who knew him and half retired. Oddly, no one wanted him to step down—least of all the patient Donovan, a Rhodes scholar who rose solemnly rather than climbed ambitiously to Luce's job.

As Donovan was flying back, the organization took over in New York. Memorial services were arranged at the Madison Avenue Presbyterian Church, to be piped into the Time & Life Building for the whole staff to hear. Luce's burial was to take place under a live oak at a Trappist monastery in Mepkin, South Carolina, the site and name of a plantation Luce had once owned. *Time, Life* and *Newsweek—Time*'s rising competitor—all did Luce cover stories.

The night of Luce's death, in Greenwich Village in Manhattan, a small gathering had taken place. Heiskell, who had been a *Life* journalist himself before moving on to the publishing side, and Jim Linen, Time's president, had invited themselves for a quiet dinner at the apartment of one of their senior editorial staff. They wondered aloud to the journalist whether, without Luce, "Hedley can handle his end of the partnership. We like it the way it's been," they said in turn. "The church-state relationship, we don't want that to change."

Church-state?

Luce had divided his empire in two. In charge of his publishing missions (he never would have called them "products") were the journalists, who worked for what he grandly christened "The Church." To support their work was "The State." It was made up of the ranks of business people who provided the wherewithal for the church to operate and the profits to make it grow. The concept gave those who lived in his church an imperious strut. For their part, the statists got profit and pride from their independence. Like so much of Luce's theorizing, the hierarchy of journalists leading and their business partners following was more a concept than a reality. In his lifetime, of course, Luce was both.

Donovan and Heiskell maintained the holy symbols of church and state more by dint of their personal relationship than by any formalities. In the ten years after Luce died, there were many problems but none between Heiskell and Donovan. "If the business side didn't interfere with the editorial decisions," Donovan later said, "I shouldn't interfere (too much) with the business decisions." Heiskell, who originated the idea for *People* and whose publishing insights helped move *Sports Illustrated* from a failing magazine for jocks into a huge success for sports-minded America, agrees with Donovan's view, adding only, "Hedley's right. But it's also true that once in a while we on the business side did feel like the galley slaves down below."

AT THE TURN OF the '70s, the two at the top were joined by another former journalist, James R. Shepley.

Once as fanatic a newshound as any in the pack, Jim Shepley made what was then a unique high passage, from editorial to business. He vaulted the wall, carrying his barking facade as a tough guy from his post as Washington bureau chief to become publisher of *Fortune* and *Time,* then in 1969, president and chief operating officer of the whole company. They were three "word" men with an inherited mission, in Heiskell's definition: "A publication depends on a great idea with a public purpose, not on there being a market out there. You start with an appealing idea. Yardsticks don't invent magazines; people do. It's not like the cereal or soap business."

In the first three years of their regime together, Heiskell, Donovan and Shepley were forced to make the most wrenching decision of their professional lives. Although profits for the whole company were strong and growing, *Life* magazine was in trouble. Long before television, *Life* extravagantly roamed the world. The weekly picture magazine was the revenue leader of the world, taking in more than half a billion dollars a year at its peak.

But newly born color television first yapped at *Life*'s heels, transporting viewers everywhere faster than *Life,* with news pictures that moved. Then it began luring away *Life*'s expensive advertising. *Life* red became the color of its bottom line, not just the trademark name of its cover ink. The magazine's agonizing death in 1972 would have made Luce miserable, as it did the people in the Time & Life Building and its outposts around the globe. (It reemerged in later years as a monthly, a pale reminder of the original *Life.*)

Donovan, a somber man of conspicuous calm, encouraged *Time* to become more thoughtful and more balanced politically. Under its new managing editor, Henry A. Grunwald, a Viennese-born intellectual, *Time* soared to heights of thoughtfulness and respectability. The new monthly *Money* was launched to a shaky start and ultimate success. Two years later at Heiskell's urging, with many Timeincers holding their stuck-up noses, Donovan's editors produced the flashy *People.* It was an overnight sensation. *People* became, and still is, the most profitable magazine anywhere, treading the narrow line between supermarket sleaze and clever mass appeal. *Fortune,* once the preeminent magazine of business, was reluctantly converted into a fortnightly, lighter-toned and more sprightly. Along the way the company had created serialized Time-Life books and picked up Boston's Little, Brown and the Book-of-the-Month Club to fill out its hardcover bookshelves.

Altogether a publishing giant to reckon with, rich in cash, its more than 12,000 employees rich in pride, free of Luce's ideological fervor without losing much of its élan. "It was some place to be," recalled one old hand who came to the place right out of Harvard, "a literary kindergarten—a class act. Why, when I first arrived, Dick Cavett was a copy boy, Joe Heller was cranking out promotion and John Gregory Dunne was a young writer."

The outlook was relentlessly American, its New York staff ensconced in settlements from Greenwich, Connecticut (mostly the business side), to Greenwich Village (mostly editors, young writers and photographers). Time was more an exporter of American ideas and news than a global publisher. Under Donovan, and especially Heiskell, the company began to install a whiff of managerial structure. In the old proprietary days, Heiskell recalls, "Harry could say, 'Nah, nah,' and that was the end of it. In our years, it became a company where someone would present an idea, and then you'd sit down and argue it."

In one corner of the publishing empire, almost unnoticed and unwanted, two alien colonies were growing that would change Time Inc. forever. The first, forest products, became a wellspring of tangible assets and capital, which enabled the other, cable TV, to take off.

For years Time Inc. had its left toe in the paper business, not for its own use but as an investment hedge. It owned the East Texas Pulp and Paper Company, whose immediate neighbor along Texas's Neches River was the older forest products company Temple Industries. As a further hedge against the cyclical ups and downs of magazine publishing, Temple's trees and land looked attractive to Heiskell and his supportive board. By stretching a bit they could fit it into what they insistently described as the need for "the company's coherent mission." Donovan disagreed.

He wondered what they were doing investing in companies that produced not a single sheet of paper Time's magazines or books could use. But he let it pass. In a sharp break with tradition, in 1973 Time swapped some of its stock for all of Temple's, leaving the Texans and their shareholders with 30 percent of Time Inc., almost twice as much as Luce ever owned. Not only was this scary ("The Texans are coming") and chancy ("What did we know or care about the manufacturing business?"), but the heavy investment cramped the company's ability to expand into the other new business, cable TV, which at first caused more grief than promise.

TIME INC. HAD MISSED out entirely in television while Luce was alive.

Although given early opportunities to become the owner of a TV network, Luce thought of himself as a print man. "Communications" was a word not much used then and "media" was never applied to journalism. He deplored his pioneer neighbor across Sixth Avenue (the Avenue of the Americas), William S. Paley, the founder of CBS. Luce scowled that Paley had "cheapened American taste with his entertainment junk." Luce even wanted to sell Time Inc.'s five profitable TV stations because he had no control over what he felt was their mindless content. (In 1970 they were sold.) But the impact of TV became unmistakable after it killed *Life*. Tentatively, the company set out to get in on the ground floor of TV's second generation, cable. In retrospect, says Heiskell, "that was the turning point."

Time had acquired a small Manhattan cable-TV franchise that eventually grew to be the centerpiece of the second largest cable operation in the U.S. It started a dreary programming service ultimately christened "Home Box Office." HBO's first programs were clinker movies, hockey and wrestling. Originally, tapes were "bicycled" from station to station. HBO transmitted its first new signal on microwave dishes spaced on towers along a pathway to 365 subscribers in Wilkes-Barre, Pennsylvania (fiftieth on the list of the top fifty TV markets).

Little did the print masters know that their wires in the ground and their dishes on stilts, which were draining so much capital and causing such executive anguish, would one day be half the company. They got a small clue when in 1975 a young visionary, Gerald M. ("Jerry") Levin, unbound to Time Inc.'s old ways, persuaded them to buy $7.5 million worth of time on a space-borne satellite that would put the whole nation within HBO's reach.

For the most part, the '70s were good years for Time—despite missed opportunities and mistakes—upholding old quality traditions, fighting good fights with the magazines (Watergate, civil rights). Although publishing growth and profit slowed down, the company was still expansive and expanding.

Heiskell, Donovan and Shepley were approaching the sixty-five retirement age, which they had themselves established for officer-directors. They had to deal with their succession—an endless, ponderous discussion—an almost theological question at Time right from the creation. Weighing, measuring qualities and values, it seemed at times to occupy almost as much attention, joint reflection and conversation as running the enterprise itself. "Andrew, Jim and I put in hundreds of man-hours, maybe thousands," Donovan recalled, "on the subject of our successors."

Two key jobs needed to be filled. First Donovan's, as editor-in-chief. Then Heiskell's, as chief executive officer. Neither they nor their successors were, or would become, nationally well known figures in the pantheon of American celebrities. Few outside the media ever heard their names or knew how they got where they did. But the voices they controlled and the result of their labors had as big an impact on American life as any partnership in the private sector. The first appointment, of the new editor-in-chief, was easier than the second, of the new chief executive.

BEFORE HE COMPLETED THE work on the first task, Donovan wanted to make sure the doors of his editorial church would remain locked to tempted meddlers. For months he labored over the "Donovan Charter." In his mind it was to guarantee the division between editorial and business matters, formally establishing Luce's church and state. "I started lobbying the document through the board of directors," he said, "almost director by director." It worked. In the last days of 1978, his "Role of the Editor-in-Chief" was ratified by the board. Its key provisions were that his successor would report only to the board, not to the chief executive officer. He would be solely responsible for the contents of the magazines. He also would be assured board membership and was invited to intervene "if non-publishing activities seem to conflict with editorial standards."

The board could exert no compelling influence on the editor-in-chief except its right to fire him. And the editor-in-chief alone would pick his own successor. Donovan had contracted on paper what Luce had instilled in his organization by his personal power and ownership. The formality of the separation was unique in journalism. An editorial sovereignty had been contractually established.

Having set the rules of the game, Donovan continued what he called the "almost apostolic" process of picking the person to occupy the pulpit. To many at the time, Donovan's choice seemed relatively easy. There were only two real possibilities. Yet he plotted alternatives with elaborate soul-searching, discreetly consulting Heiskell and Shepley, along with others who would not question his right to make the decision. He even compiled a dark-horse list. But all the time he was looking most closely at his two deputies, earlier put in place for just that purpose.

Each had been groomed for the job. Each had spent his entire professional life at Time Inc. Henry Anatole Grunwald, fifty-seven, the former managing editor of *Time,* had perfectionist and expensive editorial habits. He edited with the professorial breadth and the flair of a one-man graduate-school faculty. "The editor's indecision is final," read a sampler on his office wall. His pondering brain and talent were as apparent as his ample girth ("avocado-shaped Henry Ayatollah Grunwald," the staff dubbed him, mocking old *Time*-speak).

Donovan's other deputy was Ralph Graves, fifty-five, a former managing editor of *Life.* He was a much-admired, diffident but resolute journalist, a self-described "counterpuncher" of ideas rather than their inventor. Graves was incomparably a better manager than Grunwald as well as more easily approachable and less intimidating. At the time, Donovan said, "Henry, by a close margin, was a better choice." Heiskell had wanted Graves.

Six months after Donovan's charter was ratified, so was his choice of Grunwald, with Graves made editorial director and a member of the board. Done. Donovan had one caveat in hindsight: "I did notice Henry's lack of interest in anything but the magazines. But I didn't anticipate what the effect of that might be."

It was "the changed nature of the company," says Grunwald, "not my lack of interest, that dictated my attitude and actions. After all, I couldn't edit trees."

BIG CORPORATE DECISIONS ARE made formally in boardrooms or in executive offices. But they are often initiated and worked out or discussed on even pleasanter turf. In this case in the Champagne country on the scenic canals of France.

In New York, the four most senior Time officials climbed onto their Gulfstream jet in the summer of 1979 bound for Paris. There, they were picked up and driven to Château-Thierry, where they boarded the M/V *Princess,* the most luxurious barge on the 1,200 miles of French canals. Owned by the shipping and real estate billionaire D. K. Ludwig, she was ready for them. The barge was staffed by a crew of six. She was loaded to her gunwales with a gourmet's selection of fine wines and viands tended to by a betoqued French chef. The *Princess* had four large double staterooms (three wives were along), well-appointed dining and living rooms with poster-perfect picture windows. Creeping alongside on the banks of the canals was the barge's own radio-connected minivan for shore excursions exploring the cathedrals, châteaus, abbeys and vineyards along the Marne à la Saône Canal.

The ostensible purpose of the trip was to pull Donovan out of the dumps. In the year past, his wife for thirty-six years had died. And two months before the group embarked, he had retired after forty-four years with Time Inc. (The week after he formally retired, he told a friend, "I never felt more qualified for the job than I do today.") He had just been named as the senior adviser to President Jimmy Carter, reporting directly and privately to him. With his usual caution, Donovan wasn't sure it would work. He was right. The job turned out to be a flop. It produced little more than a solid Donovan book (*From Roosevelt to Reagan: A Reporter's Encounters with Nine Presidents*).

On the barge, along with Heiskell, Donovan and Shepley, was the vice chairman of the Time board, Arthur Temple. He had suggested the excursion for Donovan's sake, but he had another agenda as well: picking Heiskell's successor. The others thought it was pretty well set. But Temple wanted one last hearing.

Arthur Temple had become vice chairman after his Temple Industries merged with Time, making him and his family the company's largest stockholders. The merger, a Texas forest products company with Timeincers' stereotyped view of its leader, sent a shudder through every floor of the Time & Life Building. The New York *Times* covered the "Texans" and Time Inc. on the front page with a big picture of Temple. And later Manhattan's *Village Voice* snookered him in a story making Temple out to be a backwoods yo-yo. Among other putdowns, the *Voice* said Temple saw no reason why the company shouldn't move out of New York to the "heartland"—someplace like Texas, for example. A boob's heresy to Northeastern ears.

Temple, a lumber and forest products baron, does have a collection of well-honed homilies. ("Hell, I'm not afraid of a rattlesnake so long as he's out on the concrete where I can see him.") Or on corporate spin-offs. ("It's like owning a whorehouse. You got it. You sell it. And you still got it.") They are about as impromptu as the ones Dan Rather reads from cue cards. Should you choose to visit him in his company town, Diboll, Texas (population 5,227), Temple is likely to suggest you stay with him and his wife, Lottie. "Why waste money on a motel when you can use it to buy likka."

Temple barely touches the stuff; his vice—until he had a heart attack—was thirty fat cigars a day.

But Temple is no yokel. He is a sophisticated, enormously successful and sharp maverick businessman. His great-grandfather was an Episcopal minister in Virginia. His father went to Williams, which he also attended for one week before he dropped out to get married and start building a huge family business. As a boy he summered with his grandparents in Long Island's WASPy Quogue, spent part of the winter with Park Avenue relatives in New York learning to dance and march in New York's oh-so-social Knickerbocker Grey's, a kind of D.A.R. for boys.

Temple is certainly not a prig. But he is an outspoken proponent of standards he embraces. He insistently complained about HBO showing "dirty movies" and the "cheap entertainment flooding America." But far from meddling in Time Inc.'s journalism, he became one of its principal protectors and advocates on the board. He omnivorously consumed every word that poured from Time's presses—magazines and books. He was so proud of them.

BY THE TIME of the barge trip, his three companions were well aware of Temple's Luce-like evangelism for Time Inc.'s editorial standards and the "magic" of the place. But he was disappointed now. He had wanted Jim Shepley, who was sixty-two and Temple's closest friend and hunting, fishing and traveling companion, to take Heiskell's job for three years while they searched for a long-term successor.

But Shepley called off his friend Temple. He knew that neither Heiskell nor Donovan wanted him even for the short term. Unconfident of any single selection, and having groomed no one else for the job, Heiskell, Donovan, Temple and Shepley agreed to split the deck for the top two jobs. They picked two Time Inc. businessmen and switched around both their authority and titles. Shepley stepped aside and became chairman of the board's executive committee.

For president *and* chief executive officer, they chose Dick Munro, fifty, who attracted their attention mostly when he had taken over the beleaguered yet growing video group in late 1972. While Heiskell admired Munro's folksy honesty, he worried about his ability to represent the company to the world. To fill that perceived gap, on tap was Ralph Davidson, fifty-three, polished on cosmopolitan turf as managing director of Time-Life International and once the publisher of *Time*. They gave Davidson the figurehead title of chairman, without its previous scepter of command. Davidson, a handsome, sociable, ambassadorial archetype, was told in no uncertain terms that he would have no operating responsibilities.

Munro liked to get home to New Canaan to spend evenings with his wife and two sons. He had traveled outside the United States only once, in Korea, where he was a three-times-wounded Marine combat sergeant. Davidson, divorced and single at the time, liked nothing better than getting around, the U.S. or whatever far-off place beckoned.

Long after the barge trip, Heiskell explained the choice to hundreds of Timeincers at his characteristically stylish Time retirement dinner in the grand ballroom of the Plaza Hotel:

"The company has grown so much bigger. One word heard most often in our discussions was 'integrity.' To move from 'integrity' to J. Richard Munro is not a segue but an overlap. He has a sense of people. In promoting people, one of the dangers is in replication, choosing people like ourselves. In Dick's case I am untainted by replication. He is a man who has absolutely no interest in food or drink, who confuses Château Margaux with Château Gallo, or for that matter with cream soda. Ralph Davidson is now chairman, which includes the tremendously important job of representing Time Inc. to the multitude of outside organizations in government, business and the private sector. Like Munro, Davidson is not perfect. His natural and ungovernable inclination is to fly, anywhere, with a leaning towards London and Paris, and a preference for cities endowed with good skiing and scuba diving."

At the time, the split made sense. It never did again.

Munro was so busy, he was overwhelmed in his new job. Davidson was so unbusy, he longed for something more important to do. He ended up feeling betrayed by the company where he had spent most of his life and demanded a unique fat severance package.

IN THE LATE '70s, Warner and Time knew each other only as bitter adversaries in cable TV.

Cable franchising brought Warner into head-on bruising collisions with Time. Barely anyone at Time even knew Steve Ross, whose offices were just down the street. But from behind the scenes, Ross and Warner outstepped and beat Time at every cable-TV mating dance held by city councils and politicians, in Cincinnati, Dallas, Queens, N.Y., and most painfully Pittsburgh, where the Time sore losers accused Warner of cheating, worse, of stealing the game. The genteel folk a half block away at Time-Life got mad as hell at Warner and vowed they weren't going to take it anymore.

Dick Munro, who was manager of the Time cable team, remembers the Pittsburgh outcome with a wince. "I had been working Pittsburgh for several years. Yes, we really wanted to win it. In those days, it's safe to say—without saying something that might upset some people—whenever anybody won a franchise it was always a given that you would renegotiate it. No matter how bad it was, you felt somehow you always could get in there and retrade some things. We really decided to go hell bent for Pittsburgh and assumed we had won it. I can remember it was a very dark day in my life when I learned we lost it. We practically had the champagne open and Warner came in and stole the chickens. That was the first bunch of cable chickens that Warner stole from us. What we eventually learned was that Warner was just better at franchising than we were."

Jerry Levin, who became Time's vice chairman and chief tactician for Time's merger with Warner, was reminded of the Pittsburgh battle by a lawyer deposing him in the lawsuits that erupted after the Time-Warner merger announcement.

> *Lawyer* What I'm trying to find out is, what was it, what was it about the [Warner] franchising operation that caused you to need to look into, what were the rumors, or whatever you had heard, that caused you to say we should look into this and make sure there is nothing there?
>
> *Levin* At the time some people may have tried to impugn the Warner Cable activity.

As all witnesses are instructed to do in depositions, Levin was being as vague and conditional as he could be. "Some people" was, in fact, most especially one person. "May have tried to impugn" was a euphemism for a passionate obsession.

That person was Jim Shepley, president of Time. His obsession was Steve Ross. Shepley had lost none of his lock-on tenacity from his days as Washington bureau chief. "Shepley, in his marvelous kind of way," says Munro, "went apeshit. He immediately assumed that Warner had done something illegal in Pittsburgh. Shepley was convinced that something must be wrong here. So he started a law-suit." With dozens of witnesses under oath, he never found the criminal ties to Ross that he was looking for and was certain in his bones existed. (Time later dropped the case.) "We always thought when we were in competition with them," recalls Munro, "that they were a little shady. I'm not sure they were at all."

But Shepley would not give up. Shortly after the Pittsburgh fran-chise was lost, he took on a new responsibility. As a kind of expensive farewell reward for Shepley on his old stamping ground, and because Time always was eager to own newspapers, especially one in Wash-ington, Time bought the Washington *Star* and made Shepley chair-man of the daily. Shepley carried his vendetta with him.

Shepley kept after Murray Gart, former chief of Time-Life cor-respondents, who had been installed as the *Star*'s editor, to prove his case against Ross. "It may have been the tensest argument we ever had," says Gart, "and it lasted for a year. He wanted me to put together a task force to investigate Ross, kept dropping clippings on my desk and raising hell with me." Gart told him it was a local, not a national story, that Shepley was giving him no real evidence of any Ross criminal connections and finally, "You'll be using the *Star*'s news columns for Time's commercial purposes." Gart refused to pursue the Ross story.

The *Star,* a much improved but uncompetitive paper against the Washington *Post,* folded in 1981, three years after Time bought it. But Shepley never stopped complaining about Ross or gave up on his Ross obsession. He took it with him to the grave when he died of cancer in 1988, five months before the Time-Warner merger an-nouncement.

His questions about Ross lingered on.

chapter 3

Steve & His Company

ACROSS SIXTH AVENUE, DOWN the street from the Time & Life Building, past granite walls, manicured flower beds and roaring fountains, stood the Warner Communications Building at 75 Rockefeller Plaza, in the older part of the complex. No one spoke aloud of succession there. Steven J. Ross was in charge.

By the late '70s, Ross had built the company in less than twenty years from a mixed—and mixed-up—collection of ventures into an international leader in movies, records, popular publishing and cable. When he started out, Ross was street-smart, even though he knew more about the opportunities on the streets of New York than Broadway or Hollywood Boulevard. As important to his success as his intricate dealmaking talent was his beguiling "charm." That was the word everyone used to describe him. A weekend neighbor and friend, the movie producer Steven Spielberg, made a picturesque comparison from his landmark movie. "I think of Steve as a six-foot three-inch 'E.T.' "

At Warner, Ross and boss more than rhymed. No one ever disputed that. Ross was boss, despite the noise level in and around his huge office. Warner without Ross was almost unthinkable to his chorus of well-paid operating managers and aides. Nor did they hint in his presence that they wanted it any other way. After noisy disagreements and four-letter-word clashes, salted with Yiddish argot, they would recite in public the company's anthem: "We love Steve Ross"—*love* was always the verb—"he's like a father to us."

At Time Inc. in those days, love on the premises was more often the high-tension emotion of interoffice affairs than a term of endearment for bosses. But Ross was different. Deals and endearment were his lifelong game. He was a hugger, a kisser (of men and women), a wooer. "Heartfelt" is his favorite adjective for toasts. His largess of spirit and pocketbook for the chosen knew few bounds. Ross too had a mission, different but as driving as anyone's at Time. He wanted—needed—to be loved; to be successful; and by all kinds of benefactions, large and small, to hold sway over those around him. "Steve was a charming host, a slightly uncomfortable guest," one of his now departed office claque says.

He was truly known only to his family and the executives who worked for him closely, some from his earliest beginnings. Their feelings and views were refracted through a prism of affection, awe and suspicion. To discuss their experiences and insights outside their inner circle was considered an act of disloyalty, a risk few would take. Most who really know him speak candidly about Ross only behind a shield of anonymity. "We all sort of plead the Fifth Amendment, when you ask us about Steve," says one of them.

"No one from Warner," says the company's accomplished music impresario Ahmet Ertegun, who heads the Atlantic Records Group, "will say anything to outsiders that's critical of Steve. He takes such good care of everybody." Ertegun, for example, says, "I would never leave Steve. Everybody has always offered me big deals. Now I just go in to Steve when my contract is up and say, 'Here's what my lawyer says I should ask you for. But I'm telling you if you don't give it to me I'm staying here anyway.' "

Another Ross intimate, who has watched him admiringly at every phase of his life, says of him, "Steve got his training in business from working for his father-in-law at the funeral parlors where he met you on the worst day of your life. The day when your parents or your children or your loved ones dropped dead. He was there to make you feel good. And he learned how to do that better than anyone in the world because he had the best training in the world. He took that ability into show business and made it work better than anyone I've ever seen in my entire life. He would carry your bags, light your cigarettes, open the door, smother you with gifts, let you use the company's airplanes, overtip all the time, listen to your life story no matter how bored he was, without telling you anything about himself. You need a word beyond just obsequious to describe him."

David Geffen, the precocious and stormy entertainment whiz who defected from Warner in 1990 and made close to a billion dollars after selling his company to competing MCA, had worked under

Ross's wing for twenty-three years. Geffen once said to him in the midst of one of their many disputes, "Steve, do *not* light my cigarette. It's costing me too much." Someone who has bitterly opposed Ross says, "Steve has this uncanny quality of making you feel sorry for him even when you think he's screwing you."

WHEN ROSS STARTED TO collect the companies that became Warner Communications, they were a motley lot of enterprises that defied definition.

His company developed from his father-in-law's Riverside funeral parlor ("expanded service with traditional dignity") and limousines into the Kinney Service Corporation, named after Kinney Street, around the corner from its first Newark office. Kinney's divisions and subsidiaries came and went almost as fast as cars in its parking lots. Its bosses referred irreverently to the funeral part of their business as "our permanent parking division." Kinney's central engine was an array of stock swaps, acquisitions, successes, failures, spin-offs, warrants, mergers, buy-outs, tax write-offs, trades, or whatever deal device was handy, inching by chance toward coherence. "There were few conventional acquisitions," one of Ross's marveling lawyers remembers. "There's almost no major deal we did that we weren't creating new tax laws. It was heady stuff."

With the funeral parlors and limousines came car rentals; parking lots; hotel, hospital and office cleaning companies (including a contract to tidy up Rockefeller Center—RCA's David Sarnoff was the uncle of one of Ross's early executives); printing; dry-wall partitions; real estate; security guards; painting and plumbing contracting; window washing; comic books (*Superman, Batman, Wonder Woman*); *Mad* magazine; licensing (cartoon characters and sports memorabilia); movie cameras (Panavision); periodical newsstand distribution; a New Jersey bank; paperback books; data processing. Close to 160 Kinney whatever units in the conglomerate. Kinney called itself "The Servicemakers—a unique one-stop shopping complex for banking, corporate, institutional and real estate communities." The annual report in 1966 proclaimed, "Service is our business and people are our asset."

The go-go 1960s found Kinney going at high speed. Ross's crazy quilt of companies was growing and prospering. But a service company—what was that? Even Wall Street couldn't figure it out. Then in 1967, with advice from a few of his corporate friends, Ross bought a Hollywood talent agency named Ashley Famous Artists with deep roots in the movie and TV business. Its boss, Ted Ashley, an able executive, pointed Ross to a decaying Hollywood movie company, Warner–Seven Arts. It was ailing in its film department. Barely visible at first to Ross, it had a successful popular record business. Ross grabbed the package. With Ashley at its head, the company started making hit films again (*Summer of '42, Klute, A Clockwork Orange, Dirty Harry, The Exorcist*) and restored the legendary Warner Bros. studio name.

Within two years, Ross dumped, mostly at a profit, almost all of his unrelated companies and operations. Along with movies and records, Warner Bros. made and distributed TV programs. Ross began buying cable-TV monopolies. He soon dropped the "service" slogans and redefined Kinney as a "leisure and entertainment company." The Wall Street analysts understood that, the more so when he renamed his company Warner Communications Inc. Ross was now off and running. Behind his desk he had a motto: "More is not an illusion."

In the years following, his high-rolling acquisition bent had few limits. Leisure and entertainment were a broad charter. He built Jungle Habitat, a New Jersey animal park which was such a disaster that it quickly closed. That "dispelled forever," remembers one of Ross's sharp-tongued former cronies, "the popular illusion that lions eat only Christians." Ross collected Knickerbocker Toys, a major interest in the Pittsburgh Pirates, Malibu Grand Prix (auto race-tracks), Ralph Lauren perfume and cosmetics, the moribund New York Cosmos soccer team, which he brought to life by paying the Brazilian soccer superstar Pelé millions to join the roster. He tried two-way pay TV in Columbus, Ohio (QUBE), MTV, Nickelodeon, the new Atari video games. All are gone from Warner's group now, all but one—its cable-TV franchises.

Ross was acclaimed for his daring and generosity. To oblige itinerant visitors and executives, he later bought five Trump Tower apartments; an air force of planes and helicopters; the Villa Eden in Acapulco, a memorable full-service retreat perched high on a hill overlooking the resort's harbor. In Ross's New York office, the conference table for the executive suite was so big and shiny that one of his top managers closed a meeting with the wisecrack "We've got to clear out of here by noon so the Rangers can use the table for hockey practice." Ross was hanging out with Frank Sinatra, Barbra

Streisand, Spielberg and Clint Eastwood. His business was booming. He was a hero to Wall Street and his stockholders. He was courting presidents of the United States and a governor of New York.

Little did he or anyone else know he was on the edge of becoming the leading character in a drama that would have taxed Hollywood's most mournful tragedian.

TIME'S succession process was as judicious and balanced as a 5–4 Supreme Court opinion. Steve Ross's history during the same period reads more like a Greek tragedy. Ross had a series of disasters. Only the first involved his succession.

Under chairman Ross, Warner never had a chief operating officer. "I'm not a manager," Ross says. "I'm more of a dreamer." His management style, explains someone who has experienced it, "is not hands-off. That's misleading. He inspires rather than runs or curtails. He's in many ways a Jewish mother. Some people just *appear* to be generous. He really is."

But he couldn't face elevating one of his four top headquarters executives at the risk of losing the affection of the others. Below his sovereign throne he also resisted bureaucratic layers of command. To fudge both problems, Ross set up a four-man office of the president (there was *no* president), all four vying for his attention. "They were not the best people in the world," says an ex–Warner executive who knew them all, "but they were devoted to Steve, as I still am. Steve always picked people who were completely within his control." Each of the four was loosely in charge of overseeing financially the impresarios who ran Warner's creative and other divisions. Within a hectic few years, in a series of personal and corporate thunderclaps, all four would be gone, none retired.

While they were still there, it was a dazzling life. "So overwhelming," one of them remembers. "When I left the office to go on a trip to the coast, my driver didn't take me to LaGuardia, which is fifteen minutes away. He took me a mile crosstown to the helicopter so I shouldn't have to—God forbid—get in some traffic. The helicopter would take me right onto the field where the plane was, a steward and all those things waiting. So you go on your own plane and you are picked up by a limo at the other end, driven to the Beverly Hills Hotel and you get into Bungalow 10 with four bedrooms, whether you're alone or with two other people. Then you walk into a movie studio where you're kind of a king. And you're telling me our life didn't change—these little guys from Brooklyn and the Bronx!"

The youngest and newest arrival to the quartet was thirty-five-year-old Ken Rosen, handsome and dark-haired, whose father had wrenched himself from Manhattan's Lower East Side ghetto to become a modestly successful lawyer and a politically connected administrative judge. Rosen was a fast-moving young deal maker. "Around Steve he was deferential and always looking for direction," says a contemporary. "With others, he was developing into a sort of Steve Ross junior."

He came to Ross's attention early, as a financial operator in the first big show-biz acquisition of Ashley Famous Artists. Ross kept his eye on Rosen as he cut a small swath in the financial side of entertainment investments. When Ross brought him to Warner, it was to do mergers and acquisitions. He quickly became Ross's constant companion and protégé, "the younger brother Steve didn't have," says one friend. Carmen Ferragano, Ross's longtime assistant, told a reporter that "Kenny absolutely worshiped Steve. Steve was receptive to being worshiped." Rosen's executive companions in the office of the president were drawn to the apparent new crown prince but wary of his close relationship to Ross.

"Kenny helped us all," one of them says. "Under Steve's wing he showed us how to live." Soon they all had extravagant contracts with a rondo of short-term and long-term bonuses, incentive stock plans and severance insurance that would convert the pain of leaving into an enriching experience. These were not just severance packages, recalls another of the four, "they were more like suitcases or steamer trunks." One of their compensation consultants, who fled in dismay, describes the executive enrichment process with all its new gimmicks as "lowering the top of the tennis net from its regulation height to two inches from the ground."

As Warner entered the '80s, Ross's lieutenants were making more each year than the top executives of Exxon, AT&T or GM. The boss himself was leaping up to earnings of $10 million a year or more, higher than any CEO in a public company in the U.S. and thirty times over what anyone at Time Inc. was making.

Ross remembers the period with melancholia. "I started to groom Ken Rosen to be the president. I had no real replacement. In 1976 I negotiated four contracts with the men in the office of the president. Ken was fifteen years younger than the other three. This is the scary

part of it. He was the *only* one—they all got the same contract—
who wanted a clause for disability. That was in November. The
contract started January 1, 1977."

Three months later, on Sunday, April 3, Rosen was riding the
Central Park bridle paths. His horse suddenly bolted and Rosen
plunged head-first into a tree. He was near death, in a coma for
months. Ross rarely left Rosen's bedside. "Steve would actually
shake him out of his semi-consciousness," one friend remembers.
"Steve talked him alive" was the sentimental consensus. Another
Ross business confidant said to a reporter, "Steve loved Kenny and
I also think he's addicted to helping people. He relaxes from his own
problems by helping others, and he gets satisfaction from being
needed."

Today Rosen, fifty, lives in Innisfree Village, a family-style collection of cottages for the mentally handicapped, seventeen miles
outside Charlottesville, nestled in the foothills of Virginia's Blue
Ridge Mountains.

AT TIME INC., THE GENERATION of new managers had never
really known their company's founder. At Warner, even though Ross
owned less than 1 percent of its stock, the company was dominated
by Ross's personality and the roller-coaster of his life. Like every
other Warner trip, the company's odyssey through the '70s and '80s
was as much personal as it was corporate. It is impossible to know
Warner—past and present—without knowing Steve Ross in a more
personal way than chronicles of business history usually demand.

"Why," wonders a member of his family, "is it that Steve is the
only mogul uncomfortable on the top of his mountain?"

To most casual observers of Ross in action, he is an exemplar of
self-assurance, charm, command, with the grace of a man in pos-
session of his success, abundantly offering his own blanket of security
to those around him. One longtime intimate explains, "Steve gets
loyalty. The people who work for him swear by him and they'll jump
off mountains in order to please Steve Ross because he makes damn
sure they get rewarded for what they do." One of his former executives explains the jump in a different way. "His relationships with
people are a combination of incredible sincerity and total insincerity.
If Steve told me to go jump out the window, I would, not because
I'd do whatever Steve told me but because I'd know there would be
a safety net two floors below."

Yet there is another Steve Ross—as there is another everybody. Ross himself is enclosed in a protective wall by his staff. He is a master of promotion sizzle and ballyhoo, yet his Warner operation has been a fortress of silence and secrecy. When Ross meets for a reluctant interview with the press, he is accompanied by a public relations person. Although at his first lunch with the editors of Time's magazines he was told by the journalists he would do better coming alone—as he did. In some interviews, he makes vague, unsupported accusations against people, always following the slanderous tidbit with "That's off the record." "We do a terrible job PR-wise," says Ross. "Primarily I'm the reason. I don't give interviews. Newspapers get angry at us. Magazines get angry at us. So finally I give an interview and we make a hundred more enemies." (He was interviewed extensively for this book.)

When a reporter recently routinely asked for Ross's prepared factual biography (every CEO has one), he was told, "We're working on it." Eight weeks later it arrived in its latest version, without a single biographical word about the man himself, only about his company. The lead sentence said, "It is almost impossible to separate the 20-year history of Warner Communications Inc. from the business career of Steven J. Ross." Asking to see a Warner telephone directory available to some 35,000 Time Warner employees, a reporter who regularly covers the company was told it is a "private document." Ross's seven-line *Who's Who in America* entry lists only his year and place of birth, "N.Y.C. 1927," and that he is married (no name) and was a "Student, Paul Smith's Coll., 1948," no other personal data. Ross, who has made an impressive climb from hardscrabble anonymity to radiant celebrity, displays his glitzy present more than his humbler past.

When word got back to him that one reporter writing about him told a Ross associate that she didn't feel she ever got "behind the mask," Ross summoned her immediately to his office and heatedly inquired, "What mask?" Certainly not uniquely—but even more than with most fabulists who star in their own imaginative scripts—Ross appears to be a devout believer in the stories he tells about his own life. He seems to embrace whatever tales he once told no matter how incorrect they are.

"I think everybody is afraid of being found out," says one longtime Ross admirer, "except those people who finally decide that they are who they invented themselves to be. Steve is extraordinary at those things he's good at, making you want to be his friend, his ability to work financial magic, making you feel that you have a privileged and a special relationship with him. Actually, there's no such thing as being close to Steve, because nobody's really close. On some level he's a visionary. But it's odd. He obviously doesn't think very highly of himself. You can see it in the way he behaves, the way he holds himself, the way he constantly services people."

Ross tells his own life story earnestly, with a belief and conviction reinforced by repetition. Separating the facts from the fiction requires more excavating than merely asking.

THE FLATBUSH SECTION OF Brooklyn, where Steve Ross was born on September 19, 1927, was populated largely by Jewish immigrant families, most living on marginal incomes in solid two-story row houses, where young boys played stick- and stoopball on tree-lined streets. They were characterized in *The New Crowd*, a lively account of the roots of Jewish financial success in America, as "the first-born sons of middle-income or working-class families headed by a self-employed father. They were expected to do far better than their parents, most of whom were immigrants or the children of immigrants—many from Eastern Europe."

Young Steve fit the specs perfectly. His father, the son of Russian and Alsatian immigrants, at first earned a good living in the home-building business. When the 1929 stock market crash and the Depression hit, Ross's family was left penniless. They moved from their house on Carroll Street to a small apartment house on Newkirk Avenue, surrounded by brownstones. While young Steve was in kindergarten, his father changed the family name from Rechnitz to Ross, in order to get a job as an oil burner salesman in 1932. "He couldn't get a job with that name, so he changed it," Ross says.

"We were poor, poor," Ross remembers. He will never forget, he says, "Sometimes we had rolls for dinner—and that was it." But his proud, dignified mother, he says, always insisted on having finger bowls on the table, symbolism to him of a self-esteem that she engraved on his memory. She also had strict rules about good manners. "If I ever sat down before my mother or my sister and I didn't help them by holding their chair, I didn't have that roll." His grandfather taught him magic tricks, which he still can do today.

"My mother," with her finger bowls and standards of polite behavior, Ross says, "taught me dignity and self-respect. When you

grow up in the Depression and on the streets, you always remember."
Steve attended the neighborhood P.S. 152 on Glenwood Road, then
later Erasmus High. (In those days New York City had the best
public-school system in the U.S.) He was, even then, a mixture of
shyness and overconfidence. Young Steve was well liked by teachers,
who remembered that the subject he excelled in was math.

After his father began to pull himself out of the hardship of the
Depression years, he and his wife decided "for the children's sake"
to move to "the city," i.e., Manhattan, a nickel subway ride away
but a big step up. With his family still unable to afford the tuition,
Ross transferred, on an athletic scholarship, he says, to the predom-
inantly Jewish private Columbia Grammar School, where "you could
meet new people."

Already over six feet, Ross played varsity football, baseball and
basketball and managed the swimming team. He was elected vice
president of the student council and a member of the junior prom
committee, where his flair on the dance floor made him a natural.
He was co-winner in the vote for the "most popular" boy in his
senior class. In the yearbook, Ross's way with the girls was attested
to by a joking reference to him as "the noted bigamist."

Ross graduated from Columbia Grammar in June 1945, three
months short of the World War II draft age. He has often told friends
he "lied" about his age when he was fifteen so that he could get into
the Navy "for the adventure" and service to his country. Actually,
he was seventeen and eligible for the Navy, so instead of waiting to
be drafted, he chose his own service and enlisted.

After six months of basic training in New York and Virginia, Ross
boarded the USS *Hopping,* a destroyer escort converted into a high-
speed transport. "We were shallow draft," Ross says, "so that we
could get close to islands." His recollection of his wartime service is
that "We carried supplies and Marines into landings in the Pacific,
then the war ended. Because of having overseas duty most of my
time, which was very unusual," Ross explains, "we had all these
points, so I got out early." ("Points" were awarded to servicemen
and women, with bonus awards for combat and overseas duty, to
determine in what order they were to be discharged from the service.)

Ross, who wears almost invisible hearing aids, attributes the need
to his Navy service. "I have a hearing problem," he says. "I love to
have a dinner for six or eight people. That's fine. I have trouble

hearing more. At cocktail parties if you're a tall person with a hearing problem you get all the background noise of a cocktail party without hearing anything. I'm about six foot three and a half. You stand there with a smile on your face hoping you're shaking your head at the right time." He says his impairment became noticeable "ten years after the war when I was twenty-eight or twenty-nine. It was caused by the firing of guns off the ship. They didn't have the type equipment they have now to protect you."

Ross's official service record tells an entirely different story. In fact, two weeks after Ross began active duty in the Navy, and more than six months before he joined his ship, the war in the Pacific had already ended. Seaman First Class Steven Jay Ross, 7172226, spent five months of his one year and eleven days in the Navy lollygagging aboard the USS *Hopping.* Nearly two months before Ross joined her crew, Navy records say she was in the Charleston, South Carolina, shipyard, where "ammunition was unloaded" and the ship began a "pre-inactive overhaul." She went from drydock to an anchorage in Norfolk, Virginia, where Ross boarded. She was underway at sea with Ross aboard for only two days from Norfolk to Charleston for more shipyard work, then at sea five more days to Green Cove Springs, Florida, where she was decommissioned.

The *Hopping* had indeed seen heavy action in both the Atlantic and the Pacific. But a hyperactive Warner press agent embellished the myth even further, obviously confusing, as Ross does, the ship with the man, when he wrote that "During World War II, Mr. Ross saw action with the U.S. Navy in the Atlantic and Pacific theaters."

AFTER THE WAR, VETERANS were given tuition-free access to schools and colleges under the GI Bill of Rights. They could attend any accredited school that would admit them. But for those like Ross who hadn't yet started college, it was hard to break through the crowd that was going back. A number of new schools sprang up to capitalize on the oversupply of applicants.

The headmaster at Columbia Grammar, whose advice Ross says he sought, thought he would be best served by the advantages and personal attention of a small college. Ross remembers the headmaster recommended that, "as opposed to a triple bunk-bed in a gymnasium at a Duke or Wisconsin. He didn't think my education would be very good going to a class with 120 or 130 others." The academic intimacy and privacy of a small school appealed to Ross.

"He told me it didn't matter, Yale, Harvard or anything else. We were living in an unusual time and it was best to find the best professors with a small amount of people. After the war you sort of deserve a room by yourself or with only one other person."

Paul Smith's two-year junior college, on the site of an old resort hotel in the isolated north woods near Lake Placid, New York, was just such a place. No matter that it specializes in "resorts management," "hospitality" and "forestry," with a background program in liberal arts. Or that it gave only an A.A. (Associate of Arts) degree, upped in old Warner handouts to B.A. (the more conventional four-year Bachelor of Arts).

Ross entered its first class in 1946, surrounded by other ex-GIs. When they weren't studying, they went snowshoeing, skiing, hunting, trapping, fishing or partying on weekends in Saranac Lake. "It was fantastic," Ross says. "You could go fishing or hunting with your professors." Ross is Paul Smith's most famous graduate, remembered fondly by classmates and professors for three attributes: 1) "He was brilliant in my field of high-powered mathematics, particularly calculus," one professor recalled; 2) "Ross was one handsome dude," a classmate says, "good-looking, articulate, quiet—he stood out, young ladies paid a lot of attention to him"; 3) "Touch football was very popular and he was an addict," says another.

In the fall of 1947 the college paper reported:

Taking full advantage of Deerwoods' weak line, the Campus Commandos scuttled the Deerwood Devils 14 to 6 Saturday, November 1st. [In the] third quarter Steve Ross, who had been playing a wonderful game at right end, was injured while attempting to knock down a pass. During the bitterly contested battle on the gridiron, after many brilliant receptions while playing end for the Commandos, Steve was once more in the center of a scramble for the pigskin. When the mass of players untangled themselves, he was alone on the turf with the first major injury incurred on the field of competition for Paul Smith's College. Steve was admitted to Saranac General hospital. After a physician's consultation, it was decided Steve's left arm was badly broken below the elbow, and a steel plate was used to strengthen the joint which was torn. The injury was serious and the patient will have to remain there for at least three weeks. Let's hope the radio given to him by his fellow students affords him some of the interest he has donated to all school activities in which he has participated.

Ross has a different recollection of his broken arm and football career, which reached its apogee when playing, not touch football in college, but end for the professional Cleveland Browns. At one time in his life, the children's bedrooms were festooned with Cleveland Browns banners and souvenirs, supposedly a reminder of those dreamy days. He also explained to his friends and family that the metal plate in his arm came from a bone-breaking collision in a Browns play called "the cross," more often known as the "Statue of Liberty," in which a passer raises the ball, which is snatched from his cocked arm by one of his own teammates coming around behind him. The Cleveland Browns, the local newspapers and his putative teammates have no recollection or records of him or anyone with a name close to his ever playing with the team.

Over the years, Ross has scaled down his tale of his playing defensive end for the Cleveland Browns, as it had been repeatedly, but not directly, questioned. "I tried out and was accepted in 1948," he now says, but "I broke my arm in training camp with the Cleveland Browns—I have a plate in my arm." His career with the Browns was short-lived, he now claims, "Because of the arm it went fast. I got in and out of the camp fast. It was all over." Where was the Browns' training camp? "Cleveland—somewhere."

Dozens of people who have been close to Ross sympathize with more than criticize his mythmaking. "Steve invented all that stuff," says one of them. "Steve's accomplishments are really extraordinary. He does not have to invent any false history. I think it speaks to his lack of feeling good about himself. I don't say he's unique in this regard, not at all. Nor do I hold it against him. It makes me feel sad for him."

IN THOSE DAYS, even after World War II, American business was largely segregated. Blacks, who had been totally segregated in the armed services (in sports as well), were still virtually inadmissible in the white-collar working world. First- or second-generation Jews were incomparably better off but still mostly shunned in businesses run by more assimilated Jews and WASPs. Irish and Italians were in similar confinement. Steve Ross and his striving friends, raised in

the Bronx or Brooklyn, and from "the wrong" or no colleges, had
to make their own way in a harsher hustling world.

"Machers," they were called, a half-derisive word for "doers" in
the Yiddish idiom Ross never uses. "They were self-made New York
Jewish businessmen," one of their more privileged colleagues says.
"A few were either working in secondary positions in good investment banks or senior positions in bad ones—they were deal-
oriented." They heard the usually unspoken but clear message that
they should "stay with their own" and not invade established businesses. So whatever his prowess on the playing fields and his charming presence, Ross found himself in New York's garment district.
He started as a stockroom boy and was later a salesman for a sports
slacks manufacturer, then a children's bathing suit salesman in a
company owned by an uncle.

He courted a Westchester beauty from a German-Jewish family,
who rejected him because her family wanted their daughter to do
better. In 1954 when he was twenty-six, he married Carol Rosenthal,
the handsome daughter of the owner of The Riverside, an expanding
West Side funeral parlor empire. The Rosenthal family offered their
new son-in-law a job in the business. Ross at first said no. "I said I
can be cut twenty-two places and it's fine with me," recalls Ross.
"But I can't stand to see anyone else cut. I could pass out." They
understood and told him, "No, not downstairs, upstairs in administration." From upstairs, away from the embalmers, Ross built the
Riverside into the mini-conglomerate Kinney Corporation, that cra-
dle-to-grave service company.

At home, things weren't going so well. "When I was in the funeral
business," Ross says, "I sometimes worked a night shift. That's not
very conducive to a good marriage." By the time Ross was expanding
Kinney into the movie business, he was spending much of his time
in California or working on deals in New York. Even fewer hours
were left for his wife or son and daughter. Absence made Carol's
heart lonelier if not colder. In 1974 they separated and in 1978 divorced. Of the marriage, a chastened Ross says today, "I have a
thirty-four-year-old and twenty-nine-year-old and now an eight-year-
old. I always said I'd give them more time. So I just hope that we're
all right in saying quality is more important than quantity, when
you're given a second chance."

. . .

BY THEN ROSS WAS a risen star in the corporate-movie world. He met Courtney Sale, the daughter of a Texas Coca-Cola bottling family. An attractive Skidmore graduate, she had run her own small art gallery in Dallas before transplanting herself to New York. She began working as an art dealer for several galleries and was an aspiring documentary filmmaker who later scored with a Public Broadcasting documentary, *Strokes of Genius,* a film on modern artists. A Warner friend had introduced her to Ross. For two years they were inseparable until one night at that favorite expense-account watering hole, '21,' he met Amanda Burden.

In Orson Welles's landmark film *Citizen Kane,* the key to unlocking the mysteries of Charles Foster Kane's life is a child's sled hauntingly referred to at the beginning and end of the movie as "Rosebud." "If there's a Rosebud in Steve's life," says someone who knows Ross well, "it will take you back to Amanda."

Amanda Mortimer Burden at thirty-one was finishing a postponed college education at Sarah Lawrence College in suburban Bronxville. Amanda was as beautiful an undergraduate as ever graced a college campus, with social credentials to match. She was the daughter of the socially registered Stanley Mortimer and the impeccable style setter Barbara ("Babe") Paley, second wife of CBS Chairman William S. Paley and one of New York and Boston's "fabulous Cushing sisters." Each of the three sisters had married "well": Babe to Wall Street and Standard Oil heir Stanley Mortimer, then to Paley; her sister Minnie to Vincent Astor, later to the painter James Fosburgh; and Betsey, first to James Roosevelt, FDR's eldest son, and then to John Hay ("Jock") Whitney.

Amanda, who had divorced Carter Burden, another New Yorker high in the Social Register, was introduced to Steve Ross by her friend William vanden Heuvel. Ken Rosen had suggested the encounter.

Courtney Sale was no match for the alluring, flirtatious Amanda. Ross instantly set Courtney aside. Within months, he had moved into Amanda's apartment at 10 Gracie Square, overlooking the East River. Ross became her round-the-clock companion, embraced her two young children, showering them with treats and attention.

When Ross flew to China with a group of Warner cronies and their wives, Amanda went along. She accompanied Ross with the children on a trip to Disneyland. When he took friends on the Warner plane to Las Vegas, she and other friends watched him, glistening with sweat under his three-piece suit, chips overflowing every pocket, happily distributing some of his card-table winnings to his guests. Second only to his movie studio, Ross's biggest enthusiasm was the Warner-owned Cosmos soccer team. He was such a rooter at every game that aides as a joke gave him a parachute-type harness, supposedly to keep him from falling out of his box as he cheered the Cosmos on. Amanda went with him to every game, knew all the players and enjoyed becoming a soccer groupie.

From the Beverly Hills Hotel pool in California to the charity ballrooms of New York, they became the talk of both coasts. Her mother, Babe, who had no fondness for Jews in the abstract, liked Ross less in person. Bill Paley, who had grown up in a Chicago ghetto, was rich and a young man about town by the time he and his family settled in Philadelphia. He was prouder of his broadcast eminence, his friendship with Jock Whitney, his finely hewn taste in art and the cultural artifacts of aristocracy, than his Jewish roots. At a small CBS meeting, Paley once asked an incredulous executive who used the word "kvetch" what it meant. Ross was simply not Paley's kind of Jew—"tacky," he said. "Paley was very imperious and thought of himself as a king," says one former Warner executive, "which just heightened Steve's sense of unworthiness."

Amanda had been a neglected child, tended by nannies, never close to her mother. Amanda's conspicuous public displays of affection for Ross seemed to her friends to be her way of striking, in one amorous blow, at both her mother's and stepfather's snobbery. "She was sticking it to them," speculates one intimate.

She arranged Ross's lavish fiftieth birthday party. It was described by one awed Warner executive: "Three hundred of Steve's closest friends were there at the Waldorf. It was one of the greatest parties of all times. Governor Hugh Carey and Sinatra. [*Sesame Street*'s] Joe Raposo composed a special song. Clint Eastwood sent a telegram. It was written up in the social pages. I was so privileged to be there. It was mostly corporate people—a pecking-order party, all corporate and divisional. Those kinds of things made you feel like family."

Ross's family was always at Warner, never at the Paleys', where he was treated with condescension. Sally Bedell Smith reports in her biography of Paley that in 1978 when Babe Paley died of cancer:

Moments later, Bill Paley picked up the phone to call Steve Ross, then chairman of Warner Communications, who was dating Amanda at the time. In the early days of his career, Ross had been an undertaker. "Call me when it is over and I'll be there," he had said to Amanda. Arriving within minutes, Ross said, "If you go out of the bedroom, I will take care of it all." So the family filed out, leaving a silver-haired movie mogul to tend to arrangements for Babe Paley's lifeless body.

Ross, several of his associates say, "still gives great funerals." But marriage ceremonies were a different matter. He wanted his ex-wife Carol to marry again (she did in June 1979) before he himself did, so as not to alienate the Rosenthal family, another friend explains. Ross was a reluctant groom, more comfortable with the people who worked for him than in the salons of Amanda's or the Paleys' friends. Their potential marriage created a fiery on-and-off tension between them. At one moment, on her deathbed, Babe Paley was told by a friend that the marriage seemed to be off. Babe beamed, the friend says, rose weakly from her bed, and "danced a little jig," chanting happily, "They're not getting married, they're not getting married."

But in November of 1979, after four years of vacillation, they were married privately. Later Paley gave the wedding party in his opulent apartment. The guests were mostly Amanda's and Paley's friends, with a small sprinkling of Warner executives. Once when one of Ross's office mates rose to deliver a tasteless toast suggesting that since they had been living together so long what was so exciting about their getting married, Paley harrumphed to a guest close at hand, "Brooklyn comes to Fifth Avenue."

If the long courtship had been often romantic, the marriage was tense. Although Ross was one of the most handsomely rewarded executives in the country, within the family he incessantly complained to both his wives about being short of money, never failing to display his high living elsewhere. Apart from his business, Ross seemed to have no other interests. Backgammon, at which he was a whiz, was his favorite diversion.

Although the glamorous couple showed up in the gossip columns mostly at charity dinners and political fund-raisers, they spent more time with Ross's Warner pals, cultivating his show-biz and growing political connections, than they did on Amanda's turf. There were no quiet moments of reading, since Ross doesn't read; four longtime Ross associates say separately that Ross has *never* been known to read a single book in the years they have known him.

On the evenings Amanda and he were home alone, Ross, often clad in a bathrobe, watched movies, played with Amanda's children or sat in a corner scribbling notes for deals on small pads. When they went out evenings, if he hadn't had his hair coiffed in the office, a stylist took care of him at home. Everyone who knows him says he has always been meticulous about his appearance.

No one had yet coined the term "trophy wife." But Amanda was the comeliest trophy of that species. Although she was simply if tastefully adorned—the "Halston look"—before she met Ross, he did spend to redecorate her. Ross bought her wardrobes of clothes from Giorgio's of Beverly Hills on golden Rodeo Drive. He also gave her a few baubles (two pairs of earrings, a ring and bracelet), liked to see her "dressed up" when they went out.

Even her fine piquant features were emboldened by enhancing new makeup right down to her newly reddened fingernails. Whatever their troubles at home, in public Ross carried her on his arm with the proud look of the possessor of the finest pick in the aviary. "He became different when he married Amanda," says a close friend. "He was a Brooklyn boy and he was basking in her glow." Another friend who knew them both says, "It was the start of Steve's public persona when he met Amanda. And when they married, he thought he was getting Babe Paley. She hoped she might be getting another Bill Paley. They were both wrong. Steve changed dramatically after the marriage. He loved the social aspect of it. He was all caught up in it."

Nonsense, says Ross, "that's wrong." It was Warner's growth and his new relationship with Paley that was the main difference in his life. "Other than my lunches or dinners with Bill," things were the same, he says. "Bill and I used to have these discussions about cable versus networks. He had CBS Records. We had Warner Records. We were both in publishing. He was a customer of ours. We sold them some TV shows and movies. So that we had interesting business and personal discussions. We got along very well. My life didn't change at all."

IN THE EIGHTH MONTH of his marriage to Amanda, Ross was suddenly rushed from his office to nearby Lenox Hill Hospital, struck down by a heart attack. After treatment and a summer of recovery, Ross took Amanda off on a convalescent cruise to the Caribbean aboard the *QE 2*, amidst tourists and holiday revelers. Amanda hated it; Ross surrounded himself with the strangers aboard and charmed them.

When they returned, with Steve nevermore to indulge his addiction to five packs of Parliaments a day ("I was never without a cigarette," he says), Ross had more than his health on his mind. He had put his sadness over Ken Rosen behind him and handsomely remarried. But the month after their return from the Caribbean, one week after they moved into a gargantuan Park Avenue triplex previously owned by Seagram heir Edgar Bronfman, Ross got another stunning blow. After barely sixteen months of married life, Amanda had had enough. She walked out.

Ross was angered, hurt but powerless. He flew off to Warner's Acapulco haven with his lady-in-waiting, Courtney Sale. In the spring of that year, Ross demanded a divorce *immediately*. Granted.

Amanda Mortimer Burden Ross had her pick of surnames. She chose to be known thereafter as Amanda Burden.

Ross then enticed some of her closest friends onto the Warner payroll, including her brother. Her pal Bill vanden Heuvel was scouting deals for Warner. Within the year he was made a Warner director and later became chairman of its executive compensation committee (a position he still held years later on the Time Warner board). One divorced friend had to choose between Amanda and a much-needed salary for managing the Warner house in Acapulco. She took the job. "I was deeply hurt," Amanda told a confidante, "but I guess I understood they all needed the work. It was a bad summer for me. It was part of the wooing away by Steve of a lot of my friends." His attention to her children was unflagging.

A year later, in October of 1982, close to three hundred guests gathered in the ballroom of the Plaza Hotel, including Governor Carey, Steven Spielberg, Cary Grant, Barbara Walters and Quincy Jones. They heard another wedding toast, this time to Courtney and Steve from Warner Bros.' Ted Ashley: "To Steve Ross, who for all his success, has continued to find true happiness elusive—until now."

Not quite. It was only intermission time.

chapter 4

Munro:
A "Unified Vision"?

WHEN DICK MUNRO MOVED into his thirty-fourth-floor corner office in 1980, he was overjoyed to have the job as CEO of Time Inc. but was to be rarely content doing it. "I don't think he had a happy day the ten years he was there," says one of his colleagues. "That's an exaggeration with some truth in it," Munro says. "It was not fun. The '80s to me were exhausting." And if "the truth be told," Steve Ross added, "Dick was often panned for his efforts."

One of the first things Munro did was to announce his intention to retire at sixty in ten years. Some board members were flabbergasted. "He made himself a lame duck the day he came in," says one of them.

From the beginning, he had a vexing management problem. Ralph Davidson had been made chairman only to take care of the world outside. Munro was left to run the business. He had no authoritative second-in-command, no designated real chief operating officer. With his gregarious nature, he let too many people report directly to him. He felt the inside-outside formula with Davidson was a mistake from the moment he heard about it. But what was he to do? "It was hard for me to tell Heiskell that's not acceptable," he explains. "I wouldn't have got the job."

The first three years "were relatively relaxed," Munro remembers. "There didn't seem to be enormous pressure on us. We didn't think much about the stock price." One early portent of what was ahead for him was the rumor that a California investment house was buying a lot of Time stock. Was it even remotely possible that some outsider could march in and take over the company? Should they take out some insurance?

Unlike the Warner practice down the street, Timeincers had no employment contracts. No one seemed to mind. It was traditional Time paternalism. And the employee benefits and profit-sharing were the best in journalism. In an off-the-cuff and off-the-wall speech Luce once gave to a large staff dinner he convened to raise morale, he began: "There are no contracts at Time Inc., are there? No. I guess I could fire any one of you if I wanted. No one can fire me." It was a stunner—but quickly forgotten as one of Luce's pot-stirring eccentric pronouncements.

With rumors of takeover, Munro was advised in 1981 that contracts for top executives might be useful in discouraging a raider from making a move on the company. Munro bought the plan. He gave himself and six other senior executives identical separation agreements, including Henry Grunwald, by then installed as editor-in-chief in the matching corner office down the hall. The contracts were in place for less than a year.

Time's own *Fortune* blew them off Time's executive benefits map when it ran a cover story questioning the new "golden parachutes" created by some American companies for their top executives. The article had a list of "The Most Generous Agreements." Munro's name turned up ninth from the top, with a $3 million bailout severance package. Embarrassed to appear in one of his own magazines looking like such a fat cat, Munro cancelled his own and everybody else's agreement. There was not a peep of protest. Until the start of the Time-Warner discussions, Time executives and staffers never had contracts again.

"A STATE-OF-THE-art goy," one of the Warner crowd later called Munro. He was, to be sure, an Episcopalian raised in Skaneateles, New York, upstate a hundred miles from the Thousand Islands of the St. Lawrence River in the quiet wooded north country. But his early childhood and adolescence were hardly serene.

When Munro was five years old, his mother and his father, the black sheep of a landed-gentry farming family, were divorced (her first husband had committed suicide). His father's family had fought in the American Revolution and been rewarded with valuable tracts of land. Munro, a history buff, says without a trace of hubris that "at the battle of Lexington, I'm told there were something like ninety-one soldiers and seventeen of them were Munros." But his father rebelled against his patrimony, said to hell with all this blue-blood stuff. He bought and ran a two-pump gas station.

Although his father never paid much attention to him, young Dick hung around the filling station. He found out that despite his father's perversity, he was a sentimentalist, a one-man local welfare department, supporting from his legacy a neighborhood of dirt-poor families. "I had a strange relationship with him. When I reflect on him," muses Munro, "I guess that's where I got an awful lot of my liberal tendencies. I'm an outspoken Democrat in a Republican world. A lot of my very good friends—most of them—are basically racist. I've been able to live with that. When people start telling black jokes, I just walk away. I'm a crazy liberal who thinks he can fix things."

He lived with his mother, once a slightly dizzy Broadway actress, a "swinger, a wild lady," he says fondly, who reached a brief peak singing a role in Sigmund Romberg's *Blossom Time*. A family gene for the musical theater was her only inheritance. Her father had been America's leading Gilbert and Sullivan performer, married to a chorus girl. Show biz was in Munro's background, but it never showed up anyplace in the foreground of his life.

When his mother moved to Florida to try to make a living as an interior decorator, they lived in a row house. The small houses "looked kind of like slave quarters," he says, slapped up in the shadow of Palm Beach's towering Breakers Hotel. He parked cars at a local night spot, caught sight of Gary Cooper and the Duke and Duchess of Windsor. "Make no mistake," says Munro, "I wasn't a Palm Beacher. We were a poor West Palm Beach family, a very different thing in those days." In high school, he was a terrible student. "I was a free spirit. I loved my mother," he says, "and she loved me, but she just let me raise myself. She didn't care if I went to school or not. I wasn't wild. I just had no direction." No father and a distracted mother.

At Colgate University, where generations of twenty-six other Munros went, Dick assumed he would have no problem getting in despite his dreary high school record. When Colgate suggested he first take some tests, he refused. Aimlessly he joined up with some high school buddies and hied off to foreign territory, Western Kentucky University.

Within a year he dropped out, joined the Marines as an enlisted man and was shipped off to the Korean War. Wounded twice, he was back on the firing line again near the thirty-eighth parallel when an enemy grenade blew up at his feet, putting him in Navy hospitals for almost a year. In 1953 he was discharged with a $55-a-month 30 percent veterans disability pension. He still has shrapnel in his feet, and in his mailbox his monthly pension check, raised to $240.

On the GI Bill, he had no trouble getting into Colgate. By then he was a mature war veteran with a more serious purpose and a passion for reading. Korean War vets with college degrees were in demand, although a colleague jested at Munro's retirement party that "his Colgate grade average made Dan Quayle look like a Rhodes scholar." Munro had a job offer from GM, could have had one from IBM. "I was so tired of being poor," he says, "and now I could get a job." A.C. Spark Plug flew him out to Flint, Michigan. Nice people but all they talked about was spark plugs. So he answered the call of a Time Inc. campus recruiter. He was hired and started out selling blocks of magazine subscriptions to college agents. Home base for his traveling salesmanship was New York, a city he had visited only once or twice before in his life.

For Munro it was all on-the-job training when he moved on as a business manager in the promotion department and then to *Sports Illustrated*. "In those days," he recalls, "all you had to do was add and subtract. Almost no one ever heard of a balance sheet. Business then was all profit and loss." The *Atlantic Monthly* beckoned him to become its publisher, but by then he had higher hopes. "At Time Inc.," he says, "it was very WASPy, Williams, Yale, a little blue blood. No question about it. I never knew it, because I never knew what WASPs and Jews were. It also helped to be tall." Munro was short. But that didn't stop him in 1962 from marrying his boss's secretary and becoming publisher of *Sports Illustrated*.

After Munro's four years as publisher, Andrew Heiskell was so taken with his conviviality that he handed him a really tough one. He was put in charge of what Heiskell called "the cats and dogs we loosely call video"—the fledgling cable and HBO video group, a poor orphan creature. There he worked with two other videophiles, Nick Nicholas and Jerry Levin, the new boy who developed HBO. Their job was to make something of the dream or get rid of the nightmare most old Timeincers felt cable was. The three expanded HBO programming and subscribers. They also built and bought cable franchises, even though they consistently lost out to Warner. The total growth in video and cable was so great that their effort began to bring in a big share of the entire company's revenue. Munro himself was an effervescing, untainted success.

TWENTY-THREE YEARS after he was hired, in 1980, with Munro sitting on the peak of the Time Inc. mountain as the CEO of the whole company, the climate around him began to get foggy. An army of Time business school graduates, squinting at printouts from their new computers, teamed up with McKinsey management consultants and discovered a company "identity crisis."

It was spelled out most pointedly, two years into Munro's term, by the brightest Harvard MBA of the bunch, Nick Nicholas, who had worked for Munro in the cable and video group. Nicholas's staff report, spiral-bound between heavy covers like the bookshelf of strategy reports that were to follow, was labeled: "Confidential, New Strategic Objectives for Time Inc., March 1, 1982." First, the report to the board took a deep bow to the past, "magazines, the historical heart of the company." Nicholas's report gave a round of applause to the overall gains made by Time Inc. in the ten years past, from $660 million in revenue to an impressive $3.3 billion, a compounded rate of growth of more than 18 percent.

Then it got to its real message. Magazines and books now accounted for only a third of the total. Cable and video had galloped to almost the same level. Forest products contributed more than a third. Nicholas's conclusion was jargon-encrusted but had a cutting message: "There is no evidence that the persistent undervaluation of Time Inc. common stock relative to its intrinsic value achievable in the public market will change unless we fundamentally alter the current mix, objective and strategy." Translation: We'll never get our stock up on Wall Street unless we sell forest products and do something better with our money.

The report read as if the final chapter had been forgotten; it hinted at what the company should get rid of but left out in what direction it should move. The report called for an end to the "adhocracy," the kind once described as dreaming up a new magazine while shaving in the morning. "In 1982," recalls Nicholas, "we had a company that made no sense, no rhyme or reason to it. It was like owning jock straps and the New York *Times*."

Tact and internal politics required that the report not say what to do with the close to $2 billion that could be available after selling all those trees, land and mills. To those who knew, there was not much doubt about what Nicholas or Munro or Jerry Levin wanted to do.

Arthur Temple, the leader of the tree crowd and a born-again magazine man, got huffy. "They were like a woman who gets bored and she goes out and buys a new hat," says Temple. "Some of the hats they bought in those days were very funny-looking hats. They were starving our business while they were feeding those greedy pups over on those other tits." Some of the print boys worried that the fresh pot of money would be ladled out to the video group.

Grumbling aside, ten months later Time Inc. spun out of the forest products business. Then it went hell bent, by cable and satellite, toward the tube. And, in the most visible embarrassment of the decade, toward cable TV in print.

A CAT THAT SITS on a hot stove, Mark Twain wrote, will never sit on a hot stove again. But neither will he sit on a cold one. The red-hot stove Time Inc. jumped on in 1983 was *TV-Cable Week*. The company got burned so publicly that not until just before the Warner merger did it have the confidence to touch another such stove again— hot or cold.

For three years, the magazine group publishers had looked enviously at the striding pace of their cable-TV brothers and sisters. The magazine people were frustrated; there must be something in TV's growth for them to translate into print and profit. Kelso Sutton, forty-one, the brash and bright cigar-smoking business boss of Time's publishing group, was a candidate to run all of Time Inc. one day. Urged on by Munro and others, Sutton found the swelling cable-TV market an inviting new opportunity, especially with Time pouring money into both cable systems and programming. How could aggressive magazine publishers crack it?

Walter Annenberg had done it with *TV Guide*. By publishing weekly program listings and mostly editorial fluff, *TV Guide* had become the largest weekly in the U.S. Time thought of buying it in 1981, but the $900 million price seemed too stiff (Rupert Murdoch later bought it for $2.8 billion). Time by then had overcome its cable franchising woes and was the second-largest cable-system owner in America. It also had HBO, by far the leading pay-TV channel. *TV Guide* gave short shrift to cable in those days. Why not put out a guide that covered both TV and cable, adding to the mix, one prospectus said, the "snap and wit" of Time's clever and experienced mass-market wordsmiths? It could have a weekly circulation of eight or ten million.

A high-level joint business and editorial duo (Jason McManus, who later became Time's editor-in-chief, and Reginald Brack, who became McManus's publishing partner as head of the Time Inc. Magazine Company) had explored the market for such a weekly around the country. After three months they came back and said, No way. That was the wrong answer. Sutton later named a much larger task force to get a better one. For months computers turned out projections, editors laid out dummies, applying their "snap and wit" to the TV fare they screened. "It was intense," says Munro, "we really beat that son of a bitch to death."

A brooding and talented editor from *People,* Dick Burgheim, who could create just the right popular touch, was picked to head the editorial team. It could be the last new mass magazine—a home run for Kelso Sutton's publishing group, earning eye-catching millions. The local cable operators would be the distributors. It barely occurred to Time's senior planners that the cable operators wanted their programs honestly reviewed about as much as car dealers wanted Ralph Nader paying them a visit. One of the casualties of the effort recalls that "The operators didn't want some smart-ass New York reviewer saying, 'If you watch this you'll be sorry.' "

Although *TV-Cable Week* fell under Grunwald's writ, he considered it a "service" magazine, not the kind of publication he should get too agitated about. It was, after all, more dependent on untried computers generating hundreds of timetables with local listings than on tried-and-true editors and writers commenting on them. Grunwald could have vetoed the weekly. But he never said yes or no. "I wish I'd acted differently," he says. "But there was always a question, especially among the board members, of why do we have church and state. So I felt it was important that the editor-in-chief not be obstructing the business side, which was pushing hard. I could not make a case the magazine would be demeaning to Time Inc. Okay, they want to do it, let them do it."

Grunwald's deputy, Ralph Graves, disagreed. He thought *TV-Cable Week* was a "factoid," not a magazine. As Decision Day approached, Graves sent Grunwald, Munro and Sutton a powerful memo:

What worries me most about this project is the sheer number of different gambles involved, every one of which we have to win.

Competition Not just *TV Guide* but also newspapers, free guides, free TV crawl and whatever technology may be coming down the road.

Pricing *TV Guide* is losing ground at 50 cents, and we will be asking 79 cents from people who are used to getting a lot of this informaton free.

Partnership We have to depend on the cable system operators, a most hazardous dependency.

Postage Apparently we can now count on qualifying for second class, but we have to be absolutely certain, since first class or third class would kill us.

Penetration We have to have the highest ever.

Renewal Rate We have to have the highest ever.

Listings Even if we bring off every one of these gambles—and we have to win them all, not just six out of seven—we could become obsolete by the time we reach breakeven, thanks to some electronic delivery of the same information.

This is like Russian roulette, where we have to keep pulling the trigger and all chambers (the gambles) have to prove harmless.

Grunwald spoke to Graves about the memo, said he was "inclined to leave the publishing decisions to the business side." Munro and Sutton never responded.

On the eve of a decision, one final fish-or-cut-bait presentation, choreographed with state-of-the-art graphics, was shown to Munro and an audience of forty or fifty staff. When it was over, there was a burst of applause, mostly for the performers, who were more persuasive with their marketing know-how than with the magazine itself. Sutton said that one final laborious and expensive test was needed to be sure. Munro was tired of spending more money on inconclusive tests, so he said, "Let's just do it."

And they did. The whole editorial staff with its high-tech computers was shipped out kicking and screaming to suburban White Plains. Their new office building was as unfinished as the advanced computer programs that went with it.

When it came out in 1983 with a fanfare of promotion, Time Inc.'s *TV-Cable Week* was an instant dud. The managers of Time's own cable systems wouldn't buy it, synergy be damned. After five months of chaos and anguish, it was closed down, the worst magazine flameout in publishing history. It was a laughingstock outside of Time, a trauma inside. "We blew it, we screwed up," says Munro. "The real flaw was with the distribution system. I should have said to our cable companies goddamnit you're going to love this magazine. Go out and distribute it. We don't operate that way and sometimes we look like damn fools. I'm on the Kellogg board. They bring out three or four new products a year that fail and nobody notices."

But Time was not trying out a new brand of cornflakes. Everybody noticed that the haughtiest magazine publishing company in the world had the biggest magazine flop of the century, arrogant big shots due for their comeuppance. It was all chronicled in a hilarious and whimsical but wicked account of the farce written by Christopher Byron, a former member of its staff. Grim Time bosses saw nothing funny in *The Fanciest Dive,* either the book or their humiliating plunge.

Ralph Graves, the author of the unheeded memo, turned out to have been right on target. Only one of seven barrels in his Russian roulette analogy ever fired the way it was supposed to: *TV-Cable Week* at least got a second-class mailing permit.

Graves chose early retirement six months later. (Retrospectively, no less than six senior retired Time Inc. executives who were there at the time now feel that Graves should have been made CEO instead of Munro. But no one ever seriously suggested it because Graves was thought of as "editorial.")

The theme of the annual report on 1983 was "Quality."

Nick Nicholas, with his cable and HBO background then, and as co-CEO of Time Warner today, has a revisionist's view of the *TV-Cable Week* debacle. "It was a non-event," he says. "I had nothing to do with it, but it's still a non-event. Forty—forty-seven million bucks." Artful bookkeeeping aside, it was more like $100 million. Nicholas feels what mattered most about the failure was that it "shook the confidence of the magazine group."

• • •

"WE LOST OUR NERVE after *TV-Cable Week* and we had to go through a period of expunging fear," says Dick Stolley, a longtime *Life* correspondent and editor who was the founding editor of *People*.

Time's magazine group had not brought out a successful new magazine since *People,* ten years earlier. A monthly science magazine, *Discover,* started in 1980, was foundering and in 1987 was sold at an announced $30 million loss (the actual figure was closer to $50 or $60 million). Quietly, a task force of editors repeatedly tried to create a magazine for women but it never jelled. For three years Grunwald pushed his own pet project, *Quality,* aimed at an affluent educated audience. The numbers crunchers defeated him. They said there was not enough of a market for such highfalutin stuff.

Tony Cox, a young, sharp business strategist who has since left Time and is now chairman of Showtime Networks, watched it all. He remembers that when *People* was first suggested, his new generation of MBAs thought it was "one of the stupidest publishing ideas we'd ever heard of." They resisted, dragged their feet. "But when the chairman, Heiskell, keeps popping by and says, 'What ya doing with my *People* idea?' you've eventually got to do something." It was launched after one brief newsstand test. "The financial models could be manipulated to produce any outcome," Cox says. "What sort of assumptions would you like? What was missing in later years was the advocacy of a goal. Who was the advocate?"

When in doubt, form a committee. In effect, that's what Time did. The editors and businessmen called it the "Magazine Development Group." In theory, Grunwald was its navigator, but in fact Kelso Sutton, the publishing head of the magazine division, was its helmsman. Aboard the exploration vessel was a crew of more than thirty editors, writers, designers and publishers, the best talent they could find. Most of them were to the company born. In those days, to be hired on the business side of Time, and even to a lesser extent for editorial, you had to be a "Time type." In the middle and upper ranks, people were rarely hired from "outside." The personnel department was still using that old rejection code scrawled across the top of interview forms, "NFT," not for Time—one step away from the dowager's codeword admonition "NOCD," not of our class, dear.

The new Magazine Development Group would show the world that Time still had creative publishing muscle—but cautiously this

time. Time's reputation couldn't suffer another public embarrassment. An alumnus of the group says that "*TV-Cable* so horrified
everybody, including the board, that there was a feeling we must
never let this happen again."

The top executives of the company split ranks on whether to pursue
smaller "niche" magazines that were being successfully launched
around them, or stick to big books that could lure people away from
TV screens. "We started to believe," says a Timeincer who was there
at the creation of the Magazine Development Group, "that we could
produce magazines in a laboratory, wearing white coats. It was 'market driven,' the new buzzword. Before, you had surveys after the
fact. Now you had them before."

The passions of the editors in their crumbling church were no
match for the state businessmen with their numbers, rates-of-return
and tests of potential readers. The group tested and dummied more
than ten new magazines, everything from *Home Office* and *Total
Health* to *Good Cook, Investment Week* and *Picture Week*. The last,
a supermarket pink-collar weekly, was tested, redone, tested again,
redone and throttled after spending more than $15 million on it. At
one desperate point, the Magazine Development Group played Pen-
tagon-like war games: an A magazine task force competing against
a B.

Everything they tried turned out to be too small to make any
difference or too big to take the risk. "Once you've created a magazine development group, you're going to have magazines to consider," another alumnus of the group says. "The computer," adds
Marshall Loeb, who ran the group for a while and is the present
managing editor of *Fortune,* "gives you a marvelous reason to run
all kinds of studies." Reg Brack, who now heads the Time Inc.
Magazine Company, has a more caustic verdict. "The odds of a new
idea making it through that system or that fast-paced environment
were slim to none." It turned out to be none. Brack, who replaced
Sutton in 1986, wiped out the whole operation and its gestating
magazines as soon as he moved into his new office. He had no use
for "those little things."

What was not missing were ideas and resolve. Television was the
hot medium. The print advocates had to do something new to prove
magazines were not an endangered species—that Time was still the
best magazine creator around. No lack of ideas and prospectuses
prevented them. Fair to say that Time's fertile staff had over the

years dreamed up and proposed just about every magazine imaginable. If they overlooked anything, outside entrepreneurs brought it to them. Focus was what they lacked. After *TV-Cable Week* it was making a commitment that scared them.

When he retired as editor-in-chief in 1987, Grunwald reflected on the period in his farewell speech to the staff. He remained bothered by what went wrong. "Did we simply fail to come up with the right ideas? Did we try too hard for the big weekly casino? Were there too many task forces, was there too much bureaucracy? One thing I am particularly sure of: too often there was an absence of the unified vision. The editors and our business colleagues rarely agreed."

One playful office wag provided another explanation. He passed around a list of the "Six Stages of New Magazine Development: 1) Exultation 2) Disenchantment 3) Confusion 4) The Search for the Guilty 5) Punishment of the Innocent 6) Distinction for the Uninvolved."

TO THE WORLD OUTSIDE, the TV and cable group was the "Uninvolved." The "Guilty" were the people in the publishing half of the company—always more in the public eye than their video partners. The existing magazines were viewed as "mature," meaning mostly okay but with little growth potential. Time-Life Books, once a vigorous money-maker, was just pulling itself out of the red. The effort to bring new luster back to publishing with innovative magazines had flopped.

TV and cable were supposed to be the vibrant new heartbeat of the slumping company. It was a naive view. Deep inside Time they knew otherwise.

Hungry for new movies, HBO couldn't get enough of them. A surge of new home video players began to make available fresher movies on cassettes. HBO hit a wall of slow growth. Under Levin, a disastrous long-term deal with Columbia Pictures for exclusive showing of its new films cost hundreds of millions without helping HBO. The contract was for a base fee per film, plus a sliding scale upward without limit based on box-office success. In Hollywood lingo, they were not "capped." Without the cap, some of the films were blockbusters costing HBO a fortune at a time when HBO's subscriber growth had slowed down. Capital for expanding cable franchises was also hard to come by. Costly ventures in subscription

television (STV) and print information by TV (Teletext) bombed
and sputtered away.

It was a period, says one former senior Time executive, when "a
lot of shit was hitting the fan. Our earnings started to go down.
Things began looking bad."

On a wintry evening in early 1985, Dick Munro and his chief
financial officer at the time, Nick Nicholas, were headed on foot for
Grand Central Station—a regular commuting couple. Munro, be-
moaning all the bad news, suddenly turned to Nicholas and said,
"Next Monday you're going back to video." Nicholas understood.
"There were about five bad years," Nicholas says. "Four, five or six.
The company was flat. We had the board of directors dissatisfied.
Whenever we seemed to do something good over here, we'd shoot
ourselves in the foot over there. We couldn't get all the cylinders
going at the same time. Those were tough, tough days."

On Wall Street and in the offices of hustling investment bankers,
new takeover rumors were heating up the phone lines.

NICHOLAS TOOK TO THE task of shaping up cable and HBO
in a hurry. "Hey, we've got a problem. Let's go fix the goddamn
thing instead of pretending we don't have it." He renegotiated the
sour Columbia Pictures deal, clashed with HBO's chairman, Frank
Biondi, and fired him. (Biondi is now president and CEO of Viacom,
a big HBO competitor.)

Then he applied his muscle and his quick financial mind to cable.
He lost out to Warner again when Time tried to buy American
Express's interest in Warner-Amex Cable, but pocketed a $12.5 mil-
lion reward for Time from Amex just by standing in the wings as a
potential buyer and forcing Warner to pay Amex a higher price. In
"one three-way $2.1 billion deal, concluded on my kitchen table,"
he bought Westinghouse Cable, "the biggest deal of my life up to
then," Nicholas recalls with retrospective glee. Then he sold a chunk
of Time's huge wholly owned American Television Corporation
(ATC) to the public, netting a tidy profit and new capital.

Nicholas, for all his fast-moving success in cable and financial
reorganizations, was a conservative operator, averse to risk and unwilling to court failure. He missed at least one giant opportunity,
which he has been trying to remedy ever since.

The Atlanta buccaneer broadcaster and yachtsman Ted Turner,
whose CNN would become the most important journalistic invention

of the past twenty years, was roaming the media and entertainment seas, often running straight into the wind. In 1985 the eccentric entrepreneur was buying MGM and was hard up for cash. To help finance his adventures, he offered Time a half interest in CNN for $300 million. Time didn't like the cut of his jib, called him the "Mouth of the South." One of Munro's advisers who knew Turner said he's not a "Time Inc. type. He drinks too much, spends money crazily and chases women." Munro even hid, trying to avoid meeting with him, when Turner repeatedly came cap-in-hand to the Time & Life Building.

Nicholas was amused by Turner but just didn't like the numbers. The calculated return on investment for CNN then was zero or minus. Cautiously he offered Turner $225 million, with the $75 million balance to be paid out if Turner met his budgeted projections. Turner, of course, had no credible projections, just dreams. Anyway, he needed the full $300 million in cash. Nicholas was wary of dreams when it came to all-cash deals. Turner sailed away. "It was the biggest business mistake of my life," said Nicholas later, as he longs for Time Warner to own CNN. Time eventually accumulated a frustrating 21.5 percent ownership stake in Turner Broadcasting, with 10.5 percent voting power. The company today is estimated to be worth in the $5 billion range.

THE WINTER of 1985 brought chilling doubt not only to the executive suites and boardroom of Time. In the editorial precincts, it produced an even harsher climate. *Time* magazine, the company's standard-bearer, was hit by the most punishing libel suit in its history, *Sharon* v. *Time Inc.* The division of church and state would never be the same again.

The case unfolded in one agonizing Manhattan federal court session after another. The attacker was the burly Ariel Sharon, Israel's voluble defense minister and the zealous leader of his country's disastrous war in Lebanon. *Time* accused him in a cover story of "reportedly" condoning the worst massacre of the war, the bloody, premeditated slaughter of hundreds of Palestinians in Lebanon's Sabra and Shatila refugee camps. Sharon, who needed vindication to restore his damaged political career in Israel, cannonaded back full bore, charging *Time* with a "blood libel," "lying," "anti-Semitism" and worse.

On principle, financially secure publications do not settle libel suits or retract when they think they are right, no matter what the cost. *Time* thought it was right, although it could offer no convincing proof. It set out to prove both the wisdom of the principle and the validity of its facts. It failed on both counts. Its sources melted away and the magazine never could produce the evidence it needed in court, nor was it willing to yield any ground in print. The magazine's few defenders had to answer critics who said *Time* was being "arrogant," "sloppy," "unfair," "hiding behind its First Amendment privilege." At the trial, *Time*'s proud system of reporting and checking was ridiculed and unraveled. Its editors, reporters and researchers were held up to disdain. The case produced humiliating front-page news and devastating editorial criticism around the world.

Under the Donovan Charter that separated church and state, Time's editor-in-chief, Henry Grunwald, was free ultimately to call the shots. Although they deferred to Grunwald, Munro, Sutton and others badly wanted to settle. Grunwald and his editors rejected several proposed settlement statements drafted by Time. But it is doubtful whether Sharon, with his own political agenda, would have settled on any acceptable terms. Grunwald stood his traditional ground.

In the end *Time* "won" on an important issue of constitutional law. It lost everyplace else in the more damaging court of public opinion. The jury did uphold the magazine's complex legal rights of not "knowingly lying" or having "reckless disregard for the truth." By that special definition, *Time* was granted First Amendment protection for not having committed what had been confusingly defined by the Supreme Court as "actual malice." But more significantly, in a most unusual caveat to its verdict, the jury deplored *Time*'s journalism. "We find," the jury foreman read in open court, "that certain *Time* employees acted negligently and carelessly in reporting and verifying the information which ultimately found its way into the published paragraph." *Time* won in law but flunked in journalism.

What happened after the trial was over? Listen to these accounts.

Grunwald "The Sharon trial was very punishing to me but not inside Time Inc. In hindsight I find it extraordinary the extent to which decisions were left to me. It was scrupulously church-state."

Munro "There were some people on the board who never understood church and state. It has to be in your genes. You have to be raised here. Not only does it work but it helps us on the business side to dodge a lot of bullets. Sharon was the incident that triggered a light bulb going off in the boardroom. Jesus, the outside directors were saying, the editor-in-chief works for us and we ought to have him report to us occasionally. It may have been a milestone. As a result of Sharon, the board members really felt they should be more informed. We're talking about more oversight by the board—that's right."

Nicholas "The venerable notion of church and state had gone from a safeguard of editorial integrity, which was a good idea, into a *Kramer vs. Kramer*–style divorce, which was a bad idea."

William M. Guttman, Time Inc. general counsel in 1985 "I never fully appreciated what church and state meant until this turning point for everyone."

Donald S. Perkins, one of Time Inc.'s outside directors "There never was a discussion at the board level about the seriousness of the Sharon case. The separation was involved. I wondered whether this would have happened had this been organized differently. I couldn't find any company that had anything like this. After the case was over and after we'd won in the law and lost in the newspapers, the subject was being closed. The chairman of the board said 'The next subject is—' And I interrupted him. I could not in good conscience let it pass without asking questions. I wasn't aware of the Donovan Charter. Even if I'd seen it, it wasn't very meaningful to me before this discussion. I asked whether it would be appropriate to have an editorial audit at *Time*. I just farted in church."

AMONG THE TWELVE OUTSIDE directors of Time Inc. in the late '80s, by far the most active and involved was Don Perkins, the retired head of the Jewel Companies, a large Chicago-based grocery distributor. "He was the main driver on the board," says Nicholas. Perkins is a "professional director." He served on ten other boards and has been invited to join dozens more, a "Mr. Midwest" of the business world ("I've been to more board meetings than most people you'll ever talk to"). Perkins is a graceful, philosophical mediator who spouts homilies from his deep experience ("A problem should be brought before the board even before management knows the answer") and writes essays on corporate governance. Management policy is his game, and boards are his arena ("I am as concerned about the human beings as I am about the situation"). He has also brought his presence to dozens of such non-business boards as the Ford Foundation, Brookings Institution and Harvard Business School, where, after Yale ('49), he was in the class of '51.

Perkins seemed just the right Time director to take on what he called the "audit" of the tricky church-state relationship, which puzzled him and so many of the other directors. "Some people on the board," Grunwald recalled, "thought it made no sense in any corporation to have more than one boss." He was dead right. One of the outside directors puts it more pungently: "You could have all this horseshit you wanted about church and state. But directors can be sued and you can't adopt an absolute philosophy like that."

For his part, Perkins felt "there are clearly some purely editorial things on which the editor-in-chief should be solely responsible." No one was in the mood for a confrontation. So Grunwald, in the aftermath of the Sharon case and, more important, facing his own retirement within two years, was more than willing to talk things over for the future. Over an amiable dinner at Manhattan's Four Seasons restaurant, he and Perkins began to discuss how to improve the relationship between the board and the editors. "More communications" was the bromidic formula.

Grunwald is a masterly diplomat (which he later became) and an impressive advocate of the abstract. He agreed to try his hand at some editing and amendments of the Donovan Charter. His objective was to preserve the independence of his own and, more especially, his successors' office. The company had expanded and changed since the Donovan-Heiskell partnership. He and Munro were two peas in different pods. "I don't take Dick to the opera," Grunwald said, "and he doesn't take me to the ballgame."

He conceded the charter needed some fine tuning. Time-Life Books had already slipped away from his supervision. After failing to create new magazines, Time was acquiring interests and ownership in a rack of magazines that were independently put out by their existing managements. HBO and cable had barely any editorial raison d'être that was plausibly within his reach. Grunwald, unlike Donovan, who had been managing editor of *Fortune,* knew little about business and appeared to care less. Editing words and ideas was his passion, especially those in *Time.*

In one draft memo, Grunwald pointed out that "If one started Time Inc. from scratch today, one might not opt for the church and state structure." But he convinced Perkins and the others that the unique editorial sovereignty of the editor-in-chief over the six New York-based magazines (*Time, Fortune, People, Sports Illustrated, Money* and *Life*) had best not be thrown out. Instead they agreed on two major revisions to the charter.

The first was benign enough. After the fallout from the Sharon case, a paragraph was inserted mandating quarterly reporting to the board of any libel litigation. The other revision was more fundamental. It changed the editor-in-chief's working relationship. In the future he would work "in close consultation with the Chief Executive Officer of the Magazine Group" and only "when appropriate with the CEO of the Company." Down a notch for the editor-in-chief.

The change ratified for the first time in writing what Grunwald had been doing in practice, concerning himself not much with the tone and strategy of the whole company but mostly with the magazines he edited. In the much expanded company, henceforth the editor-in-chief would stick to Time's homegrown magazines and not get involved in what the rest of Time Inc. was doing, except as one member of a large board. Partnership at the top of what was once a journalistic pyramid would be formally dissolved. As textual and even trivial as it appeared, the spirit of the change would matter mightily to the people and the events ahead.

The board happily embraced converting the church into a chapel rather than the sanctuary of the whole damn Time Inc. cathedral.

THE HALLS OF THE Time & Life Building in the '80s were alive with the sound of buzzing management consultants and the thud of strategy reports. Reorganization charts were rolling off the drafting tables onto the Xeroxes. One such scheme, which looked like the disorderly loading dock of a box factory, called for appointing more than half a dozen new executive vice presidents. Members of the board, patiently and affectionately, told Munro to try again. After one strategy report on acquiring newspapers and TV stations, Arthur Temple slapped his hand on the board table and said, "Dick, I love your strategy. I just wish you'd thought of it ten years ago."

Time's own *Fortune* again nailed the problem. In the magazine's annual report on how corporate executives rate the "perceived innovativeness" of American companies, Time had plummeted from a radiant third place in 1983 to fifteenth in 1984. It would be forty-second in 1986 and a dismal ninety-sixth the year after.

The threat from outside predators still did not seem menacing. The wildfire of takeovers, raids and restructuring was warming up, but the heat was mostly turned on heavier industry, not on trademark publishers. When American Express had tried to buy McGraw-Hill in the late '70s—including its *Business Week*—McGraw-Hill wrapped itself in the flag of press freedom. American Express backed off. Time had an even bigger flag, so it was reassured.

Warren Buffett, the folksy Omaha-based investment guru who owned more than 2.5 million shares of Time stock, 4 percent of the company, came in 1984 to Munro with an offer that at first seemed hard to refuse. Buffett had—and still has—a reputation not only as one of the smartest investors, but as someone who makes quality investments for the long run. He is widely known as "one of the most celebrated friends of management in American finance." If invited in, Buffett would offer his welcome financial advice, as un-prickly as a Nebraska cornflower. Both the Washington Post Company and Capital Cities had thrived on his quiet partnerships.

Buffett made a courtly, generous proposition to Munro. If Time would find it welcome, he would buy on the open market even more Time stock than he already owned, affording the company protection from the money-grubbing world around it. His assured shield would be guaranteed in writing. At Capital Cities/ABC, where Buffett owned 18 percent of the company, he irrevocably turned over his voting rights to the management. If he should decide to sell, he also volunteered to offer the stock first to the company—an agreement similar to the ones he also has as a big stockholder in the Washington Post and other companies.

Buffett recalls that when he came to see Munro, "I may have very mildly suggested that the climate for takeovers was changing. I might smell that a little faster than they would because I was more in tune with the financial community. But I didn't want to talk them into anything." He also had an idea that could give the stock a big boost, at the same time making the magazines invulnerable to takeover by putting them in the equivalent of a trust.

"He was a couple of steps—not surprising—ahead of where we were," says Munro. "Boy, if he'd come along two years later, we would have been terribly interested." But not then. At an informal dinner the night before the next board meeting, Munro casually—

without pushing it—dropped the Buffett carrot on the hors d'oeuvres plate. In less than five minutes, with no more than a shoulder shrug, the board sniffed the offering and turned it away. The reaction, Nicholas recalls, was "Why would we want to do that? What does he bring to the party?" Heiskell, long retired when he heard about the proposal, remembers thinking, "They were then so high and mighty and cocky that they spurned it."

Munro had an altogether different explanation for his irresolution. "In this period," he said, "we were trying to figure out where this animal called Time Inc. was going to go." To find out, Time troops went off to strategy retreats in everywhere from Cambridge, Massachusetts, to a shooting and fishing club in Eastport, Long Island; the sunnier climes of Charleston, South Carolina; and Lyford Cay in the Bahamas. Time's then general counsel, Bill Guttman, who was later made staff leader of the strategy group, felt that "we needed a compass more than we did numbers."

ENERGETIC AND BRIGHT SECOND-TIER managers, with the help of outside consultants, ground out series of literate, stimulating documents—written by the editors in the groups, backed up by analysts of every stripe. Taken together, their reports affirmed or denied proposals in just about every direction.

The reports were closer to road maps than driving instructions. More creativity inside; no, more acquisition outside. Get into the movie business; no, stick to what we know. More information purveying; no, more entertainment or a combination of the two. Go global; no, Time had never been any good at that. Vertical integration; no, horizontal expansion. Buy newspapers; no, Time doesn't know how to deal with local news. Buy a television network or affiliated stations; no, cable or fiber optics is the wave of the future.

One internal task force of younger business staffers and editors, eight of the best and the brightest from every part of the company, was later commissioned by the management to do a retrospective candid assessment of the period. They spared no one's feelings when they reported back in their sixty-seven-page assessment:

> There are no visible high-potential areas emerging within the company to fuel future growth. A perceived "home run" orientation toward innovation has contributed to a fear of failure among managers who come to believe that the risks of inno-

vation are unacceptable. As a result the company is perceived on both Wall Street and internally as uncreative, overly cautious, investor-driven and risk-averse. Throughout the company we have found a disquieting gap between management's rhetoric and management's actions. Senior management has not communicated a galvanizing vision of the company's future growth opportunities.

Throughout all the reports was one constant theme: video. But what in video?

Like most managements, Time's earnestly read the impressive thick reports, sent congratulations to the reporters, then went about their business. The ABC network looked as if it might be on the market. One small Time group was put to work to consider whether the FCC rules barring cross-ownership of cable and TV properties could be overcome. While they were considering, ABC was snatched right from under their furrowed brows. In quick succession within nine months, a friendly CapCities acquired ABC. Turner and right-wing Senator Jesse Helms each made a hostile feint at CBS, which investor Laurence Tisch then bought. And General Electric gobbled up NBC. The internationals were also coming in—Bertelsmann, Sony, Hachette, Murdoch, Maxwell, Thompson. Time started really to worry.

Time's apprehension was not lessened by "Bid-'em-Up" Bruce Wasserstein, the disheveled but dazzling takeover superstar. He became the management and board's investment adviser, the heavyweight who suggested their financial scripts for the next five years, right up to the final curtain of the Time Warner merger. Wasserstein regularly appeared before the board, giving primers on the new hostile takeover environment of leveraged buy-outs, "creeping acquirers," poison pills and "seductive two-tier offers."

Munro took the hint. Working from a consultant's list of a hundred possible companies, he started an informal tour of the media map of the U.S. with an unaggressive and vague message. "We're in the same business. We have a good relationship. If you ever thought of doing anything with us . . ." When he called on the New York *Times*'s Punch Sulzberger, the Washington *Post*'s Kay Graham, Warren Phillips of Dow Jones's *Wall Street Journal,* Los Angeles *Times-Mirror*'s Otis Chandler, Knight-Ridder and a list of others, he was just sort of "kicking the tires," says Munro. No one he talked to could quite figure out what he was doing—except the folks at Knight-Ridder, who thought Time might be moving on them and called their lawyer. The approaches were as pleasant as they were inconsequential.

One newspaper acquisition attempt by Time got more earnest. Al Neuharth, the self-declared "son of a bitch egotist," was grand pasha of the tempting eighty-two-paper Gannett newspaper group, largest in the U.S. Neuharth, who is the splashiest export ever to come out of Eureka, South Dakota, was an unlikely match right from the start for Dick Munro ("We're kind of Calvinistic here").

WHEN AL NEUHARTH MOVED into penthouse suite 38-H of the Waldorf-Astoria Towers in 1984, he made some changes. He had his own ideas about decor.

Among some other upgradings in his new sleepover pad, Neuharth embellished the pool table where Frank Sinatra used to shoot eight-ball with a golden glitter more appropriate to his taste. It matched the full-sized pair of golden-faced sheep, with Godiva chocolates wrapped in gold foil underneath their hind legs, that stood in the foyer outside his lavish headquarters in Rosslyn, Virginia.

Although Neuharth was hardly his style, Munro enjoyed lunching with him in the Waldorf digs. Munro didn't have eight-ball in mind. "Gannett was riding high," he says. "Their local papers were just booming—local monopolies like cable. We had 135 cable systems all humming. We knew what it was like when there wasn't a competitor in the marketplace. Neuharth had exactly the same situation in newspapers. We looked at his record, seventy-eight straight quarters of growth, amazing, and said, 'Boy that's pretty exciting stuff.' "

It could be a match. Time's magazines, books, cable and HBO with Gannett's profitable newspapers. The complete media company with no FCC problems of cross-ownership. The numbers both their staffs were running looked inviting. There was the flamboyant Neuharth to worry about. But after breaking bread a few times in the suite, Munro and Neuharth talked of each other as "friends." Munro told the Time board about his preliminary encounters.

At the same time, Tom Wyman, the CBS boss, embattled by Ted Turner's advances and Senator Jesse Helms's ideological threats, approached Munro. He wanted to know whether Time might be interested in becoming the white knight who could save the Tiffany Network from invading barbarians. Again Time staff ran the numbers—not great this time. Munro and Nicholas jousted with Wyman and his chief financial officer in an Essex House hotel suite. They all decided it was a mismatch, banned by FCC rules, fuzzy as to who was buying whom, along with that eternal Time question in viewing combinations, Who would end up as boss? No satisfactory answers—no deal.

One day a few weeks later, an agitated Wyman called Munro again. A lawyer from Cravath, Swaine & Moore, the law firm they both used, told him Neuharth was negotiating with Time. Munro vividly remembers the "famous" phone call: " 'Dick you aren't talking to Gannett are you?' And I said well actually we are having some conversations. And he said, 'Well I've got Al in the next room and we're about to do a deal.' That's when he hung up the phone. That was the end of that."

It's hard to tell who was more indignant, Wyman, who had been assured by Neuharth he was negotiating with no one else; or Munro, who had the same assurance and was warming to the idea of a Time-Gannett combination. Both angrily broke off with Neuharth, who himself was madder than he was chagrined. "There were never any negotiations with Time," he says, pooh-poohing the uproar, "just friendly discussions. It was Munro's preppie morality that blew things up." Unlike Munro, Neuharth saw no conflict in his fencing with Time while at the same time he was negotiating a deal with Wyman. (Three months later, Wyman was fired when the gray knight, the New York investor Larry Tisch, stepped in and took control of CBS.)

Munro and company were disillusioned with what they called Neuharth's "double-dealing." But the "asset fit" was still beguiling, and Neuharth himself was near retirement. Both Gannett and Time participants say some back-channels were also helpful. Clifton Wharton, a member of the Time board and chancellor of the State University of New York, was married to a member of the Gannett board. Maybe now that everyone had cooled off, "even though this terrible thing had happened," they should try again, especially since the latest strategy group was pushing a newspaper acquisition.

So, with faint heart, in the following November 1985 they tried again—this time in a more rustic setting.

EIGHTY-TWO MILES EAST of New York City, off a back-country road, slumbers Eastport's Long Island-Wyandanch Club, a three-hundred-acre shooting and fishing wildwood built more than a hundred years ago by old money. Its sprawling two-story clubhouse, sided with weathered gray shingles, is surrounded by three well-stocked trout ponds, trap and skeet towers for clay birds, pheasant and chukar walks for the real thing.

If the tweedy members are inclined, the clubhouse can be used overnight. In its musty twin-bedded guest rooms on the second floor, wire hangers dangle from rusting wall hooks. Shared bathrooms are equipped with a footed bathtub and primitive wall showers. Downstairs in the living room, a full set of the esteemed 1910 eleventh edition of the *Encyclopaedia Britannica* yellows on the bookcases. Game birds mounted under vintage glass line the walls and perch stiffly on the large stone fireplace. The only concessions to modernity are a single telephone and an old TV set with a rabbit-ear antenna sitting on the floor.

In these quaint surroundings, in the fall of 1985, yet another Time shotgun strategy group met with its sights set on TV stations and newspapers. The gabfest was inconclusive. Most of the group whirled back to New York, helicopter-borne, cheered on by a gaggle of curious neighborhood kids who had turned out to see the high-flying evacuation. Remaining behind were Time's four big guns, Dick Munro and his trio of competing successors: Time's three executive vice presidents, Nick Nicholas (in charge of cable and HBO), Jerry Levin (strategy) and Kelso Sutton (publishing).

All four stayed in place for the main event, the airborne arrival of Al Neuharth and his two heirs, Gannett chief editor John Curley and Douglas McCorkindale, Gannett's chief financial officer, who Neuharth calls his "goddamn bean counter."

Curley, a down-to-earth journalist, had driven out earlier in a rented car. Sutton, the leader of the publishing group, was the only enrolled member of the club and hence quartermaster for the event. When Sutton returned from a brief supply mission to his nearby weekend home, he was met by one of the club's excited staff. "Mr. Sutton, Mr. Sutton," she anxiously blurted out, "Mr. Curley tells us that Mr. Neuharth can't share a bathroom." "Well," replied the resourceful Sutton, "we'll just have to get Big Al one of his own." With dispatch, he solved the problem by commandeering an equally rundown cottage alongside the main clubhouse.

Neuharth dropped down in a Time helicopter. Accompanied by his financial chief, McCorkindale, he was toting two briefcases and was dressed in his trademark work clothes: gray-and-white sport jacket, white shirt with pearl-gray tie, gray pants and black shoes. Sutton greeted him with a reservation clerk's apology, "Mr. Neuharth, your room isn't quite ready yet." They marked time for a few minutes. Then Sutton and a club attendant walked Neuharth over to the cottage. As they tried to enter, the screen door popped its hinges and fell on Neuharth's head. Startled, Neuharth mumbled an oath and Sutton an apology. Neuharth was no more pleased when he managed to get through the doorway to discover that the bed inside was hospital rigged, permanently set with its head higher than its foot. "By then," says Sutton, "Al was obviously pissed off. So we beat a hasty retreat." On the way out, the club attendant solicitously suggested, "Mr. Neuharth, perhaps you'd like a golf cart to get back." Casting a glance at the twenty-yard walk, he grumbled, "Whadya think, I'm an old man or something?"

Overlooking the rocky start, Neuharth showed up in good humor for drinks around the crackling fireplace, as casually dressed as the others. He spurned Sutton's offer to make him a martini, with an old putdown: "I'm the only one who can make *my* martini." To lighten things up, the Time group suggested that Jerry Levin, then the head of Time's strategy group, don the outfit he had been wearing that afternoon. Levin scurried upstairs and came down decked out in a New York Mets baseball uniform. Neuharth, a Yankee fan, fell into the spirit, sprinted back to his cottage and promptly returned in a wild psychedelic New York Yankees T-shirt. Drinks in hand, costumed like a softball team, they all watched the Reagan-Gorbachev Geneva summit on TV, then sat down to a friendly dinner.

Over roast lamb, onions, carrots and potatoes, downed with delicate Trefethen (1983) and Grgich (1982) chardonnays, Munro, Nicholas and Levin bantered back and forth with the Gannett trio about each other's business. So far so good. Neuharth did wonder why Time spent so much money on things like taking businessmen on an Asian Newstour, from which Nicholas and Levin had enthusiastically just returned. But the real heavy lifting began after dinner, when Neuharth said to the group, "You are the guys who are going to have to figure this out and then do it." Nicholas recalls responding to a surprised Neuharth, "If you really mean that, why don't you and Dick go to bed." And so they did, leaving their generals behind with a fridge full of wine and their heads full of questions.

As the bibulous exchange continued, McCorkindale popped a few too many corks. He authoritatively described such Gannettisms as buying a newspaper, then paring the editorial staff and raising the ad rates to keep profits growing. "We liked each other and all had a good time," says Levin, "but we basically saw the Gannett essence. The guys didn't hit it off philosophically. It was a long shot anyway. The meeting put the nail in the coffin."

At sunrise, Curley had a courier-delivered copy of their flagship *USA Today* for Neuharth, with whom he was chatting outside the cottage. Sutton, also up early to do some fly fishing in the pond while the others jogged, overheard Neuharth ask, "What about this guy, the editor-in-chief Grunwald?" "We'll be able to handle him," Curley replied.

Over breakfast they explored whether and how they should try to do something together. They evaded the answer by agreeing that they'd all go back and discuss it among themselves, then "be in touch."

After some morning bird shooting and strolling through cornfields, the Neuharth threesome headed by limousine to the nearby Suffolk Air Base. On the way they stopped at a local bar and grill for lunch before flying off in Gannett's black-and-white Gulfstream. Curley remembers the consensus: "My conclusion was we would never agree to any of their terms and conditions, and they probably wouldn't agree to ours. It was our presumption they'd want to run things and our presumption that we'd want to. It didn't surprise me, because I went to school [Columbia Journalism, '63] with fellows who worked for Time. I had a sense from things they were saying about their corporate culture. Dick Munro repeated several times that Time is a grand old company with a grand old tradition, in the vision of Henry Luce. They said the Time Inc. name will always stand first, control its own destiny, sees itself as the main media in the U.S."

Nicholas has a shorter version: "We concluded our cultures were dramatically different. We woke up the next morning, shook hands and went our ways."

Neuharth says he still had hope. "But I got suspicious when Munro cancelled three follow-up dates. Finally, I got a call from Munro and he said no, not now."

Neuharth, who swears he liked the old-boy club, retired three years later, naming John Curley his successor. When Curley asked Neuharth what he wanted from Gannett as a memento, Neuharth answered, "a nice diamond ring." Today, on the ring finger of his left hand, Neuharth sports an outsize one-inch rectangular black ring, embedded with two rows of diamonds spelling out "Al Neuharth/ Founder USA Today." He was named chairman of the Gannett Foundation, which he relocated in 1989 to ostentatious $20 million new quarters more suitable to his taste. Within two years, no longer so impressed with a company that he wasn't running, Neuharth saw to it that the foundation sold all of its more than half billion dollars in Gannett stock. The foundation had to rename itself, choosing "Freedom Forum."

"I think Munro thought he was getting close to a deal," was one director's delusion, "although no terms were ever proposed or reported to the board."

That was the end of Time's newspaper strategy.

SURPRISING INEPTITUDE AND EXECUTIVE foolishness? Not altogether. At the top of any pyramid of power—government, corporate, military or whatever—there is usually unimpressive, even loony confusion. The long march of Time through the '80s was no exception.

Chapter 5

Nick, Jerry and Jason

NICK NICHOLAS IS FOND of quoting that old saw about the 2,000-year-old man. When asked his main means of transportation, he answers, "Fear—if you don't move quickly enough you get eaten."

Time Inc. was moving fast enough in the '80s but zigzagging so erratically that it made little headway. On the executive thirty-fourth floor, the fear of takeover sharks whipped up the frenzy. "I still can't believe that when Dick Munro became CEO," says one of his executive advisers at the time, "he had no sense of where he wanted to take the company. Nicholas didn't either. Success, after all, is not a vision. Neither is market share."

Munro met privately with restless directors at breakfast, lunch and dinner. They urged him, above all else, to get executive help. "I'd sit down with Dick," recalls director Don Perkins, "and I'd say I think you're part of the problem. Not because you're not a good executive but you just can't be in all the places this company requires." Everyone admired Munro's outspoken, open manner. But, adds Perkins, "When I could see the blood rising above Dick's collar line, that's when I wanted to put my hand over his mouth."

Always candid, Munro confessed his problem to other CEOs at a closed Harvard Business School seminar. He told them of his frustrating sessions with individual directors. "This time," he recounted, "they were more forthcoming than in the past, saying that I was overworked and really should appoint a chief operating officer to share the load. The pressure is also beginning to mount internally as well as on the board. We'd been taking a real pounding in the business press." But Munro kept delaying. One of his big problems was that he didn't know what to do with his titular chairman Ralph Davidson.

Munro needed to be nudged. After he presented his 1986 goals to the board, they added one imperative he had not included: Get yourself a chief operating officer. Munro had always been grooming his protégé Nicholas for the job. But as he had told his Harvard seminarians, "I have three excellent candidates. They are all the same age, forty-six, eight years younger than I. The risk is that by naming one I might lose the other two." The other two were Jerry Levin, who plainly had the brains and vision—"one of our intellectual provocateurs," Nicholas calls him—but was thought not to have the financial know-how and executive record; and Kelso Sutton, who had only magazine experience and was carrying the heavy baggage of the *TV-Cable Week* failure.

In March of 1986, one month after the board leaned on him to make a decision, Munro called in Nicholas and told him, "I'm naming you president in the fall." He added, recalls Nicholas, "You're going to run this place one day. I've made my last appointment. I'm not going to do to you what they did to Davidson." Munro talked one-on-one with each of fourteen outside directors and reported them "all pleased."

At its July 17, 1986, meeting, the board ratified the changes at the top. Munro continued as the boss with the new title of chairman, Nicholas was made president and Ralph Davidson was moved aside to another hollow title, chairman of the executive committee.

Less than a year later Davidson quit, demanding and getting a then unprecedented—for Time—$4 million severance package, as well as millions in stock options and profit-sharing. On top of the Time stock he owned, his income from his pension and profit-sharing alone would yield him more than $1 million a year. Feeling guilty for what it had put Davidson through, Time went another embarrassing step further. It paid the outside lawyer Davidson hired to extract the special deal from Time an $18,500 fee. Old Timeincers, including Donovan and Heiskell, were "aghast." Davidson was named chairman of the Kennedy Center in Washington, where the board removed him three years after he was hired.

Four years later, looking back on the period from his present post as president and co-CEO of Time Warner, Nicholas told an interviewer flatly, "I've been running Time Inc. since 1986."

True enough but not too appreciative of his mentor Munro, who has a more complex view: "My humility may end up biting me. What happened was I gave Nicholas an awful lot of leeway and people thought he did it all by himself. I do get kind of annoyed when people say I was obviously a puppet. The troika in the last few years really worked beautifully. Everybody contributing. We had some lousy ideas coming from Nick and he'd be the first to admit it."

He might well admit it. But he might not be the first.

WHEN NICHOLAS IS GAMBOLING barefoot over the Saltaire dunes of his Fire Island weekend retreat, skiing the slopes of Vail, Colorado, with his psychotherapist wife and their five kids, or having dinner with his journalist friend Nick Gage, the "Nick the Knife" of repute is nowhere in evidence.

Nick Nicholas knows that his superficial reputation as a tough guy follows him like the contrails of the Time Warner jets. "Not many people know me well," he explains. "I've been self-reliant my whole life. I don't think people get me wrong because they know me. They get me wrong because they don't know me."

There's more truth than self-defensive dodging in his explanation. Nicholas has many friends and admirers in business, along with his detractors. But Nicholas at work sometimes sounds more narrowly focused and harder than he means to. "I'm supposed to be the icewater-in-the-veins guy," says Nicholas. "What am I going to do? Go around and deny it? I'm the ultimate realist. I don't think I'm the slightest bit mean. You have to separate that from 'We bought too much of this stuff and we've got to get rid of it.' Or, 'Let's not sweep this problem under the rug. Eight people aren't pulling their oars. All those young people under them are pulling—let's change it.' That's different."

Nicholas knows a lot about pulling his own oar. He is the grandson of a penniless Anatolian Greek cabinetmaker who emigrated to Portland, Maine. Nicholas's own aspiring immigrant father embedded himself in the New World by an unusual route—for those days. He applied and was admitted to the U.S. Naval Academy. His son Nick was born the day in 1939 that Germany declared war on England. Young Nick was a navy brat from birth, rarely living in the same place more than two years. His father, a submariner during most of his life and a much-decorated World War II sub captain, was as steeped in Greek classics as he was in battle tactics. "The Quiet Warrior," Nicholas recalls, "who would just as soon put a torpedo in your gut as talk to you about Homer."

After the war, the family lived in Denmark, traveled and moved all over Europe. One summer at camp in Switzerland, playing the kids' game of capture the flag, Nicholas says, "I wanted to win so much that I made a sideway foray on the hill." He tumbled from the top and crashed, permanently disabling one kidney. Dad picked him up in a government DC-3, took Nick off to Capri to recuperate. When his father was reassigned to the Portsmouth, New Hampshire, naval base, Nick went to public high school.

Nick, with solid grades but none of the social background of affluent preppies, got himself into Andover. He says he had the wrong clothes, the wrong shoes, the wrong school background but the right work habits. Nor was he much of an athlete, so instead of playing on the football team, he managed it. He did learn the "right" schools and went off to Princeton to study engineering. Every summer of his life since thirteen he had worked—as a tailor, as cook in a naval prison, as a vacuum cleaner salesman, night manager of a gas station. Some vacations he spent in the Caribbean, where his father commanded the Navy's Sea Frontier Group. From Guantánamo to Panama, Nick picked up odd jobs—from selling water coolers in the Dominican Republic to scrubbing hulls in shipyards.

At Princeton, he was bored with engineering formulas for bridge stresses. He switched to economics, more to his liking, and was bickered into Tiger Inn, an eating club, many of whose members spent more time at football and hockey than at course work. Not Nicholas. He graduated magna cum laude, at twenty-three, married, had a daughter and got a scholarship backed up by a loan that took him to the Harvard Business School. "About all I ever remember doing most of my life was work," he laments. "I was not gregarious. I was very serious, but once I loosened up, whether at the card table or over a bottle of tequila or whatever the hell it was, I fell in with the crowd and played hard. I learned to do that. It was like a liberation for me."

The same ubiquitous Time recruiter who had found Munro at Colgate found Nicholas at Harvard, signed him up as an assistant in the controller's office. His work at first was mostly trying to allocate the seconds and minutes registered by departments of the company on the massive Time Inc. telephone bill. There were no computers back then, and the job got him acquainted with telephone connections all over the building.

He was a whiz-kid financial analyst and caught the attention of Time's president, Jim Shepley, who made him his assistant in 1970. It was the year his father suddenly died. "My father's death really shook me up—shook a lot of things out of my pocket," including his own unhappy marriage. "I reordered my life, began to deal with some of the issues I really should have been dealing with all along. Like what's important to me. All work and no family is part of it."

Two years later, he remarried and moved into the tumultuous new territory where Time's cable and television was being scouted. His boss turned out to be Dick Munro and his guide the new boy named Jerry Levin. Before long, Nicholas was running Manhattan Cable and later HBO. He had his first taste of management and learned even more about business strategy to go with the numbers he had already mastered. The combination catapulted him to the top of his world. He became chief financial officer for the whole company and then in 1986 its president and chief operating officer.

His friend Nick Gage, a miner of his own Greek heritage and the author of *Eleni,* finds Nicholas a kind of American Odysseus, the wandering warrior of the Trojan Wars, known for his cunning and his wise counsel. Nicholas himself is doing some reexamination of his roots. These days when he visits with his mother, over a glass of wine he tape-records her reminiscences of what it was like in her little Greek village in the old country.

Nicholas thinks of himself more like his namesake father, a proud man who wore only his submariner's pin, never the fruit salad of decorations he was entitled to wear. "To this day," says Nicholas, "I'm not a grab-the-roses guy. A lot of my friends criticize the way I deal with the press."

Others of his friends—and all of his critics—cock an eyebrow at the way he has dealt not only with the press but with other moments in his career.

BEFORE ASCENDING TO THE presidency of Time and becoming heir-designate, Nicholas had only one serious competitor, Jerry Levin. In the accelerating momentum toward videoland, Kelso Sutton had been sidetracked. He was a magazine man, with tough edges. And he had made some tactical publishing mistakes, which caused him to stumble on his way to the chief executive finish line. As far

back as 1983, Nicholas, Levin and Sutton had all been marked as
promising up-and-comers by the Time board. Sutton had rarely gone
head-to-head with Nicholas. Levin had.

Although Levin, by common agreement, was the most interesting
mind on the business side of Time, as onetime head of the video
group he had run into trouble. In 1984–85, HBO's growth was slowing down, starving for better movies and harassed by the explosive
growth of video cassette players. Cable too was straining. "We were
fighting with each other," says Nicholas, "it was a goddamned disaster." That was the moment when Nicholas was reassigned f:om
chief financial officer to take Levin's place in video.

Levin was shunted aside and given what in the corporate world is
often an empty job, head of the so-called strategy group. The trouble
was there was no group—and there was no strategy. "I wasn't happy
about doing that," says Levin. "Dick, who has other fine qualities,
is not the kind of CEO who would point you in a direction. I had
no resources. It was very clear there was some competition between
Nick and me. There wasn't any longer much of a base for me to
operate from." After the *TV-Cable Week* disaster, Sutton was also
relieved of his commanding magazine duties and stepped down to
run Time's book publishing.

Even more humiliating, three months after Nicholas was named
president, Levin and Sutton were suddenly dumped from the Time
board. "I was somewhat upset," says Sutton, "but I wasn't slitting
my wrists the way Jerry was." Nicholas ducks responsibility for Levin's being severed without anesthesia. But he has said he "was running the company since 1986." And when reminded of the episode,
he bobs and weaves, saying, "I might not have done that today. But
removing Jerry from the board was Dick Munro's call. Did I agree
with the decision? Absolutely. I also thought strategy was a great
job. Who gives a shit what it looks like? Am I a little bit more mellow
today? Yeah, I am. Am I a little bit more forgiving today? Probably.
Jerry and I and the rest of us are working together very well today.
I wouldn't have predicted that back then. My betting was that Jerry
was not going to stay." Nicholas's updated view today is that "I
persuaded Jerry to stay. It wasn't Munro, not anybody else. It was
me."

Betting on Levin's quitting wouldn't have been a long shot. As
Levin remembers it, "At the time Nick had a fairly mechanistic way
of looking at the world and Dick wasn't going to change it. I thought

it was a terrible thing obviously. And under normal circumstances one would just up and say fuck it. I think Nick acted too quickly. Let's face it, Nick, who I think has changed in some ways, liked and wanted the exercise of power. Those things are fundamentally inimical to me. I didn't think I should have gone off the board. That's for sure. Nick's logic had a stainless steel quality to it that was wrong. I think Nick is a less abrupt person today than he was then. The reason I didn't quit was not just because of blind love for the company. There was some unfinished business. It was finding the destiny of the company. I was going to do it."

With Nicholas moving to the top of the headquarters building and Levin in search of Time Inc.'s destiny, the company was only half staffed for the '90s. Editor-in-chief Henry Grunwald was a year away from retirement in 1986. The company needed a new editorial chief to polish up its worldwide identifier, the Time-Life editorial escutcheon.

Even under the terms of the revised Donovan editorial charter, it was still a choice the incumbent Grunwald alone could make.

NO MATTER THAT the dealmaking of video brought in half the company's revenue and was the focal point of Wall Street futurology; that *People* and *Sports Illustrated* were its most successful magazines; or that it published a revamped biweekly *Fortune,* the self-help monthly *Money,* a monthly version of the old weekly *Life* and a couple dozen magazines it had acquired; or that it owned the Book-of-the-Month Club, Little, Brown, and Time-Life Books. Only *Time* magazine stood for the name of the company Time Inc.

Time was the place where Grunwald, sixty-four, the immigrant son of "Vienna's Oscar Hammerstein," had spent his entire professional life, from office boy to managing editor, and finally editor-in-chief of the whole magazine group. As he prepared for retirement, he needed to pick his successor. Who would succeed him as editor-in-chief—or, as many said in Time-speak, "the Pope" of Time's editorial church?

As Grunwald himself had, both his potential successors had served as managing editors of *Time,* once one of the most potent jobs in journalism. But their modes were very different.

First, there was Ray Cave, who had been moved over in 1977 from *Sports Illustrated* by Donovan, first to be assistant managing editor, then, within a year, at fifty, managing editor of *Time.* "It was a gamble I wouldn't have taken," says Cave. "The *Time* staff was shocked. No one on the magazine thought I could edit anything but the sports section. I was an outsider in *Time*'s terms." By naming Cave, Donovan passed over Jason McManus, forty-three, a *Time* veteran, Grunwald's longtime deputy, and the most apparent heir for the job. McManus, Donovan thought, could wait his turn. "I was enormously disappointed," recalls McManus. "Most of the staff thought I would be the next managing editor. Many wise and good friends said you've got to get out of here within eighteen months. Your career is finished. But Hedley even had it put in the *Wall Street Journal* that this is not the end of McManus, it may just be the beginning."

Donovan, who moved with the force and relentlessness of a louring locomotive, always had a plan in mind. "I considered Ray Cave a very close choice to Jason. Despite the good changes Henry made in *Time,* there was, as there will always be, a lot of unshakable habit, ways of doing things. I thought Jason, although very sensible as a manager, was a little inclined to go along. Jason was obviously better read in politics and foreign policy as a journalist, but Ray was smart enough to pick that up. I just thought it would do *Time* good to have a little more jostling. I was also troubled by *Time*'s profit squeeze, not unrelated to Henry's editorial extravagances. I wanted to get Grunwald on the thirty-fourth floor and put him in stronger contention for my job," which he got when Donovan retired.

Cave pulled *Time* out of its late-'70s slump, even with Grunwald looking over his shoulder and second-guessing him much more than he should have. He cut back some of its pondering intellectual content, sharpened its news edge and gave the magazine a more up-to-date look with a colorful array of pictures and new graphics—his proudest accomplishment. In 1985 the traditional *Time* dinner trumpets sounded at the Plaza Hotel. After twenty-six years of unobtrusively striving and biding his time, including seven years serving as Cave's deputy on *Time,* McManus, fifty, got Cave's job as *Time*'s managing editor. Cave, fifty-seven, moved upstairs to be editor-in-chief Grunwald's principal deputy.

AN EXPERIENCED EDITOR ONCE remarked that a new editor has two years to get acquainted with his job, three to leave his mark and after that it's all maintenance.

McManus had no need to get acquainted. "I was very surprised,"

he says, "how easy and comfortable the job was. If I had gotten it
in 1977 I probably would have been modestly terrified. But by 1985
I had reached a stage in my career that I felt none of those things.
I knew exactly how *Time* worked. I knew all the people. And I
felt I had this kind of secret. I was really supposed to do my job to
do something else," i.e., stand in line for the editor-in-chiefship.

Clinging to his secret, McManus, unlike all those who went before
him, never did leave his editor's mark on *Time,* although he loosened
the reins to give his editors and writers more freedom. "Jason could
sit in the subway and tell you which way the wind was blowing on
the thirty-fourth floor," recalls one of his top aides. "He ran *Time*
as if he were ahead in the marathon for editor-in-chief and didn't
want to blow his lead."

But his lead was shorter than he may have thought. Running
slightly ahead of him at the time was Ray Cave. "I've never heard
Jason say anything at our lunches," Donovan once said, "that you
couldn't find on the editorial pages of the New York *Times.*" Cave
was different. A wiry, bearded curmudgeon with a classical education
from the St. John's College Great Books program, he had served
with Army counterintelligence in Korea and had been a reporter and
editor for ten years on the Baltimore *Evening Sun* before coming to
Sports Illustrated. There he fell under the spell of Andre Laguerre,
an inspired editor and a loner who got fanatic loyalty from his staff
and built a moat repelling all outsiders from the editorial kingdom
he ruled.

Laguerre, says Cave, "certainly ranks with the greatest editors
Time Inc. ever had. But he had a tremendous weakness in not trying
to get along with the upper establishment. That was his fault, nobody
else's, his fault."

Although Cave today recognizes that shortcoming in his mentor,
he rarely saw it in himself. Instead he displayed many of Laguerre's
talents and almost all his faults. On the thirty-fourth floor as Grunwald's deputy, Cave had an office alongside Munro's. They never
exchanged a word. In two tours of duty on the thirty-fourth floor,
Cave remembers that "I rarely talked to the business bosses—Dick,
Nick and Jerry—unless my boss, the editor-in-chief, asked me to. I
didn't want to appear to be going behind his back. In hindsight that
was probably a mistake."

Munro and Nicholas certainly thought it was. Munro got panicky
at the possibility that Grunwald would pick Cave for his successor

as editor-in-chief. Grunwald refused to reveal his leanings on the
succession. So Munro took matters into his own hands. He had a
series of breakfasts and lunches with each of the managing editors
to solicit their suggestions. One of them recalls Munro saying, "I've
decided to get into this process. It's too important to be left to the
journalists and editors." He found they too resented Cave's per-
emptory ways. When Munro sent word to McManus, Cave and one
long-shot candidate, Gil Rogin, also a former managing editor of
Sports Illustrated, that he wanted each to write the job description
for editor-in-chief, Cave alone refused. He felt the whole inquiry by
Munro was improper, since it was Grunwald's bailiwick and decision.
With Grunwald undecided, Munro got even more worried.

Munro trashed Cave so badly at one board session that afterwards
Louis Banks, an outside director who had once been managing editor
of *Fortune* and editorial director of Time Inc., wrote him a "Dear
Dick" letter:

> I thought your rather strident attack on Ray Cave was out of
> order. He may not be the man for the job. But I saw him turn
> *Time* into a well-managed operation, change the whole edi-
> torial system to break the top-editing bottleneck and give him-
> self time for graphics; enlist, promote and develop outstanding
> by-line writers and lead *Time* into the writing and the graphics
> that brought a miracle of rejuvenation. He may chew up people
> for breakfast, but he successfully nursed one staffer out of his
> alcoholism with the patience and kindness I would have found
> difficult. A guy with that kind of record deserves more even-
> handed consideration. Ray is a Welshman, and while he doesn't
> sing, he suffers from the awful moodiness of his countrymen.
> Maybe more than his share, and that might be a fatal flaw. But
> you must remember all the misgivings we all had about Grun-
> wald's management talents.

"WHAT DROVE ME BANANAS," says Munro, "was the way it
got dragged out."

Cave's perversity didn't make it easy for Grunwald, who thought
Cave the more imaginative and creative editor. Most of the managing
editors below also resented Cave's didactic, unpredictable manner;
and Munro and Nicholas couldn't stand what seemed to them his
scorn. Despite reservations about McManus, Grunwald decided that
"given the choice it had to be Jason." Munro's "devastating view of

Cave made it very difficult for me to turn that around although not totally impossible." As he did all the years he edited *Time,* Grunwald waited until the clock was about to run out before he closed the book. McManus, he finally said. On April 17, 1987, Time announced Grunwald would retire at year's end. He would be succeeded by McManus, who inherited Grunwald's title *and* his seat on the Time board as well.

By then it was too late to avoid three unintended consequences. All three involved the future role in Time Inc. of the editor-in-chief.

First, Munro vowed that "this can't go on—this is the last time" such an apartness and last-minute monastic choice would be tolerated. Even the Church, after all, has a College of Cardinals to pick its Pope. Grunwald's agonizing succession solo led a chorus of the board to raise an old question. Should McManus, the next editor-in-chief, be on the board at all? "It was never a more serious question," says Perkins, "than having board members say that if we're ever going to change this we should when Grunwald retires. That was said, sure, but that's a lot different from saying, Hey, let's all get together and make sure the editor-in-chief is not on the board."

Perkins is half right. It wasn't exactly a lynch mob, but it was more serious than he allows. "There was," says Louis Banks, a director at the time, "a real movement to get the editor-in-chief off the board. It was part of a structural redesign to reduce him to the level of the publishing head of the magazine group, not on a level with the CEO of the whole company as he had been." To claim otherwise, as McManus and others do, says Banks, is "garbage."

Even when McManus's role was set, the announced changeover date had to be moved up much earlier than planned. Strobe Talbott, then *Time*'s well-connected Washington bureau chief and top diplomatic correspondent, heard that Grunwald was about to be designated by President Reagan as ambassador to Austria. Pledged to secrecy by the White House, Grunwald had told no one. "Nothing stays secret at Time or anywhere else for that matter for more than five minutes," Grunwald reasoned. "I thought the minute I told Dick or the board it would be all over the place." Although Grunwald and Munro worked in offices just down the hall from each other, "one could have been on Pluto and the other Mars," says one confidant of both. When Munro, with no inkling of what was going on, suddenly heard about the ambassadorial fait accompli, he was furious. "I felt blind-sided," he says. "I couldn't understand why Henry hadn't picked up the phone and called me."

The day after his discovery, Munro was visiting Nantucket. Grunwald was across the sound separating the two islands at his summer house on Martha's Vineyard. A series of emergency telephone conference calls was set up among Munro, Nicholas, Levin, McManus, Bill Guttman—Time Inc.'s general counsel—and members of the board, led by Perkins. In the furor, all agreed Grunwald would have to resign his job immediately to avoid the taint of conflict of interest, even before his Senate confirmation hearing. Grunwald at first was reluctant to leave six months early, since the FBI hadn't even begun its security check. He was quickly turned around but not before again offending the imagination of Munro, Nicholas and other board members.

They remembered his conduct of the Sharon trial plus the cliff-hanging process by which he had chosen his successor. When they found out about Grunwald's ambassadorial designation, they were aggrieved with what became accepted Time lore that "Henry used Time's Washington corporate office to lobby for the job."

Grunwald can be criticized for other missteps. But lobbying to be ambassador was a bum rap. In fact, Grunwald was appointed by Reagan through an unlikely intervention. *60 Minutes* correspondent Mike Wallace, an old friend of Nancy Reagan's, was a regular telephone pal of Mrs. Reagan's in her habitual gossip collecting. Wallace was also a friend of Grunwald's. Without Grunwald's ever knowing it until long after he arrived in Vienna, Wallace suggested to Nancy Reagan that Grunwald, with his cosmopolitan Viennese background and his intellectual depth, would make a first-rate ambassador.

Ten days after Wallace talked to Mrs. Reagan, the president's chief of staff, Howard Baker, called Grunwald and surprised him by offering the post. By every account, Grunwald did indeed make an excellent ambassador to Austria.

Looking back on those events, Munro—ever generous in his recollections of the past—says, "After all, his appointment was a wonderful coup for Henry and a coup for America—and that's coming from a Democrat. I think Henry was less than courteous with me. But he had no real obligation to do that. He didn't work for me. The lobbying thing I later found out was bullshit. Sure Henry was a little distant from me. But he was older and an intellectual, which most of us aren't."

· · ·

WITH GRUNWALD GONE AND McManus fully in charge of the editorial side of Time Inc., there were still some nettlesome burrs McManus thought needed grinding down.

As much as both Munro and Nicholas had resisted the possibility of Cave's getting the top editorial job, they were no more comfortable with him as their thirty-fourth-floor neighbor in the second slot of editorial director. A disappointed Ray Cave, who had been McManus's boss on *Time,* tried to solve his role reversal by a rigid rule. "I didn't know how to establish myself with Munro and Nicholas," says Cave, "without appearing to undermine the editor-in-chief." His solution was to have nothing to do with the businessmen.

Cave, a talented editor with strong views, is no office diplomat, nor an attendant lord. Neither did he have much support from the editors below him, who were exposed to his frustrated cantankerousness. "I was bored," says Cave. McManus was not bored. He was busy trying to make amends with his business partners, at the same time softening the inadvertent blows Cave was striking at the editors below him. The combination was more than a taciturn McManus would tolerate.

The morning Cave returned from a late August fishing vacation, thirteen months after he became editorial director, he was called into McManus's office. McManus recalls that "I liked Ray and didn't think he was happy." That may explain how he could say to Cave the awful cliché words that are in management textbooks on how *not* to fire someone. "This is the hardest decision I've ever had to make," Cave remembers being told, "but for your sake and mine I'd like you to leave by the end of the year. You're not happy here shuffling papers. I'm sure this does not come as a complete surprise to you." Cave coldly replied that it certainly did. Within ten minutes he was out of the office, suffering the conversation mostly in typical resolute silence. "In Jason," Cave later said, "they got exactly the editor-in-chief they wanted. I'm not even sure it wasn't the best decision for Time Inc."

McManus prepared and released the standard sugar-coated announcement. Cave would have none of it. "If you're going to fire me you're not going to tell the public that I suddenly decided to write novels or some goddamned thing. You want to fire me. Fire me." When the Time public relations office was pressed by the *Wall*

Street Journal to give the real reason for Cave's departure, Cave instructed the spokesman, "Tell them I was fired." And so they did.

Nine months later, McManus also fired Pat Ryan, another Laguerre protégée and Ray Cave's putative wife—having lived with him for fifteen years without ever formally getting married. Ryan had been managing editor of *People* and had been persuaded in 1987 to try to rescue the monthly *Life,* which has had five managing editors and four publishers in the twelve years since it was reborn as a monthly. Ryan says she well knew "it was a poor, weak creature" in need of radical treatment. She was as unyielding as Cave with her publishing partners, who kept barraging her with reader surveys and focus-group opinions. McManus himself sent her a memo asking whether "you accept the sense of urgency" for skewing *Life* toward larger audiences.

She did—but not to her bosses' satisfaction. So McManus in August 1989 summoned her to his office, closed the door and told her, "My friend, I think it's time you left." For half an hour, Ryan unsuccessfully protested. Then, dejected and upset, she called her staff together and in tears told them, "I've been fired."

Few could remember two such summary firings of long-Timers from the top rungs of the editorial ladder. Looking back on the puzzlement the firings created, McManus explains: "From my point of view that's directly dealing with problems as opposed to papering them over. Now there is much more straightforwardness and honesty. I'm criticized for not being tough enough for this job. But getting rid of Pat and Ray was not easy."

The top editorial managers of Time, along with their business partners, were all now in place for the '90s. Some blood had been spilled. But who knows of a major operation where the chief surgeon and his aides finish up without some splatterings of blood on their working clothes?

Chapter 6

From Westchester
to Silicon Valley

T IME'S SLOG THROUGH THE 1980s remained profitable but surrounded by confusion and angst. Yet it was no worse than many another middle-aged company's performance during the decade. Most were struggling to find fresh focus and leaders amidst the wrenching new worldwide environment in finance and technology. Many—like Time—were trying to overcome the traditions and momentum, hanging around like fond relics, of their long-dead founders and proprietors.

But Warner as it began the '80s had vastly different problems. In the midst of all Ross's other personal upheavals, he and Warner suffered their two worst humiliations. Both are memorialized today at two dump sites.

JUST OFF WHITE PLAINS Road, in suburban Tarrytown, New York, behind a camouflage of well-tended trees, is a rock-strewn lot overgrown with weeds and sumac, littered with piles of dirt. A growling bulldozer occasionally invades the fenced-in premises to deposit or take away debris from a nearby highway construction project.

The site has seen even dirtier days. In the early 1970s it was the location of gangland's Westchester Premier Theatre, the most embarrassing small investment Warner Communications ever made. Steve Ross would never be allowed to forget it or stop being asked to explain how it could have happened. It was a tale strewn with crooks, broken hearts and broken lives.

To this day the extent of the involvement of Ross and Warner— then a $2 billion company—in a piddling $250,000 investment scam makes no sense and probably never will, despite years of criminal trials and investigations.

In the American legal system, under the threat of severe punishment from government prosecutors, those accused of crimes seek their own survival. As a result, plea-bargaining deals, with admissions, denials and evasions, often have more to do with legal maneuvering than with what really happened in an actual crime. Al Capone went to jail for tax evasion, not for his murderous record; Michael Milken was as severely judged by the public for some of the dozens of crimes with which he was originally charged but which were never proved as he was for the six securities felonies to which he admitted. So it was in the conflicting accounts of those indicted in the infamous Westchester Premier Theatre cases.

FROM ITS EARLIEST DAYS, the project reeked. Neighbors complained of the smell of rotten eggs from the garbage, sewage and coal ash that was used to fill the swampy sixteen-acre site. The theater's financial brokers smelled just as bad as the site. The original front man and promoter was a small-time Wall Street hustler (who ended up in jail). He was secretly backed by two Mafia soldiers from the Gambino and Colombo crime families, who also went to jail.

The stock salesman raising money for the venture in 1973 was Leonard Horwitz (his friends called him "The Fox"), a sometime stockbroker as well as a $60,000-a-year Warner "marketing consultant." He too went to jail. One of Horwitz's first personal investors in seed stock was his friend Jay Emmett, a top Warner executive. Emmett was a friendly, popular and handsome guy—a "good buddy"—with the amiability of the best bartender and the quick palaver of a door-to-door salesman. Horwitz was not just one of Emmett's stockbrokers, his gin-rummy playing partner and holder of Emmett's football pool stakes. Horwitz often borrowed money from Emmett to settle gambling debts and, later, $100,000 for legal fees, plus $165,000 to finance Horwitz's new house.

But Emmett had a much more important relationship. The man he described as his "closest friend" was Steve Ross. The closeness was no exaggeration. "No one at Warner has ever been that close to Steve," says someone who knew them both well. At Warner, Emmett was second only to Ross himself. He occupied a lavish office across the hall from Ross. He was Ross's constant lunchmate and after-hours companion.

Horwitz, Emmett's friend and a Warner consultant, was having trouble raising enough money to get the Westchester theater built. He found he couldn't sell all the required 275,000 shares. So he went to see his pal in Emmett's Warner office. He had a brown paper bag stuffed with $50,000 in cash in his hand and a shady proposition on his lips. Could Emmett find a way for Warner to buy more of the inflated Westchester Theatre stock? If he could, the cash Horwitz carried was to be the first payment on a "loan"—actually a bribe—Horwitz would pay Warner to encourage the stock sale. According to his later testimony, Emmett marched across the hall and told Ross that Horwitz was willing to give a loan or cash payment in return for Warner's buying theater stock. Emmett quoted Ross as saying that Warner couldn't accept such a loan but suggested that "Len ought to meet with Sol Weiss, and maybe he could be helpful in the Warner cash fund."

Ross later described the meeting to a reporter: "I approved the purchase of the Westchester Theatre stock because Jay asked me about it during a ten-second conversation. It sounded like a good fit because of what we could get out of the theater for our cable operations."

Sol Weiss, to whom Emmett says Ross steered Horwitz, was the right functionary for a small Warner investment. A certified public accountant, he was Warner's assistant treasurer and an unlikely co-conspirator in what turned out to be a criminal fraud. He was a small, mousy and devoutly observant Orthodox Jew in yarmulke and rimless glasses, a "minnow" among whales, his own lawyer said. Weiss's main job was helping Warner executives with their personal investments and taxes—especially Ross. He also held Ross's power of attorney, the key to his safe deposit box and, along with other Ross aides, was a token beneficiary in Ross's will as was Emmett. "Sol," an acquaintance said, "was a lovely, quiet, religious man who never did anything he wasn't told to. He was Steve's diligent, diminutive troll."

Over time, $250,000 of theater stock was bought with checks issued from the Warner treasury over Weiss's signature. But Horwitz couldn't come up with the cash bribes he had promised. So he was given the kickback bribe money in a series of different Warner checks. These payments were authorized in phony vouchers, signed by Emmett, for services never rendered. The checks were used by Horwitz to pay the promised bribes. The secret Armstrong Report to Warner's board described them as "$222,000 in purported consulting fees to Leonard Horwitz and others." The checks in turn were cashed by Horwitz and the cash given back.

Complicated? Not really. The stock was bought by Warner as a $250,000 company investment, fully reported as such. Another $222,000 in cash was raised from phony Warner work orders, then turned back in "purported" cash bribes. The cash went either to Emmett or to what the prosecutor said was Warner's "secret cash fund."

NONE OF THE MONEY-laundering shenanigans helped speed up building of the theater. At one point the state environmental commissioner halted construction. The FBI, IRS and county district attorney all poked into charges of payoffs, corruption and mob connections in its financing, building and carting contracts. After money-draining lawsuits and much sparring with investigators, the theater finally opened in 1975, a year late and $2.5 million over budget.

The 3,600-seat arena, with the look of a sugar-frosted birthday cake, was promoted as a Las Vegas–style entertainment center for suburbanites. But it had a bigger lure to the sharpies cutting corners off-stage. Its box office and concessions were a cash cow, ripe for skimming. Among many other scams, the theater had 136 extra portable and unrecorded folding seats. Ticket income for them was not counted in the theater's receipts or in tax records. The cash was split up and looted.

Despite repeated full-house appearances by Ross's friend Frank Sinatra and dozens of other stars, from Liza Minnelli and Johnny Carson to Linda Ronstadt and Diana Ross, the theater was so milked by mobsters that it filed for bankruptcy within two years and was finally torn down. But financial failure and the wrecker's ball were the least of it.

The hoods around the theater drew the attention of a thirty-two-year-old federal prosecutor, Nathaniel H. ("Nick") Akerman, a Harvard law graduate and former member of the Watergate prosecutor's team. Starting with tipsters, Akerman got a stunning series of convictions of crooks who profited from the theater. Sent to jail were close to a dozen thugs convicted of skimming box-office receipts, bankruptcy fraud and obstruction of justice. At one embarrassing moment, *Life* ran a picture of Frank Sinatra grinning in his Westchester Theatre dressing room, arms locked with a rogues' gallery of Mafiosi, including Carlo Gambino, Paul Castellano and hit-man Jimmy ("The Weasel") Fratianno, who proudly claimed credit for eleven mob murders.

Almost from the beginning, Akerman was after a bigger prey, the celebrated Steve Ross. Through menacing plea bargaining with Horwitz, Emmett and Weiss, he hoped to squeeze out of them evidence against Ross. Akerman had enough on Emmett and Horwitz to make them plead guilty to criminal charges, postponing their sentencing until after Weiss was worked over. Weiss refused to give in. Instead he went to trial and testified that Emmett was a liar. Weiss said neither he nor Ross ever knew anything about the $222,000 in bribes. Ross, who was listed as a "co-conspirator" but never charged or formally declared a "target," assumed the Fifth Amendment protection against self-incrimination and refused to appear before the grand jury.

Emmett, whose $700,000 legal fees were advanced by Warner, hired the country's leading trial lawyer, Edward Bennett Williams. He had been recommended to Emmett by Ross's lawyer Arthur Liman. With Williams' guidance, Emmett couched his confession in terms that never directly implicated Ross. Instead, he spoke only of payments to the "cash fund."

At Emmett's sentencing, Akerman melodramatically charged in open court: "In our view the real culprit has not been brought to criminal justice. The real culprit in this instance is the chairman of the board of Warner Communications and the investigation of him is still continuing." Ross angrily replied that "I have done no wrong and the accusations are outrageous." Predictably, the charge made front-page news. "ACCUSE WARNER EXEC OF FRAUD," screamed a banner headline on page 1 of the tabloid New York *Daily News,* accompanied by a picture of Ross. Despite relentless probing and threats, Akerman never succeeded in nailing Ross and damaged his own reputation by making accusations without legal proof.

When the Warner-related confessions, trials and appeals were finally over:

- Horwitz was sentenced to three years in prison for stock and tax fraud. After his cooperation with the government, his sentence was reduced to nine months, and he served only four.

- Emmett agreed secretly to tape-record a conversation with Ross for the prosecutor. But even more secretly he warned Ross of the trap in advance. "Greater love hath no man," says a mutual friend of Ross's and Emmett's, "than one who would secretly tell you he would be wired by the feds when he next talked to you." When Emmett pleaded guilty, he admitted he signed false invoices, diverting at least $23,000 from Warner. Akerman dropped the charges that he took $150,000 and that he accepted $70,000 in bribes. (Amanda Burden, who had by then separated from Ross, sat with Emmett's wife in the courtroom and comforted her.) After his guilty plea, Emmett resigned from Warner but was allowed to keep his $7.5 million in Warner stock as part of his plea bargain, along with a couple of million more in other Warner benefits. His sentence of five years in jail was suspended and he was given three years' probation, plus community service and the maximum fine of $20,000. Emmett became a shareholder and director of his lawyer Ed Williams's Baltimore Orioles; backed "Jake's," his son's midtown Manhattan restaurant that failed; does volunteer work in Washington for the Kennedy family's Special Olympics and continues to do his own investments and deals. Ross will no longer talk about Emmett who he hasn't seen in ten years. Emmett, who like everyone else, still lauds Ross to friends for his "generosity and genius," also has been known to add, "I walked through minefields for Steve."

- In 1984, after losing an appeal, the badly shaken and hapless Weiss got a three-year suspended jail sentence and was ordered to do forty hours a week of community service for five years. He also was fined $58,000 and forfeited his $2 million in Warner stock. Weiss now does tax work and accounting for clients who are sent to him by Ross's chief financial adviser, Oded Aboodi.

AFTER THE CONFESSIONS AND the trial, in 1983 Steve Brill, the best reporter on his own *American Lawyer* (in which a majority interest, six years later, was sold to Warner), came upon a sealed court document. It had been judged inadmissible at the Weiss trial. In it were two letters from Edward Rosenthal, Ross's eighty-year-old ex-father-in-law and deputy chairman of Warner, who remained a director emeritus of Time Warner and regularly attended meetings until he died in 1991.

Rosenthal had written to Emmett right after his indictment: "Jay, with a deep feeling of guilt in my heart that you must suffer because of what you did for me and my company and all of us at WCI [Warner], including my family, I write to beg your forgiveness for what we have put you through. We just pray that the knowledge of your innocence, that what you did, you did for us, not yourself, will help you continue the great courage you have shown." A second letter from Rosenthal offered to help Emmett, "since you took the rap for all the WCI [Warner]."

When Brill asked Rosenthal about the incriminating letters, he said, "Jay took nothing for himself. He did it to set up a cash fund. Every major company has a cash fund. We needed cash for record deals, for unions at the parking lots. It's standard. And now they're all trying to cover it up. Steve is. And the lawyers are too. The letters I wrote are beautiful letters." After further conversations, Brill decided that "Rosenthal is articulate but widely believed to be capable of the kind of erratic behavior and judgments that might be called senility." Kindly and loyal sentimentality toward Emmett would have been a more apt description. Others who knew Rosenthal at the time found him not a bit "senile." His daughter, Carol Maslow—Ross's first wife—says the description is "nonsense—a lie." But from his reporting, Brill concluded:

> The jury was wrong; the prosecutor was wrong; the defense counsel did a poor job; the press headlined the accusations without looking behind them, a mistake I nearly made, as I, like the prosecutor, set out to nail the big targets—because reporting, like prosecuting, thrives on big targets.

Today, Brill is in partnership with Warner and knows Ross much better. From that perspective he says, "Steve's weakness is that he tends to fall in love with people who are glib, articulate, attractive, can move in his kind of show-biz circles. Every once in a while he gets suckered in by them. That's what happened with Emmett." Wily Ed Williams spread the blame around, placing it on an undeniable abstraction, which could be applied to Warner and too many other companies. Emmett's role in the fraud, said Williams, only reflected "a part of the venality of the corporate scheme in American life."

Another star lawyer close to the case was Arthur Liman of Paul, Weiss, Rifkind, Wharton & Garrison, Ross's longtime adviser and

confidant. As Warner's senior outside counsel, Liman had advised
Emmett to waive his Fifth Amendment rights and testify before the
grand jury; he advised Ross to refuse. "Arthur is more than a
lawyer," says Ross, "he's one of the world's great businessmen, a
great sounding board, also godfather to my daughter." Among his
other public services, Liman was the highly visible chief counsel of
the televised Senate Iran-contra committee hearings. In early 1990,
Liman wrote about Reagan's role in the Iran-contra scandal for the
New York *Times*. He could just as well have been writing about
Ross, the Westchester Theatre scandals and why Ross never has
been able to get out from under its cloud.

> The disappointment that accompanied the release of President
> Reagan's Iran-contra testimony is unwarranted. If there were
> no revelations, no smoking guns, no sudden confessions, that's
> because we have known since the hearings ended in the summer
> of 1987, all that is knowable about the affair. What was known
> was disturbing and ugly enough. What was unknowable could
> be inferred with a little common sense and imagination.

Early in 1985, U.S. Attorney Rudolph Giuliani announced that the
long investigation into Ross's Westchester connection was ended with
"insufficient evidence to bring charges."

When a reporter asked Ross whether other jarring events in his
business life were as hard to take as his Westchester misery, Ross
answered without a second thought: "I don't think there's any comparison. I think the Theatre was more painful."

Another catastrophe brewing at the same time may not have been
as painful, but the combination was enough to make a lesser soul
plead for mercy.

Consider the second dump site.

THIRTY-EIGHT YEARS HAD passed since the first explosion of
an atomic bomb near Alamogordo, New Mexico ("Trinity Test").
In September of 1983, twenty heavily laden semi-trailer trucks made
their way to the same gravelly desert land for a doomsday delivery
with an infinitely more mundane purpose: the burial of Warner's
bombed-out Atari, once the most successful enterprise in the company's entire history.

The trucks were laden with tons of discarded electronic games and consoles from Warner's El Paso Atari plant, ninety miles south. While guards stood by, fifty cubic yards of cement were poured over the crushed and buried remains to entomb them forever. Today, overgrown mesquite shrubs and creosote bushes whistling in the desert wind are the only vegetation marking the site—a grave of mismanagement and duplicity.

As in most other landmark events in Steve Ross's memory, it was framed by bookends of homey anecdotes. On a visit to Disneyland with Amanda and the kids in 1975, Ross noticed that the youngsters were more interested in the brand-new Atari coin-operated video games than the other attractions. He scribbled a note to remind himself of the company's pending acquisition. Warner bought the fledgling Silicon Valley Atari company for a mere $28 million, the year after the Disneyland excursion.

Ross filled his houses in Manhattan, East Hampton and Acapulco with Atari games and Warner's coffers with its millions in profits. Six bountiful years later, one night at Walter Cronkite's house in Manhattan, Ross noticed the CBS luminary, an electronic gadgeteer, fiddling with a video game. A product for all ages, Ross concluded with his congenital optimism and faith in ever-widening markets.

With its Atari subsidiary, Warner became the company most touted by the Wall Street analysts' cheering section. It was a phenomenal success, the fastest growing big company in the world. By 1982, Atari was bringing in more than half of Warner's total $4 billion revenues and close to 70 percent of its profits, making Warner bigger than either of its midtown Manhattan neighbors, Time Inc. and CBS. *Time* christened the period "The Age of Atari." Thomas ("Tip") O'Neill, the white-thatched speaker of the House of Representatives, called the new young members of his brood "Atari Democrats." At the peak of its success, the name Atari became almost as recognizable a part of the American language as Jell-O, Scotch Tape, Frigidaire or Baby Boomers.

THEN IN A SINGLE disastrous year, Atari's games headed toward the oblivion of hula hoops. The feckless industry trade press, which had proclaimed Ross "Adman of the Year" in 1981, did an about-face for 1982 and found him "one of the ten worst executives in America."

Even without the overwhelming rapid-fire agonies of the tragic disabling of Ken Rosen, a heart attack, a broken second marriage and quick remarriage, plus the pain and public ignominy of the Westchester trials, Steve Ross never would have taken much interest in Atari. The company was not his style. He loved the profits. But it was a dull manufacturing business with plants around the world, 10,000 employees and polyester retailers, bereft of celebrities, romance or glamour. He barely gave it a nod, except to revel in its success. He never visited its plants and only twice, belatedly, its headquarters in Sunnyvale, California.

Ross turned over supervision of Atari to Emanuel ("Manny") Gerard, an overbearing former securities analyst who had risen to be one of the two chief operating officers of Warner (the other was Jay Emmett). "Manny," says a former colleague in a widely endorsed description, "was intolerant, abrasive, foul-mouthed and was always talking, ya-da-ya-da-da, dumpa dumpa, never listening." His motto seemed to be When you talk to me you shut up. Gerard was arrogant and intimidating, recalls another victim of his snarling tongue. "If you told him something he already knew, he would insult you with 'Welcome to the twentieth century.' And if you didn't know something he knew, he would holler, 'Where the fuck have you been' or 'What the fuck are you talking about, schmuck, you just don't understand anything.' "

Gerard doesn't really disagree. "I did mouth off," he says. "I was fucking impossible then, but I've learned a lot since." Although he still radiates unbounded self-assurance, on his desk he keeps what he calls his "humility reminder": a small carved ivory skull, the Warner emblem on its mounting, with the fateful Atari crash date "December 8, 1982" inscribed across it in bold letters.

By early 1982, intoxicated by the success of its Pac-Man cartridge, Atari kept shipping more video games than the stores were selling. Inventory control was close to nonexistent. Overproduction, long-term credit, discounts and a freewheeling return policy created tons of oversupply. To keep up with sales, production and management, more than 1,000 new recruits a week flooded into its California offices—so many that no one could keep track of them or what they were doing.

When a *Wall Street Journal* "Heard on the Street" column asked in May 1982, "Is the home video game market close to saturation?" Warner's public relations staff went to work. It was a plot by short sellers, said Warner's flacks, to drive the price of the stock down. Although warning signals were flashing in Sunnyvale, with cancellations mounting as fast as orders, in June of 1982 an inattentive and always upbeat Ross reported to the stockholders on "Atari's excellent performance," "another record quarter," "unprecedented rate of sales of Pac-Man."

But even before then, there were forecasts of a devastating storm darkening the skies over Sunnyvale. And by July executive memos reported "cancellation activity almost doubled, three times greater than in recent weeks." The fall sales reports warned of the "frightening realization that inventory levels are dangerously high." Atari's chief of operations urged that "we take a very hard look, quickly, to devise further cut-backs, possibly take some involuntary vacation." Marketing analysts at Atari wrote with dismay, "We have run out of answers, foresee major cancellations in November and December." Meanwhile, in New York at a board meeting, Ross was predicting that Atari was "heading for a good Christmas."

Afraid to go over Gerard's head to the big boss, no one dared to tell Ross the bad news. It might not have mattered anyway. Ross's executive dictum was to "let the managers manage." He was also preoccupied with the Westchester Theatre investigation and his marriage to Courtney Sale. Gerard's bulldozer optimism overwhelmed any dissent. *His* dictum was always "Steve doesn't like anything negative."

Ross's one intervention was characteristic. In July, he was cozying up to Steven Spielberg, whose Universal Pictures *E.T.* was a smash-hit movie. Ross had little trouble interesting Spielberg in a staggering $23 million offer for the video game rights to the movie, along with a promise to produce a game from it in less than three months. Both the price and the timetable were unheard of in the industry.

WITH THE GLEAM OF REBOUND in their eyes, the week before Thanksgiving, embattled Atari executives recklessly shipped $100 million worth of games to retailers for Christmas. They seemed to be overlooking the elementary lesson they could have learned in the months before. It's not what you ship; it's what gets sold. They quickly learned again. Overnight, telephone reports of actual sales—especially of the new "E.T."—were ominous, one-fifth of what was expected. Atari's version transformed the lovable E.T. into a household varmint. The new game was a complete flop.

On December 7, 1982, a date, Warner old hands say, that "will live in infamy," Manny Gerard got a late emergency phone call at his Manhattan apartment. Ray Kassar, Atari's CEO, was calling from

California to tell him the forecast for Atari fourth-quarter sales would be far below what stockholders, the public and, most especially, the favored security analysts had been led to believe.

Next day in painful meetings all over the Warner building, executives told each other and staff that Atari sales just "fell off the cliff." They never conceded that they hadn't seemed to notice Atari had been tumbling down its mountain of success ever since June. Nor had they satisfied the SEC rules of formally alerting the stockholders to any early signs of bad news. Now it could no longer be kept a secret. Trading was halted in Warner stock at 2:50 P.M. At last, satisfying SEC requirements, Warner put out a shattering press release:

> New York, N.Y., December 8, 1982—Warner Communications announced today that earnings for 1982 will be substantially below previous expectations. Disappointing sales of Atari game cartridges and substantially lower sales of Atari coin-operated games were major factors in this decline.

The market response was instantaneous. Before the day was over, Warner stock had plunged to a battered and astonishing low point. The Los Angeles *Times*, reflecting all the amazed press coverage, reported:

> Warner Communications Incorporated, one of the most glittering performers on Wall Street for the past two years, stunned investors with the news that Atari might make less in pre-tax profits than analysts had been expecting. Warner's spangles turned to sackcloth. Its stock lost one-third of its value, or over one billion dollars. "Credibility with the analysts is going to be a big problem," said one of them.

For weeks before, Warner had been assuring analysts of record sales and profits. Ross himself could hardly believe what he was hearing. "How could this have happened?" he kept repeating trancelike. "It's the most amazing thing I've ever seen. The orders just stopped and stopped dead."

Gordon Crawford, the most prominent analyst in California's Capital Group investment funds, on and off the biggest institutional shareholder of Warner and later Time Warner, saw the Atari light dimming a year before it blew out. "It was obvious," he said, "that everybody's expectations including Atari's were grossly excessive. We started selling our $200 million stake in Warner in January of 1982. In June, after the electronics show and hearing Steve's optimism, I told our people to accelerate our getting rid of the stock. By the fall we didn't own a share. Then came Warner's equivalent of Pearl Harbor Day. The next day the stock collapsed."

AT WARNER, BAD NEWS is considered unbelievable. So, following Ross's lead, it is simply not accepted. Ross set the tone.

A month after Atari's collapse, at the next consumer electronics show, Ross assembled a few dozen California Atari executives in a massive suite in Las Vegas's Caesars Palace hotel. Their jaws were set, ready to catch hell from the boss. Not so. Ross said, "I wish to thank each and every one of you for a good year." He told them not to be discouraged by the press and rumors—"because that's truly the only way we could lose." Yes, they had growing pains, but now they would do better. He patted a few backs, then, smiling, left for dinner with his friend Frank Sinatra, who was staying in a suite on the floor above. (Sinatra often paraded around the electronics show with Ross to add a little glamour to the flickering hardware on display.) The next night Ross had another genial dinner with his financial hero and ally, the junk-bond king, Michael Milken. "Steve idolized Milken," says a friend, "thought he was the greatest thing since chocolate-chip cookies."

One Atari executive leaving a morale-boosting meeting in New York was astonished. "They sent a Warner jet plane for us to tell us we lost $400 million and on the plane they served crab meat, shrimp and lobster. God, imagine what we would have gotten if we made money."

Deane Johnson was a squeaky-clean brand-new Warner director and executive vice president, married to Henry Ford's socialite ex-wife Anne Ford. Johnson was brought into Warner from an establishment California law firm, largely to give polish to the company's reputation after Westchester. He echoed the Ross sentiment. "I have every confidence," said Johnson after the 1983 plunge, "that Atari will continue to be a very dominant force in the games business. I promise you we're through announcing those huge losses."

It was a hollow promise. Losses got catastrophically worse. As a result of Atari, Warner in 1983 lost $417 million; $586 million in

1984—more than a billion dollars in all. Ray Kassar, the Atari CEO, and one of his chief lieutenants were haled before the SEC accused of insider trading, unloading Warner stock before the public announcement. They were forced to "disgorge" their illegal profits and were severely reprimanded.

Beverly Sills, the celebrity opera star, joined the Warner board in the last months of 1982 as the female replacement for Bess Myerson, a former Miss America and ex–New York City commissioner of consumer affairs. It was one of diva Sills's most memorable debuts. "When Atari collapsed," she recalls, "it was my first board meeting. My mouth dropped open. I couldn't absorb what was happening. Steve was angry but his mind was already moving on to the solution, the next step. He was furious, frustrated but ready to go on to the next thing."

On he went, undaunted, reporting several months later in his annual letter to Warner stockholders: "At Atari there are already indications of renewed vigor." He exuberantly announced the hiring of a new chief for Atari, a high executive from Philip Morris. But before Atari's new broom could even start sweeping in California, Ross sold Atari out from under him. It went for a collection of paper, warrants and notes.

Despite his mismanagement, not to say the charge of insider trading, Atari's boss Ray Kassar left with an estimated $9 million in Warner stock and bonuses, his mansion in San Francisco and a chauffeur-driven Rolls-Royce.

In the year following the Atari disaster, the company bought five Trump Tower apartments for about $9 million (not including the costs of staffing them), as "an investment and for corporate usage," the company said, including one for Kassar who had been fired.

Manny Gerard hung around for two years, during which he received a contractual bonus of $717,000 for the year of the Atari disaster. He then left the company with a potful of stock estimated to be worth $7 million, and compensation of more than $40,000 a month for six years. Gerard went back to being a securities analyst and investor. His ardor for his old company's future cooled. He repeatedly warns against buying the new Time Warner stock. "I wouldn't pay a nickel for assets alone," he said.

Ross also collected compensation of $1.7 million for the Atari disaster year of 1982, plus a contractual bonus of $1.95 million. Serendipity too was on his side amid all the corporate wreckage. He explained convincingly to the SEC that his sale at a handsome profit of 360,000 shares of Warner stock during the year that Atari collapsed had been the result of a "personal financial and tax-planning" program, which had indeed been announced publicly a year before any Atari trouble.

Eighteen stockholder suits, alleging everything from mismanagement to fraud, were consolidated into one and settled for some $18 million.

And how did Ross handle it all?

Listen to a friend who, with his wife, visited Ross right after the Atari bomb hit home: "The world had fallen in on him. The company that was once worth more than CBS suddenly was on hard times. Steve was on the edge of physical and corporate extinction. He reflected on all of it. There was the Ken Rosen tragedy, a massive heart attack, Amanda leaving him, the Westchester Theatre. My wife and I and Steve and Courtney were all together. I could have kicked my wife's ankles black and blue. She said, Steve tell me about this Westchester Theatre thing. And for two and a half hours he in the sweetest kindest way went into his life. The seven good years, the seven lean years, the biblical stuff. And he said everything happened. The prosecution and persecution by the feds. He convinced us, perhaps one of the faults of his executive style, a $50,000 item would never even have reached his desk. That wouldn't even be a tip. He wasn't defensive. But he said, in Courtney's presence, how she came back in his life even though all those other terrible things had hit him. And he was the most gracious host imaginable."

Chapter 7

Murdoch, Siegel and a Lawyer Named Armstrong

THE WORLD OF business watched with morbid fascination in 1983 as Steve Ross's and Warner's golden financial record turned to dross.

Then suddenly from the world of the big news media Rupert Murdoch surfaced as a threat of a different sort. The "Magellan of the Information Age," a journalist in his native Australia called Murdoch, "splashing ashore on one continent after another." Harold ("Harry") Evans, who is now president and publisher of Random House, and bolted as editor of the *Times* of London after Murdoch's takeover of the paper, had a harsher analogy in his book *Good Times, Bad Times*. "One minute he's swimming along with a smile, then snap! There's blood in the water and your head's gone."

Ross was a tempting bleeding morsel for Murdoch's voracious appetite. An adventuresome hands-on editor, Murdoch has as sly an eye for popular taste as he has for dissecting a company's balance sheet. His forthright, matey manner, grafted to an Oxford education, never prevented him from angling profitably for readers in the sludge at the bottom of the barrel. He rarely gave them less than they lusted after. From Australia, where he owned two-thirds of the news media, he had moved out to Britain and the U.S. His London *Sun* and *News of the World* were respectively the biggest, raunchiest daily and weekly in the world. In the U.S. he picked up and jazzed up the New York *Post*, Chicago *Sun-Times* and Boston *Herald*. He founded the *National Star*, as wild a supermarket weekly as its competitor, the *National Enquirer*. In Manhattan he took over *New York* magazine and the *Village Voice*. His TV, movie, big book and magazine acquisitions came later. (So did his big retrenchment in 1991 to reduce his $8.2 billion debt.) When he met with Ross, he had already launched Sky Cable, a direct-to-the-home satellite with a need for pay-TV movies.

Murdoch began nibbling at Warner by Ross's casual invitation. Allen & Company's Stanley Shuman was one of Ross's many financial-community friends as well as Murdoch's banker. He suggested Murdoch and Ross get together to discuss their mutual interest in pay TV. In early August 1983, Ross sent his helicopter to bring Murdoch and Shuman out to his house in East Hampton. After three hours, Murdoch was unimpressed. "He spent about half an hour teaching me to play Atari games," said Murdoch. "I find it hard to believe that the chief executive of a company in the process of losing $400 million could be taking an eight-week break in East Hampton at the time. I felt like no one was running the company." Ross was, however, as usual, "a very charming host."

And Murdoch was a very polite guest. On his way out the door he told Ross he'd like to buy some shares in Warner and "hoped he wouldn't mind." Ross replied, "Be my guest." Next day, Murdoch bought a paltry 47,500 shares for a million dollars and change. Then day after day, in small bites, he gobbled up more and more at the depressed average price of $21 a share (down from a pre-Atari high of around $60). By early December, Murdoch owned 7 percent of Warner to become its largest single stockholder.

No one would ever think of Murdoch as a "passive" investor. But "I never knew," says Ross, "whether Rupert was going to do something or not. I didn't have a feeling of comfort he would not." Ross invited Murdoch to his coziest conference room and sang his favorite melody. If Murdoch tried to take over the company, Ross crooned, stars like Streisand, Eastwood, Spielberg and others would leave once Ross was not in charge.

Murdoch was again unimpressed and impatient with the view that the ties binding the Hollywood stars were anything more than Warner's golden chains. Their "loyalty to Ross," Murdoch thought, "was nonsense. I never considered his relationship with the creative community or talents as being of any relevance."

Murdoch had an intermediary check with Hollywood stars, who, he says, replied that they didn't care one way or the other. Nevertheless Ross's stars and friends wrote letters, signed petitions, shouting that they would never work for Warner if Ross were not in charge. "I did everything I could," says one of the big Warner show-biz protesters, "to assist him and speak to analysts and large blocs of shareholders. I said, as did all the others, that we would not work for the company. It was all bullshit, by the way. But we were playing the game on Steve's side as Rupert was playing it on his. But Steve believes things that just aren't so. People want me, they need me, without me they wouldn't stay here, blah, blah, blah. It's just not true."

ENTER HERBERT J. SIEGEL, the son of a prosperous Philadelphia overcoat manufacturer, husband of CBS heiress Ann Levy. Frank Sinatra, who seems to turn up everyplace, sang at their wedding.

Siegel, a big businessman of medium build, talks in bursts and is described by many women as "sexy." He is a tenacious deal entrepreneur, one of the most litigious and successful investors in the country. After graduating from Lehigh University ('50), he quickly slid into dealmaking, getting in and out of companies that made everything from jukeboxes and car polish to beer and films. His beloved and hardworking Romanian-immigrant father thought his son's work was all paper shuffling, because "What do you produce— you don't make anything."

Young Siegel also bought a sizable talent agency whose clients included Jackie Gleason, Nat "King" Cole, Perry Como, Sidney Poitier, Eydie Gorme and Steve Lawrence. But it conflicted with bigger opportunities he saw in the movie business. He had put together a small chemical and plastics company to use as an investment base for other deals. Likable and unpretentious in repose, Siegel can be a holy terror within the walls of a boardroom.

In the middle '60s, long before takeovers became the financial fashion, he started a series of raids. His most prominent early major-league target was Paramount Pictures, where he rattled the teeth of its aged board until Gulf + Western came in and bought Siegel out, yielding him a tidy profit. He merged his chemical and industrial company with Chris-Craft, later sold its boat business but held on to its valuable TV stations.

Deals were his real meat, served up at frequent lunches in Manhattan's '21' Club, with such friends as Norton Simon's David Mahoney, car-maker John DeLorean, the National Football League's commissioner Pete Rozelle, all members of his Chris-Craft board.

When he tried to acquire Piper Aircraft in 1968, it revved up all its propellers to blow him away. For seven long years, with Arthur Liman (who also seems to turn up everywhere) as Siegel's lawyer, they fought in the courts, winning appeals until they got to the U.S. Supreme Court, where they lost. Unsuccessful in taking the company, in 1977 he moved on to 20th Century-Fox, withdrew—and walked away with a $100 million profit and a piece of Fox's TV stations. With each thrust and parry, in the wondrous ways of shrewd investors, Siegel eventually amassed a larger fortune. "Herbie's a genial sore winner," one of his close friends says.

At the height of the Piper battle, hostile takeovers were still frowned on by much of the business establishment. Siegel needed an expert financial witness to support him. Siegel's lawyer and weekend neighbor in Westhampton Beach, Long Island, had long been Arthur Liman. And Liman's biggest client was Steve Ross. At Liman's law firm, Paul, Weiss, Rifkind, Wharton & Garrison, there is an office ditty, "Just remember who's the boss/ It's clients like Steve Ross." Liman brought Ross into court to testify in support of Siegel's unpopular takeover case.

SIEGEL NEVER FORGOT THE favor Ross had bestowed. When Murdoch was threatening Ross and Warner in 1983, Siegel called Liman, who suggested that Siegel and Ross—acquaintances at the time—should have a friendly talk. After calling Ross and asking, "Are you having a problem?" Siegel dropped by on a cold December Sunday at Ross's apartment, where they watched a little pro football. Then they got down to more serious business. Siegel liked Ross and liked even more Warner's core businesses (films, records and cable), which he could buy into at a bargain price.

Within weeks they worked out an intricate deal in which the two companies would swap stock, giving Siegel nominal control of Warner. It would also give Warner a big interest in the TV stations that Chris-Craft owned. Murdoch, still an Australian citizen, would then be barred from taking over Warner under the FCC rule that prohibits foreigners from owning more than 20 percent of American broadcast properties.

Siegel's role as a white knight for Ross was so amicable that Liman's firm represented them both in the negotiations. At the time, Ross repeatedly and improbably denied that he was even worried about Murdoch. Instead, he insisted Warner joined up with Siegel for better reasons. Ross announced that "Herb's philosophy is the same as ours. He wants to build this thing from the broadcast side and he understands we want to do our own thing."

Roger Smith, one of Ross's few irreverent and droll advisers, who was eased out shortly thereafter, remembers saying to Ross as the battle against Murdoch heated up: "What's so terrible about Murdoch? Don't tell me he puts out lousy newspapers, because we put out lousy movies. Let's assume we have to have a boss. Would you rather have a man like Murdoch who can get Maggie Thatcher, Ronald Reagan or the Pope on the telephone in half an hour or a man like Siegel who can get the best table at '21'?" Ross, he says, replied frostily, "We're not going to have any boss."

Murdoch was loopy at being blocked by what he considered low blows. So he uncorked a few foul punches himself. Challenging the Ross-Siegel deal in court was only a Marquis of Queensberry jab. He had other resources. As a publisher, Murdoch bought black ink by the barrel and poured it on anyone he disfavored. He had not the slightest scruple about using his newspapers to hammer Ross personally.

Murdoch's New York *Post* and his other papers ran a series of stories accusing Ross of insider trading in Warner stock when Atari collapsed; replaying the Westchester Theatre scandals; and questioning Ross's and other Warner top executives' investments in "scandal-scarred" government-financed New York housing. Murdoch attacked with wads of information gathered by his best investigative reporting team. They worked in the guise of journalists but actually, in Murdoch's word, were "seconded" to his lawyers. The rest of the press cried foul, came down on Murdoch for outrageously using his sensational journalism to try to slaughter a business adversary.

Siegel accumulated more than 20 percent of Warner's stock, giving Warner protection against a knockout punch by Murdoch. But Ross, stung by the blows in print, worried about where else Murdoch would strike. Not wanting Murdoch in the ring at all, against most advice Ross bought out Murdoch's interest for a $40 million premium even after he'd beaten him. With his new friend and partner Herb Siegel in his corner, Ross thought he could again go back to the good old days when he made all the big decisions and the background lyrics came from Frank Sinatra's "My Way."

Imagine "my surprise," Ross says, at the first board meeting Siegel attended. Ross routinely put up the slate of directors for board committees. Siegel said he wanted to hold off approving Ross's choices until he got to know the directors better. Never, never in the history of the company had Ross been so confronted. "I took some offense at that," says Ross, in fact "I could have fallen right out the window." It got steadily worse. In Ross's mind, Siegel quickly went from white knight to gray knight to, as was later said from the bench in court, "a Trojan Horse."

The rancorous feud eventually forced their marriage broker, Arthur Liman, to choose one or the other. He picked Ross. Siegel got himself another lawyer.

ROSS SAYS THAT EVEN before they came together, he had explained to Siegel, "my management philosophy, the nature of a creative business, the necessity in my mind of things like airplanes, the house in Mexico, the way we treat people, the million-dollar decisions on gut." Answers Siegel, "I was in show business when he was in parking lots." A canny show-biz veteran who is no admirer of Siegel's adds, "Herb's made more money in the movie business, having never been in the movie business, than anyone in the history of the movie business." Herb Siegel, says Liman, "is an investor with few equals. I don't think of Steve the way I think of somebody like Herb, Warren Buffett or even Larry Tisch. They're fundamentally stock market people and very good at it. Steve is a builder."

But right from the start, recalls Siegel, "I never had seen a company run like that." The board "got no monthly financial statements, we were losing a million dollars a day and I wanted to follow the Lazard Frères asset redeployment plan that we'd agreed on for selling off the cats and dogs. I never wanted to interfere with the creative people or hurt the operating companies, but I wanted to see some numbers." He did noisily object to the $100 million in New York staff corporate overhead, demanded that it be cut by more than half, pronto. He thought "$6 million was a lot to pay" for the Acapulco retreat with "a $24,000 bill for tennis sneakers."

Siegel says he didn't "object to indulging the people in the core businesses." But did a company with Warner's huge losses need to invest $48 million more to tone up its air force of two Gulfstreams (later upped to four), a Hawker Siddely, plus three helicopters? "This company," Siegel told the board, "is not an airline." (Under his prodding, Ross sold the biggest helicopter to Donald Trump at a bargain price of $2 million.)

And what about the "$8 million in decorative paintings and $700,000 to redo one executive's office"; a $950,000 fee to Ross's pal, Warner director and chairman of the board's executive compensation committee, Bill vanden Heuvel for a negligible role in the sale of their Ralph Lauren cosmetics company? A $500,000 contribution to director Beverly Sills's New York City Opera? Five company apartments in Trump Tower? Siegel says most of the worst excesses were invisible to the stockholders because Warner defined them as "not material" to the company's operations.

"He was nickel-and-diming me to death," says Ross, "penny-ante, picayune, it was terrible, nightmarish." Ross thinks the trouble was that "Herb is a hell of a good investor. He's just a lousy manager. There were no big risks in his business. The profit of Warner—and this is really where I made a mistake—was larger than the total revenue of Chris-Craft."

THEIR BOARDROOM BATTLES WERE legend.

Siegel was astonished to learn from a reporter the secret, kept from the outside directors, that Warner bought Gadgets, a group of failing restaurants run by a convicted felon. The association with a felon could cost Chris-Craft its TV licenses, as well as $70 million in losses from the investment itself. "Maybe I'm crazy," says Ross, "but I never got the feeling Herb wanted to force me out. He didn't want to live with me and he didn't want to get rid of me. Where we really came apart at the seams was over a very-high-ticket item." The ticket was for a ride on the fast-moving TV-cable train.

Ross says that he and his board had great faith in the future of cable, especially their Warner-Amex systems, a company jointly owned by Warner and American Express. Amex wanted to sell out and Ross wanted to buy. "It eventually turned out to be one of the greatest deals Steve ever made," a critic of Ross's admits. But Siegel said no more debt until Warner finished raising some money by finally disposing of other operations as planned, including its MTV, Showtime, the Cosmos soccer team, the Pittsburgh Pirates, the Franklin Mint, the Eastern Mountain Stores sports clothing chain and the real estate acquired to build an elaborate new "campus" for Atari.

Siegel forced Ross to fire some of his closest cronies, confronted other director-executives at board meetings. "He was very harsh with my executives," Ross recalls. When two of them at a board meeting threatened to resign, Siegel shot back, "I might welcome that. Next." By then Siegel controlled 24 percent of the company's stock (30 percent voting); Ross owned only 1 percent. Siegel threatened a proxy fight. Ross said it would destroy the company, make its stars flee. With Mike Milken's junk-bond help, Ross tried leveraged buy-out schemes, including getting rid of Siegel. They failed. Ross called Siegel's naysaying to his offers "extortionate" and tried to weaken Siegel's hold by issuing more Warner stock.

One Warner director, an old friend of Siegel's, recalls asking him one day when they were alone, "If you want to run the company, why don't you make a run for it?" Siegel answered without blinking, "I don't want to run the company, I just want to see it run better."

Siegel struck one of his loudest blows right at Ross's pocketbook. He objected to Ross's proposed new employment contract, the fattest in the executive world, an average of $14 million a year. *Fortune* commented that "the entire U.S. Senate gets paid only $9 million." Siegel called the proposed contract "obscene," "outrageous," "abominable." The Ross directors approved it anyway, with one calling Ross "godlike." All nine of Ross's directors—five of them Warner officers—voted for the contract; all six of Siegel's voted against it.

At the stockholders' meeting, the music producer David Geffen, who regarded Ross as a father figure, went to a microphone and said on cue, "I am actually shocked at how low the chairman's compensation is compared with the kind of money earned in Hollywood. The loss of Steve Ross to this company would be incalculable." Four years later Geffen left Ross in a huff after twenty-three years when he sold his Warner-backed record company to rival MCA for $555 million.

Siegel thought Ross ran Warner like a "private fiefdom." Mild-mannered former U.S. senator and Connecticut governor Abraham Ribicoff, a Siegel director on the Warner board, described the atmosphere in more vivid terms after he quit in 1987. "I have never in my life been with a board so subservient to the chairman or the CEO. I couldn't take it any more. I think Steve Ross's contract is one of the most outrageous things that has ever happened. Nobody is worth that kind of money. You have a bunch of morons on the board completely manipulated by Steve Ross, stooges to give Steve Ross anything he wanted."

Siegel's pressure on Ross, who was unaccustomed to having his authority challenged by any member of his own board, finally made Ross say, Enough! He succeeded in cutting four of Siegel's hostile directors off the board, reducing him to two seats, against Ross's eleven.

THE ROSS–SIEGEL FEUD hemorrhaged onto the boardroom table, into Warner's stockholder meetings, and stained reputations in the press. In the spring of 1987, Siegel reopened Ross's most painful old wound, the Westchester Premier Theatre.

At the start of the federal investigation in 1978, when the U.S. attorney's criminal division had begun digging in Warner's executive suite, the company required a credible response. Corporate practice and the likelihood of stockholder lawsuits had compelled the Warner board to conduct an independent investigation of its own management, including, of course, Ross himself. A special two-man board committee of Warner directors was deputized to supervise the study and hire an independent outside counsel. The directors were Lawrence B. Buttenwieser, a lawyer who went all the way back to the Kinney days and had been on Ross's board for twenty-two years; and Raymond S. Troubh, a financial consultant who had been a Warner director for sixteen years. "Both," says a lawyer who has known the two well, "are very good friends of Steve's."

The counsel they retained was Michael F. Armstrong, a well-known former prosecutor who had been in charge of the securities fraud unit of the U.S. Attorney's office. He also had been the chief lawyer for New York's Knapp Commission, uncovering corruption and graft in the city's police department. With his crew of three other lawyers, a detective and staff, Armstrong began marathon interviews in an inquiry that stretched over eight years. The investigation produced what became known as the "Armstrong Report," 663 pages plus 88 exhibits and close to 8,000 pages of testimony.

By the rules of engagement, created by Ross and the Warner board, only Buttenwieser and Troubh were supposed to read the Armstrong Report. They would summarize their own and the report's conclusions to the others on the board. When they did in June of 1986, one year before the beginning of the Time-Warner courtship, the committee's conclusions were compressed into 750 words covering three double-spaced typed pages.

They informed the board and stockholders that whatever else there was in the Armstrong Report, "there was insufficient evidence of illegal conduct. The interests of the company and stockholders would best be served by placing the matter to rest and the report not made public," not even shown to other members of the board.

Their sanitized summary also, in effect, retroactively reversed the criminal conviction of Sol Weiss by a jury in a United States district court—a conviction upheld by the Second Circuit Court of Appeals. Despite the courts' verdict on Weiss, Warner found "insufficient evidence, credible to the committee, to conclude Solomon M. Weiss engaged in illegal conduct in connection with kickbacks." That enabled Warner to pay Weiss's $2 million in legal bills and expenses.

At first Siegel had not objected to the report's remaining secret. But after thinking it over, and as his battle with Ross escalated, Siegel vehemently disagreed that the report should be kept from him. He demanded, as a "responsible director," that he also be allowed to read it. Warner called Siegel's curiosity "extortionate," a "sham," a bargaining "pretext," and said that the Armstrong Report was not "relevant to current business."

Thwarted, Siegel took his beef to higher authority, the Delaware Chancery Court. His lawyers claimed, "The Report investigated, among other things, the possibility that Ross or other employees engaged in, condoned or were aware of illegal activities in connection with Warner's acquisition of stock in Westchester Premier Theatre."

Warner's lawyers replied that Siegel had "no proper purpose" in suing to see the Armstrong Report. But, they added, they would not oppose him if he and his lawyers, designated by the judge, read it and promised never to disclose its contents. The judge issued the highest restrictive "confidentiality order" requiring that "each page of the [663-page] copy of the Report shall bear a stamp referring to this Order in substantially the following form: THIS REPORT IS SUBJECT TO A STRICT CONFIDENTIALITY ORDER ENTERED BY THE DELAWARE COURT OF CHANCERY ON MAY 22, 1987. DISCLOSURE OF ANY PORTION OF THIS REPORT BY ANY PERSON IN VIOLATION OF SUCH ORDER IS PUNISHABLE AS A CONTEMPT OF COURT. SUCH ORDER IS ENFORCEABLE AGAINST ANY PERSON WITH NOTICE OF SUCH ORDER OR THIS LEGEND."

The order further provided that only Warner or the court could lift the secrecy ban. "Any application," the order said, "to make any disclosure must be made with seven days notice to [Warner, which] has three business days to advise if they object. If [Warner] does not so object, then plaintiff shall be free to make the intended use of the report."

Siegel got the report, read it and put it in a safe. To this day, under the court-imposed restriction, Siegel says, "I will not respond to any question about the Armstrong Report. My son Bill, who is a lawyer and works with me, knows nothing about what's in it. I've never even told my wife."

It is strange—even hard to believe—that those most immediately involved with Ross and Siegel say they didn't read the report. Arthur Liman, Ross's most intimate confidant, says, "I've never read the Armstrong Report and don't believe Steve ever read the whole report. Maybe in connection with Herb's Delaware proceeding Steve finally got to see it." "I've never seen it," Ross says. "I haven't the slightest idea what's in it. The most important thing is that after I testified privately downtown to [prosecutor] Akerman's superiors in the U.S. attorney's office [in a secret, closed hearing] everything was dropped." Cravath's Samuel C. Butler, the firm's presiding partner, was not only Siegel's counsel but has for years been Time Inc.'s most important lawyer and "legal conscience." Cravath was specifically designated by Chancellor Allen as one of Siegel's two law firms permitted to read the report (the other was Cravath's Delaware counsel). Butler says that neither he nor anyone else at Cravath read it. A few months later when the Time-Warner negotiations began in earnest, Cravath stopped representing Siegel in the matter to avoid a conflict of interest.

Ross considers the whole outcome a public relations failure but an important victory. Siegel may have got what he wanted, Ross says, "but he didn't get it under his terms. You see we were so bad with public relations at Warner that we won something in the Delaware court and we were seen as being the loser."

The two Warner directors charged with reporting on the investigation proudly said it "was broader and more thorough than the Department of Justice, SEC, any defense counsel or press" ever conducted. Their conclusion was only—*only*—that the eight-year-long study of Ross and the company's management produced "insufficient evidence of *illegal* conduct." And that Weiss should never have been convicted, despite what the jury and the appeals court said. The Weiss exoneration by Warner may well have been compassionate. "There's no way," says one of the Armstrong investigators, "that Sol Weiss would have done anything without instruction," strongly implying that the instruction came from Ross's right-hand man, Jay Emmett, who had pleaded guilty to the criminal charges.

What did the report indicate about Ross's involvement and the way he ran the company? From what the report of Warner's own independent investigator revealed, it is not hard to understand why Ross availed himself of the Fifth Amendment against self-incrimination, or why he and his board's special committee wanted to keep the contents of the Armstrong Report secret. Yes, it contained highly personal revelations about Ross. But they were neither irrelevant to the theater scandals nor to Ross's style as Warner's boss.

Contrary to Ross's account of his public relations "victory," Siegel did not go quietly into the night after reading the report. A month later he filed another request with the court to get the full 8,000 pages of testimony that Armstrong and his staff collected to reach their conclusions. Siegel was turned down.

But the most damaging contents of the report showed up in court records—in a letter to the chancellor—of this Siegel appeal to the courts on June 16, 1987, the same month that Ross and Time began their first talks about getting together. The pages of this court record were made available to this reporter as the result of a routine request for the "public documents" in *Herbert J. Siegel* v. *Warner Communications, et al.*, Civil Action No. 9005. They have never before been made public.

The report homed in on a mysterious briefcase that Ross kept in his office closet, including around the time of the Westchester Theatre payoffs. The briefcase was stuffed with tens of thousands of dollars in cash. The Armstrong Report to the Warner board's two-man special audit committee said, "It was necessary to investigate the briefcase issue in order to determine whether Ross was being truthful." It took the investigators a while to ferret out the answer to that question. The report said:

> During our first three interviews, Ross denied that he had
> maintained any such cash reservoir. In our last interview with

Ross (January 14, 1985), however, when pressed on this point, he asserted for the first time, that he had kept excess gambling winnings in a briefcase in his office. This surprising shift in testimony raised new questions about Ross' credibility, as well as his participation in the [Westchester Theatre] kickback scheme.

Ross claimed he used the cash in the briefcase for "various purposes," including "cash and gifts" to a woman with whom the report said he had a "relationship." (*Her name is withheld here by the author, since it was not suggested she was involved or knew anything about the Westchester Theatre. She is referred to here anonymously in bracketed italics—R.M.C.*) At the fourth session, when Ross remembered the briefcase:

> During this interview, Ross revealed for the first time that between 1973 and 1975 he had kept a briefcase in a closet in his office, unknown to anyone else, in which he had kept cash from his gambling winnings. He said that he had used the cash for various purposes, including giving cash and gifts to [*the woman*]. As noted above, Ross' statements about the briefcase significantly departed from his earlier comments as to the sources, maintenance and use of cash. Although Ross maintained that the cash in the briefcase had nothing to do with any cash allegedly delivered by [Leonard] Horwitz [later convicted and sent to jail], the Committee felt that it was necessary to investigate the briefcase issue in order to determine whether Ross was being truthful.

In collecting evidence, Armstrong and his team were circumspect and thorough:

> We have discovered nothing to indicate that the Government had any evidence that Ross masterminded the kickback scheme, and nothing to show he was even aware of it other than the somewhat cryptic statement to which Emmett testified and one piece of documentary evidence—a "credit card" at Caesar's Palace in Las Vegas, Nevada, indicating that Ross had lost $40,000 in cash playing blackjack during the weekend of June 1–3, 1973, just after the alleged $50,000 payment from

Horwitz. Ross has repeatedly challenged the accuracy of the entries on the credit card and has flatly denied ever having lost $40,000 at blackjack. He has maintained that he is a "card counter" at blackjack [someone who remembers every card played] and has suggested that the entries were made to justify either the complimentary treatment that he and his party received on that weekend or the casino's extension of credit to him. However, trial counsel for [Sol] Weiss decided the card posed too much of a cross-examination threat and did not call Ross to give favorable testimony for Weiss.

The investigators couldn't believe that Ross was as successful a gambler as he said he was:

Our refusal to accept Ross' contention that he regularly won $60,000 to $90,000 each time that he engaged in card counting is based upon our interviews with persons who accompanied Ross on his gambling trips, and with Ross himself, who was inconsistent on this issue. The weight of the credible evidence indicates that Ross probably won between $10,000 and $40,000 on a consistent basis. Since even these more modest amounts would have been sufficient, depending upon how the gambling winnings were split, to have accounted for [the woman's] support and gifts, our rejection of his higher estimates of winnings does not mean that he would have had to resort to other means to fund [her] expenses. Of course, he still could have used [Westchester Theatre] kickbacks for that purpose as well.

We are not convinced that Ross maintained a briefcase in his office throughout the period [with the woman]. We believe that Ross might have exaggerated his use of a briefcase to store cash in order to explain where he must have kept the surplus from his claimed winnings of $60,000 to $90,000 per each gambling trip. We simply do not believe that Ross regularly won that much money playing blackjack, and suspect that he made such estimates in an effort to explain how he funded [the woman's] expenses.

When Armstrong went to Ross's lawyer Arthur Liman for an explanation of why it took so long for Ross to remember the briefcase, Liman reported that Ross said he had been "confused about the 'timing.' '' Liman and Ross's lawyers had an additional explanation, the report said:

> At the time we interviewed Ross, they said that he was under considerable strain from other events and was also taking heavy amounts of medication for health reasons. They said that they had recommended to Ross that he postpone our interview because of these problems, but that Ross had insisted on going forward. They argued to us that Ross had not been as sharp or accurate as he would have been under normal circumstances, and that his demeanor, as well as the surprising content of his answers, were largely attributable to the side effects of medication. Indeed, Liman dismissed Ross' claim that he had won between $60,000 and $90,000 each time that he gambled seriously as "ridiculous."

But Armstrong was skeptical about whether Ross had been himself or not when he was being interviewed. "While it is true," the report said, "that Ross appeared somewhat subdued as compared with prior interviews, it is also true that our questions often touched upon sensitive topics. However, in our view, he seemed to have fully understood our questions and to have been fully capable of responding to our inquiries."

Armstrong conceded that there could have been a confusion on dates:

> As we understand the modified version of the briefcase story, Ross did not repudiate his statements about having kept large sums of cash in a briefcase in his office closet, but said simply that he had not initiated that practice until 1976 or 1977. We were told that Ross associated his first such use of the briefcase with a gambling trip he had taken with [Ken] Rosen [Ross's heir-apparent who was severely injured in the 1977 Central Park riding accident].

Like many another gambler—large and small—Ross also told the U.S. Attorney he was his own informal income tax accountant:

> We are also troubled by the fact that Ross' explanations are inconsistent with his statements to the U.S. Attorney. When

he was questioned by the prosecutors about his gambling successes, Ross said that he had not reported any gambling winnings on his income tax returns because: "I felt at the end of the year that I netted out. I was neither a winner or a loser with all my gambling." Ross' statement that he "netted out" could not have been true if a substantial portion of his winnings were used to pay for [*the woman's*] expenses or to buy her gifts. The prosecutors did not overtly challenge Ross on this point, presumably because, as far as we know, when Ross appeared before the prosecutors they were unaware of [*the woman*]. Indeed, they still may not be aware of her existence, or of her possible significance to these events.

Armstrong and his staff found that Ross's "inconsistent statements regarding his own gambling and uses of cash are troublesome," but inconclusive:

> The $110,000 in cash kickbacks allegedly paid to Weiss during Ross' relationship with [*the woman*] occurred at disparate times, and most of the alleged cash deliveries (but not all) do not appear to have coincided with the timing of Ross' expenditures [*for the woman*] (at least as recollected by [*her*]). On the other hand, if Ross maintained a receptacle for cash (as it seems he must have done if his gambling winnings had been his source of cash), he could have also kept a portion of the kickbacks in the same place.
>
> Our willingness to accept Ross' explanation for how he defrayed [*the woman's*] expenses is tempered by the fact that he did not raise [*her*] name despite our repeated inquiries about his uses of the cash. It was not until we located and interviewed [*her*] and then told him about her statements, that he was prepared to acknowledge that he may have given her substantial sums of cash.
>
> While Ross' failure to tell us about [*the woman*] could have been explained by an understandable desire to protect the privacy of his personal life, Ross disclaimed such an excuse. Instead, he said that he simply had not recalled that he had given substantial sums of cash to her.

Finally the report concluded:

Our inquiries in these areas unearthed conflicting evidence, as well as several instances in which we believe that Ross was not completely candid. Despite our reservations about Ross' credibility, however, we have been unable to establish that any of the alleged kickbacks made by Horwitz were intended for the private benefit of Ross or for an entertainment slush fund.

On the other hand, if Ross had substantial gambling winnings during the period [*of his relationship with the woman*] (and we believe that he did), it is unlikely that Ross lost back his entire retained share of winnings in casual gambling. Thus, while certain aspects of the briefcase story are implausible, Ross may well have used a briefcase (or some other depository) from time to time in order to store suplus winnings from successful gambling trips.

Our concerns about Ross' credibility have prevented us from reaching any definitive conclusion about his possible involvement in the [Westchester Theatre] scandals. Although Ross' reluctance to disclose and to discuss his relationship with [*the woman*] may be understandable to some degree, his inconsistent statements regarding his own gambling and uses of cash are troublesome.

And its summary:

In summary, we continue to believe that the weight of all the available evidence does not support the charge that Ross received or knew of the [Westchester Theatre] cash kickbacks. Indeed, the only person who actually made that charge—Emmett—also knew the essential details of the episode [*with the woman*] and does not appear to have ever related the alleged [Westchester Theatre] kickback to any need by Ross to pay [*her*] expenses. Emmett's testimony invoked the notion of a corporate, not a personal, cash fund.

Two years later, on the eve of the Time-Paramount battle, Siegel went back to the Chancery Court again and asked that his new lawyers be allowed to read the Armstrong Report. Warner replied: "We view this as a thinly veiled threat to resurrect the Westchester Theatre inquiry, which dates from 1973 and [is intended] to intimidate [Warner]." Siegel again failed.

From the evidence in the Armstrong Report extracts, it is hard to quarrel with the conclusion that no criminal case against Ross was sustainable or that a jury would convict him of culpability in the theater scandal beyond a reasonable doubt. The evidence was so circumstantial that any experienced defense lawyer would have left the prosecution reeling.

If only legal innocence of criminal conduct is the standard for choosing a CEO, continuing him in office and rewarding him with huge compensation packages, then Ross was indeed home free. But by the standards more customarily applied to the head of a public company, if a really independent board had been allowed to read such a report, no matter how successful the company, the CEO would have been quietly eased out, fired or allowed to retire. Not Ross.

He received a ten-year contract with compensation averaging $14 million a year, plus incentive bonuses and stock options potentially worth hundreds of millions, then the largest such executive package for a public company in the U.S.

One of the many senior legal advisers to Time muses: "My view of the law is that if you're not indicted or not convicted—Ross wasn't even indicted—you're entitled to the benefit of our system. But I agree that's not the only test for a CEO. All I can say is that it didn't occur to me then that Time should have done more than they did. Looking back in retrospect, maybe it was something we should have done."

MOST CLICHÉS ARE TRUE. As Warner regained its financial health and stock market value, the cliché that "nothing succeeds like success" ended for the moment the Ross-Siegel feud.

Siegel does use bare knuckles in the boardroom. But his opposition to Ross's traditional one-man rule contributed to welcome results. "Herb Siegel was a pain in the ass," says one Warner insider close to Ross, "but the mere fact he was there caused a lot of smart things to happen. He made Steve be careful at a time when he needed to be careful."

By selling off a baker's dozen of its operations, taking advantage of tax write-offs, cutting back New York overhead, concentrating on movies, records and cable systems, Warner climbed into the black once more. In the second half of the '80s, Warner was again riding high. Its cable investment began to pay off. Record and tape sales rose. The studio was turning out hit movies, foreign and TV program sales were rising. Its stockholders were getting dividends and Warner stock was heading toward pre-Atari peaks.

Ross had his spectacular new salary. His biggest stockholder, Siegel, had been silenced by the court and his representation cut down in the boardroom. But even more important to Siegel, his $400 million Chris-Craft investment had grown more than five times over to $2.1 billion. Ross could rightly say his company was "one of the best turnaround stories I've ever seen." And so could Siegel.

Ross has an uncanny ability, says one intimate, to pull himself together and do a "positive reframe" of his life no matter how gloomy others might find the outlook. Donald Oresman, a shrewd lawyer-executive and Paramount's second-in-command, who fought Ross in a later battle, puts Ross's ability to bounce back primarily in business terms: "Because he is so entrepreneurial, his career has been checkered, but in the long run, he's hit more home runs than he's struck out. He's not a manager, he's a handler. His business history is like cotton candy. He's the quintessential entrepreneur who basically bought companies. If they worked he had a hit, if they didn't that was it. It's more than charm. He has a capacity for making people feel safe in the insecure product-driven world where one day you're hot as a firecracker and the next day you're in the dumps."

A Warner director and friend who has worked with Ross for years close up puts it more personally. "He is capable of having very deep feelings, but I think he is first and foremost a fighter, a born survivor. I've seen him at board meetings at various times very angry. He gets cold, ice cold to the person he's angry at and to the people who haven't performed up to his expectations. It's part of the game. A lot of people say he runs a hands-off operation. That's nonsense. Since the Atari disaster, I've never seen him when he didn't know exactly what was going on. He's older, more matured, knows he's vulnerable—in terms of health and anything else. When he expects to be most hurt, it doesn't really trouble him as much as he expected. Primarily he's a people dealer. He convinces you that he's terribly interested in *you,* immediately makes you feel that he's your friend. If you're in trouble, call him. He exudes a tremendous amount of self-confidence in being able to fix up anything. He does make you feel that he'll stop everything for you if you need him. It's personally very flattering."

Whatever the explanation, in modern times few, if any, corporate chieftains of Ross's scale and visibility have bounced back from such a series of personal and business disasters.

Steve Ross did.

Warner's 1988 annual report, as usual more hyped than other companies, shouted its theme about Warner's future on a pullout poster: "Today, 1980 is ancient history."

Now a rehabilitated Ross needed new and more exonerating fields to conquer. That opportunity presented itself with a twenty-five-cent call from a phone booth placed by Time's Nick Nicholas.

part 2

COMING TOGETHER

chapter 8

On Tiptoes

O N DOWNTOWN MANHATTAN'S FOLEY Square, abutting Chinatown, stands the colonnaded New York State Court Building. One spring day in 1987, Nick Nicholas climbed its long steps to answer a citizen's call to civic responsibility. He was on jury duty.

He had come equipped to fill the empty hours waiting either to be empaneled or dismissed. Armed with a briefcase full of office reading matter, Nicholas was lucky. He earned his twelve dollars and was let go early. No time waster, he went to the phone booth to continue making close to forty calls. "I carry around with me," he recalls, "a list of lots of things to get done one day." One of those things he had jotted down was a suggestion from HBO's boss, Michael Fuchs, that he should get to know Steve Ross. So, among others, "with no special expectations," Nicholas called Ross to see if he could fill the unanticipated free time by going up to see him. Sure, Ross amiably replied. Nicholas hopped in a cab, plowed up the East River Drive to Ross's Park Avenue apartment.

The conversation was pleasant and general. Nothing special. But in the forefront of Ross's mind was something big and quite special. "One of the problems we recognized Warner had," says Ross, "is that we were in no-man's-land in cable." He describes it in one of the familiar, often used Ross aphorisms: "We were too small to be large and too big to be small." He also felt that "we were both in the same business. We dealt with each other so far as Warner and HBO were concerned." Ross thought that a combination of some kind with Time could be just what he had been looking for.

Time's appetite for *something* was high, but its choice was limited. Although executives worried every day about rumors of hostile take-over moves, the Timeincers had already shredded, one by one, a list of expansion and acquisition plans. A single sticking point always got in the way. Time's top and bottom line—as well as every line in between—was constantly that if they merged or made an acquisition, Time would have to dominate, be the boss so that the preservation of the "Time culture" would be assured. They said just that in so many words. "It was always," recalls one high Time staff executive, "like the scene in the Broadway musical *Evita,* where the generals are marching around the chair jockeying for who gets to sit down last. That's the way it always was with CBS, Gannett, ABC, and later Ross."

But remaining at the head of one of Time's dwindling lists of acquisition possibilities were two companies, Warner and Gulf + Western (later renamed Paramount Communications). Both owned big movie studios, natural potential mates for Time's HBO and the company's consuming appetite for films. Yet there was a traumatic old barrier between Time and an entertainment partner. Time had repeatedly been burned when it got close to movie studios. There were the hundreds of millions of dollars from the Columbia Pictures–HBO debacle and a failed effort with Tri-Star Pictures as a joint venture with CBS and Columbia. Much earlier, Time had coveted Universal and MGM, with thoughts of ownership, only to be stopped dead by Luce in a withering memo. He vetoed any such thoughts because they could create "conflicts in the fields of tastes and standards." Just to make sure, he had added, "I would also exclude the service of anaesthetizing people by TV."

Time's disillusioning experiences with Hollywood folk were heightened by trying to work with David Susskind, whose Talent Associates Time owned in the '80s, only to find there wasn't room for Susskind's show-biz temperament within the orderly, tradition-laden halls of the Time & Life Building. (Susskind's chauffeur-driven car often cruised by fuming Time executives waiting at bus stops.) Movie people were just not "Time types." In fact, the management's entire Hollywood experience led Time's top staff strategy group, as late as 1988, to exclude, in mapping alternatives for the company, any path that would lead to the acquisition of a movie studio. The staff report conclusively said that "Time Inc. has considered and rejected trying to acquire a major studio."

Not that many a movie mogul hadn't courted Time. One persistent suitor even earlier and more ardent than Ross was Martin Davis. His Gulf + Western conglomerate owned Paramount Pictures, Simon

& Schuster, Madison Square Garden and other enterprises, as well as a huge financial company. At chatty breakfasts in the Ritz-Carlton Hotel—midway between the Time & Life and Gulf + Western buildings—Munro held Davis at bay. He confidently assured Davis that Time wanted to remain independent and didn't cotton to Hollywood's ways. He meant it. "Dick probably reflected our confusion over the movie business," says Jerry Levin. "We were always ambivalent and schizoid about that." After each amiable standoff, Munro and sometimes Nicholas would hoof it south eight blocks back to their office. A frustrated Davis traveled three blocks west to his and other places in the back of a town car.

But the one Time executive who had *never* given up on movies was Jerry Levin. He was a relative latecomer to Time (1972), the developer of HBO with its breakthrough satellite in the sky. In the race for the top job, Levin had been shunted aside to the backwater of strategic planning. But he managed to make it the mainstream, becoming widely known in Time's executiveland as "our brain," and became the prime mover in what he called the need for a "transforming transaction" to bring the company into its new era.

From the beginning it was a determination realized only by intricate, dogged maneuvering. "Jerry," says a former Time executive who knows him well, "is the most interesting, thoughtful, best mind in all of Time, but the better angels of his nature don't always win." A newer Warner subordinate finds him vaguely puzzling. "I sometimes feel as if I'm communing with the Delphic Oracle." Still others at Time and Warner say they have found him "smart as hell," but at times "devious" or "building tunnels in back alleys."

GERALD M. LEVIN, among others, refutes the cliché that Time's business leaders were a homogenized collection of buttoned-down WASPs who learned their dogma on the premises and were determined to observe it.

Although in college (Haverford, '60) he was a Bible student who once had the intention of becoming a rabbi, Levin is also a lifelong movie, sports and TV addict. Framed on a shelf of his booklined Time-Life office was a quote from George Orwell's *1984*:

> The voice came from an oblong metal plaque like a dulled mirror which formed part of the surface of the right-hand wall.

The instrument (the telescreen, it was called) could be dimmed,
but there was no way of shutting it off completely.

Levin knew before anyone at Time that the TV screen Orwell envisioned would never be shut off. The "ineluctable growth of television," Levin calls it. Unlike his senior executive brothers, Levin
had not spent his professional life at Time. Nor had he grown up in
the old Time print tradition, although he had undoubtedly read more
than any of his fellows. He was an outsider, with different personal
and professional roots—entirely different.

Levin was the son of a religious Russian-Romanian family. His
hardworking father became a Pennsylvania "butter and egg man,"
with a head for business and high hopes for his son. Even though
young Jerry's father's grocery business thrived, Levin remembers
that the family was turned down for an upscale house in a better
section of town bordering the Main Line. When they were finally
accepted in an economically middle-class community, Levin found
himself in high school with youngsters who hung out at restricted
country clubs. He resented their exclusiveness, and to this day has
never played golf, a virtual heresy among many Time businessmen.

At Haverford, a first-class small college with a strong Quaker
tradition, he turned to philosophy, wrote an honors thesis on the
consistency between the Judaic and Christian traditions. "I was trying
in my own mind," he says, "to blend them because I had a sense I
was leaving home. That knocked out any notions of being a rabbi.
It certainly made me a secular Jew—intellectually engaged by Christian philosophy. The symbol of Jesus, the notion of humility, ego
submersion, the meek will inherit the earth, became so powerful to
me that, although I was first in my class, I refused the award that
went with it. To this day I'm not sure why, but I also burned every
paper I wrote in college including my honors paper on the theory
that no one needed to applaud it or read it. It was obviously significant because it irks me now." (He is now chairman of Haverford's
board of trustees.)

A quiet rebelliousness throbbed within him, best expressed by the
seminal author in his life, Albert Camus, whose protagonist in *The
Stranger,* says Levin, "was basically an observer of things, not really
a participant." Camus believed that "you can't defeat the system,
but the act of rebellion, the fact of action, that's where you get
meaning."

In his senior year he married and withdrew his applications to Oxford (which today he regrets) and for a Fulbright Fellowship so he could study law at the University of Pennsylvania, where his young wife was a student. He still thought he would teach philosophy or write. But he did so well at law school that the Wall Street law firm Simpson Thacher & Bartlett offered him an inviting job. He went to work for one of the firm's most publicly involved senior partners, Whitney North Seymour.

After four years of high-visibility cases (e.g., civil rights, First Amendment), he found the law ungratifying "because you were giving advice to people who were really doing something." He thought of going to Washington, perhaps the Peace Corps, instead ended up in the stimulating company of David Lilienthal, the chairman of the New Deal's Tennessee Valley Authority and later the Atomic Energy Commission, who had turned his talents to the quasi-private sector. "I learned from him," says Levin, "how you take things with the force of an idea and put them into action." Lilienthal sent him to Iran, where he worked on an ambitious project converting the Shah's southern desert into agricultural areas, a sort of mini-TVA. Returning from Iran in 1972, he had been divorced and was remarried. At thirty-two he needed a new job.

Through a friend he heard about cable TV and Time. He remembers, "I became fascinated with it because the concepts had many of the same principles as the work I'd been doing on massive flood control and electrification. My fascination with that technology is some clue to my subsequent interest. There's very little difference between water, electricity and television." Time hired him to join the frazzled tiny band of pioneers who were threading cable through the hard rock of Manhattan.

While working on new cable programs and tactics, the obviously bright new boy was invited to explain his HBO dream to a senior Time eminence. He was gently told the company was not interested in his old movies and wrestling programs. "But you're not going to stop me, are you?" he asked, quietly protesting. "It will really grow into something important." Go ahead and try, he was told with faint encouragement. Three years later Levin announced he was moving movies and sports programs up from primitive dishes twenty miles apart on the ground and bouncing them off a satellite thousands of miles in the sky. It was an exciting first for pay TV and put HBO far ahead of its competitors.

The news made the front page of the *Wall Street Journal*. Sluggish Time stock bounced up. At a meeting of security analysts shortly after, Munro, who was then in charge of the new venture, remembers, "We were at the Harvard Club, where the management was hosting the analysts. It was sort of a turning point for me and maybe Time Inc. All our senior guys were on the dais. Suddenly that whole meeting began to be HBO-oriented. Magazines were ignored. Everybody was looking down the table at me. I didn't know a hell of a lot, but I was the only one who had any idea of what they were talking about, satellites, dishes."

Kelso Sutton, who headed the magazine division, remembers the moment. "I was sitting there with the biggest operating unit in the company," says Sutton, "and barely getting a question. Finally someone said would anyone like to ask Kelso a question? That was a big change." Within two years the infant HBO was making money. Within fifteen years, the Time trio—Munro, Levin and Nicholas— who made the HBO and cable project work were running the company, heading it toward a new destination.

There was, says Levin, "some destiny inherent in the transaction with Warner."

FROM BEHIND THE SCENES, Levin focused on the glimmerings of opportunity in Nicholas's brief jury-duty visit to Ross. The possibilities became even more obvious when Ross quickly phoned and said, as Ross recalls, "Gee, I think I've got this idea and I've got it down on paper." He invited Munro and Nicholas to walk down the street to get together with him in his Warner office. Once they arrived, from his notes on a yellow pad Ross rambled on enthusiastically about a bewildering array of combinations and possible deals that would bring the two companies closer together.

For Nicholas, Munro and the other Time videotropes, at first Ross's scribblings were not at all clear. Time was wary. Maybe some joint ventures in cable, or possibly between Warner's movie company and HBO? It was all inchoate and tentative. Nicholas and Levin met with Time's house lawyers, financial and cable executives. They were even more skeptical than their bosses appeared to be.

One of those present remembers that at their first luncheon meeting "We were asked to express our views on what was being called the 'Ross entertainment joint venture.' Everybody unanimously felt it was a mistake. We didn't like the sound of Ross. And no one could conceive of how you would unwind something like this if it didn't work out." As a counterproposal, a limited cable joint venture was mentioned. Over the summer the group worked only on a possible combination restricted to cable. Time wasn't even ready for a joint fifty-fifty cable venture with Warner. But by summer's end, appetites at the top had been whetted, even though on the surface it appeared that both proud companies had backed off.

Levin and Nicholas did not give up. On August 11, 1987, while others were on vacation, Levin wrote a memo to Munro, who was not yet fully on board, that spelled out a future entirely different from their negative discussions with their staff:

> *Confidential Memo*
> To: J. Richard Munro
> From: Gerald M. Levin
> cc: N. Nicholas
>
> I am now convinced our primary objective should be merger. Like IBM or GE its size and range of solid franchises would make it an institutional "must carry" stock. The combination could be accomplished through a no premium merger, shareholder value would be enhanced without the insanely pricey dilution so prevalent in the purchase of assets today. Most of our asset base and expansion possibilities center on entertainment and on our established position in cable and programming. Publishing is more limited. The new Time Inc., then, would be an entertainment oriented communications company. At long last, the company would be a major motion picture producer and distributor. Principal issue is still Steve. Can we work with him? Can we communicate comfortably? Will *we* ultimately be the survivor company and management focus? Can suitable divorce provisions be worked out in advance? If Warner is not do-able then the only other option would be G + W.

Then Levin raised the crucial questions that would dominate all the future negotiations, even though not one of the specific doubts he raised would ever be investigated:

> As we saw with Gannett, the potential asset combination can be compelling in theory but meaningless in the real world

if the cultures are incompatible or the CEOs cannot relate. What about Steve? He has had health problems. His lifestyle is sumptuous, his perks lavish. Any inquiry into Steve's past must include the Westchester Premier Theatre scandal, although presumably that is behind him. Also there is a period of remarkable franchising success with Warner Cable, including a very close relationship with Donald Manes in Queens [the New York borough president who committed suicide after a bribery scandal]. And on a business level, the Atari debacle illustrated some glaring defects in Steve's delegated management.

Levin was pragmatic as well as far-seeing. By now he well knew the people at Time and its board. He concluded the memo with a piece of realism:

> A word of caution and reality: neither our senior management nor our board will presently proceed to the end result I have described. The memorandum is intended to provoke debate and not detail the mechanics.

When a lawyer later asked Levin whether it was "fair to say that this memorandum outlined the subsequent course of action that Time followed," Levin replied, "I am a self-effacing individual and I don't think I could answer yes to that question." Levin was expressing more than modesty. At the time he wrote his memo, Levin knew from past disappointments that he and Nicholas still lacked the internal support and consensus that would allow them to push hard for movies and entertainment against Time's old print journalism tradition. Levin was not only trying to entice Ross but, as important, to get backing from the key executives and board members in his own company.

So while Time executives pondered, talked among themselves, did staff studies pointing toward more video involvement, and played shy with Warner, Ross wondered. To try to advance their discussions, he proposed a working meeting together. Time stalled, trying to figure out its best move. Levin, by now a kind of pitching coach for Munro and Nicholas, wrote another delaying memo:

> Munro should go see Ross today, October 5, one on one, and not by telephone to explain that we have a major project

(undisclosed and no hints!) we are working on, so we should push back a meeting until November. The cable joint venture didn't really result in any positive conclusion. We have no present intention of merging with Warner in any respect. It would be helpful to know why Steve is so anxious to meet. Didn't he get the message that we're not prepared to do anything at this point? [Levin cannot recall what the "major project" was—or even if there was one.]

Munro put the eager Ross off for a month. Then the two, this time along with their top film and operating executives, met again on the neutral ground of a suite at the Helmsley Palace Hotel. Ross and his team were beckoning, but Time was still playing it cool. After the meeting coach Levin wrote another memo to Munro pointing out that the meeting "had been a good and satisfactory *preliminary* step 'in getting to know each other.' " But he added the tactical warning that at Munro's next meeting with Ross "the key here is to keep our options open with Warner, cool Steve's ardor somewhat but maintain a deepening relationship."

Both sides were talking separately, occasionally meeting together in hotels and private clubs, spinning out possible deals. But whether alone or with Warner, the Time group was finding problems for every solution. Ross decided he was confusing Time instead of winning them over. So he did something he had never done before (and never did again until the deal was concluded). He paid a visit to the Time & Life Building to see Munro and Nicholas.

"It was similar to the first meeting I'd had with Nick," Ross says, "but this time I got a quick response." What was different "was that I brought with me a little pamphlet in a blue binder. Maybe one of the few pamphlets I ever made—or had made—in my entire life. It was a big joint venture with a lot of details spelled out in the ensuing pages. I didn't do that the first time, so that I could understand why there could be confusion. My booklet showed a structure of what I'd been talking about. Now they had something in front of them. I left it behind. Asked them not to distribute it but to read and destroy it." (Ross says no copies remain. Unlike his potential partners at Time, Ross leaves no paper trail.)

Ross proved to be right. The pace of the executive meetings accelerated—at such places as the Dorset and Berkshire hotels, the Rainbow Room's Rockefeller Center Luncheon Club and other venues away from curious underlings. The proposed joint venture, with all its tax, legal and control problems, grew in size, not to say complexity. Munro began informally to tell Time board members what they had in mind. Several warned of the hazards of a noncommittal, makeshift partnership, but they were eager for new ideas and willing to hear more.

STRATEGY GROUPS, STAFF STUDIES, task forces, executive retreats are a relatively modern corporate invention. Not so many years ago—and perhaps even today—the most important work was done on the premises of the workplace. But from the early '70s on, the bigger the company the more it was likely to indulge in such lofty séances in far-off places.

Time, like many another bureaucratized company, specialized in them. Warner, which remained a proprietor's place, hatched most of its strategies within Steve Ross's head. No matter that Time's volumes of reports rarely, if ever, generated specific results that were acted on by the decision-making executives or the board. Their texts provided stimulation, information and, most of all, confirmation for the bosses.

The Lyford Cay Club in the Bahamas was a favorite Time seedbed for strategy meetings and retreats. The twenty-some-member strategy group—transported on Time's jets—that met to work and play at Lyford Cay in May 1988 was made up of the brightest operating managers from every part of the company. They were well prepared by an earlier Lyford meeting and several other retreats in northern climes (some wore golf shirts emblazoned, "Free the Lyford Cay Nine"). Like most such Time groups, they were given few instructions—and no inside information. Except for their leader, general counsel Bill Guttman, they were even kept ignorant of the ongoing secret discussions with Ross and Warner.

They were also victims of a corporate cultural lag, strategists under the confining delusion that acquiring a movie studio was a no-no to the Time management. "Damn right, correct," says Nicholas. "They were totally in the dark, using information a couple of years old. They believed that. What happened was we went to Lyford, spent three days there in vigorous discussion yelling, with temper, emotion and strong feelings. They told us we were wrong in not wanting a studio. I think we probably nervously laughed."

"Nick and I," explains Levin, "tried to keep them away from what we called 'our taint.' Frankly we saw their leanings toward video as part of the advocacy process convincing the board. By the time they met, we were in a transactional mode." But subliminally the group got the message. "Nick and I could have written the group's presentation ourselves," chortles Munro. Nonetheless, they had a spirited, freewheeling seminar on the sixty-seven-page draft report the strategy group had already prepared. Then they signed off on its plain-spoken analysis and recommendations, including:

> Time Inc. lacks the palpable passion that once inspired creative energy throughout the company. That passion—for excellence, impact and public service—needs to be restated and rekindled. the vision we embrace must emphasize our commitment to create quality. Internally, our own managers believe we are not managing for innovation. The television screen provides in excess of 65% of the words consumed from all media forms by the American public. Magazines represent 2.4%. We can challenge the precision of these figures but the balance between print and video will tip further from print in the years ahead.

They finally concluded:

> Given the consumer market we face today, we believe Time Inc. is significantly underleveraged in video programming. We will be more so in the years ahead unless we make this the focus of our investment strategy.

Bingo! "The report served its purpose," says Levin. "The Warner deal would be consistent with its recommendation." So much so that the top sheet of the report was removed and replaced by a covering letter from Munro, the recommendations were moved to the front, and the entire report was promptly sent to every member of the Time board. Munro's letter said:

> Last month twenty Time Inc. senior executives met four days off site at an executive retreat, to consider and discuss the implications of [these] recommendations. My colleagues and I enthusiastically endorse most of them wholeheartedly.

In the same envelope to the board, both Munro and Nicholas enclosed a more memorable letter—not just the strategist's blind-sided generalizations but a pinpointed proposal:

> Our recent internal review concluded that if we want to remain the preeminent source of information and entertainment, we must acknowledge the increasing dominance of video as the medium of choice worldwide. We do not believe, however, that Time Inc. has the experience and depth of management to evolve into a fully integrated major motion picture and television company. Thus we have concluded that the only practical means to achieve this goal is to acquire or merge with a major studio. To that end we have been examining some form of combination between Time Inc. and Warner Communications, but to date have reached no conclusions. Warner is characterized by excellent, stable management.

By that time, Munro, Nicholas and Levin had reached a far more advanced conclusion. "Merger Now," Levin called the new phase in a working note. On an early June day in 1988, Munro and Nicholas visited Ross again and said that the joint venture they and their staffs had been working on was too complicated, with technical issues that could not be resolved. "Dick was a full participant in the discussion by then," says Nicholas. "We said to Steve, you know there's another way to do what we're trying to do. It's a bolder move, but since we both, you know, share a point of view about the future. . . ." So they asked Ross, Why didn't they merge the companies altogether— get married instead of just living together?

Ross was no reluctant groom this time. "I always like to take things a step further," Ross says. But wait. Before posting the wedding banns, the Time side needed to get endorsement for their interfaith corporate marriage from the outside directors on the Time board. That would not be easy.

AMONG THE BLUE-CHIP boards of American corporations, few were bluer or more densely populated by establishment outside directors than Time Inc.'s. Around its inlaid board table sat the CEOs of IBM (John R. Opel), Xerox (David T. Kearns), R. H. Macy (Edward S. Finkelstein), Borg-Warner (James F. Beré), The Henley Group (Michael D. Dingman), two college heads (Radcliffe's president, Matina S. Horner, and the State University of New York's chancellor, Clifton R. Wharton, Jr.), plus a constellation of other business leaders, past and present (Arthur Temple, Don Perkins, Temple-Inland's Clifford J. Grum, Sonat's Henry C. Goodrich and the son of Time's founder, Hank Luce).

Time's two salesmen for their Warner merger plan were Munro and Nicholas (not their chief strategist and negotiator, Jerry Levin, who as usual was behind the scenes crafting the deal itself). If managers want to get the endorsement of a big change in course when their board meets formally, they had best do some individual politicking in advance. The Munro-Nicholas lobbying schedule went right down to the last day, July 21, the date of the next Time board meeting. Their whirlwind schedule brought them to each of the dozen outside directors, in person and with follow-up phone calls. Their itinerary:

JUNE 23	CLIFF WHARTON 12:00/LUNCH IN WHARTON'S OFFICE
	HENRY GOODRICH 2:00 P.M./DICK MUNRO'S OFFICE
JULY 5	TEMPLE, DINGMAN AND OPEL
11:30 A.M.	NICHOLAS AND MUNRO DEPART FROM WCAP (NO PLANE YET ASSIGNED)
12:00 P.M.	ARRIVE MANCHESTER, NEW HAMPSHIRE, HENLEY COMPANY HANGAR
	ARTHUR TEMPLE WILL MEET THEM AT HENLEY HANGAR AND THEN THEY ALL BOARD HENLEY HELICOPTER (TAIL #N14HG) FOR A 15 MINUTE FLIGHT TO HAMPTON, NEW HAMPSHIRE
	MESSRS. NICHOLAS, MUNRO AND TEMPLE WILL BE MET BY DINGMAN'S DRIVER AND TAKEN TO DINGMAN'S OFFICE:
	THE HENLEY GROUP, INC. LIBERTY LANE HAMPTON, NH 03843
	AT THE CONCLUSION OF THE LUNCHEON MEETING HENLEY DRIVER TO TRANSPORT ALL BACK TO HAMPTON HELICOPTER FLIGHT BACK TO MANCHESTER, NH AIRPORT
2:30 P.M.	NICHOLAS AND MUNRO DEPART MANCHESTER

3:00 P.M.   ARRIVE INNOTECH AVIATION, BURLING-
              TON, VT AIRPORT, MR. OPEL WILL MEET
              THEM AND DRIVE THEM TO HIS HOME (30
              MIN. DRIVE) SHELBURNE FARM, ADDRESS:
              ORCHARD POINT SHELBURNE, VT. AT THE
              CONCLUSION OF THE MEETING MR. OPEL
              WILL DRIVE MUNRO AND NICHOLAS BACK
              TO BURLINGTON AIRPORT FOR RETURN
              TRIP TO WCAP

              NO DEPARTURE TIME SET

JULY 6   DAVID KEARNS   2:30 P.M./DICK MUNRO'S
          OFFICE

JULY 7   HANK LUCE   11:00 A.M./HANK LUCE'S OF-
          FICE, 720 FIFTH AVENUE, ROOM 504

JULY 18   JIM BERE/DON PERKINS   12:00/LUNCH,
          BORG-WARNER OFFICES, 200 SOUTH MICHI-
          GAN, 21ST FLOOR

JULY 19   ED FINKELSTEIN   9:00 A.M./FINKELSTEIN'S
          OFFICE

JULY 20   CLIFFORD GRUM   2:30 P.M./DICK MUN-
          RO'S OFFICE

MATINA HORNER   TO DATE (JUNE 21) NO CONTACT HAS
                BEEN MADE TO RESCHEDULE

WHEN THE DIRECTORS ASSEMBLED for their July 21 meeting in the boardroom atop the Time & Life Building, only one of their number was missing, Arthur Temple. He was convalescing from a heart attack he had suffered barely a week earlier. His bumptious views had already been expressed to the board: "If all you want is to make money by whatever means, let's just open a string of whorehouses across the country. I don't think we've got to make money that way."

With Temple absent, the meeting was peaceful. First they handsomely remedied a past mistake. After having kicked Levin off the board two years earlier, they reelected him, this time making him vice chairman. Most of the meeting was devoted to a routine show-and-tell. Those attending were shown slides on movie companies, demonstrating in full color that Warner, Paramount and Disney were the three most attractive, with Warner even more so than the other two. Munro and Levin, reading from scripts, reviewed their past strategies including the "brief conversation with CBS and more serious talks" with Gannett. They emphasized the need—repeated incessantly—"to assure control by Time Inc. management to preserve editorial independence." Bruce Wasserstein and other investment bankers, plus Cravath lawyers, were invited in to outline financial and legal questions.

There was little dissent expressed at the table. Temple and Hank Luce had already questioned the strategy of going into movies altogether. The others were more concerned about Ross personally and how the deal would be crafted so that Time's management could stay in control.

No one was asked to vote. But Munro & Co. were encouraged to try to negotiate the merger if: 1) they could satisfy themselves about Ross's record and character; 2) assure that the "corporate governance," without any doubt, would end up in Time's hands; 3) Nicholas would promptly succeed Munro and first be co-CEO with Ross of the new company and then sole boss; 4) Ross would retire at a date certain; 5) the exchange ratio of the shares would be fair to Time; 6) "Time culture," always defined as the "journalistic independence and integrity," most especially of *Time* magazine, would be assured; and finally 7) that all the key merger conditions would be guaranteed by requiring, to change them, a two-thirds vote of the board (known as a "supermajority," originally defined by Levin as "a surrogate for uncertainty about Steve and a pocket reservation about the deal itself").

There was tough discussion, questioning and caution expressed but little or no formal dissent. Of course, the formal board minutes, so as not to reveal anything except what was legally required, were deliberately getting briefer and more sterile with every meeting. They had the routineness of a Miranda Rights recitation. The directors reserved their most outspoken views for private conversations, in the meetings they had on the Munro-Nicholas visits before the board meeting and in the follow-ups after.

And what did Munro, Nicholas and Levin find when they told their friendly directors individually that they were no longer just planning to have the affair with Ross they had talked about in the past? Now they wanted a full-fledged marriage, complete with a binding prenuptial agreement and a joint checking account.

"We got encouragement everywhere we went," recalls Nicholas, in a reediting of current events worthy of a new edition of the Soviet encyclopedia. "The strategic thing they bought right onto," he says.

"Okay, they buy the strategy. Steve Ross, governance, those are the issues—entertainment wasn't an issue." And what about the contrary evidence in the notes describing the reactions of the directors? "I don't take any notes so I don't know about notes," Nicholas says. If Nicholas took no notes, Munro and Levin certainly did, in their own hand, scrawled on scraps of paper. *Fortune* summarized Levin's tally: "Beré was unenthusiastic; Perkins lukewarm; ditto [Clifford] Grum; Opel was skeptical but open minded; Kearns was signed on as was Finkelstein. No read on the board's two academics, Horner and Wharton. Temple did not appear on the list nor did [Hank] Luce. There was no need."

Some samples of the actual notes of conversations before and after their July board meeting:

Munro note Dingman phone call—He has talked with Arthur [Temple] twice. First conversation was ranting and raving. Shepley [Time's retired president] telling Arthur that Steve is mafia (Remember the franchising days?) He likes the deal very much. On the premium point [of valuing Warner stock higher than Time's] he's unchanged. Warner getting lot more than they're giving. A premium demeans the deal. Mike also thinks that Andrew [Heiskell] is not helpful either.

Munro Luce call—He's bothered by the Ross compensation, the 8 year contract, the ethics and foul tongue of Hollywood types, the Westchester Theatre scandals.

Munro Finkelstein call—He describes himself as a gunslinger like Dingman—feels he understands what's going on better than most board members. After what he's been through [a leveraged buy-out of Macy's] he feels he can identify and understand Ross's motivation. He feels it is necessary to make sure Warner knows it is clearly being acquired and Steve should understand that very clearly. He doesn't feel [Hank] Luce is a problem.

Levin Temple call—Ross greedy, separation of companies polluted by show business. No one will grab you—or I would have done it, empire building.

Munro Goodrich call—He talked with Arthur and thought he made some small progress. Corrected Arthur's assumption that Steve would receive a $50 million "bonus" as a result of the merger and that Nick and I would be made instantly rich. Arthur feels Warner is simply beneath us. The sleaze factor. He also strongly favors the cable joint venture as opposed to the full merger. We should consider experience when picking board members for the new enterprise. Had real problems with Luce.

Levin Clifford—50-50. Hasn't come around yet—said nothing at board meeting.

Munro Wharton call—He finds Temple situation most disturbing but feels that Bruce [Wasserstein] is over-reacting to it. He's still troubled by co-CEOs. Not concerned about Steve's compensation. If we have to pay a premium it has to be defended and explained—what are we getting for the premium? Shouldn't be worried about Hank—he has no credibility nor influence. Arthur has both. Not a very meaningful conversation.

Munro Beré phone call—Everyone wants to do the deal. The board accepts Munro's recommendation. It's a great deal economically but he is very concerned about the "social" problems (culture etc). He feels that the reason Ross wants to do the deal is that it rids him of Siegel. That's his primary motivation. He's concerned about being put in play. He has no problem with Ross cashing in but thinks he's going to have a problem with Ross' future compensation. (This should get flushed out as soon as possible.) He mentions that Arthur thinks Nick and I are fleecing our nests ["feathering," Temple remembers he said] and that some directors are watching Nick to see signs of materialistic excess. He complimented us on putting everything on the table and on our candidness.

Munro Perkins call—He thought I came on much too strongly in my opening remarks in the closed session; that I was telling them what we should do instead of asking. He thought Dingman's remarks were terrific though feels Mike has no concern about the cultural issue. Not overly concerned with premium. More concerned with Steve—perception etc. Applauds our feelings that Nick and I should "take less." He feels we should get rich if the deal succeeds, not on making the deal.

Munro Temple meeting—Our discussion about the proposed merger lasted about one hour and half plus. It began with his

emotional discussion of why he couldn't support the merger—
a theme we've all heard before and one that he is continuing
to feel passionately about. It was both thoughtful and articulate. He did not rant and rave—similar to his New Hampshire
remarks. I sympathized sincerely since I share some of his
feelings. He mentioned that he did not want to be a spoiler
and would not be. He wasn't sure that he could in good conscience support something that he had so much trouble believing in. I'm afraid I did not make the sale but he's wavering
and I think we have a better than 50% shot at getting his
support. And if we don't get it I don't see Arthur mucking
things up behind the scenes.

Munro [David] Kearns call—I filled David in on what he missed
and he stated again that he is enthusiastically for the deal.

The Time managers were nervous. Directors had raised a full range
of tough break points involving: Ross's past; the absolute imperative
for Time's domination to be guaranteed; the price to be paid for
Warner; the governance of the merged company; and executive
succession. Most on the board liked the strategy but were wary of
its execution and of Ross himself. The two largest stockholders in
the company, Temple and Hank Luce, were threatening to vote
against it. Temple was actively lobbying his cronies on the board.

   Luce, sixty-six, whose gruff, beefy exterior conceals an inner hard
core of principle, huffed and puffed at board meetings and drank
too much outside them. He also still voted 3 percent of the company's
shares. "When Hank is lucid," says one Time senior business executive, "he's pretty good." Luce alone put his objections on paper,
his best mode of expression. In a letter to Munro he wrote:

   My father's will [said] "Time Inc. is now, and is expected to
   continue to be principally a journalistic enterprise operated in
   the public interest." In the view of [that] and many other specific factors, I don't believe I could vote for the proposition we
   discussed at our last board meeting.

A delegation was to be dispatched to see him, including Jason
McManus, a far more diffident editor-in-chief than his three pred-
ecessors. McManus wanted some heavy artillery support behind him.
Henry Luce was dead, Grunwald was serving as U.S. ambassador

to Austria. But Hedley Donovan, by then nine years retired, was a cab ride, twenty-five blocks, away. McManus called, asked Donovan if he could see him that same day.

Over martinis, McManus nervously told Donovan that this "is not exactly a courtesy call." Donovan felt a little more courtesy was much in order. "I didn't feel it entirely ingratiating that this thing had been going on at least a year and nobody had ever breathed a word of it to me until the very last moment." When McManus asked whether Donovan would help them bring Hank Luce around, Donovan said he could hardly enlist in that cause since he himself liked nothing about the plan, the partner or the leap into entertainment away from journalism. "It didn't look to me," recalled Donovan, "as if the alternatives had been adequately explored. Jason seemed increasingly uncomfortable. He said it was necessary, inevitable, too bad but things had to change." Donovan also said McManus reported that Heiskell "was not enthusiastic," that "Shepley is very much against it, not just echoing Arthur Temple, but independently thinks Ross is an elegant crook."

McManus has a different recollection of the standoff. Enlisting Donovan's aid in bringing Luce around "was not the purpose of the trip. We just felt that many of these people were simply out of touch with the realities of what was going on." Jerry Levin, to whom McManus reported on his failed mission, recorded the meeting in another scrawled aide-mémoire:

> **Levin** Hedley—[Ross has a] lifetime of bad press—something behind it. Doesn't buy eat or be eaten. Spin off magazines, merge with another journalistic enterprise like Dow Jones or Knight-Ridder. You're feckless if you can't start mags and get the resources you need. Against it—questions most of basic premises. Strict construction of [Henry] Luce.

Arthur Temple never believed there was a serious threat of a takeover. "Dick and Nick were more concerned about a takeover," Temple said, "and maybe some other directors were. I never thought there was anything to it. They often said [we] were a target. I said I think that's vanity speaking. I don't think anybody's got you in their sights. [My family and I] represented a good deal of stock and nobody ever contacted me." Even Levin agreed. Asked by a lawyer when he was later deposed, Levin said: "I think we would agree with Mr. Temple that there would not be a hostile attack, that we were just subject to a lot of rumors."

AS IN COVERT MILITARY operations, corporate mergers and acquirers adopt breezy code names to conceal their companies. In the Time-Warner negotiations, Warner was christened WONDER (as in "wonderful"), Time TANGO (as in "It takes two to . . .")

The mating dance of WONDER and TANGO had hundreds of hoofers—exectives, lawyers, investment bankers, numbers analysts, lobbyists, caterers, security guards and printers. But the principal dancers tangoing and wondering together were Jerry Levin for Time and Steve Ross's surrogate, Oded ("Call me Ed") Aboodi. The two were a well-matched pair. Even though they had never met before they had a weltanschauung in common. Each had the Middle East in his background.

Ed Aboodi's parents, Iraqi Jews who emigrated to Israel, where he was born, came to New York when he was fourteen and became citizens. After New York's High School of Commerce, then undergraduate ('63) and MBA ('64) degrees from New York University, Aboodi landed a job as an accountant at the giant accounting firm Arthur Young & Co., assigned to the Kinney account. As far back as 1969 he helped Ross acquire Warner–Seven Arts and worked on the creation of Warner Communications. With Ross's encouragement, he left Arthur Young in 1980 to form his own company, advising Ross, Warner executives and others on tax and investment strategies.

He had other clients, too, "notably at that time," he recalls, "United Brands [né United Fruit], you know Chiquita banana and all that, with people jumping out windows." The allusion was to the company's CEO, the beleaguered Eli Black, a rabbi-businessman who committed suicide by smashing with his briefcase the picture window in his Manhattan Pan Am Building headquarters office and flinging himself out.

Aboodi's Alpine Capital Company is housed in the Time Warner Building (with another office in Jersey City, closer to his home), where he has been Ross's unparalleled chief financial adviser for years. Although Aboodi has never been an officer, director or carried any title in Warner, or in Time Warner today, he regularly attends board meetings. Few would disagree that he was for Warner, and is still for Time Warner, the untitled chief financial engineer, second only to Ross himself in the combined company.

A lean fifty-one-year-old, Aboodi was an invisible mystery man to the world outside Warner until the Time-Warner deal. The only listing in any telephone directory for Alpine is for "Alpine Cap Co," which turns out to be a number in Hoboken, New Jersey, where a gruff voice answers and says, "There's no Mr. Aboodi here. But if you find him let us know 'cause we get a lot of calls for him. We make caps—the kind you put on your head." Aboodi says he has no telephone listing for Alpine because "people know me and they know how to find me. I've never thought about it."

When he gives a rare interview ("I mostly decline interviews because they don't add anything and when you read them you get upset"), his financial talk sounds more like the analytical metaphysics of a Talmudic scholar than of a man of mystery. ("When Ed went to Japan to close a deal," says Ross, with a smile, "we needed two translators. One to explain Ed in plain English and the other to translate the explanation into Japanese.") Yet Aboodi is an engaging, warm and affable figure, quick to laugh and parry with a fine wit. He enthusiastically displays to visitors the exhibit of great black-and-white photographs from *Life* mounted in the corridors of his office floor, put together for him by his new friends at Time. (The walls of the Time executive floor are less memorably lined with colorful pictures from *Sports Illustrated*.)

WHY HIS REPUTATION AS a shadowy mystery man?

"It may be," he speculates, his training in discretion at Arthur Young, but more likely "because my father, who had extensive dealings in the European markets and the business community, where confidentiality is more prevalent, may have had an impact on me." An inheritance like his barely noticeable accent, erased mostly in an English boarding school before he came to the U.S. He still speaks fluent Hebrew and some Arabic. "People with whom I speak Hebrew," Aboodi says with an easy smile, "say I speak it with an American accent. People I speak English with detect the residue of Hebrew."

Aboodi obligingly still helps Sol Weiss by sending clients his way since Weiss's Westchester Theatre conviction. "Ed Aboodi is a terrific guy and I love him," says Ross with his usual understatement. "Ed and I have fun together sitting in a room and trying to figure out how we can improve on deals. He's much better informed than I." Aboodi is also a devoted believer in, as well as the major contributor to, the Steve Ross school of dealmaking. "Steve is always searching for a way to improve a deal and make it better. There's always the search for a better solution than the one we have at present. We're creating a transaction."

In the Time-Warner tango, Ross says, "I just gave Ed marching orders." Aboodi is the man who brings reality to Ross's "dreaming," says Arthur Liman, "the one that lawyers and bankers could go to if Steve is unavailable." Another collaborator who knows them well says, "Steve Ross is the king and Ed is the knight." A longtime Ross outside financial adviser, Felix Rohatyn of Lazard Frères (who was also a retained adviser for Time), adds that "I've never seen him frayed around the edges." As for Levin's role, Munro says, "He was delegated to make this deal happen. You put Jerry and Aboodi together and their skill is mind-boggling."

What was the essential characteristic Levin and Aboodi had in common? "Since I lived and worked in the Middle East for a while," says Levin, "it was a lot easier for me to deal with Ed. He and I used to describe everything we were doing not in Bruce Wasserstein's phrase, 'a series of little black boxes,' but one hurdle, one problem after another. Aboodi's great strength is not to be a hard-edged negotiator. He tries to understand the substance of what's going. There's always a solution if you understand what people are trying to drive at. It's a more complex subtle shading—something that I don't think our Time troops were quite accustomed to."

Aboodi agrees. "I think there's some truth in that. There are many things you wind up building and you have to feel your way around. You have to be prepared to take a journey and that's a process of sorting out."

LEVIN AND ABOODI, a Delphic-like oracle and a Talmudic-like exegetist, quite a combination for an intricate modern business deal. Levin even spoke of the "thaumaturgic [i.e., mystical] significance" of some of their meeting sites.

Their negotiations turned out to be more like an Arab bazaar, where Levin and Aboodi both had experience, than a Harvard Business School case study, where neither had. The fifteen or twenty issues that Levin and Aboodi negotiated were manageable. But one was not. The Time outside directors called it "governance." The Levin-Aboodi negotiating team simply called it "Steve."

Ross himself recognized the problem. On this issue, he remembers, "We were like two trains passing in the night. We were too subtle. We missed each other. We always agreed and then we'd come back to it. And therefore I knew they were having trouble. I never thought it was Nick, Dick or Jerry. There's only one other group left. So they must be having problems with the board."

Time's general counsel Bill Guttman was asked to try to find a way to allay the doubts about Ross by drafting a "Plan of Succession," which Munro distributed to all of the outside directors. It proposed that the plan for Nicholas to replace Ross in five years be written into a provision in the company's by-laws and be submitted to the stockholders for approval. Even more important, that ironclad succession could only be changed by a two-thirds vote of the board. "Everybody would then know," says Guttman, "that Nick would be CEO in five years and there wouldn't be all this bullshit about who's going to win this horserace. The outside directors loved it. Ross hadn't heard of it yet."

When Aboodi first saw the Time plan, Levin recalls Aboodi saying, "I think we probably need a meeting with Steve." Levin got the coded signal. "That only happens when there's something ultimate with Steve, because all this had been going on between Aboodi and me." Levin had read the warning right.

Twenty-one days after the Time board meeting, despite Levin's and Aboodi's delicate craftsmanship, smoothed by the loving palaver among Munro, Nicholas and Ross, the deal crashed. Dead. "They were getting to some kind of a climax," says Don Wilson, then Time's senior public and corporate affairs officer, "and suddenly they broke down. I was stunned."

He would have been less stunned if he'd been at the passionate, tearful meeting in Steve Ross's Park Avenue duplex the afternoon of August 11, 1988.

chapter 9

Coitus Interruptus

STEVE ROSS SPENT MOST of the morning in the emergency room of Lenox Hill Hospital just up Park Avenue. He was rushed there in the midst of an excruciating attack of diverticulitis. "I'm not sure," Ross feels, "the diverticulitis wasn't caused by everything that was going on in the past two years." He was still pale and haggard when he ushered Munro and Nicholas into his snug, handsomely appointed library. Outside, first in the dining and then the living room of the twelfth- and thirteenth-floor apartment (complete with a Warner-installed screening room for showing movies), Levin and a passel of lawyers waited.

The press release Time drafted for the announcement of the merger had words and implications that made Ross choke. Make it "tough," the writers were told—enough to satisfy the Time board by making it clear that Time was "acquiring" Warner. The "dreaded A word," as it became known. In the draft release, Ross himself was a transition CEO until Nicholas took over. To assure he retired on a fixed date, in the background was the two-thirds supermajority vote of the new board required to change any such key provisions.

In the library with Munro and Nicholas, "it was very emotional," Ross says. "I remember very briefly saying what I believed. I didn't believe the Time board honestly had faith in Nicholas and me being able to operate as true co-CEOs. Therefore I don't think it will work unless the board understands me and I understand the board." He called off the deal.

When Ross, Munro and Nicholas joined the others in the living room, tears were welling up in Ross's eyes, his voice quavering. From notes, he repeated what he had said inside. He told Cravath's

Alan Stevenson, a Time lawyer whose firm had once represented Chris-Craft, "I don't want this problem again—you should know from the four or five years with Herb Siegel. I said Time and Warner could have a fantastic company. The styles are different but that makes it more interesting because we learn from each other."

"He cried?" exclaims Beverly Sills. "I don't believe that. He may have felt terrible. But I don't see him like that. In terms of emotion, the strongest emotion I've seen him display publicly is frustration. He's the essence of the deal maker because he's always ready for the next one. I've never seen him come to a screeching halt in anything we've ever done." Arthur Liman, who wasn't present, says, "I know Steve in a way few people know him. Beverly has never seen Steve with tears in his eyes. I have."

Was the display of emotion and tears all a negotiating ploy? Ross is appalled at the suggestion. "If it had been a cash deal, you might have the right to be cynical. But remember it was an exchange of equity. If I overreached, I might have really hurt the company. As to my status after the merger, I think they knew me well enough to know it wasn't a ploy. It was a very traumatic experience that shook me to the roots. I thought the deal was a thousand percent off."

"Ross," says a friend, "hates rejection." Levin, the onetime Bible student, sat dejected in the living room. At one point, he quoted from Ecclesiastes, "There's a season and a time to every purpose." A hot August day was plainly not the right time or season for their purpose.

Nicholas, who doesn't like to be let down, was seething. Munro was disappointed. Levin was predictably analytical:

"I had tried to get back to Aboodi the night before the Ross meeting," says Levin. "It was clear to me we weren't engaged, there was no back-and-forth. There was no meaningful exchange or dialogue. A curtain had come down. In effect, we had insulted Steve. Once you do that, the deal is gone. It wasn't crystal clear what was going to happen at this meeting. Whether we were going to negotiate, although in my heart of hearts I felt not. It wasn't that the retirement date was being set. You do have a fixed date and everybody knows it, but Steve is very much active and wants to be respected. It's a very subtle complex point. We used the wrong words about his 're-tirement,' the wrong phrase. He uses a set of words that just have different meaning from the ones our guys use. It was unseemly for a charter, a corporation, a board to have those kinds of provisions written in. I appreciate it now. I didn't understand it fully or I would have been more sensitive to it at the time. Our guys tend to view things in black and white with somebody reporting to somebody else and there's a fixed date. Steve's mind is more of a matrix mind."

Ross was right about at least one of the misgivings in his matrix. In the year and a half he had been talking to Time, not a single outside director ever made a move to meet him, even though he had suggested it and Munro had offered to arrange it if the directors wanted to. Not a one of them, each agrees, knew him, except to see him in a crowd. None tried to remedy, by meeting Ross directly face-to-face, their unfamiliarity with the man who was to be the new chairman of their board and co-CEO of their merged company, about whom they knew so little and had so many questions and reservations.

Ross found it more than a social rebuff. "Maybe they were giving me a message. That the board doesn't want to meet with the new CEO. I suggested I ought to meet with them. Why don't they want to meet me? Maybe they felt that you're just there on a pass through—a couple of years, a transition, then we'll try to figure out something. I felt like a lame duck."

"IT'S OFF. IT WILL not be on, it's over and we're not going back to it, we'll never merge with Warner," Nicholas told senior editorial and publishing executives after the deal crashed. He explained to them he could understand Ross's feelings. Ross was "the Henry Luce of Warner. He built it brick by brick. It was his company. I'm the fourth or fifth generation. I didn't invent the company. So the struggle that Steve was having, I couldn't even identify with. I wasn't angry with him. I was disappointed. This was about him." Nicholas told a friend, "It doesn't matter if everything else is right. The people have to be right."

If the trio on top felt let down, even in some moments betrayed, their staffs had the opposite reaction. At one senior business management lunch where Nicholas reported the breakdown, "We were troubled to hear it was ever on and pleased to hear it was off," one of those attending remembers. "People around the table didn't want it to happen. Jesus, what would we be if we became Time Warner? There was very grave concern." He recalls that "of the fourteen people there, at least thirteen, maybe all fourteen, were relieved.

We were always anxious about Steve, his character and the people who worked for him. The lifestyles were totally different."

When the New York *Times* broke an informed and detailed story on the attempt to merge, the whole worldwide staff suddenly knew about it. "The directors of the companies," the story said, "were never asked to vote on the proposal because Time board members might have rejected it." Certainly a large majority of the Time journalists, business-side people and lawyers would have been opposed. Their reaction to the startling news had little to do with strategy, synergy or global expansion. It had everything to do with their impression of Ross and the reaction of their friends. Examples:

A senior Time alumnus who knew and worked with Luce and knew Ross "Nicholas' comparison of Ross and Luce is absurd. Sure, Harry Luce and Steve Ross both dominated their companies. Sure, both started small and became big capitalist entrepreneurs. But there the comparison stops dead. Luce was a founder, a creator driven by ideas, which yielded profits. Ross is a buyer and collector of companies. He's driven by profits, money and his need to be respected. He's never created anything in his life himself except deals."

A Time corporate executive "Everything I heard about Ross was bad. About a week after the story had come out, I was at a meeting of mid-level executives where Levin was the guest speaker. One of the more outspoken executives said I just read this article in the *Times* and if there's anything that's the antithesis of what Time Inc. stands for it's Steve Ross. I can't believe we'd even consider getting in bed with him. Can't you tell me that that article was way off base. That was a common feeling."

Editor "I was stunned by the central revelation, the prospect of working for Steve Ross. I was thinking about the West-chester Theatre."

Business manager "When we first heard about the merger we were surprised. Steve Ross has had a checkered reputation, not the kind associated with Time Inc."

Time film staffer "The publishing side are babes in the woods, they're so naive, they've had so little touch with reality. They've never even run into anyone like him before. They are so seduceable that it's almost laughable. Steve is a professional seducer. They've never mixed it up with guys like that. They don't know what a killer is. I'm not saying Ross is a killer, but we all deal with killers in the movie business. You don't get to be where he is without being a killer."

Researcher "There was a lot of talk about Steve Ross—whether he was a good guy or a bad guy. Some of our stories before did not always portray him as a great hero."

Editorial executive "The early things about Steve Ross are appalling. He may be a good businessman but give me a break. He's no St. Stephen."

Cable executive "Cable franchising can get to be a dirty business. Time Inc.'s reputation was pretty good. The worst was Warner."

Writer "There was almost universal dismay. The old Time Inc. would have been dead. Journalism would no longer have been the moving force. Rumors about Steve Ross surfaced immediately. It was generally felt that he was a pretty unsavory character."

Among the outside Time directors, says Levin, "the relief was not about Ross's past." It was about his immediate and future role in the combined company. "The one characteristic of Steve that appeared was the imperial, immortal executive who would never leave his throne. That's what was bothering them. Not that he was a funny guy." Time Director Don Perkins analogizes the directors' doubts precisely. "What we were concerned about was his refusal to talk about retirement. It was like getting in bed with Armand Hammer—a specific reference that was made many times." Hammer ran his oil company with an iron hand until he died in 1990 at ninety-two.

With the news of the intended merger out in the open, the directors too began hearing from friends, on the golf course, at social gatherings, from their spouses, in shooting blinds, at board meetings of other companies. The message they heard was "You're lucky you didn't get mixed up with this guy."

Most of the doubts about Ross were based on rumors, loose talk, smoke without fire, nothing anybody could prove. No one had troubled to inquire deeply. The hostile talk even had the taint of snobbery with an undercurrent in some quarters of anti-Semitism. Without any hard evidence, it certainly was slanderous—in another era it might have been called McCarthyism. But it was over, done. There was no deal. Ross no longer mattered to them.

RELIEF, DISAPPOINTMENT, ANGER—WHATEVER the emotion over the breakup, there was one fact to face. In its strategy for the '90s, Time was back to square minus one.

The public revelation that Time had been negotiating a transaction with Warner set Wall Street abuzz again. On the New York Stock Exchange, Time stock was unusually active. Time's anxiety about hostile takeover bids came back even stronger. Such raiders as Conniston Partners and Kohlberg, Kravis and Roberts were rumored to have Time in their sights. GE was a constant worry.

One day, unexpectedly, Time's old and respected friend Warren Buffett, spurned once before when he had offered to protect Time, came around with a new, more appealing suggestion. Buffett, Capital Cities/ABC's largest individual stockholder with an 18 percent interest, thought perhaps the two companies should try to get together. CapCities, with its profitable newspaper group, plus TV stations and the ABC network, could make a fit.

One built-in obstacle made it unlikely. But maybe that could be overcome by a restructuring or a change in the FCC policy that prohibited the cross-ownership of cable and TV in the same areas. At Buffett's suggestion, Munro and Nicholas went down the street to meet with their CapCities/ABC equivalents, Thomas Murphy and Daniel Burke. Munro knew about them from riding the commuter train and thought they were "really good guys."

For two months in each other's offices, with staff help, they worked on what became known on Time's thirty-fourth floor as "the CapCities road." Then in mid-December the road caved in. It was not the government roadblock that stopped them. Again it was governance, whether Nicholas would really end up as boss, and, by the way, who was acquiring whom? Nicholas has a cryptic description of the end of that road: "Dick said, 'Time Inc. is not for sale. Merry Christmas.' End of discussion."

ON THE BOARD OF Time, Mike Dingman, sixty, a director since 1978, is known by the others as the one real "wheeler-dealer," the

"gunslinger." Hedley Donovan privately referred to him as the "gar-
bageman," more for his dealmaking antics than the fact that part of
his business was in recycling.

Dingman has bought and sold companies at a pace to match the
racing cars he likes to drive. His peace and quiet comes only as a
Sunday painter or on his hundred-foot sailing sloop—certainly not
in the roiling high-leveraged Henley Group, which he heads, or the
conglomerates he ran before. There the asset-shuffling and the lev-
eraging twist and turn faster than Dingman himself does on the slopes
he has recently learned to ski. His financial strategy, he says, is to
engage in "perpetual liquidation." (He now is chairman of the Time
Warner board's finance committee.)

Unlike his "closest friend" Arthur Temple, Dingman liked the
Time-Warner combination from the beginning. At first he objected
only to paying a premium for Warner—a ratio above what Warner
was worth on the trading floor of the stock exchange. From the outset
he thought the governance question was "horseshit." He told fellow
Time directors, "You can't preordain or set in concrete something
like that." Munro recalls those moments. "Mike Dingman cut
through this bullshit rather quickly. I think some of the more thoughtful directors agreed. When we were talking about succession, he said
why bother. Ross may be the better guy and he'll run the company.
Let's stop worrying about personalities and put these two great companies together." Dingman knew about that sort of thing from his
own personal experience. Nicholas points out that "Mike had an
ironclad agreement from Allied-Signal and look what happened."
(Dingman was eased out.)

Dingman also vigorously disagreed with the board's negative views
of Ross and repeatedly said so to anyone who would listen. "Everybody here has an opinion, but let's see what the guy looks like. I'd
like to talk to him and touch him. Goddamnit, why don't we meet
this guy? They never wanted to." And they never did.

To Dingman, when the deal fell apart it was "the tragedy of all
tragedies, like watching a couple that's in love break up after the
tremendous courtship and effort that had gone on, Christ, for years.
You see people say it's dead and you look at them and say, You
really want this thing to die? These were two lovers who wanted to
make love and probably should make love. That's when I got myself
involved in management's side of the business. I got stirred." So,
damnit, he decided to meet Ross.

Dingman had just the right intermediary to introduce him to Ross. One of his own investment bankers was the Lazard partner Jonathan O'Herron, who had been working along with Felix Rohatyn as Warner's adviser. "John," says Arthur Liman, "knew these people, and John knows and loves Steve. I don't believe this transaction would have happened without John. He worked intimately with Steve and shared his insights" as Warner's adviser.

O'Herron got Dingman and himself invited for dinner at Ross's apartment. Ross sized up Dingman right away. "He's an entrepreneur," Ross says he thought, "a true entrepreneur." They even agreed on the menu. Ross's chef specializes in the chicken potpie Steve thought his mother cooked in Brooklyn when he was a boy (actually it was chicken in the pot, a different dish). "You're so smart," said O'Herron to an amazed Ross. "You've got two Irishmen for dinner and you serve a favorite Irish dish."

Dingman told Ross he always had liked the deal. He said he knew a lot about Ross from Rohatyn and O'Herron. Something as trivial as a retirement date shouldn't keep Time and Warner apart. "He knows the company and likes the way we operate," Ross concluded from what Dingman was telling him. "He knows that I'm for making zero creative decisions and agrees with that. He said he was there to assure me that the board really wanted me. Mike was saying you're reading the board wrong."

Dingman hit a chord, Ross says, that had been pulsating within him ever since the August 11 bust-up. "That August date may have been the best thing that ever happened to me. Mike made a hell of a lot of sense to me. I started to think about what did I really want to do with my life? Why the hell am I interested in ten years? I don't think I'm a particularly good administrator. I hate personnel problems, the daily details that a CEO has to deal with. There are many better CEOs in this world."

He told Dingman that "I might do better not as a CEO if I really know that the board and I have an understanding that during some amount of years, whatever that number is, I must be co-CEO to protect my people. If they don't feel protected, we're going to have a disaster. After that, if I could be allowed to do dreaming, future planning and positioning, dealing with key people, if I could do my thing, maybe I would be happier. But only if I had an affirmation from the board that they really understood."

Dingman says *he* understood perfectly what Ross meant. "It was a legitimate concern the same way Time's was. There had to be a way to do the deal. I think I offered that opportunity." And, adds Dingman, "I loved the chicken potpie."

NEXT MORNING EARLY, DINGMAN called Munro and Nicholas. "I'm impressed with the guy," he reported after his first and only meeting. "I can understand why you wanted to make the deal. I think we can do it with him." O'Herron followed up with Munro, telling him the same story in Munro's favorite restaurant, the Time cafeteria. But when Munro, Nicholas and Levin put their heads together, they still weren't convinced Ross had really changed his views either about stepping down at a fixed date or about who would run the combined company.

Over Christmas, they had second thoughts. CapCities/ABC was gone. Despite their worries about takeover and their public talk about "global strategy," they were no place. "Wait a minute," Levin mused. "If we really go back and think about it, and if we really had our druthers, Warner is a superior fit. We like Steve. We had this problem, so maybe . . . ?" They reconsidered Dingman's account of his dinner with Ross, just maybe?

Suddenly, "Let's have lunch" became the modus operandi.

Munro, noncommittally, phoned Ross and went over to his office for a friendly lunch. Levin reached out for Aboodi, and they met at Aboodi's luncheon club next to the Rainbow Room for a buffet lunch. Munro came back from his meal bubbling, "Gee, I had this terrific lunch with Steve." Levin weighed in with "Aboodi and I were both struck by the deal—its range and importance—even though Ed never strayed from his protection of Steve. It was obvious that this had to be done right for Steve." The trouble was that Ross's role had been "trivialized." But Aboodi told him that Ross had changed his mind about having "a defined time and date" when he would give up being co-CEO of the new company. So Nicholas tried a lunch with Ross himself.

"It was rather lengthy," Nicholas recalls. "As is normal when Steve and I get together, the first two-thirds of the lunch was all about the things we were each going to do, the deals we were going to try to make." When they began talking about Time Warner, "Steve seemed to have crossed the bridge. He wanted to make Time Warner happen. I found it a really pleasant surprise."

On January 19, 1989, the Time board met again. They talked about budgets, contracts, shark repellents and increasing the number of Time shares, everything but Warner. Talk about reopening those negotiations was "not far enough along," Levin later reported, "to mention at the board table." Instead, in private conversations, board members were told that discussions with Ross had started up again.

For this round there were to be no outside lawyers, bankers or quibbling second-level executives directly involved. For negotiating sessions, Levin and Aboodi drew up the agenda, and only the two of them plus Munro, Nicholas and Ross met. At a breakthrough meeting in early February, held in Ross's apartment again, the five began at lunch and went on until the early evening. Ross made it clear he was ready to accept a retirement date and could handle the public perception of Time acquiring Warner.

The Time threesome left exhilarated. Levin stepped out into the bracing February night and reached for his cellular phone that each of Time's top executives had been given for Christmas. As he hastened on foot down Park Avenue, he dialed a Time lawyer and said, "It's going to happen."

NOW THEY WERE IN a hurry to get the reluctant directors' approval. They had only three weeks before the next board meeting.

The board members had, in effect, already killed the Warner deal once by insisting on terms that expressed their misgivings about Ross and that were unacceptable to him. But Munro, Nicholas and Levin told them about Ross's change of heart. Now he would accept a retirement date. The succession—governance—was no longer the problem it had been. "It wasn't until they renegotiated," says Hank Luce, "and reported a different deal in February that I decided to go along." For the moment, even Arthur Temple slacked off on his stiff opposition. "I thought Steve Ross was a very strong take-charge individual and that he would have his way regardless of agreements."

As for Ross's out-of-sight compensation ("the Babe Ruth" of executive pay, *Fortune* called him), that was show biz. And, anyway, they were just complying with his old Warner contract of about $14 million a year and an estimated hundreds of millions in stock options and deferred compensation. Director James Beré, chairman of Borg Warner, recalled that "the initial reaction" to Ross's compensation "was basically a cultural shock to the board." But "upon analysis, one could make the case that it has increased with the success of Warner and was linked to shareholder value. This gave me comfort, since I believed in linking executive compensation to shareholder value. If he could do for Time's shareholders what he apparently did for Warner's, we would be getting a great bargain.''

Don Perkins gave up on one condition he had insisted on before. He said he would drop his objections to paying a premium above the stock market value for Warner so long as the perpetuation of the "Time culture" could be guaranteed. Past deep reservations about Ross were overcome by the escalating enthusiasm for him repeatedly expressed by Munro, Nicholas and Levin. "He is a man," Munro said earnestly, "of character, honesty and integrity." Nicholas's estimate was "He and his executives have quality, longevity and ethics." Levin said, "Ross is not only a first-rate executive but a fine individual of utmost integrity."

Dingman alone among the outside directors at that point had seen Ross. Temple and his allies, Grum and Goodrich, who had opposed the Warner deal, were no big problem, since by then Munro, Nicholas and Ross agreed the three would not be on the board of the merged company anyway. Nevertheless, Goodrich became the only other director who met with Ross before the agreement was signed. Accompanied by Munro, Goodrich went to Ross's apartment. He remembers thinking, "He was without a doubt the most big-picture man I ever saw. He's properly cast in the movie business. He could be an actor. In an hour-and-a-half breakfast you only get a superficial feel for a guy. My feel was that he was one tough son of a bitch and that he was going to eat those guys up. They won't know what hit them." But, he adds, "I refuse to be negative on this deal because of Steve Ross. You might say he charmed me in an hour and a half. Hell, he didn't charm me. All I'm saying is he's so much better than the other two actors on the scene that maybe it's not that bad a deal." No matter, Goodrich wouldn't be around to see it.

Ask the other directors why they never took the trouble to meet the man their company was marrying, and they all agree it wasn't necessary. They explain that meeting with Ross could have been interpreted as interfering with management. Dick, Nick and Jerry were so high on Ross, they all say in similar words, that they saw no need to meet Ross.

Perkins "We'd been talking about this for a year. The board's responsibility is to work through the management. I'm not smart enough, no one is, to sit down and say the worst that has been said about Steve Ross is true or not true. I'd be perfectly happy to meet him, but I didn't think it had a purpose in the sequence of events. Had we been told it would be a plus to meet him, we'd have all gone over to meet him."

Finkelstein "Everybody knew that Dick and Nick were meeting with him. He was a very able man in the field of running an entertainment business. You don't buy or merge with a company on the basis of personality. What would you get to know from a two-hour dinner as to whether you wanted to go ahead with a merger or not?"

Hank Luce "I don't know Ross at all. But I naturally would remember the business about that theater in Tarrytown, and it's hard to believe all that could have happened without Ross's knowledge. So that was a bother and the social connections with the likes of Sinatra and from there maybe with the mob and one really didn't know. I think I gave him credit with having become more responsible with passing time, that something happened some years ago he would be unlikely to repeat. When Munro and Nicholas were recommending the renegotiated deal, they made a very strong statement about Ross as a person. They said they'd been living with him for practically two years now, that they'd gotten to be very good friends with him. That they liked him a lot. They had total reliance in his integrity and whatever else. So I, and I suppose others, concluded, well, we can't fight that. If we believe in Munro and Nicholas at all we'd better take their word for it."

Wharton "The negotiations were handled in much the same fashion as previous negotiations where we bought out smaller entities. There were no meetings with the CEO. I suspect that the same pattern was followed here."

Temple "It's not surprising if you look at the cast of characters on the Time board. Look at the relationships. Dick sits on Opel's IBM board. Nick's on Kearns's Xerox board. I certainly would have wanted to know Ross better. Henry Goodrich asked to meet with Ross. I was going to but I'd already made up my mind I didn't want the deal. It's extraordinary the degree to which management preempted the board. Directors are a bunch of wimps."

And how do the Time managers account for the outside directors' lack of curiosity about seeing Ross?

Munro "An interesting question, a very legitimate one. I don't have the answer. But I have some thoughts. Some directors pay more attention than others. Some care more than others. Some are preoccupied with what they're doing and have blind faith in management. I think a lot of them maybe have enough respect for management to feel if he's good enough for us he's good enough for them."

Nicholas "I'm on Xerox's board and if Dave Kearns, who I trust, whatever he said I'd take his word for it. They trusted our judgment. Along the way a number of them made their own inquiries. It's all bullshit. The whole issue never occurred to me. Steve is a terrific guy. It didn't seem appropriate to bring Steve around. He would have had them absolutely snowed but it wasn't necessary. What does that prove? It's not substance. It doesn't deal with the issues."

Levin "We offered Steve to all the board members. There was an open invitation to meet Steve, but other than the Dingman dinner and the Goodrich breakfast they didn't pick it up. The view expressed was that they were presumptively satisfied with the recommendation of management. It's not just accepting it at face value. This was an important but nuanced set of negotiations. I suspect—whether it was openly stated or not— that it was not appropriate at that time to meet Steve. Maybe when things moved along, then they should have. But we were into another zone of discussions: When was he stepping down? That probably wasn't an appropriate subject for them. It's part of the dynamic of how the deal and the negotiations and the subtleties are being handled."

Fortune managing editor Marshall Loeb "Even if the guy had won the Congressional Medal of Honor, was a Rhodes scholar and U.S. senator, I'd want to meet him. I find it most unusual. If I were a member of that board I damn well would want to have Mr. Ross present and ask him a lot of questions—in a non-hostile fashion."

Editor-in-chief Jason McManus "I don't understand the protocol about how such major corporate events are conducted. I can imagine like a Bulgarian wedding you don't ever see the bride beforehand."

Ross himself was puzzled by why the Time directors never met with him. "The same question," says he, "gnawed at me. I just was getting bad vibes."

CLOSE TO TWO YEARS earlier, when Time's appetite for Warner was rising, Levin had written his memo to Munro and Nicholas, which had asked, "What about Steve?" His "health problems," his "lifestyle is sumptuous," his "remarkable franchising success including a very close relationship with Donald Manes in Queens." "Any inquiry into Steve's past," Levin had written, "must include the Westchester Premier Theatre scandal," the "Atari debacle," which "illustrated some glaring defects in Steve's delegated management."

Questions about "Steve's past" were among the first that troubled Time directors, that their friends had warned them about and that tumbled out of the mouths of Timeincers when they learned of the merger attempt. "The directors," Levin said much later, "wanted to know as much as we could provide them about Ross." To satisfy them, Nicholas said, "we talked about the due diligence Dick and I had done on Steve." Nicholas also told one of his own magazine reporters, "We have some pretty good investigative resources around here." True enough, says Munro. "We kept reporting to the directors we had done our due diligence, that we made a hundred phone calls, checked him out seventeen ways from Sunday." To the Time-Life Washington bureau, full of skeptical reporters, Munro explained, "We had three separate investigations and he came up clean."

But in their enthusiasm for Ross, they wildly exaggerated what they actually did. Nothing they did could in any way be characterized as an "investigation." A partial "reference check," their own personnel department would have called it. The *only* inquiry Time or its agents conducted into Ross's background, Munro says when his memory is jogged, "wasn't a hundred phone calls, it was a handful." He says he "didn't make that many phone calls because most of my peer group among CEOs were not in the entertainment business and wouldn't have known Steve. I called people like Jim Robinson

(American Express) and the Tisches (CBS and Loews) and people who had had a relationship with him. I got nothing but rave reviews. There was never a negative word."

Nicholas and Levin called only a handful of others like Arthur Liman (Ross's lawyer), Felix Rohatyn (a Ross financial adviser) and Cravath's Robert D. Joffe (who was new to the Time corporate account). No report on Ross was written. No inquiry other than the phone calls was conducted. "You don't give a bum rap in those phone calls," says Goodrich. "I do not consider that an investigation."

Kroll Associates, the international corporate detective agency, later hired for Time to investigate the private life of Paramount's Martin Davis when his Paramount Communications made a hostile tender offer, was never retained to find out anything about Ross. (Time Warner did hire Kroll again a year later to investigate the record of a crooked movie investor with whom it was doing business.) Nor were the investigators that Time often called on in other discreet matters used. But even in retrospect, the present Time directors are not a bit defensive about their lack of curiosity about the background of Ross and his company.

"I don't think it was odd at all," says Mike Dingman. "Nick and Jerry worked forever on the issue of Warner and covered the subject ad nauseam, humanwise. To feel that Dick is not accurate or fair or open, or that Nick isn't or Jerry isn't would be a fallacy. These guys do their homework and I did check, myself. The friends they and I talked to were pretty important friends. Knowing the fraternity that exists in this city and other places, there are some honorable people. I instinctively felt that our guys were on the right track. They were having a tough time with a bum rap. What kept going through my mind is how is it that Steve Ross has made so many successful things in an industry so goddamned full of crooks. I said to myself there's got to be something in this guy that's got to be positive. I was once a director of a company which was Kinney's biggest competitor. And I understood more about that business than anyone. It's the cleaning business—New York. The fact is, Steve's ability to get himself up from that level to where he is today is absolutely extraordinary."

Director John Opel was less informed but just as unruffled. When he was later asked under oath in a deposition whether he was "aware of the Westchester Theatre scandal," he replied, "I don't know what you're talking about." IBM, which he headed at the time, had its headquarters office in Armonk, New York, and his home is in Chappaqua, New York, both barely seven miles from the site of the theater. Gannett's Westchester dailies gave blanket coverage to the theater stench, as did other New York newspapers.

Director Don Perkins "was not under the impression that any formal investigation of Ross had been conducted. It was by analysis." He suggests, "It would have been wrong to use an editorial approach to personify a business through the CEO. Granted that Warner has always been described as more of a function of one person. There wasn't a lack of curiosity about Ross but it was expressed to the Time management."

"If the board had an aversion to Steve Ross," director Ed Finkelstein feels, "they had a right to say they didn't like this guy. I never heard anyone say that. Ross is a guy who's not convicted of anything—he's running a company successfully. His own company was investigated thoroughly [in the Armstrong Report]. Why dig all that up—unless you were against it and wanted to screw up the deal. It would have been a good technique for somebody to kill the deal."

NO ONE DID WANT to kill the deal. The 663-page internal Armstrong Report on Ross's management of Warner, which grew out of the Westchester Theatre scandals, was not discussed by the Time board. Jerry Levin, in a sworn deposition statement when the merger was later challenged in court, didn't sound as if he knew much about it himself:

Lawyer Are you aware of something termed the Armstrong Report?

Levin I am not.

Lawyer Are you aware of an investigation that Warner did concerning incidents relating to the Westchester Theatre?

Levin Yes, I'm aware.

Lawyer And are you aware that there was a written report made to at least certain members of the board of Warner?

Levin My knowledge is based on what I have read about it.

Lawyer Did Time ever ask for a copy of the report?

Levin No. It wasn't necessary.

Lawyer Why wasn't it necessary?

Levin It wasn't a report of anything that we either had knowledge about, what its origin was, what it related to, so it was outside our own experience, and we used every available avenue to satisfy ourselves about the nature and quality, indeed, the distinguished quality, of Mr. Ross.

Lawyer Are you aware of any information concerning governmental investigations of either Warner or any management personnel at Warner? [E.g., SEC on Atari insider trading.]

Levin I don't have specific knowledge.

Lawyer Do you have any general knowledge of such investigation?

Levin As to the Westchester Premier Theatre, I know there was an investigation of Warner officials.

Lawyer Any other investigation that you are aware of?

Levin Not that I'm aware of.

Lawyer Any other investigations that anyone else at Time has told you about?

Levin No.

Lawyer Did you reach any conclusions as to whether those issues were behind Steve?

Levin We did. There was an extensive process conducted in part by Dick Munro and Nick, and to a certain extent myself, in satisfying ourselves by meeting with and talking to many, many individuals who had known Steve Ross for his entire business career, and without exception, that inquiry, which was undertaken, led us to the conclusion, and indeed our board reached the same conclusion, that there was nothing behind what was in the public record and Steve Ross is a man, an executive of immense probity, integrity and character, as well as a fine businessman.

Lawyer Something else you looked into was the period of remarkable franchising success at Warner Cable, including a very close relationship with Donald Manes in Queens. Is that correct?

Levin With respect to cable franchising during the '70s and early '80s, we are satisfied that there was nothing at all to indicate that those franchises weren't received on anything but merits.

Lawyer Did any of the directors or former heads of Time Inc., I am sorry, the magazine, ever express any concern that Mr. Ross either had connections with the Mafia or that there were rumors that Mr. Ross had connections with the Mafia?

Levin I never heard that.

Of course everybody had heard just that, but no one bothered to correct him. It was all unproved anyway—even a rotten question for a lawyer to ask with no backup except talk. As for the outside directors, they were flying blind. Since director Opel says he had never heard of the Westchester Theatre, it is not surprising that neither had he heard of the Armstrong Report or the SEC investigation of inside trading in Warner stock. Perkins questions "how far you go to embarrass someone you're trying to merge with." Even Temple, the cantankerous leader of the loyal opposition, knew nothing of something called the Armstrong Report or the SEC Atari investigation until he was off the board. And no one—not the management or the directors—ever mentioned that Ross had relied on his constitutional right against self-incrimination under the Fifth Amendment when the grand jury was investigating the Westchester Theatre, or that he was officially listed as a "co-conspirator."

Time Inc.'s senior counsel, Cravath's Sam Butler, explains: "It certainly wasn't discussed at the two board meetings I attended or the dinner the night before. My recollection is that we [Time executives and he] talked about the Armstrong Report very briefly and it wasn't my view that it needed to be disclosed. If you're not indicted, or not convicted—Steve Ross wasn't even indicted—you're entitled to the benefit of our system."

Fortune managing editor Marshall Loeb, Time's senior business journalist, is surprised in retrospect that no one asked to see the Armstrong Report. "It's easy to pass judgment months afterwards," he says, "but by all means had I known of that report, had I been a senior manager of this company, had I been a director, I surely would have wanted to study that report or if not I personally, I would have wanted to assign one of my primary deputies who was an expert in the law and all manner of things to study that report and give me a précis."

Why were these questions not pressed? Why didn't the Time management ask Ross at least to let a surrogate of theirs read the Armstrong Report just to reassure themselves? Ross coolly answers that it would have been a waste of time. "There was Herb Siegel," he says, "the most bitter enemy I ever had, who has read the report and has done nothing about it."

Cravath partner Robert Joffe, who was Time's litigation counsel in the merger, thinks Ross's past history wasn't really relevant. "As time passes, Steve Ross's character with every passing day is more and more unimpeachable. This was a corporation, to be run as such, with a joint board, equal power, co-chairmen [he meant co-CEOs, not chairmen], provisions for retirement, so it wasn't exactly as if they were handing the company over to some masked man." And he echoes Ross. "If Herb Siegel with all his resources couldn't prove that there was a problem with Steve Ross, why should anyone think that there was?" (Siegel had repeatedly been forbidden to make any use of the report by court order.)

Levin is comfortable with what was *not* done. The board had volumes of information on the record about Warner. "Is there an AIDS test that you can give or a morals check or even a business practices check?" he asks.

Jason McManus, who was mostly a spectator on the negotiations, speculated that, "Given the intimacy of the negotiations and Steve's touchiness about a lot of things, my guess is that maybe we thought that even asking for the report would have been embarrassing."

Dick Munro agrees, adding an important imperative. "There's a fascinating issue here. I'm not sure I have a very logical answer. I guess by that point we were pretty well satisfied that Steve Ross was a guy we could live with. As long as we had a comfort level with that, there was no need to get into things like the Armstrong Report. Everyone is looking at this man's past and no one has found him guilty of something illegal. So let's get off his back, let's consider him innocent and get on with it. If I'd read the Armstrong Report, it may have told me some things that were a little less than positive about Steve. But to me it was kind of ancient history. That was then. This is now. There was no signal anywhere that, uh-oh, we'd better look deeper. I thought people had looked deeply enough. I found Steve highly acceptable personally. My private due diligence satisfied me. I did want to make this deal happen, not at any cost but to me the biggest part was just making it happen. Let's make this goddamn deal happen.''

In the rush, in Munro's words, to "make this goddamn deal happen," there was another jolting nightmare. This time it was papered over by evasion and nonchalance.

chapter 10

We Surrender, Dear

SEVEN MONTHS EARLIER, WHEN Time had thought it had a deal with Warner, Ross had broken it off in a vale of tears. He wouldn't accept the language of the succession agreement and the change in the company's by-laws requiring him to step down in five years so that Time's culture, supposedly personified by Nicholas, would run the combined company. But on reflection, Ross had dried his eyes. Everybody was told that he had changed his mind. He was ready. His transition was no longer supposed to be a problem.

Not quite. In the matrixes of Ross's mind there are always swirls of variables.

In early March 1989, on the eve of Time's and Warner's scheduled ratification of a new agreement, the merger came close to crashing again. It was the same old issue: succession. "Steve just kind of turned off," says Levin. He was hearing from Aboodi that Ross was once more balking at the guarantee that in five years he would let Nicholas take over. "Every time Steve gets to the moment of truth," Levin worried, "he agonizes. The first time we broke off. I thought it was going to happen again."

To try to keep the deal alive, this time they didn't meet with cozy intimacy at Ross's apartment. Instead they went to Ross's office accompanied by stony lawyers from both sides. Time's insisted on preserving in the by-laws of the new corporation the provision requiring the supermajority, a two-thirds vote, to change the succession. Ross's lawyers were equally adamant that the board and Ross shouldn't be committed to such formal language. An agitated Warner general counsel, Martin Payson, flushed with anger, declared, "No way. Now let's just cut this out." It seemed to be a dealbreaking impasse again on the same old issue.

When things really go awry for Ross, he often turns to Arthur Liman. So at the end of the stormy day in Ross's office, that night, at eight, Levin and Liman repaired alone to the quiet of Liman's law office, away from what Levin says were the "sensitivities and legalese." Together they worked on Liman's draft of a peace treaty. It gave Ross just what he wanted.

He would not "retire" at the end of five years. Instead he would remain chairman for ten and be an "adviser" for five years after that. Nor would the Time Warner board be handcuffed by a two-thirds majority vote to assure Time's domination. The "A-word," acquisition, suggesting that Time was taking over Warner, was not to be used. The "Statement of Principles" they wrote and Ross signed was to be kept secret from everyone but board members. What became known as the Liman Letter said in part:

> The merger is a true combination of two great companies. For either company to be looked upon as anything but an equal partner in this transaction would sap that company of its vitality and destroy the very benefits and synergy that the combination is intended to achieve. It was not a condition of the negotiations that [Ross] retire at the end of five years. When [Ross] resigns as co-CEO in 1994, [Nicholas] will become sole CEO and [Ross] will remain as sole Chairman of the Board of the combined companies and will continue to have an active role and provide leadership and guidance to the businesses that he helped build.

The piece of paper was not a contract. It had no standing in law. It was not a part of the merger agreement. By then, for Munro, Nicholas and Levin it didn't need to be. They said they had confidence in Ross's word and what they called the "signed-in-blood" letter. "Ross is absolutely good to his word," Nicholas says. "In the final analysis it did require some leap of faith—putting all the contractual stuff aside. I said if it feels right you do it. If it doesn't you don't. That's a question of business and personal judgment. Ultimately that's what happened."

Indeed, "I signed it in blood," says Ross. "It was a matter of honor with me. My word is my bond," he repeats.

The minutes of the Warner board meeting described Ross's victory less dramatically:

> Mr. Liman further reviewed the Statement of Principles pursuant to which Mr. Nicholas would become the sole CEO of Time Warner in five years, *unless the board determines otherwise.* Mr. Payson described earlier drafts of the Merger Agreement that contemplated a special majority requirement of two-thirds action by the Board of Directors to make any changes in the charter, by-laws or plan of succession, but said that at *Mr. Ross's request, these provisions had been eliminated.* [Italics added.]

The Time directors, who by then were tired of the whole question and confused, got fuzzier language. At their board meeting Levin evasively told them:

> A major area of concern to us during our negotiation with Warner was governance. As I mentioned, this topic caused us to break off talks before. Today we have agreement on the following governance issues: the composition of the board and its committees, the initial organizational structure and executive succession provision.

In simpler, more accurate words, the guarantees that the Time board members had insisted on from the beginning had slipped away without their knowing it. The controlling Time Warner by-laws say it in plain language: "Any officer may be removed, either with or without cause, by the Board at any meeting called for the purpose." A simple majority vote of the board at any time could make the change.

Not only did board members not understand what had happened to their treasured two-thirds-majority insurance policy, neither did Munro and Nicholas. The obfuscating point was that the two of them and Ross had lengthy employment contracts. Their agreements provided that if the board decided to fire any one of them or to violate their agreements, then—and only then—for them to get *fully* compensated, it would take a two-thirds vote of the board. The contracts were purely and simply about money—nothing else. The two-thirds vote had no bearing on what their roles would be or for how long, but only on how much money they would get if the succession or governance plans changed.

"They're like baseball contracts," a Time businessman said when he found out about the change. "They don't assure that the manager will manage or the player will stay in the same position. Only that he will get paid no matter what."

Levin and the Warner people well knew what the change meant. But the contract clause was so complex and so buried that Nicholas and Munro didn't understand until more than a year later when a reporter pointed it out to them. As for the Time directors, they were confronted with a 253-page fine-print agreement, the texts of even denser employment contracts and a thicket of financial projections. "I didn't think it made any difference anyway," says Dingman. "The objective was to get these two lovers together, not to worry about the details. I can't remember being aware of it. I never paid any attention to it."

The change also escaped the notice of editor-in-chief Jason McManus. "I didn't know about the elimination of the supermajority on governance until I read about it later. I hesitate to say that, because it makes me an inattentive director. I don't know why I didn't know about it—whether it was explained and I missed it, or whether it wasn't explained. I'm embarrassed as a journalist that I don't know the answer to that question."

Perkins, the Time director in charge of the board's governance committee, gingerly glides over the fact that the negotiators had surrendered on what they repeatedly said was their rock-bottom cornerstone condition. Perhaps he confused the employment contracts, which concerned only money, with the two-thirds succession guarantee, which was now gone.

A new twenty-four-member Time Warner board, evenly matched at the start with twelve Warner and twelve Time directors, could fire Nicholas or Ross and change who would be boss any time it wanted—by a simple majority vote. "A CEO, even if he has a contract," says Arthur Liman, "serves at the pleasure of the board. If you remove him you have to honor the contract but you can always remove him."

HAVING ROLLED UP AND put away the governance safety net, the negotiators had to agree on price. No cash was to be involved. Originally, Time had wanted to buy Warner flat-out for cash. Ross said absolutely not. Warner was not for sale. Furthermore, the tax burden on the Warner stockholders and the debt in the merged company would be too high. If they just exchanged stock, he said, and did a "pooling of interests" (an accounting term) they could all be better off.

If Time could not buy Warner for cash, then from the start it wanted a "market-to-market" swap. On Wall Street that means the value of Time shares would be determined by their stock market price as compared to the price of Warner's. When one company acquires another, it often pays a premium, some percentage over the market price. Premiums are paid for various reasons, usually because that's what it takes to get the stock. Time's directors and executives felt at the outset that Time was the prestige company and should pay no premium for Warner.

Levin had started out against any premium. But he loosened up and was willing to be "flexible" if they could reach agreement on the succession issue. Levin told the board they had such an agreement. His negotiating handwritten note to himself had said, "15% OK premium, 20% not okay." Dingman, the consummate deal maker, had insisted earlier that "a premium demeans the deal. No way there should even be a premium." Beré thought, "The non-premium issues are all fluff and the premium is the one concrete issue." Finkelstein was willing to pay a small price above market "to make sure Warner knows it's being acquired and Steve understands that very clearly to protect the 'Time culture.' "

Gradually, as their hunger to complete the deal grew, the Time side folded again. Time started the share exchange and premium negotiation with a bargaining willingness to go up above the market value for Warner shares by about 15 percent. Warner started with a demand for more than 22 percent and stuck to it. Ultimately, Time agreed to the Warner price. As a result, Warner stockholders would end up owning more than 62 percent of Time Warner (some share-holders owned stock in both companies).

Felix Rohatyn had advised Warner that a premium of 20 percent "would be a hell of a deal." When Ross walked into his board meeting and announced that Nicholas and Levin had agreed to an even higher premium of 22 percent, Rohatyn was ecstatic. He announced that the exchange ratio makes "an even more fantastic" deal for Warner, adding that "Time is now an entertainment company." The market, he said, would react to the whole deal with "euphoria and acclamation."

Accepting would have been a more accurate prediction. Time stock dropped two points, then rose nine. Warner went up only two.

OUTSIDE DIRECTORS ARE required, in theory and in law, to take seriously their assigned roles as guardians of the corporation for the shareholders. In recent years, directors also have expressed responsibility for the employees and the public—"stakeholders," as the three groups together were called in the fast-moving acquisition euphemisms of the '80s.

Outside directors are also supposed to be well enough informed and involved to challenge as well as support the management. Time's outside directors did challenge the management and were frequently consulted. They asked many questions but failed to follow up on the answers they got. If they had, they might have been just as satisfied with the real information they received as they were in their ignorance when they abdicated that responsibility. They just trusted a management which saw glory in finally making the kind of deal it had been floundering around for close to a decade.

Over the issues the outside directors originally said mattered most (Ross, succession, governance, price), from their own accounts, they wearily seemed to give up with an attitude bordering on terminal indifference. In the end, no one could accuse them of the rigorous "due diligence" they were supposed to represent.

One Time director gave the most realistic assessment: "The average guy or woman on a board devotes 95 percent of his time to his own business. A board can't tell an operating management how to run its day-in and day-out business. If you don't like the business, you should get off."

Robert Townsend, the investment banker who took over Avis Rent a Car and made it "try harder," once wrote, tongue-in-cheek:

> While ostensibly the seat of all power and responsibility, directors are usually friends of the chief executive put there to keep him safely in office. They meet, gaze at the financial window dressing, listen to the chief and his team talk superficially about the state of the operation, ask a couple of dutiful questions, courteously recorded and subsequently ignored, and adjourn.

Time's outside directors did better than that—but on the record of their involvement, not much better. A chancery lawyer reached back to the Bible's Book of Psalms to describe such conduct by directors and executives: "They have eyes, but they see not/ They have ears, but they hear not."

AFTER AN INFORMAL DINNER the night before, Time's board met to ratify the agreements. They convened at 11:30 the following morning, Friday, March 3, 1989, in their forty-seventh-floor boardroom atop the Time & Life Building. Two days earlier each had been sent reams of detailed projections and draft agreements.

Munro, Nicholas and Levin skated through the deal in front of a backdrop of slides, charts and summaries, aided by a platoon of investment bankers and lawyers. Time's leading outside financial advisers, Bruce Wasserstein and his group, affirmed that Time was the "surviving" company, but the deal was neither an acquisition nor a merger, more of a "hybrid." When the presenters were done and questions answered, in the spirit of things, the board unanimously approved. Hank Luce, who could not attend the meeting, gave his approval later by phone. Several directors congratulated the management.

For a bang-up finish to the meeting, the room was darkened, on the screen flashed selections from memorable Warner movies, including *Dirty Harry* and *Chariots of Fire,* with its inspirational soundtrack. As the lights came up, there was an exuberant round of applause.

A month later, Temple resigned, saying that it was no longer the "type of business in which I can feel pride, which is not to say that it will not prove profitable." His two allies, Goodrich and Grum, were not renominated. Selecting twelve directors for the combined board from sixteen on the Time board was, says one of the directors, "like a comic opera. It would put the *Mikado* to shame if someone could put it to music."

Time's outside directors, except for Dingman and Goodrich, still had not met with Ross. They never did until five months later, after the transaction was finally completed.

The Warner board meeting down the street stretched over two days before the deal was ratified. Because of Siegel's hostile presence, Ross says, he could not consult in advance with his outside directors. Warner's chief outside financial advisers, Lazard's Felix Rohatyn and his team, acted as cheerleaders. Rohatyn said that he had attended many extraordinary meetings in his thirty years at Lazard but never one as extraordinary as this one. He exalted Ross for the "vision" to "conceive and propose the merger." Rohatyn called the proposed Time-Warner merger a "block buster," "the best deal I've seen in thirty years," "a seminal transaction," a "great new powerhouse," which "will break the logjam open." He also pointed out that he had been an adviser for fifteen years to Time, whose management had "integrity and style." Two years earlier, he added, he never thought the deal could be made to happen at all because the companies were so different.

In the early days of the negotiation he had remarked in exasperation to Bruce Wasserstein, "If Time's the church, what are we, the synagogue?" But he hadn't reckoned with the changes in Time. Munro and Nicholas, he said, "were different from their predecessors," Heiskell, Donovan and Shepley. The '80s generation of Time executives, says Rohatyn, "came to feel that the future of Time Inc. lay with a major entertainment company." Describing himself as someone who "rarely gets excited" and is "known as a pessimist," Rohatyn said the deal "could accomplish what no one could have imagined."

Warner executives went over Time's assets, including *People,* whose Princess Di special issue alone, the directors were told, made more in profits than *Vanity Fair* did in all of 1988. The magazines were said to be "mature" (business double-speak for little growth prospects) but producing enough stable cash flow to be "invested in operations that would allow higher rates of return" than magazines. When asked why only two-year financial projections were used, Lazard's John O'Herron said any longer would be "meaningless." Wasserstein's group used projections for Time that went out as far as ten years.

Director Merv Adelson, who had just sold Lorimar-Telepictures to Warner for $1.3 billion in an all-stock deal, said the new company would be "awesome." Ross waxed enthusiastic about a brilliant future sparkling with laser disks and pay TV reaching for global encirclement. When it came time to vote, it was unanimous but for two abstentions: Siegel, who asked about "the cost savings" and, in effect, was being bought out; and Ross, who, along with Siegel, had a tangle of obligations that lawyers advised them both made it unwise for them to vote.

Now both boards had approved. And "It's Westward Ho! toward movieland," cracked one Time executive.

SHORTLY AFTER 7:30 THAT EVENING, Ed Cannon, a night security guard in the Time & Life Building, got an emergency phone call. "Go to the lobby and meet some people from Warner," he was ordered. "Forget who they are. It's a secret."

In minutes, Steve Ross, visiting the Time office for the second time in his life, accompanied by a Warner retinue, streamed through the lobby and was whisked up to conference room 34-34D on the executive floor. More than a dozen Time executives, lawyers and staff were waiting to witness the signing of the merger agreement. "It was to be an informal affair," recalls one of the witnesses, not "like the signing on the battleship *Missouri* in Tokyo Bay."

"Find a photographer," Munro whispered to Cannon, presumably an easy task in the birthright company of photojournalism. But the Time-Life darkroom told him none was available. "I couldn't say, 'Nothing's available,' to Mr. Munro," Cannon says he thought to himself. He called Rockefeller Center security, which was happy to hear from him. Coincidentally, at that moment they were rescuing a free-lance photographer freezing in the winter night on the eighth-floor setback outside the building. Clad in a Navy jacket, jeans and gloves cut off at the knuckles, young Casey Bailey had been locked out while shooting a story for *FYI*, Time's house organ. "She didn't look too respectable," Cannon remembers, "just coming in from the cold and all that."

Dressed for the occasion or not, she was rushed up to photograph the historic signing, with no idea of who or what her subjects were. When she started to work, she said, "I don't know what to do to make you guys smile. How about the word 'money'?" "Can't I say 'stock'?" Ross shot back. With that she got the laughs and smiles she wanted. Ross and Munro sat down at the conference table, posed and signed. Everyone joined in for more pictures. Levin and Aboodi, arms around each other; Aboodi, who brought along his son and daughter; Payson with his daughter; a grinning Jason McManus. Snap, snap, snap. When friendly Dick Munro ambled over and asked the photographer who she worked for, she joined in the merriment and answered, "the *National Enquirer*." Silence suddenly surrounded her. Munro sharply broke it with, "Where *are* you from,

young lady?" She quickly recanted, "Oh, *FYI*." "That sounds better," Munro said, relieved.

"Who were those guys, the CIA?" she asked as she was shown
out.

The signing of the merger agreement was a champagne (Moët &
Chandon) and shirtsleeves affair. "Even Dick Munro," a teetotaler,
"had a sip," Ross recalls. "It was a wonderful, exciting occasion. It
was a culmination, on second thought," he adds in view of the challenge that came three months later, "let's put it this way, it certainly
was a conception."

THE "CONCEPTION" DRAFT ANNOUNCEMENT did not use
the word "acquisition," so as not to offend Ross and his Warner
people. When Munro was asked before a large Time audience
whether Time had in fact acquired Warner, he replied, "Technically
it's an acquisition of Warner by Time but in spirit it's a merger. It's
very important that the Warner people feel it's a merger and that
our people feel it's a merger. That we go off together hand in hand
and that nobody has the upper hand."

In the fine print of the merger agreements, there was no doubt
who had the upper hand:

- Within a year, Munro would take his long-planned early retirement
  at sixty as co-CEO. For five years thereafter he would be an officer
  with the nominal title of chairman of the executive committee. For
  an additional five years he would serve "in an advisory" capacity
  at a $750,000 fee per year, plus whatever bonuses the board chose
  to award him.

- Ross was to have the senior title, chairman and co-CEO. Nicholas was to be president and co-CEO "but not Co-Chairman of
  the Board," the agreement specifically said. Both Time Inc.'s
  own house organ and the New York *Times* were so confused
  by all the titlemanship that each mistakenly called Nicholas "co-
  chairman."

- Ross's $14 million-plus annual compensation would continue, but
  Time would immediately make good in cash his $125 million ac-
  cumulated stock, rights and benefits.

- Munro, Nicholas and Levin, who had been granted (as had McManus) whopping new options just before the merger, declined to look "greedy." For the moment they would continue their comparatively paltry $1 million to $1 million-and-a-half take. But everyone agreed that after the merger Nicholas's and Levin's compensation would have to be massively adjusted upward, "to take into account the disparity" compared to Ross and other Warner executives.

- Although not in the formal agreement, there was an understanding, later carried out, that the "principal" executive headquarters would be in the Warner Building, where the entire Time senior corporate staff moved in the summer of 1989. Munro did not join them. Instead he was given an office in Stamford, Connecticut, close to his home, in a building housing the company's cable subsidiary. He also retained a visiting office in the Time & Life Building, which he rarely used.

- At the last minute, Warner's general counsel, Martin Payson, protested his status and was elevated to vice chairman of the board, with the same title as Jerry Levin.

- The chief financial officer, the general counsel and the secretary of the board all were to come from Warner.

- The chairmen of the board's key compensation committee (three Warner directors, two Time) and audit committee (3-3), were both to come from Warner.

- Not only was the requirement for a two-thirds (supermajority) board vote to change the succession eliminated; so were the same voting restrictions that Time originally insisted on: to sell major assets, to change the editorial committee and to elect new directors.

- The merged company committed to invest up to $150 million in a fund managed by Aboodi's Alpine Capital, in addition to paying him an $8 million advisory fee and later making him the company's principal investment adviser.

- The first annual meeting after signing the agreement was held in the Ziegfeld Theater, a new location for Time but an old site for Warner meetings.

- The Warner directors who wanted to stayed on the combined board. Two Time directors who might have liked to stay (Goodrich and Grum) resigned. The Warner board also had three directors emeritus, who were invited to attend Time Warner board meetings (one was Ross's former father-in-law). Time has no directors emeritus, only retired directors, who are not invited to board meetings.

- Time's HBO, which saw an opportunity in the combined company to make films not only for television but for theatrical release as well, was sternly told to stick to its knitting. Warner Bros. would take care of all the theatrical movie business. ("I would dare say," Munro did dare to say, "HBO's future may be behind it. It's got to do something for an encore.")

- Unequal cosmetics: In Ross's seventy-nine-page contract he was referred to as the "Executive." Nicholas's new contract, half the length, calls him the "Employee." Ross's also provided he could be dismissed after "conviction of a felony which is not subject to appeal." Nicholas's doesn't mention appeals.

- The "Role of the Editor-in-Chief," the editorial charter establishing his independence, was not included in the merger agreement. In the rush to put the paperwork together, says one senior Time executive, "we forgot." The editor-in-chief would now report to an editorial committee of the board, where he is a member, rather than to the board itself. "At least once a year" the committee would review "editorial staffing and policies."As a trade-off for this change, a new entertainment committee of the board was created to "ensure the creative and artistic independence" of the company, implying that journalism and popular entertainment required the same standard. In the first year of the new company's coexistence, the editorial committee met once to hear a report from McManus; the entertainment committee never met. The compensation committee met six times, three times more than any other committee of the board.

- As a result of the 22 percent premium Time offered for the Warner stock, Warner's board crowed in a formal resolution: "The stockholders of Warner, after the business combination, own a greater interest in the combined business than the existing stockholders of Time."

Except for his "blood oath" promising a 1994 date for an insignificant change in his title, Steve Ross had yielded not a single consequential negotiating point. How did he manage that? "Dick, Nick and Jerry wanted very badly to do the strategy," says one legal adviser to Time. "They believed in the vision. They concluded the game was worth the candle. They weren't going to get it otherwise. I would have been tougher. But lawyers are hired to advise, not to decide."

A longtime friend of Ross's and a sometime Warner executive explains: "I think the fact that Steve is where he is today is a tribute and payoff of his ability to romance and make people feel that they want to be decent and kind to him. He is better at that than anybody I know. If he wants to woo you, he is willing to devote the time, attention and incredible care it takes. In the end, he'll almost always get you."

chapter 11

A Question
of Culture

WHAT OF THE SURVIVAL of the "Time culture," that most important rubric under which all the major points and lesser issues of the negotiations were repeatedly subsumed? The so-called Time culture, which Time put at the heart of the merger, exists as do other companies' cultures. It is not easy to describe or to pin down. People at Time have treasured *whatever it is* for years, without ever quite defining it. It has always meant at least a certain way of doing business, certain standards of behavior and a set of formal or understood benefits to its staff. "We tried to treat people very well personally so that we could push them to the limit professionally," a former executive says. A longtime writer explains it: "Everyone worked like hell, but there was a real sense of submarine-crew adhesion and loyalty."

The place had a touch of snootiness to it. "Time would just not do business with some people if they were below our standards," says another alumnus. Such swaggering became widely known as Time "arrogance," in person and in print. "If we were arrogant it's because we were good," says Time publishing's Kelso Sutton, without a trace of self-conscious irony. "I really object to the arrogance thing."

Time had a certain "class," which even its detractors acknowledged, not just in New York but stretching to its editorial and business outposts around the world. "Time," recalls its longtime Washington bureau chief John Steele, "was always the most elegant and substantive social transaction in town." In a smoke-filled room to raise money for a political candidate who Ross and Warner executives were backing to the limit, New York wheeler-dealer lawyer

William Shea was asked, How about going after Time's chairman
Andrew Heiskell and Time people for hefty contributions? "No, no,
that's big stuff," Shea said dismissively. "You don't put the arm on
him or them."

Hedley Donovan described it to a large group of Timeincers as
well as anyone: "This 'company' is not just a legal or business entity.
I am also using the word in the older sense, as in company of scholars,
adventurers, or a company of voyagers. I think our companionship
partakes of all those things. To spend your working days among—
please forgive old-fashioned words—among gentlemen and ladies,
people of thoughtfulness and honor, and at the same time people of
real intellectual force and professional dedication—that is not necessarily the usual experience out there in the corporate and institutional world."

Some of Time's paternalism toward its staff eroded after a Newspaper Guild strike in the late '70s. Later a wave of cost-cutting, plus
the entry into new businesses where snobby standards could limit
opportunities, brought on more atmospheric changes. But Time always was and remained, by common consent, one of the best and
most prideful places to work in America. "Time Inc. is like having
sex," says one of its younger staffers. "When it's great it's fabulous.
When it's not so good it's still okay."

The other part of the Time culture was easier to define. It had
everything to do with journalistic independence, strength and primacy. That part of the culture was uniquely committed to paper in
the editor-in-chief's charter, giving him "the sole" responsibility for
the content, staffing and standards of the magazines Time published.
Independent, quality standards of journalism came first; profits followed in the wake. Not only the journalists spouted that priority.
Advertising space salesmen and publishers alike bragged about it to
their customers.

The centerpiece of that part of the culture was always *Time*, the
newsmagazine that dealt with world and national affairs, and after
which the corporation itself was named. In the long course of the
Warner transaction, when pressed to define the Time culture by
lawyers, judges and adversaries, Time's advocates always fell back
on *Time*, the magazine. They never invoked the names of even
Fortune or *Sports Illustrated*. Or of *People, Money* or *Life*, which
could hardly be put forward as American imperatives. The banner
they raised was journalistic independence in the public interest.

Other atmospherics of the corporation were too indefinable. Sturdier and more convincing was the "integrity" of Time's journalism, the separation of church and state, the singular role of the editor-in-chief.

Munro passionately described it as a unique asset. "Ever since the early days of the conversations about putting these two companies together," he says, "the thing that separates us from the pack are our journalists. It gives us the panache, the prestige, the credibility that no entertainment company, communications or media company will have. We've got it and it's the keystone of this whole corporation."

IN THE ACTUAL WRITTEN agreements between Time and Warner, neither Time journalism nor the editor-in-chief fared well. The magazines and publishing would shrink from being more than half of the Time pie to a much smaller wedge in the new Time Warner bakeshop. Nevertheless, to make its case more compelling in its pleadings for the uniquely radiant value of the merger, Time's emphasis on its journalism loomed far larger, even essential, in justifying the combined company's special merit.

The merger agreements themselves meticulously crossed every "t" and dotted every "i," dealing with virtually any eventuality short of nuclear war. Contracts, "outs," compensation, exchange ratios, options, insurance, indemnifications, directors, committees of the board, management, valuations, taxes, certificate of incorporation, medical and retirement plans—everything except the primacy of Time's journalism and its standard-bearer, the editor-in-chief.

Every one of the seven most senior Time executive officers had elaborate binding contracts written into the original agreement. But not the editor-in-chief, Jason McManus. Why not? McManus's explanation strains credibility. What matters about the editor-in-chief, McManus explains, was insulating the "office, not the person who occupies it, so there was no need in the merger to provide special contractual arrangements for me as an individual." The board, he said, "properly focused on provisions for the leadership of the combined companies, where the individuals were indeed what mattered most. The continuity of the role of the editor-in-chief is guaranteed" in the editorial charter. The fact that they "forgot" to put the charter into the all-inclusive merger agreement did not matter, McManus argues. "It was part and parcel of all the discussions. For that reason in an odd way I'm even more protected than Nick Nicholas and harder to get rid of."

Where did he stand on the ladder of importance? Nowhere near where he stood before. His employment contract was for three years; his seniors' were for ten and fifteen. Theirs are part of the merger agreement. His was a routine employment contract that was not. Measured by the yardstick of compensation alone, McManus was handsomely paid, $1.3 million in 1989, with deferred compensation and stock options, making him the highest-paid editor in the U.S. He also received a million dollars in new stock options just before the merger announcement. But he was at the bottom of the list of the five most highly paid executives of the combined company. He also earned far less than a number of entertainment and TV executives, who were not officers of the parent company and therefore not required to divulge their earnings.

For years at Time, the editor-in-chief and CEO earned exactly the same amount. As late as 1988, in salary they were not far apart. Warner was certainly a different kind of company from Time Warner. But in the combined company, the editor-in-chief's total compensation in 1990 was less than one-fifth of Nicholas's and one-thirtieth of Ross's. Time's managing editors, the chief operating guardians of the culture, now earn salaries in the neighborhood of $250,000 a year with bonuses of 75 or 100 percent of their salary. "If your bonus was only 50 percent," says one of them, "you wouldn't last as a managing editor very long."

By tradition, McManus still sits on the Time Warner board, but there is no assurance in the agreement that he or his successor will remain beyond his present term. He is the lone member of the twenty-four on the board from journalism, other than Hank Luce, who was made chairman of the board's editorial committee at McManus's request. Luce was admittedly put there largely as a piece of name symbolism rather than for his weight on the board or the confidence he instills among Time journalists.

BY STRICTLY NUMERICAL RECKONING, the shrinking role of Time's editor-in-chief in a combined Time Warner was plausible.

Jason McManus was editorially in charge of only the seven New York–based magazines (*Time, Fortune, Sports Illustrated, People, Life, Money* and the start-up *Entertainment Weekly*). A powerhouse lineup for sure, but small stuff in the total business of the Time

Warner company. Altogether these magazines brought in less than 15 percent of the conglomerate's revenue—and much less of its profit. In the late '80s, before the merger was contemplated, editor-in-chief Grunwald had lost authority over the publishing of books and regional magazines that Time had acquired. The seven home-grown magazines, including the company's namesake *Time*, were nonetheless the linchpin of Time Warner's reputation in the world, its rationale for the assertion of a public purpose and a special culture.

Warner by itself was different. "It is basically a collection of deals smartly banded together," said one top Time executive, who affirms that "Warner has been mostly about making money, having fun and living well." It "certainly wasn't what the old Time Inc. was," he says. The sum of Warner's parts added up to no compelling purpose, brand name or franchise. Warner's public identification, outside the trades it plied, was as a big entertainment company, known largely by the name of its studio and its most visible personality, Steve Ross. But no one went to a movie (*Batman*), bought a record (Madonna), a comic book (*Mad*), or subscribed to cable because it was identified with Ross, Warner or even Warner Bros.

In reality, over the years, major movie studios like Warner didn't even "make" the movies to which their names were attached. They financed and distributed them, backing independent producers who were responsible for the creative ingredient. Films that Warner proudly proclaimed for their quality and social impact such as *The Color Purple, Chariots of Fire, Driving Miss Daisy,* or adventure stories like *Robin Hood,* were bankrolled and distributed by Warner but put together by independent producers who sold them for fees and percentages of the gross revenues. Studio heads, to be sure, needed the wit and feel, sometimes even the taste, of the market to decide which projects to back. But their creative role had largely vanished as the major studios became more bankers, distributors and dealmakers than filmmakers.

When Time and Warner came together, they trumpeted a new superlative: *the* biggest media conglomerate in the world with the largest variety of media products. But size and variety are not identity. The trademark homegrown Time magazines had been. No argument ever erupted, even from Steve Ross, that the merged company should be called Warner Time instead of Time Warner. Everyone knows, says Levin, that "the core is not Bugs Bunny, it's *Time* magazine."

· · ·

AS THE GUIDING COMPASS for these trophy magazines, Jason McManus had a claim to a larger role in Time Warner. But McManus, a trim, laid-back six feet three, is neither a claimer nor a declaimer.

He was a first-rate journalist who, unlike many of his breed, is unassertive and barely visible. He presides more than dominates. To explain his style of leadership, he has framed on the wall of his spacious corner office a maxim on selfless leadership by the sixth-century B.C. Chinese Taoist philosopher Lao-tzu.

> A leader is best
>   when people barely know he exists.
> Not so good
>   when people obey and acclaim him.
> Worse when they despise him.
> But of a good leader
>   who talks little
>   when this work is done
>   his aim fulfilled
>   they will say:
> "We did it ourselves."

McManus is one of the two most eminent graduates of Presbyterian Davidson College, near Charlotte, North Carolina. The other is former secretary of state Dean Rusk. Both became Rhodes scholars and both reached the top of their calling. Although separated by twenty years, they have much in common.

Of Rusk's autobiography, a reviewer wrote, "He was circumspect, cryptic, proclaiming very little with an infinite capacity to adjust to the inevitable, a skillful facilitator of policy but rarely a maker of it." McManus's admirers, as well as his detractors, say the evocation of his fellow college alumnus fits McManus perfectly.

The son of devout semi-rural Missourians of Scottish stock, he was a studious, earnest boy with a touch of mischievous ribaldry buried deep within him. A diligent churchgoer, at the precocious age of fourteen he fell under the spell of the British Christian apologist C. S. Lewis (*The Screwtape Letters*). McManus devoured his graceful books, which brought into harmony logic and faith.

With intensity but apparent ease, young Jason rose to the top of whatever class he joined, first grammar school in Kansas City and then high school in St. Louis. "I was much into sports," says McManus, "highly social, elected high school president, voted most popular boy, Eagle Scout, car-hop and all that American Midwestern 1950s stuff. I didn't study all that hard—you didn't have to, though they were excellent schools—and my guess is that my peers thought I was brainy but not a brain, agile with words but hardly bookish."

His high school English teacher inscribed a birthday gift book "To Jason, because he 1) is now 17; 2) smiles wisely when told he resembles Gawaine more than Galahad; 3) coined the phrase 'the sanctity of all that is subjective'; 4) understands T. S. Eliot and C. S. Lewis and can manage mermaids better than either; 5) and especially because he can read Plato and sell root beer." Underneath his picture in the high school yearbook is the caption "He is all things to all people and never anything but Jason." From high school he went on to Davidson ('56, literature and philosophy) and Princeton's Woodrow Wilson School of Public and International Affairs ('58, Master of Public Administration in international economics).

His Time career was just as steady. McManus had started out in an entirely different direction, like Jerry Levin who thought he wanted to be a rabbi. "You should know," McManus says, "that I'm a Presbyterian minister manqué." He forsook a career in the cloth only after preaching for a summer in a small suburban St. Louis church, where he became convinced "that if you want to change the world, the ministry is not the place to do it." He decided to switch to journalism and writing even before he got to New College, Oxford, in 1958 (social sciences and goofing off to try a novel). McManus never finished at Oxford but says, "It's like the Marines—once a Rhodes always a Rhodes."

With summer internships from Time Inc., including reporting in the London news bureau, he easily signed on at *Time*, extracting a promise that he would be sent abroad again in a few months as a foreign correspondent. But he did so well as a writer that his editors wanted to keep him in New York, which was not what he had in mind. Within two years, McManus had despaired of getting overseas. He was lured away from *Time* by an offer, at more than twice his $12,500 writer's salary, from a public relations guru, the elegant Edwardian pretender Ben Sonnenberg.

Nine months was enough of public relations. McManus remembers that a Time editorial executive called him one day and said, "We've lost some people by mismanagement in the past few years that we shouldn't have. Why don't you come back." He snapped up an offer to become chief of a new Common Market bureau, based in Paris. From there he went steadily up the *Time* magazine editorial ladder as correspondent, writer, foreign and then national affairs editor for more than nine years—his finest hours, when he edited sixteen *Time* covers, many crash efforts, on the Watergate scandals. He was made assistant managing editor in 1976 and executive editor two years later. Then after a setback when he was passed over for Ray Cave, he became *Time*'s managing editor in 1985, and the company's editor-in-chief in 1987.

His passage through the Time Warner merger was much rockier. Unfortunately for him and Time journalism, his reputation as a leader came close to hitting bottom. His first big involvement in the merger led to what today he calls "serious trouble" and a "bad decision."

FOR WEEKS, TIME AND Warner had been planning the tactics of the merger's public announcement. The plans included news media arrangements; schedules for lobbying visits; call sheets to let key employees, advertisers, big investors and other CEOs know; clearances from government agencies; even a glowing letter to the president of the United States. One big concern was how and when *Time* itself would report the news—McManus's domain.

Time and *Newsweek* both go to press on Sunday for Monday distribution. McManus, in consultation with Munro, Nicholas and Levin, wanted a Sunday announcement of the signing that had taken place on Friday. By that schedule, neither the Sunday newspapers nor his competitor *Newsweek* would have the story. On that timetable McManus reasoned that *Time* too would be able to skip it and write a full story the following week when there would be reactions to report. Like many a well laid plan to hold back information, the timetable got derailed.

In the office of the Los Angeles *Times,* Kathryn Harris, an astute business reporter, had just returned from maternity leave. She noticed unusual activity in Time stock. By 6 P.M. Friday she was on the trail of a Time-Warner merger. By midnight New York time, she had enough confirmation to make the front page of the last edition of Saturday morning's paper with the headline "Time Warner Reportedly on Verge of a Merger." A "done deal," the story quoted one source as telling her. The industry is "in awe" of the proposed new company—a "career capper" for Ross. No one at Time or Warner saw the coverage.

Knowing there would be hectic office work on Saturday, getting ready for the Sunday announcement, Jerry Levin had stayed at his midtown Manhattan pad that night instead of being driven to his home in Port Washington. Up at six for a jog in Central Park, he stuck to his daily regimen. At 8:30 he walked the fourteen blocks to his office. In the lobby he was startled when a guard flashed a copy of the tabloid New York *Post* at him with the banner headline "TIME-WARNER MERGER REPORTED CLOSE." He didn't stop to read the story, a pickup of the Los Angeles *Times* coverage. "Is it true?" the guard asked him. "Must be a rumor," Levin replied, quickening his step.

Before Levin could do anything, the diligent Katie Harris called from Los Angeles and told him what she had. All their careful plans for a Sunday announcement would have to be junked. After a blizzard of telephone calls, it was quickly decided a noon announcement that same day was now an imperative. McManus phoned his deputy, Dick Stolley, who had replaced Cave, and said, "All plans are off. The L.A. *Times* has the story. We're going to have to have the press conference in two or three hours."

While McManus agreed with the accelerated press conference plans, he still did not want *Time* to print any story. "My primary concern," he says, "was that basically we would be rehashing the press release, that we could not bring anything to this party. It would have been feeble journalism subject to criticism for advancing the cause." He had a second concern, which had never bothered *Time* editors before in responding to late big news. "Frankly I had long planned to do the editor's letter and I didn't want to be upstaged. I wanted to be the first person to explain this to the readers of our magazines. And I had not written the piece yet."

Time bells were ringing around the world. Washington bureau chief Strobe Talbott called one correspondent and said, "Well, we've got a new boss." "Oh, who?" he was asked. "Steve Ross," Talbott replied. *Time* managing editor Henry Muller, who had taken McManus's place on *Time* and was vacationing in his Swiss condo near Geneva, got the news at dusk as the sun was setting over the Alps. In one conference call Muller's stand-in, *Time* executive editor Ron Kriss, told other senior editors the news. "What about a story?" one of them asked. Kriss explained McManus's view, and his added worry of running afoul of the SEC with a self-serving *Time* story. No one objected. "I was so stunned by the central revelation of the merger altogether," says Dick Duncan, another executive editor, "that it never occurred to me to fight." Chief of correspondents John Stacks says he thought not running a story was a mistake, "but I stayed out of it."

The younger business section editors and writers of *Time* didn't stay out of it. They were already in place in their offices on Saturday finishing a routine late-breaking story. They twice volunteered to write and report the big Time Warner announcement. No, they were told. A decision has been made by McManus, "It's a fait accompli."

Down the street at the *Newsweek* Building there were no doubts about what to do with what they thought was "the biggest media merger ever." They went right to work, interviewing Munro, Levin, Nicholas, Ross, Wall Streeters, Time directors and Time staffers. They found full-color pictures of Ross, Munro and Nicholas to illustrate their full-page story. Later they put together a full-page ad needling *Time*. "We're not afraid to say it. *Newsweek* was the first newsmagazine to report on the proposed Time Warner merger. We stay ahead of the competition—even when the competition is the story."

Levin was the one senior Time executive who opposed the decision McManus had made not to run a story. "I felt strongly about it," Levin says. "By this time I had adopted some of the Warner style of speaking passionately in a loud voice. If church-state means anything, you have to cover this. I thought it was a very juicy story." Levin was overruled. "I found it absurd," he adds, that "I was being interviewed "by *Newsweek* but not by *Time.*"

Saturday on TV, Sunday and Monday not just in *Newsweek* but on the front page of the New York *Times,* the *Wall Street Journal* and other papers across the country it was "topic A." One columnist wrote that if media "news were measured on a seismograph, the proposed Time-Warner merger would have registered 8.0 on the Richter scale." Munro and Nicholas were startled. "This was not curing cancer," Munro says. "Just a merger, an acquisition or whatever the hell it was. Nick and I were kind of looking at each other and saying, Jesus, what have we got here, they're treating this like a major event." Right, says Nicholas, "I didn't expect all that coverage." Levin did. "I can't say that I was highly prophetic, but I thought this is going to be the biggest media story and it was going to continue."

TO EXPLAIN THE WEEKEND editorial decision, early Monday morning McManus assembled in his office his two deputies, Stolley and Rogin, his managing editors and *Time*'s chief of correspondents. Then he made his second—even more remarkable—mistake. He announced there would be no story again in *Time,* only his editor's letter published in each of the magazines. *Time*'s Stacks and Kriss disagreed, as did *Life* managing editor, Jim Gaines. McManus stuck to his view that he didn't want to be "talking to our readers in two different places, my letter and in a news story."

When Kriss and Stacks went downstairs to tell their startled staff of the decision, there was what everyone agrees was a "shit storm." The staff was already humiliated at being beaten by *Newsweek* on their own story. How could they not cover it again? "The first thing you *say* to us," one editor moaned, "is that the merger won't affect *Time,* and the first thing you *do* is turn around and muzzle us." From the Washington bureau and other outposts came incredulous protests. From Switzerland, managing editor Muller registered his own distress at the decision.

By noon, Stacks knew that something had to be done. He called McManus for a second meeting. Back in McManus's office again, Stacks described the anguish of the *Time* staff. McManus said he didn't want to look like a shill for the deal. Stacks replied it would be much worse to do nothing, "a terrible mistake." Gil Rogin, the grizzled McManus deputy, growled sarcastically, "You're not going to give us this integrity shit, are you?" (Rogin later explained, "I have a general hostility to appeals to journalism as if it were some kind of religion.")

Tempers were rising. Stacks pointed out that "we're not going to do an investigative piece on Steve Ross, just the expectable *Time* business story." *Fortune*'s Loeb said he didn't know what such a story, done so quickly, could add to what was already known. Stacks replied that on those grounds *Time* would have to skip a lot of stories that run every week. Editorial director Dick Stolley, McManus's other deputy, weighed in acerbically saying, "If you do a story, you're not going to fuck it up, are you?" Stacks hit back, "You mean the deal or the story?"

McManus relented. Hearing of the "mortification of the *Time* staff," he says, turned him around. "I've now heard all this," he remembers concluding to the editors at the meeting, "and all things considered I think that I made a bad decision before and I think this one is no better, so go ahead." *Time* did its story, producing few of the criticisms McManus had feared.

"Jason," one of his senior staff observes, "is really a splendid human with democratic instincts. But when he was passed over and had to wait eight years to become managing editor of *Time,* it emasculated him. He has no style. He just blends in." The view became a disappointed consensus, with few dissenters. "Jason doesn't assert himself against powerful people," says another member of his editorial crew. "He's just there to make things work the way the higher-ups want them to work. The editor-in-chief should be a man of heft and authority."

For everyone involved in the announced Time-Warner merger there were far rougher days ahead.

chapter 12

Star Wars

F EW EXECUTIVES IN HISTORY have felt their company's
merger with another to be so important to the nation as to
require a letter, the same moment as the announcement, no-
tifying the president of the United States. Ross and Munro did, using
specially designed stationery bearing both their names. "Dear Mr.
President," they wrote to Bush, unfurling their American flag:

> Our new company enhances the overall international compet-
> itiveness of U.S. business at a time when debate over foreign
> ownership of assets has raised important questions. This trans-
> action strengthens our ability to meet the increasingly complex
> challenges of a world economy without the devastating effects
> of an LBO or a hostile takeover. We will do so without dis-
> mantling our companies or incurring a crippling debt structure
> that would subvert our ability to secure the long-term growth
> of our business.

In a follow-up joint statement read before the televised congressional
subcommittee on economic and commercial law, Munro and Ross
began with a drumroll of *Time* magazine's "significant influence on
journalism." Right at the top they invoked the name of Henry Luce
and declared,

> We have never lost sight of our deep journalistic roots, and as
> Time Inc. is transformed into this new venture, we pledge that
> the new company will remain committed to the practice of
> independent journalism.

Levin testified before the Senate subcommittee on antitrust,
monopolies and business:

This merger creates a company with the strength and vision to enter the 21st century as a competitive force breaking new ground both here and abroad.

Briefs were filed with the FCC, FTC and Justice Department. It was easy street all the way. Approvals came tumbling out. Of the government agencies that had to be satisfied, only the SEC, which takes at least thirty to forty-five days to approve the paperwork, had not finally signed off. But, through skillful advance work and lobbying, everything on the government front was going smoothly.

On two other fronts, however, there was high anxiety.

WITHIN TIME ITSELF, STAFFERS from top to bottom were in an uproar. They didn't know Ross, worried about what they thought they knew. The sentiment ranged from damning slander, at worst, to deep apprehension at best. "My mother told me," said one correspondent, "that she never would park her car in a Kinney lot because it was controlled by the mob." An editorial staffer joked, "I have a feeling of both melancholy and optimism. It's like watching your mother-in-law drive your brand-new Range Rover over a cliff."

Up over an office in the Washington bureau went a streamer with the sign-off words of Warner cartoons, "Th-Th-That's all, folks." One senior editor, who had been on vacation, remembers that "I came back to confusion, hand-wringing, rudderlessness and a feeling we were cast adrift." Even at HBO, where joy would have been expected, there was deep resentment at no longer being king of the Time film hill. From every quarter, the caterwauling got so loud that Munro, Nicholas, Levin and McManus were sent on missions to visit offices at home, around the country and the world "to quiet the Indians," as one staffer said.

At one such meeting, editorial staffers were pressing McManus about the multimillion-dollar executive rewards. He had the misfortune to repeat the hoary cliché that "we journalists didn't get into this business for the money," provoking groans from his audience. (Time was in the midst of tough negotiations with the Newspaper Guild, offering 3 percent and 4 percent wage increases.) Jason was "looming small," one of his old friends lamented. Others sourly recalled the *Time* cover story only three months before on the RJR-Nabisco takeover, titled "A Game of Greed," in which the CEO Ross Johnson would have walked away with $100 million. (Steve

Ross stood to make twice as much.) About the RJR-Nabisco deal, *Time* had railed: "The sums are so vast, and so apparently out of line with foreseeable benefits that the deal may bring to American industry, that they raise deep and disturbing questions about the direction of U.S. business. Seldom since the age of the 19th-century robber barons has corporate behavior been so open to question."

To combat the doomsday mood, Nicholas talked of the new horizons that would open up for the combined company, including one he had once booted at a bargain price. "Now," he told a group of Time managers, "we're going to get Ted Turner. CNN and Ted Turner are next. You'll be hearing us talk about it in the next year— that's where we're going." Another group he told, "Ted loves Time Warner because it's the only company he deals with that is journalistic and is also in the cable business." To reinforce his point, he reported that Turner had sent him two dozen long-stem red roses when he heard about the merger. Three years later Turner was sending flowers to and marrying Jane Fonda, not Time Warner.

In one conversation with a senior journalist about Ross, Munro repeated a thought that had been expressed at board meetings. Ross, he said, was not in good health, and probably wouldn't be around for the full ten years (five as co-CEO and chairman, five as chairman but not co-CEO). Never fear, Munro speculated, the deal was Ross's way to achieve legitimacy—the capstone of his career. He won't be tempted to meddle. He needs to be known as a great man, not just a great operator.

Some of the Timeincers' initial skepticism was expectable griping about change. The doubt was compounded by the fear of being swallowed up by an entertainment company run by a man none of them knew but about whom they'd heard plenty of whispered gossip. If inside there was skepticism bordering on disdain, from outside came a rush of assaults that drove the Time leaders into almost manic activity.

THE ANNOUNCEMENT OF THE intended merger "was like slicing your wrists and bleeding into a shark pool," said one commentator.

Time's bankers in analyzing the merger's hazards had warned that the deal with Warner could put Time "in play," making it the target for a hostile takeover bid. Time and its directors knew they were taking that chance. They had built up their defenses. Just in case, they lined up $5 billion in emergency financing. They also paid a group of banks "dry-up" fees of more than $5 million for guarantees they would not finance anyone who tried a hostile move. (This new tactic, known as "bankmail," was defined by an economics professor as "using shareholder money to bribe a bank not to finance a lucrative tender offer to your shareholders.")

But prepared and warned or not, as soon as the action started after the merger announcement in March 1989, Time went bananas—especially its top banana, Dick Munro. "The rumors were reaching a frenzy point," Munro says. "I must admit we were really getting fairly nervous here. We would track everyone down. We were over-reacting to some of the stuff." Headlines shouted, "Time Inc. Soars Amid Takeover Rumors."

"Whadya hear, whadya hear," Munro said to everyone he could reach. Martin Davis, savvy in the takeover game and the head of Gulf + Western, which had not yet changed its name to Paramount Communications, was Munro's constant telephone pal. "Martin is a friend, a supplier" of films for HBO, Munro explained. Davis says Munro "told me he was consumed by the problem—at one point I think he even said he was paranoid about it." ("Concerned—occasionally concerned, would be close to it," Munro corrects Davis.)

Not all of Munro's chats with "my friend" Davis were so friendly. Munro said that Davis called him in the middle of the frenzy to complain about some of Time's cable programming plans. Munro told Levin that "it was a screaming telephone call, probably the rudest, most unbusinesslike" he had ever received. Many of Munro's other calls were not fielded by Little League rules either.

After the Salomon Brothers investment banking house bought 150,000 shares of Time, Munro immediately called Salomon's boss, John Gutfreund, to tell him nicely that "Time Inc. is not for sale, we're going to pull this off and it's not in your best interests to be stirring the pot." How did Gutfreund reply? He was icy. "He told me to stick it up my ass," Munro reported back. The big investment bankers everywhere were out hustling Time for a takeover, Morgan Stanley, Salomon, Conniston Partners, Merrill Lynch. Munro called Morgan Stanley's Parker Gilbert, who he says told him, "If I need your advice I'll ask for it."

Texas's Robert M. Bass Group bought 2 percent of Time and announced it had not ruled out a takeover. Munro tracked Bass down in Hawaii, only to be left with the useless impression that "he was not technically active," i.e., he had not bought 5 percent. Rupert Murdoch invited bankers to see if he should try to pick off a piece of Time. Allen & Co. was rumored to be making a move on behalf of Coca-Cola. With each whine from the smoke alarm, Time stock bounced between less than $109 after the announcement was made up to a high of $135. "The final curtain has not come down," said one money manager, "but the play has been terrific." Another said, "It's insane, the amount of Time stock traded yesterday." Time even called on the SEC to investigate the frenetic trading. Doggedly, Munro and company told everyone to go away. One observer of their pleadings said, "They sounded like that old blues line 'You've got the right string, baby, but the wrong yo-yo.'"

Munro reached Jack Welch, chairman of General Electric, who wanted only to talk about the new cable service his NBC was launching and "kind of laughed, made a joke of my question about GE and Time." Jerry Perenchio, a former MCA agent, boxing promoter and movie mogul, teamed up with Charles ("Chuck") Dolan, who had originally dragged Time deeply into cable. (Ironically, Time found Dolan "incompatible" in the early '70s and pushed him out, enabling Dolan to make a large fortune with his own big Cablevision Systems.) Perenchio and Dolan unsuccessfully looked everywhere for backing, including at the doorsteps of Murdoch, MCA and Gulf+Western. This time Levin phoned. "Dolan is an old friend, having hired me into the cable business in 1972," Levin recalled, "so I began by asking how Chuck, his family and his wife were." It went downhill from there.

"Poor Dick," said one of Munro's staff, "he was like a guppy swimming among sharks." Nor did Time get relief from the SEC, which was still doing its paperwork. The company had to call off its scheduled stockholders meeting, which could have sealed the merger had the SEC been finished.

One investor seemed to have a personal motive beyond takeover. Donald Trump, for his egomaniacal high-flying, was slated for a cover story in *Time*. He was worried about what the magazine might say. Still flush with apparent success and even more visible chutzpah, Trump started noisily buying Time stock. Munro, who barely knew him, asked Martin Davis to call Trump to find out what was going on. "You want my advice," Davis said, "call him yourself."

When he did, Munro recalls that Trump didn't make his standard threats about the upcoming story. "I have no plans at all—all of this

is strictly an investment," Munro heard him say. "It's really nice of
you to call me. I do this kind of investing all the time and nobody
ever calls me. I never hear from anybody. How nice to hear from
you, Dick. I've heard all sorts of nice things about you. We ought
to have lunch."

Trump's wife, Ivana, before their divorce, told friends that after
Trump read the *Time* story, he said, " 'Those bastards. I'm going
to buy Time.' He was so mad he bought $100 million worth of Time
stock. But then he got involved in other things and said while he
wasn't looking he had made $150 million."

And what was Steve Ross doing during this tumultuous period?
"We were getting calls about the rumors, sure," Ross says. "But we
weren't following up on them. I didn't believe that anyone in his
right mind would make a hostile attempt, because they'd lose all the
management. And then they'd have nothing." From where she sat,
Warner director Beverly Sills had a similar reaction. "These rumors,"
she says, "weren't taken seriously by the people at Warner." Ross
also had a preoccupation. He needed to settle with his old adversary
Herb Siegel before he could conclude the Time deal. After more
bouts in court, Ross succeeded by giving Siegel everything he wanted
including an added "ownership adjustment" of about $23 million. It
was a small sum, peanuts, crowed Warner press agents, compared
to the money involved in the Time Warner merger, which could be
delayed unless there was first a settlement with Siegel.

Ross and Siegel, two experienced hardballers, both knew the standard inanities of ending a mutually profitable, if nasty, business feud.
In press releases Ross announced, "We are delighted that despite
our earlier differences, the relationship between Warner and Chris-
Craft is ending on a constructive and amicable basis." Siegel added,
"Time Warner will be the premier media and entertainment company
in the world, and I wish it well."

The decks temporarily cleared, with interlopers fading away, a
calmer Munro sent a memo to the entire Time staff: "We anticipate
that the merger will be completed this summer, right on schedule—
indeed ahead of schedule." The memo was dated June 5, 1989. That
night, at home in New Canaan, his feet up, Munro was relaxed and
confident. His goal was in sight.

The next day—June 6—the roof fell in.

. . .

THE DAY STARTED HOT and muggy, followed by a drenching downpour that cleared the late spring air. Alone in his northwest corner office at twilight, Dick Munro got a brief, devastating phone call. "It was the fulfillment of your worst dream," says Munro. In one motion, he hung up and headed down the narrow hallway to Nicholas's office in the opposite corner. "I call it the 'Bridge of Sighs,' " says Peter Quinn, Munro's speechwriter, who occupied the only cubicle on the corridor.

In a state of disbelief as he came through Nicholas's door, Munro thundered, "Goddamnit, Nick, he did it. Martin did it. Martin Davis. He lied to me. He's making a hostile bid." Minutes later a fax arrived confirming Davis's call, a $175-a-share offer to buy at close to 40 percent above the market price all of Time for a total price of $10.7 billion. "We were all shellshocked when Dick told us," Ross says. So were the Time directors he reached, Munro adds, "stunned and outraged."

Car phones rang; cellular circuits crackled all over the area; commuters cancelled their evening plans and turned around; aides scuttled through the labyrinth of tunnels beneath Rockefeller Center interconnecting forty-five investment banking houses, forty-five law firms, thirty-two banks and sixty-nine Fortune 500 companies—the greatest single nexus of corporate power in the world. By eight o'clock, close to a dozen incredulous Time executives were joined by a small army of investment bankers, lawyers (one in black tie), advisers, all gathered in conference room 34-34D, rechristened the "War Room."

Wilma ("Willie") Jeffreys, director of conference and restaurant services for Time, was surprised to see her husband standing in the doorway of the Korean nail salon two miles down Sixth Avenue where she has her weekly manicure. Before her polish was dry, he told her she was needed back to feed the gathering troops. For the next six weeks, she fed up to sixty people three times a day.

"That night," recalls Levin, "we started to mobilize. It was like a circus. No one was in charge. The animals were trying to get data. There were no Warner people—but I was on the phone with Aboodi. He found out who Paramount's bank was [Citibank]. Someone coming away from that meeting would say, 'Holy shit, it's absolute chaos.' It was really a bizarre scene. People were floating in and out. Even such a simple thing as meals. Suddenly we had food right out in the hallway, for breakfast, lunch and dinner. It was as if the food chain—cookies and certain sandwiches—was a symbol of a total disruption in all our living habits."

HBO's boss Michael Fuchs joined the melee and was astonished. "You think these high-priced investment bankers would just go click, click, click," says Fuchs. "I had the feeling no one knew what the hell to do. That was quite unsettling. Maybe my expectations were off. But I expected there to be a plan of action. There were at least twenty suggestions of what to do and how to do it."

Munro sent the embattled group home to sleep on their new problem. He spent that night on the couch in his office. At seven the next morning, on every desk, under every door and out on the worldwide Time transmission circuits went another memo: "For now, we ask only that you continue to demonstrate the loyalty, dedication and diligence which have traditionally made Time Inc. such an exceptional enterprise."

At the opening of the New York Stock Exchange, trading in Time stock was suspended for an hour to catch up with the heavy volume. After Time stock opened, it leaped up forty-four points, from $126 a share to $170.

The thirty-fourth floor of the Time & Life Building was sealed off by security guards and signs at the elevator banks. "The cross-over [elevator-changing place] on the 34th floor is temporarily closed. We are sorry for the inconvenience." (A staffer scrawled across the sign "Double-Cross.") Munro, the former combat Marine, imploded, "This is war." Right, added Time's corporate relations vice president, Louis Slovinsky. "A day at the beach, only our beach was the bloody sands of Iwo Jima. Our strategy one day will come to be known as 'in-your-face strategy.' "

MUNRO'S LETTER OF REPLY to Davis was right in the face. By comparison, it made George Bush's later ultimatum letter to Saddam Hussein read like a valentine.

Munro bypassed the advice of his bankers and lawyers and threw away a boilerplate draft by the outside public relations counsel. He was angry, felt betrayed. The high-voltage missive he sent was written word-for-word by Peter Quinn, his skilled speechwriter and confidant, who admired his boss's plainspoken style and knew his low boiling point. (The Time outside directors didn't see the letter until after it went out.) This time there was no "Marty" or "Martin" but a frosty "Dear Mr. Davis":

> On a professional level you've changed the name of your corporation [that week, to Paramount Communications] but not its character. It's still "engulf and devour." Hostile takeovers are a little like wars. Once they start, it's impossible to tell where they'll end. On a personal level, I'm disappointed that I can't rely on you as a man of your word. Live and learn. On a professional level, I regret you've chosen to stake your company's future on an ill-conceived deal that is cynical if not downright deceptive. Your tender offer raises serious questions about your integrity and motives. It smacks more of spite than strategy. You knew this company wasn't for sale. Your statement that you believed our acquisition of Warner put us into play is so much rubbish and no one is more aware of that than you. Time will not ignore the public interest. The journalistic integrity of our publications, the independence of their editorial voice isn't window dressing. It's the essence of who we are and what we do. Over nearly seven decades, Time Inc. has built a unique bond of trust with the American people and we're determined to preserve it.

Munro expressed his feelings in pungent shorthand next day when his secretary announced that Davis was calling. "Tell him to go fuck himself," Munro shouted. "Mr. Munro is busy," she told Davis, then pulled the phone away from her ear at arm's length and heard Davis hang up. A lawyer later described the call as "the only communication there has been between the two parties" after the Paramount offer. Munro and Nicholas pronounced a three-word verdict on Davis: "He's a liar."

"Lie" is a word, either as a noun or verb, used both ways by Nicholas and Munro, that should be invoked sparingly. Its meaning is narrow: a statement that is known to be untrue by the person making it. In their three years of friendly talks, did Davis *lie* to Munro about never making a hostile move on Time? Or did Munro *lie* to Davis when he said that Time 1) wasn't interested in owning a movie studio, 2) was not for sale, and 3) insisted on staying independent?

On the evidence, neither appeared to be lying. Munro came late to the conclusion that owning a studio was okay. In his last conversation on the subject with Davis, Munro still had not been brought around by Nicholas and Levin to becoming a movie fan. "Dick is incapable of lying," says Levin. The Warner opportunity and desperation to expand had belatedly changed Munro's mind about movies. As for Time's staying independent, in Munro's view, joining up with Ross was not violating that basic conviction. Finally, in his heart more than his head, he felt Time would be the "surviving," dominant company and there was no way the deal could be viewed as "putting Time up for sale."

For his part, Davis had good reasons, if he needed any, to view Time's Warner deal as a "betrayal" of what Munro had been telling him. First, the new Time Warner company would own a movie studio, despite Munro's past denials. Second, Warner stockholders would hold more than 60 percent of the combined company and Davis had no doubt that Ross, by dint of his personal force alone, would be in command. And finally, with Time in play, being sought by at least half a dozen other companies, why should Davis's Paramount stay out of the game? Furthermore, Paramount had long been considered by Time and its advisers as the second most attractive acquisition candidate after Warner.

"When one party ends up with the bulk of the shares," said Davis, "a substantial part of the management, key positions in the financial area—the guts of any organization—in the legal area, I think it's quite clear, especially when the determination is made prior to the transaction."

Even before they took their arguments to court, Time's real reason for spurning Davis became obvious. It was more personal than corporate. Time executives didn't mind being Paramount's biggest customer with HBO buying millions in films. As a vendor, Davis was all right. They just didn't want him as their boss. They were convinced in any combination with Paramount that's exactly what he would be.

Nicholas says flatly that there was "no question, Davis told me I'd be a wonderful guy to run the company *after* him." Davis confirmed that understanding when he said that Munro was "obsessed with who was going to succeed him—not who but basically Nick. On co-CEOs, I never saw one that worked." Nicholas also had other reasons for not wanting Davis. "I didn't know him as a liar before he made his move. But I knew in advance he was not a guy I'd ever want to have as a partner. I always thought of him as a guy who'd just as soon shoot you through the head as deal with you. And I didn't like the way he treated his own people."

Munro agrees. "I went into this goddamn debate with the *Fortune* editors and they said what's the difference between Martin Davis and Ross? I said I'll bring Martin in and you'll find out what the fucking difference is. Ross is a *good* guy." Standing amid another knot of Time staffers, Munro told them, "People say there's not much choice between Davis and Ross. That's not so. Ross is a gentleman. Davis is a son of a bitch."

DAVIS'S HISTORY AS A manager gave some legitimate cause for concern. For a decade the business press—including *Fortune*—had chronicled his rough, intimidating executive ways. Davis's personal background was similar to Ross's, but his foreground seemed to the Time trio as different as Darth Vader was from Luke Skywalker in the movie *Star Wars*.

Bronx-born, of immigrant parents, Davis was a college dropout who began his entertainment career as an office boy and later headed publicity of the company run by the legendary Hollywood pioneer and studied malapropist Samuel Goldwyn. Davis, shrewd and hard-shelled, wily not only in public relations but in the ways of the movie business, rapidly rose through publicity, advertising and sales at Paramount Pictures to become chief operating officer until he brought Paramount to Gulf + Western's Charles Bluhdorn, who bought it in 1966.

Bluhdorn, known *un*affectionately as the "Mad Austrian," was as gruff and foul-mouthed a conglomerator as ever was. He made Davis a senior executive, his right-hand man, and, by Davis's own account, he was labeled Bluhdorn's "hatchet man." Bluhdorn's acquisition binge in the '60s brought under his leaking roof more than a hundred unrelated companies that dealt in everything from panty hose and cigars to chemicals, resorts and cement. He also spent seven brutal years being investigated by the SEC. Accused of a variety of corporate trickeries, he finally settled in 1981, neither denying nor admitting guilt, but not before he was shredded in a front-page series by the New York *Times*'s giant-killing investigative reporter Seymour Hersh.

Davis himself was not a target in the SEC investigation. But he managed Bluhdorn's defense, masterminded by none other than Steve Ross's lawyer, Arthur Liman, and Edward Bennett Williams.

Davis's role, Liman told a reporter, "was like a rock, a needle on the compass of the magnetic field of Charlie Bluhdorn." Don Oresman, a lawyer from Simpson Thacher & Bartlett, Gulf + Western's outside counsel, described Davis as the "Elmer's Glue of the Bluhdorn era, Charles's security blanket."

In 1983, when Bluhdorn, fifty-six, suddenly died of a heart attack, the board passed over Gulf + Western's president and picked Davis to be boss. Probably no one has ever deconglomerated a company as fast as Davis did Gulf + Western. He sold most of its untidy subsidiaries. With the $2.6 billion proceeds, he consolidated the company, focusing it on its Paramount movie and TV program assets, Madison Square Garden and the publishing business (including Simon & Schuster, the publisher of this book). "Not Just Another Charlie Bluhdorn," the New York *Times* headlined a profile of him, but an executive who "has come to embody a new generation of strategic thinking that places a premium on size, focus and managing businesses rather than trading them like commodities."

If Ross left the work of management to others, Davis did his own. After a series of battles, and having their bonuses cut, the two top Paramount Pictures executives quit. Michael Eisner went on to be the most successful film executive in the country, rebuilding ailing Disney. Barry Diller became an executive superstar at the helm of 20th Century–Fox. (In 1991, Davis fired Paramount's chairman, Frank G. Mancuso, a thirty-year veteran of the studio.) An investment banker who has worked with him says, "Davis is not the kind of guy you'd call up if you had a personal problem, thinking he'd come rushing over to help you solve it."

Unlike Ross and his Warner executives, Davis grew up in the publicity and public relations business and liked talking to reporters. But he kept his own public relations people on a short, even strangling, leash. At one interview with a reporter, Davis's PR man, after a half hour of silence, interjected an explanatory phrase. "He talks too much," Davis said to the reporter. Then to his PR man: "You're here to back us up, not to do your own interview. Don't put words in my mouth." The PR man was out the year after.

TO NICHOLAS AND HIS colleagues, any gentler side that Davis displayed to reporters was just another example of his skillful press agentry. Martin, they joked, "is short for martinet." "By nature and disposition," Levin said, Davis "is what I consider to be an unimaginative CEO, primarily a public relations technician, and therefore not suited to superintend these great publications at Time Inc."

The Time board agreed. In the month following the Paramount offer, they met formally in day-long emergency meetings six times, as often as they would normally convene in an entire year. Levin recalls: "The emotion outside the boardroom on a daily basis was intense because events were happening dramatically. I must have screamed at people several times. Given the negative press we were getting, we felt embattled. Combine that with being on the defensive and for a period of time we hadn't selected the course of action. There were several options. There was a lot of emotionalism in various camps, trying to get the right result. We did get a lot of conflicting advice. I think it's the most ultimate business experience you can have. When you reach a point that involves the continuing existence of your company, it's a disorienting thing for people. It resulted in bizarre or inconsistent behavior at times. One option was to take Paramount on. That certainly got the most attention. We could make a run at Paramount—Pac-Man style. Another was to try to make a deal with Warner in a modified fashion. I believed our future had to be with Warner, and that wasn't a universally shared view. A third option was to just say no." They had some meetings, says Munro, "that were just crazy, where one rainmaker said go to the mountains and another said go to the valley."

Refusing publicly even to consider Davis's offer, the board said no, no, a thousand times no, by every means they could muster. At $175 a share, they said they considered the bid an insulting undervaluation of Time's assets. The press gleefully covered each rebuff and rebound.

Variety bannered across its front page, "NO BIGNESS LIKE SHOW BIGNESS, *Size is the ultimate prize.*" Its story began, "Ego, hostility, greed, fear and power-lust: suddenly the war over the singular prize of Time Inc. has all the elements of a silver screen epic." *USA Today* weighed in with "Henry Luce wouldn't be very happy. Time Inc., Luce's beloved empire, is on the block like a side of beef. Critics point fingers at Time's management and board of directors." The *Times* of London called it a "Hollywood takeover epic." Interest in the daily shot and shell ran so high that on the newsstand in the lobby of the Time & Life Building, the *Wall Street Journal* sold out before 8:30 A.M. every day.

The excesses were described by Robert Lenzner, one of the most knowledgeable financial reporters on the beat. Under the headline "A Circus Maximus," he wrote in the New York *Observer,* "The battle of the three entertainment combines has become the greatest spectacle in the history of the takeover game. The epic proportions of the drama attracted Wall Street's investment bankers sweeping the world for bidders and big bucks, while the legal eagles invent new offensive and defensive strategies that will change the Hollywood landscape."

In all of the Time Inc. magazines' coverage, *Fortune* ran the first blatantly self-serving report. "Davis knows a good business strategy when he steals one," said the biweekly in its first story on the battle. The supposed news story editorialized: "Time considers its editorial independence a national trust not to be trifled with for mere coin. The editor-in-chief, Jason McManus, sits on its board and reports to the directors, not to the chief executive. Neither Paramount nor any other major U.S. media company has such an arrangement." For some semblance of balance, the magazine did give Davis a one-sentence hearing. "Davis told *Fortune* he is willing to guarantee in writing that he will not meddle with the magazines' editorial independence."

There were other editorial worries—including those of the managing editor of *Time,* Henry Muller, and some of his staff. McManus was taxed for sitting on the Time board at the same time he was editing *Time* and *Fortune* stories. He was accused inside and outside of dragging the editorial church into state affairs, which could appear as a "conflict of interest." That had never bothered Luce when he was in charge, and McManus replied that it would be "irresponsible" for him to remove himself from his normal role.

After one long interview with *Time,* which the weekly ran as a straight text, Davis was not satisfied. He bitterly complained that in the editing it left out his assertion that "Editorial integrity is something I've been identified with. Time Inc.'s present policy is completely consistent with ours and will prevail." He also grumbled about the story accompanying the interview. It quoted a *Fortune* article from four years back which said Davis was "thrilled" to be on the magazine's annual list of toughest bosses and that a business associate said about Davis, "He exceeds all of the qualifications for the category of s.o.b."

. . .

IT'S A WONDER—NO, a mark of professionalism—that under severe personal pocketbook stress the staffs of Time's magazines got anything right.

The 21,000 Time Inc. employees had millions in stock mostly as a result of a variety of stock-participation plans. For many, it was the only substantial savings they had. When the Paramount bid came in, the stock jumped up and down wildly as speculators, institutional investors and others bought and sold, responding to daily rumors about a new raid or Paramount-Time maneuvers. "Rumortage," the tangled daily grapevine was called. After Davis later raised his price, the stock peaked at more than $182, from the $135 high it had reached before Paramount's tender offer.

Throughout the Time & Life Building and its outposts around the world, as much attention was paid to Quotrons, Dow Jones and other stock reports as to the news of the day. Writers, researchers, editors and correspondents split their attention—and some their word-processing screens—from Beijing, where the high drama of the Communist violent suppression of students was taking place, to Wall Street, where the big news was the rise and fall of Time stock. Even a ceiling painter perched on a ladder in the hallway of the Time offices, as he dipped his brush, asked his partner holding the paint can, "Is the stock up or down since noon?"

"Except when people were researching and writing," one writer says, "every minute as far as I could tell was spent in the halls or in somebody's office figuring out what's going to happen, should we sell, are we going to be taken over, what's the difference between Marty Davis and Steve Ross?" One *Sports Illustrated* staffer talking to an editor, found that "she always had the financial news services stock quotations on her TV. I'd be talking to her and as if by some intuition she'd glance over and say, 'Ooops, four and a quarter,' then go right on talking about the story we were discussing." Business specialists on *Fortune, Money* and *Time* suddenly became in-house financial consultants to their co-workers.

At morning editorial meetings, gains and losses in the paper value of the staff's stock was a prime topic. As many telephone calls seemed to be outgoing to stockbrokers as to news sources. One staffer with options at $13 sold all his shares at $180. Several employee stockholders cashed out and bought long-coveted new houses. Others were not so free to make a profit; their shares were still locked up by mandatory waiting periods. Foreign correspondents and retirees called in for advice. The person-to-person codes of the internal electronic message system were abuzz with reports, advice and such tart comments as "A sage investor opines that Time's cash flow sucks. Ain't it wonderful to work for a *communications* company?"

McManus made a morale-building tour of the editorial staffs, which had the opposite effect from what he'd hoped. He kept using the apology, said one *Fortune* writer, " 'You guys know more about this than I do.' We'd seen what his salary was and that didn't wash. He was on the board and ought to bloody well understand this stuff."

INVISIBLE IN THE BATTLE with Paramount, to all but the senior Time executives upstairs, was a barrage of dirty tricks, unworthy of Time, not altogether returned in kind by Paramount.

The first Scud missile was fired by Time. It had its lawyers hire Kroll & Associates, the leading worldwide private investigative and detective agency, to dig up dirt on Davis and look into his past. When he heard about it, Davis bitterly snapped, "The only thing Kroll will find out about me is that my ex-wife hates me." Levin excuses the tactic by explaining, "It's part of the standard line of defense. Your investment banker, your lawyer, your PR person and some investigative effort. But beyond what is the ritual in these defenses, there was a feeling that Paramount and Davis would be fertile ground."

No such investigative agency had been used to explore Ross's or Warner's history.

A low point was reached when Time leaders, aggrieved at most of the press coverage, whispered widely that one high Paramount executive was having an affair with a prominent reporter covering the story. One Time executive went to the paper's boss with the charge; another asked Kroll agents what they knew about it. "The only place that Paramount guy is screwing that reporter is on the phone," a Kroll operative replied. He also reminded the Time senior corporate executive who was seeking more information that it would look horrible for Time, a proud journalistic organization, to be ordering up an investigation into the sex life of a reporter. The quest was dropped.

The personal recriminations erupted more formally in a complaint to the FCC filed by Time. It claimed that Paramount's "character qualifications," on the face of it, made the company and its leaders "unfit" to hold a franchise for cable because of a record of "untruthful and unreliable conduct." The brief claimed it was "inconceivable" for the FCC to "wear blinders to the undisputed evidence of [Paramount's] criminal and fraudulent misconduct." The charge included the company's past financial interest (up to 1983) in the RKO broadcast group, which was "full of miscreants." One reader of the brief said he got confused. "For a moment I thought it was about Ross and Warner, not about Davis and Paramount."

The brief personally attacked Paramount directors for their business conduct in other companies. It also made the farfetched conflict-of-interest charge that one Paramount employee was married to an executive of the Times Mirror Company, which was also in the cable business; another Paramount director was described as an officer of NYNEX, a company "under government investigation for fraudulently overcharging ratepayers." Time also brought up "antitrust violations" by Paramount, twelve years earlier.

Two can play that game, Paramount decided.

Ten days later it filed a counterclaim to a Time suit in Manhattan's U.S. District Court. It revived the Westchester Premier Theatre scandal, pointing out that "the assistant treasurer of Warner was found guilty of one count of racketeering, three counts of perjury and three counts of mail fraud and went to jail." (He did not. Sol Weiss's prison sentence was converted into community service.) The brief reminded the court that the criminal investigation "also led to the guilty pleas of another Warner executive and a Warner consultant, as well as the conviction of several organized crime figures." And it asked, What about the mysterious concealed "internal 663-page document known as the Armstrong Report"?

The brief questioned "the integrity" of Steve Ross in "Warner's Atari insider trading scandal." Even though the SEC had cleared him, Paramount charged that "Ross himself unloaded more than 60,000 shares" before the public knew about Atari's disaster, "receiving $1.4 million more than he would have made from a similar sale" had he waited.

Paramount also slammed Time for having "failed to disclose Ross's 'self-enrichment' package." Finally, it "faulted Time for imperiling its 'journalistic integrity' by going into business with a company which in the recent past has been the subject of criminal investigations, prosecutions and in some cases convictions."

Time called the Paramount charges "an act of desperation."

Paramount's second-in-command, Don Oresman, described by Davis as "the senior sage of the company," was in charge of Paramount's tactics. In Oresman's noncombat hours, he prefers reading the classics and poetry he keeps in his office filing cabinet or contemplating the bust of Henry James alongside his desk. But there was nothing Jamesian in his demeanor when he was called upon to slug it out. "We kept getting this dirty stuff," he explains, "and through Time's Cravath lawyers we couldn't get them to lay off. It was clearly coming from Time. So I said fuck 'em, let's go after them and maybe they will come to their senses."

The Paramount countersuit, he says, "was entirely designed to be a shot across their bow with not the slightest desire to hit anybody. Just to say, Hey, pay attention." Oresman says he was just seeking a truce. "After we filed our countersuit, I called Arthur Liman, with whom I had worked closely for seven years on the Bluhdorn case. I instigated a truce. I said, Arthur, this thing is ridiculous, and I read off to him a list of things, Kroll and the whole laundry list of the other crap. I said, Jesus Christ can't we end this? I don't have the slightest desire to find out anything about Steve Ross's past. We don't give a good goddamn about it. You've got to put an end to this thing." Liman instantly agreed. He says he called Cravath immediately. There were no more personal dirty tricks.

Liman confirms Oresman's account and says he added, "Look, Don, this case is going to be decided in a Delaware court and throwing mud at each other is not going to affect the outcome." Then Liman, who was trying an unrelated case in California at the time, immediately phoned Cravath managing partner Sam Butler, "and I then explained to Steve, who supported me." There were no more dirty tricks. "Yes, we're tough guys," admits Oresman, "but there are certain things—it's like playing chess by upsetting the chessboard, that's not a form of chess."

Steve Ross vows he had nothing to do with those moves and says he was told that Paramount shot the first personal foul. He was misinformed. Time did. "The rule in that kind of a battle for survival," says Levin, "is all's fair."

PARAMOUNT'S TENDER OFFER TO buy Time demolished the planned cashless tax-free and debt-free Time-Warner stock swap. The havoc Paramount's intervention wrought was financial, not managerial. The command structure in the new company was to remain the same as it had been under the original merger plan. But its financing was transformed.

To complete the new deal, the most crucial problem for Time became its stockholders. In corporate combinations where there are stock transfers rather than cash payments, the New York Stock Exchange (NYSE) rules require a stockholder vote. Cash deals most often do not. The original Time merger with Warner needed such stockholder approval—virtually a sure thing. But after Paramount barged in with a cash offer of $175 a share, Time's board knew its stockholders would jump at the instant profit of Paramount's cash-in-hand offer rather than Time Warner's long-term promises of even greater returns in the years ahead. "The merger proposal," shouted Paramount, "was doomed to be overwhelmingly rejected." As offensive as that prediction was to Time executives and board, they knew Paramount was right.

A high percentage of the company's shares was held by financial institutions and trusts, who see their role as making as much money as they can for their own investors. Also large blocks of Time stock immediately were snapped up by arbitragers ("arbs"), who earn their living by gambling on the rise and fall of stocks and other securities involved in exchange offers and takeovers. Neither group is much interested in elegant claims about a company's long-term possibilities or "independent journalism," or the "Time culture," or what one of Time's investment bankers called "the church-state cathedral." The institutions and arbs invest for money. The funds and arbs "don't buy stocks," said one banker, "they rent them." That seemed all right to Time's jilted old friend, Gannett's Al Neuharth. The Paramount offer, he wrote, was just "a bigger bag of lettuce."

Gordon Crawford was the senior vice president and a senior analyst at Los Angeles's Capital Group funds, Time's biggest institutional investor, owning 7 percent of the company's shares. Crawford was repeatedly quoted in the press saying such things as "I would rather be a long-term owner than cashed out [i.e, sell stock] of one of the world's most exciting companies at $175 a share." But SEC records told a different story. They showed that the investment funds Crawford advised at the Capital Group sold unobserved all but 18,000 of the 4.6 million shares of their Time holdings. The records also indicate they bought back their stake at lower prices and a profit before the first Time Warner annual meeting.

Crawford says that's not true. He argues they sold only 600,000 shares. "The SEC reports are wrong. We made a mistake in our filing when someone in our back shop picked up the wrong identification number. All during this period we are and have remained the largest stockholder in Time, Warner and now Time Warner. We make lots of filing mistakes with the SEC. If everybody believed everything that's filed with the SEC they'd be crazy. It's too late now to correct the records."

Ross was so enamored of the original merger and so convinced the stockholders would be making a mistake in voting against it that he suggested getting the NYSE to change its rules to make a stockholder vote unnecessary. Time disagreed but let Ross try anyway. He reached out to friends in Washington and Europe, looking for someone who knew the stock exchange president personally to try to get him to set in motion a change in the rules. The NYSE firmly said no.

The only way to avoid putting the deal to a stockholder vote was for Time to buy Warner outright rather than exchanging stock. In a ten-hour all-day meeting, after exhausting every other alternative, Time's board decided. It agreed to pay $70 a share for 100 million Warner shares—a total of $7 billion and fees. Warner was then selling for $55 a share on the open market. Another $6 billion or so payment for the rest of the shares was to be worked out later in a mix of preferred stock, bonds and possibly cash. The total cost of the acquisition was $14.9 billion including half a billion dollars in banking, financial and legal fees, plus other expenses, to pay off options and other forms of compensation.

Ross also demanded that the sale must be a "come-hell-or-high-water" contract with "no outs" for Time. This meant that no matter how much anyone else bid for Time, it would still have to buy Warner. Warner, on the other hand, could back out if a bid higher than Time's came along. Nicholas enthusiastically but unfortunately described it as being "strapped to a rocket that just left Cape Canaveral." On second thought he conceded his words were "inappropriate" and that the reason Time accepted being locked to Ross "was simply that we had to do it to persuade Warner to agree to put itself up for sale." To finance the deal, Time announced it had from banks much more than the $14 plus billion it would ultimately need. The total price, CBS News pointed out, just about equaled "the total U.S. foreign aid program in 1989."

The governing and management arrangements of the new agreement remained substantially the same as the original merger plan. The enormous changes were money.

Apart from the billions in debt, the most important revisions involved paying more than a billion dollars to Ross and Warner employees and stockholders, as well as potential millions in new stock options. Time Inc. employees got no cash, although its top trio of executives got new contracts and options that could bring them multimillions in capital and millions in income for the rest of their lives. The value of the stock that Time employees held dropped to almost one-third ($66) of its pre-merger high ($182). The mid-level Time Inc. employees and stockholders would have to wait for the "long term" to realize any financial benefits from the deal.

THE SUMS OF MONEY in the proposed new Time agreement to buy Warner were so large they almost seemed to the people at Time an abstraction—like the federal deficit. But the huge new compensation packages and cash payments to the senior executives of both Warner and Time were an awesome reality.

The University of California's Graef S. Crystal, a leading expert on executive pay and a *Fortune* contributor on the subject, called the managers' payments "The Marie Antoinette School of Management." *Newsday*'s financial columnist Allan Sloan said the deal was "too clever and gave too rich rewards for the managers," an "enrichment deal masquerading as a move to keep foreigners at bay."

The compensation contracts themselves were full of cosmetic masks. Salaries were made to look modest by adding to base pay mandatory bonuses in some cases of 100 percent or more, and discretionary bonuses of much more than that (e.g., Nicholas's salary in 1989 was $573,559, but his $1.4 million bonus made his cash compensation alone $1.9 million and rising). Various forms of option grants, deferred compensation, pension plans and incentive formulas made it impossible to say with assurance what the annual compensation really was. The so-called salary figure was merely the twine holding together packages of millions of dollars in add-ons. Many corporations engage in such hocus-pocus but few more elaborately than in the convolutions, mostly inherited from Warner, now integrated into the future Time Warner.

"We all wished," said one Time manager, "that those guys hadn't taken so much money. It was the unseemliness of that gap. It was a break in the family. Everything we want to do or want to spend on wouldn't buy Steve Ross's breakfast."

There were many non-Marxist reasons for the Time workers to complain about the gap between their pay and their bosses'. Under the new deal:

- Ross would receive a payout of $193 million, plus salary, at least 1.8 million shares of new options and long-term bonuses that could reach hundreds of millions more over the life of his fifteen-year contract. Compensation experts said it was the largest payout ever made to one executive in a public company. A Warner spokesman argued that Ross could actually make less from the changes in his contract which were "minor" and "technical." Ross made the mistake of saying that "everything is the same. Not one comma was changed" in his new contract compared to the old one. More than a comma was changed as it was explained to the Warner board in a "review" of all the revisions in the contract. "Probably in hindsight," Ross now says about "not one comma" being changed, "it was the wrong response, because it could be misunderstood." One big change was that Ross's bonus formula was shifted from being based on the percentage of the company's after-tax earnings to a percentage of its pretax. "He is worth every penny of it," said Munro. Ross himself is not a bit defensive about his take. "I haven't gotten more than the shareholders," he says. "I represented Warner stockholders, who got $14 billion. In my contract I was rewarded according to the stock and according to the earnings. So I don't think it needs defending and I'm just going to ignore it."

- Ross's services, his contract said, are "special, unique, unusual, extraordinary and intellectual in character." So, among other unusual benefits, his bonuses were to be paid quarterly. Munro and Nicholas, whose qualities were not described in their first contracts, were to collect their bonuses once a year, the way executives conventionally do. Ross's wife, Courtney, is also noted in the agreement, receiving a $250,000 fee for producing the movie *Listen Up*, which was a financial flop, despite a multimillion dollar advertising and promotion budget.

- Munro in 1989 took home $2,450,000 in salary and bonus, an increase of 61 percent over the year before. He also got a $7 million boost in his retirement contract. Other benefits yield him a lifetime annual income of more than $1 million. His stock and options could be worth $25 to $30 million or more. Munro says he could have made as much by selling out to Paramount. No way, answers Martin Davis. "Ten- and fifteen-year contracts on top of retirement? Unheard of. That would not have happened here."

- Nicholas's $1.9 million was a 46 percent increase over 1988. Over the life of his fifteen-year contract, he was guaranteed a minimum base pay of $16 million, but with bonuses and stock it was more likely to be worth more than $50 million, many times more, depending upon the performance of the stock and the good graces of the board.

- Levin got $1.8 million, a 50 percent boost over 1988, and was guaranteed not less than $12 million over fifteen years, with additional tens of millions in bonuses and stock.

- The biggest group windfall went to five hundred Warner executives and employees, who were paid in cash by Time in the new deal, bringing them more than $677 million, the largest payments ever made to employees after an acquisition. They were also given new options at $150 a share. Robert Morgado, a Warner executive vice president, who seven years earlier was making a government salary of $79,113 as secretary to New York governor Hugh Carey, collected $16 million. The company's chief financial officer, Bert Wasserman, got $20 million; its general counsel, Martin Payson, $20 million; and Deane Johnson, a director and officer for eight years, $20 million.

- Investor Herb Siegel came out fine as well. By then his original Chris-Craft $400 million stake in Warner had grown to $2.3 billion.

- Time employees got *no* cash payout for their stock. They would have to wait, have faith in the long-term growth of their holdings, and accept the fact that their stock had dropped to one-third its highest pre-merger value. "Warner stockholders made out beautifully in the deal," said a financial editor, "while Time shareholders got their heads handed to them."

- Three-year contracts for the most senior Time editors remained unchanged. Only at HBO were there substantial increases at the top.

- Advisory fees to Time's two main investment advisers, Wasserstein & Perella and Shearson Lehman, were $16 million each; Warner's fee to Felix Rohatyn's Lazard Frères, $20 million, and to Ed Aboodi's Alpine Capital, $8 million and a commitment to invest up to $150 million in a fund he ran. In the last month of the booming '80s decade, a *Fortune* survey of more than two hundred chief executives of America's largest companies asked, "Do you think investment bankers are putting more emphasis on deals and fees than on the long-term interests of their clients?" Answer: 95 percent yes; 5 percent no. Question: "Are they overpaid?" Answer: 95 percent yes; 5 percent no.

- Legal fees to nearly thirty law firms were more than $76 million, one of the largest payments to Time's Cravath ($14 million) and the same or more to Warner's main law firms, Arthur Liman's Paul, Weiss, and to Wachtell, Lipton. "Everybody was running around doing forty different things," says one senior lawyer. "Fee money isn't that important in a multibillion deal, depending on how you look at it."

- Financing fees and expenses to banks were $350 million. Another $29 million went to miscellaneous fees, making the total cost for services in working out the deal more than half a billion dollars.

- Pocket change: Each director on the combined board would be paid $60,000 a year, one of the highest director fees in the U.S., with $2,500 additional for every special meeting, $1,000 for every committee meeting not held at the same time as the board meeting, plus retirement benefits.

- Without a Warner merger, Time would have had a long-term debt of $1.6 billion. If the original merger had gone through, Time Warner's debt would have been $2.6 billion. Under the new deal forced by the Paramount offer, the total debt of Time Warner was $11.5 billion, averaging an interest commitment alone of more than $3 million a day. At the time, Nicholas said, with Reaganite optimism, "We're going to grow our way out of this debt."

- Rohatyn said that he could not be sure how the Time Warner stock would be valued in the future, "but the risk is primarily Time's," since the Warner employee stockholders were being paid in cash. And how does Rohatyn, the most vocal critic of the high leverage of the '80s, reconcile his enthusiasm for this deal with his other views? Easily. "I was representing the Warner stockholders," he says.

- The $70-a-share price turned out to be a 55 percent rise for Warner stockholders over the $45 their stock was worth before the first merger announcement. The Time Inc. stockholders got nothing, unless they had sold their stock during the merger negotiations.

Who came out ahead was all "scorekeeping," "a collection of trivia," say the Time executives and their board members. "This merger was a lot bigger than Steve Ross and anybody else," insists Munro. "The grandeur of putting these two enormously successful, prestigious companies together overshadowed the personalities."

"Are we selling the company?" Beverly Sills asked sentimentally at the Warner board meeting approving the sale. "Yes," said Liman in a distinctly different tone of voice, "at $70 a share."

While Warner board members were enthusiastic about the deal, there was also, said one of them, "a certain sadness in the room." Like old-Timers, Warner founding directors emeritus Jacob Liebo-witz and Ross's former father-in-law Eddie Rosenthal both said wist-fully, "Things will never be the same again." And a Warner switchboard operator, who later was told she would soon have to start answering "Time Warner," explained, "It will be hard to re-member after you've been answering 'Warner' for so many years."

When the sums of money became public in SEC filings, the Time staff and alumni, as well as the press in general, were astonished. Up on one bulletin board in the Time & Life Building went a cartoon. It showed a satisfied boss at his desk saying, "I got mine—and yours too." Someone had labeled him "Ross."

MONEY ASIDE, MUNRO AND Nicholas assured the staff in an-other memo: "The human values make this company so special. We will never stop aggressively trying to preserve them." Aggressive they were, escalating the fight on other fronts.

Time filed another complaint in Washington, making a claim rare if not unique in American constitutional history. It charged that Paramount, with its takeover bid, created the need for such huge debt that it was "threatening the First Amendment rights of Time journalism." That kind of claim was later turned down by every court, including the U.S. Supreme Court when the company stretched the First Amendment even further by suing the tiny town of Niceville, Florida, of all places, for trying to start a cable system to compete with Warner Cable.

Ross and Munro headed for Washington again for another reason, a first showing of *Batman,* Warner's record-breaking hit film, the first movie, Munro seriously says, he had seen in ten years. After a "theme" party in the bat cave of the National Zoo, where Vice President Dan Quayle greeted them, a drawn and haggard Munro stopped in at Time's Washington bureau. Earlier in the week he had suffered the indignity of being booed in the Time cafeteria when he dropped in for lunch. Those who saw and talked with him were worried about the strain he seemed to be under and concerned that "he was so embattled maybe he couldn't handle things."

There was cause for concern. Munro was under punishing stress. At one of the daily early morning meetings held in Nicholas's small conference room, there was a discussion of what to do about former Time directors who were critics of the deal, especially Arthur Temple. Munro interjected, "We've heard from everybody. We haven't heard from Shepley. It's not like Jim not to weigh in." The room fell silent, until someone reminded Munro he had delivered the eulogy at Shepley's funeral the year before. Munro banged his head in consternation.

chapter 13

In the Kingdom of Delaware

THEN, AS EXPECTED, PARAMOUNT upped its bid—to
$200 a share. Time's board rejected it without a blink. Para-
mount headed for a courthouse in Delaware where the battle
would be joined. "If the Delaware court comes out against us," a
worried Munro said, "then God help us."

Why a Delaware court?

Bobbing on moorings or at anchor, dockside or cruising the water-
ways of the world, are more than 40,000 American yachts with the
words "Dover, Del." inscribed on their transoms. Few of them have
ever been even close to that inland capital city (population 33,000)
of tiny Delaware. The boats' owners call Dover their home and
registered in that state for the same reason that more than 160,000
American corporations do, including Time, Warner and Paramount.
They all seek the safe harbor of the state's simplified incorporation
laws and its court system. What Reno used to be to easy divorce,
Delaware is to incorporation. "Incorporate While You Wait" could
be the state's motto. Delaware's governor and secretary of state
solicit the business with an elaborate full-color brochure urging companies to "take a closer look and discover why Delaware is known
as the 'Corporation Capital of the World.' "

Corporate law became the state's second-largest revenue source
after New Jersey Governor Woodrow Wilson (later President Wilson) outlawed trusts. Also changed were the state's procedures for
corporations that had incorporated there before the 1920s to avoid
just such constraints elsewhere. When the companies fled New Jersey, Delaware picked up the lucrative business. Its rules protected
directors against liability complaints, letting companies exercise their

business judgment, and imposed on them minimal fees and taxes. Disputes were settled in Delaware's Chancery Court, where judgments of fairness rather than strict rules of law govern the outcome.

In the U.S., chancery courts as such are a rarity except in what some lawyers call the "Kingdom of Delaware." Chancery springs from the old British tradition of *equity,* correcting injustices more informally and swiftly than other courts can. "Equity," wrote a seventeenth-century jurist, "is a roguish thing. For the law we have a measure and know what to trust; equity is according to the conscience of him that is Chancellor. One Chancellor has a long foot, another a short foot, a third an indifferent foot. 'Tis the same thing in the Chancellor's conscience."

Delaware Chancellor William T. Allen, forty-four, who was to hear the case of *Paramount* v. *Time et al.,* often carries a cane and does himself indeed have lopsided feet. They are the result of replacements in both legs of arthritic hips. But there is nothing hobbled about his reputation for intellect and jurisprudence or his fondness for the classical music that floods his peaceful chambers. A New York University graduate ('69) with a law degree from the University of Texas ('72), Chancellor Allen is a studious jurist with lightly rimmed spectacles, a Guardsman's brush mustache and a shirt collar secured by a gold pin. He is the chief judge of Delaware's five-judge Court of Chancery, which during the high-rolling '80s heard hundreds of takeover cases. The chancellors, who earn between $82,000 and $90,000 a year, "hold sway over trillions of dollars of corporate assets," says legal takeover specialist Martin Lipton, "and their decisions are helping to reshape the U.S. economy."

Allen would have to decide whether to accept Paramount's assertion that the shareholders of Time should be allowed to determine the company's fate. Or Time's claim that its board was building long-term value and was not required to expose its new Warner acquisition plan to stockholders' hunger for instant cash gratification. Time was encouraged by one Allen decision in which he had written, "A corporation is not a town meeting. Directors, not shareholders, have responsibilities to manage the affairs of the corporation."

Nonetheless, the outcome of the Paramount-Time case was far from certain. It was more of a toss-up. In a series of other decisions, Allen and the Delaware Supreme Court had swung back and forth, deciding in several big cases in favor of management, then swinging their gavels the other way in favor of the stockholders. For Paramount v. Time, Allen had only conflicting precedents to rely on.

At one prominent New York law firm not involved in the case, all thirty corporate partners polled on the eve of the hearing guessed that Allen would decide in favor of Paramount. At another well-known firm the partners argued the case among themselves and overwhelmingly decided in favor of Time.

DELAWARE'S MODERN COURT OF Chancery Building over-looks Wilmington's Rodney Square, a carefully tended, peaceful park enriched by colorful flower beds and—astride a galloping horse—the bold bronze figure of Caesar Rodney, Delaware's signer of the Declaration of Independence. The site's long history records only one indecorous moment. When the equestrian statue was un-veiled, a commissioner exclaimed to aghast onlookers, "Why the goddamned horse has got no arse-hole! Never seen a horse without an arse-hole." (The defect was remedied.)

Early in the morning of July 11, 1989, with the temperature pushing 100, there was a wild contretemps on the edge of the green. By 9:30 A.M., more than three hundred lawyers, arbs, corporate executives, press agents, TV producers and reporters were swarming the doors of the Chancery Court. The sweating crowd jostled for position, laden with cellular phones, laptop computers, electronic pagers, bag carriers and hired "minders" to guard their gear outside while the court was in session. "It looks as if the Rolling Stones are having a concert," one amazed security officer said, blocking the locked court-house doors. "Easy," he warned, "we're not going to have a soccer riot here."

Wilmington, a dignified city dominated by the Du Pont Company, had never witnessed such a scene. Few of its local residents knew what brought the swarm to their city. Although the case was front-page news elsewhere, it was routine to the local Wilmington *News-Journal*. The paper carried only a one-line calendar note mistakenly calling the case "Paramount v. Dunkin' Donuts"—another dispute at the busy chancery bar but not involving Paramount.

At 10:10 A.M. in the jammed paneled courtroom, with an overflow of reporters and spectators stretched out in the aisles and on the floor, a bell clanged. The bailiff chanted, "Hear ye, hear ye, all rise." Chancellor Allen limped through the door and slid into his red leather swivel chair.

. . .

AS IN MOST APPEALS courts, the real meat in Delaware's Chancery Court is in briefs served up in advance; the arguments by lawyers in court are garnishment. There are no witnesses, no cross-examination, no jury, only documents—and the less rhetoric by the lawyers the better. For the Paramount-Time case, a *Burke's Peerage* of eleven tony law firms made appearances.

"Litigation lawyers," Allen wryly remarked at one point, "have a Marine Corps mentality." Not in his court. None of them trifled with the relatively young, impassive Allen. When Warner's lawyer Herbert M. Wachtell (Wachtell Lipton) said with a flourish, "Think about it, your honor," Allen quietly put him down with "I'll try." Or when Time's Bob Joffe (Cravath) momentarily strayed off the main line of his case, Allen quietly said, "I don't think this is worth the time." Joffe nodded. "If you don't think so, I don't think so." When a lawyer mentioned Herb Siegel's name, Allen needed no further guidance. He slightly smiled and said knowingly, "He's had several applications here."

A Warner lawyer, Charles F. Richards, Jr. (Richards, Layton & Finger), referred to "sloganeering" by Paramount. Allen brought him up sharply with "I hadn't noticed any sloganeering." Paramount's Melvyn L. Cantor (Simpson Thacher) addressed Allen as "Judge," quickly correcting himself by apologizing, "Chancellor, I'm sorry, I've been told never to call you 'judge.' "

Cantor argued in person and in briefs that Time's claim of a special culture was "an apple-pie argument" having nothing to do with shareholder value. Only part of the company was in magazines, including what was sarcastically called "the majestic swim-suit issue of *Sports Illustrated.*" He disparaged all the preening about *Time,* since Munro himself had said that *People* and *Sports Illustrated* were the "huge engines that drive" the magazine division. Anyway, by the terms of the merger proposal, control of Time would pass to Warner with "breathtaking compensation packages for senior Time and Warner executives." When it made the deal with Warner, his argument went, Time clearly "put itself up for sale" to the highest bidder.

By refusing to submit their deal to a stockholder vote, Paramount claimed, "Time's board has taken away all voting rights from stockholders." The court should stop Time and its management from usurping the stockholders' rights to decide. Because Ross had insisted to Time that it buy Warner "come hell or high water," the deal was a "doomsday machine," a "vicious example of its scorched earth policy at the expense of its shareholders." For Paramount, Cantor also pointed out that in two years of negotiations between Time and Warner, the most "intensely negotiated points had to do with pay for executives and succession," not the financial interests of the disenfranchised stockholders. Let them vote, he argued, and see whether they wanted the Warner buy-out or the richer Paramount offer.

Time's Joffe replied that the Time board members knew what they were doing, had the long-term interests of the company and its stockholders uppermost in their concerns. He read a *Who's Who* of Time's business-establishment outside directors. (The court reporter got every name right, except the best known, Luce, referring to the founder's son as "Hank Lewis.") "These are not careless people," he said, "not patsies for management." Paramount was a "low-ball bidder," not getting close to the real value of Time's assets. He charged that Davis had made no plans or estimates, did not even consider how the business would be run if he took over Time. The company should be allowed to continue planning its future thoughtfully, not be subject to quick stockholder profit-taking. In the long run, he said, everybody would benefit.

Joffe charged that Paramount had "mounted a monumental campaign of disinformation and public confusion," saying that Time's offer for Warner was "the culmination of a responsible two-year-long planning process." He conceded that Time and Warner's business together did depend on different cultures. "To put it in colloquial terms, as did one of our directors," said Joffe, "show-biz people cannot be treated as button-down types and journalists are not satisfied with an artsy-craftsy atmosphere."

Michael R. Klein (Wilmer, Cutler & Pickering), a lawyer representing a large stockholder, took the podium to knock Time Warner's prediction of great future growth in the stock's value as "a wish and a promise enhancement."

At 3:24 P.M. (after a one-hour lunch break) Allen adjourned the hearing, promising a ruling by the weekend, three days away. On the courthouse steps, TV reporters peppered the lawyers with questions. What did they think? Who came out ahead? What would Allen rule? The answers were evasive, not just out of deference to the court. None of the lawyers, reporters or court buffs had any firm conviction about which way the gavel would fall.

. . .

IN NEW YORK, ALL morning the Time hierarchs, who had been advised not to go to Wilmington, sat by the phones, getting reports from staffers on cellulars in the lobby of the court. In the Warner Building, Steve Ross fidgeted in his office, taking similar phone calls while tense aides streamed in and out. Ross was straining to get away. In his office were Beverly Sills, impatiently waiting, suitcase by her side; Ross's assistant, Carmen Ferragano; and his constant shadow, bodyguard Tony Battista, who "looks like a hood and behaves like a pussycat," said one of his many fans. Crosstown a Warner helicopter was standing by to take them to one of Warner's jets for a trip to Paris

"Our emotions," recalls Levin, "were tied to the nature of the reports. We had been going up and down as the briefs came in. The form of the company's existence was now going to be controlled in court. It all came down to what one chancellor was going to say." They would have to wait three days to find out.

Steve Ross spent his waiting time in Paris, after arriving overnight. He was handsomely installed in his Paris headquarters, the Ritz Hotel's Imperial Suite, as grand as any in the world, overlooking the Place Vendôme. Business was only a partial reason for his trip. Ross had front-rank seats for himself, his family and friends to witness the not-to-be missed hyperspectacular celebration of the 200th anniversary of the French Revolution two days later on Bastille Day, July 14, 1989.

But first he gave a private party for twenty at Maxim's and paid visits to Paris businessmen, accompanied by French-speaking Beverly Sills. Ross had instructed her to begin each sentence cautiously in French with, "Pending the merger," until finally an amused Parisian said to her, "It's not necessary to keep repeating that. I understand."

On July 14—Bicentennial Bastille Day—Sills cut out with fellow Warner director Bill vanden Heuvel and his daughter for the young woman's twenty-first birthday party. It was a lunch at the apartment of ABC correspondent and former Kennedy press secretary Pierre Salinger and his wife. Also at the Salingers' were Jacqueline Onassis and her financier friend Maurice Tempelsman. Back at the Ritz, Ross slept late, stayed in the suite with his wife, Courtney, who had joined him after a brief vacation with their daughter in Europe.

In the Time & Life Building in New York, the atmosphere was tense and subdued. Munro distracted himself and joined in France's historic celebration in his own way while awaiting Chancellor Allen's decision. He dipped into *Citizens,* Simon Schama's chronicle of the French Revolution that was Time Inc.'s Book-of-the-Month Club selection for August.

By 11 A.M., a large group of thirty-fourth-floor executives gathered in Levin's office, crowding around his speakerphone. Suddenly Levin's secretary announced, "Mr. Joffe's on the phone." Levin pressed the speaker button. "Bob?" "We won!" shouted Joffe.

The group shook their fists in the air and broke into a cheer so loud that it echoed down the hallway. "It was one of the very few times," Levin remembers, "that I had a rush of emotion for a few seconds. We could tell when we began to hear the decision that it was a home run." Nicholas said, "It's good to be told you're right. Sometimes you worry that you may be deluding yourself." And Munro shook his head as he left the room wondering, "Why did I worry so much?"

When Ross got the word by phone a little after 5 P.M. Paris time, his assistant, Carmen Ferragano, summoned Sills and vanden Heuvel to Ross's suite. Elated, Ross gave them the good news. There was no need for a special celebration. That night, amidst an extravaganza of televised fireworks and pageantry, with all of France roaring "La Marseillaise," Ross and his group watched from VIP seats of honor, followed by a huge festive official dinner across the Place de la Concorde at the Hotel Crillon.

Now there was only one final obstacle to hurdle, Paramount's anticipated appeal of Allen's decision to the Delaware Supreme Court. Its final judgment was still ten days away.

TO TIME, WARNER AND even Paramount, Allen's written decision seemed unlikely to be reversed. His seventy-nine-page opinion, handed down so quickly after the hearings, had obviously been drafted more from the briefs than from any oral arguments heard in his court.

He assumed that since institutions and arbs, not individuals, held most of the Time stock, "It is reasonable to suppose that most such money managers would be tempted by the cash now." However,

> While some shareholders, even a majority, may disagree with the wisdom [of the Time board's] choice, that fact provides no reason for this court to force them to take another, more popular course of action. The long-term strategic plan of the Time-

the Kingdom of Delaware

Warner consolidations is plainly a most important corporate policy. Reasonable persons can and do disagree as to whether it is a better course from the shareholders' point of view collectively to cash out their stake in the company now at this (or a higher) premium cash price. However, there is no persuasive evidence that the board of Time has a corrupt or venal motivation in electing to continue with its long-term plan.

At the heart of his argument was the Time journalistic "culture," which, he pointed out, Paramount argued was "nothing more than a desire to perpetuate or entrench existing management disguised in a pompous, highfalutin claim." He understood, said Allen, "the risk of cheap deception." But,

There may be at work here forces more subtle than a desire to maintain a title or office in order to assure continued salary or perquisites. The mission of the firm is not seen by those involved as wholly economic. Time's traditional business of the publication of magazines, most notably *Time* magazine, but also numerous others, had developed a unique structure in which the editor-in-chief reports directly to a special committee of the board in order to protect the "culture," the first, and central requirement.

Editor-in-chief Jason McManus later reversed the view he had expressed in his own affidavit where he said he didn't need a contract in the merger agreement. After the decision, he changed his mind. "It's quite clear now," says McManus, "that we would have had a stronger case—despite the fact that we won it—on the editorial front if I had been given the same kind of contract" as the non-editorial executives, whose contracts, binding on the board, were part of the merger agreement.

In Allen's court, as well as in other venues, an easy target for bashing was Time's investment banker, Bruce Wasserstein. His firm's projections of what would happen to Time Warner stock after the merger ranged from a low of $133 (the low actually turned out to be $66) to a high of $402 in 1993—a range, Allen quipped, "that a Texan might feel at home on."

He noted that Ross's contract was "munificent" and that "Munro's compensation enjoyed a $7 million increase over ten years."

But he had no reason to believe that "self-enrichment" or "management entrenchment" was their principal motivation. Nor was it his job to "try to evaluate whether Mr. Ross and his negotiator, Mr. Aboodi, out-negotiated Time's Mr. Levin and Mr. Nicholas."

Approvingly, he noted that Gordon Crawford, a senior analyst at Los Angeles's Capital Group funds, the largest single stockholder in both Time and Warner (7 percent of each company), said in an affidavit that the "proposed Time-Warner combination is superior for Time shareholders to the $200 per share Paramount cash offer." (Allen did not know that at the same time Capital was invisibly selling hundreds of thousands of Time shares at a handsome profit.)

> The Time board may be proved to have been brilliantly prescient or dismayingly wrong. The shareholders will bear the effects for good or ill. That many, presumably most, shareholders would prefer the board to do otherwise than it has done does not, in the circumstance of a challenge to this type of transaction, afford a basis to interfere with the board's *business judgment*. The [Paramount] action will be denied. IT IS SO ORDERED.

With all that good news, six days later Steve Ross at last met for the first time with the outside directors of Time. He stopped over at the Time & Life Building (his third visit ever) for lunch with the Time directors after their last board meeting as Time Inc. Four of the outside directors left before lunch. To the remaining four, their new chairman-to-be was a complete stranger but certainly well met. It was all chitchat, with Ross beaming, nothing of any consequence. Altogether they found him a "very engaging guy." Ross "was charming," one of them recalls, "tall—taller than I thought he was and very talkative, smiling a lot. It went very, very comfortably."

AND SO DID ANOTHER milestone event the week following.

On July 24, for the first time in its history, the Delaware Supreme Court allowed its proceedings to be televised (by CNN)—the first takeover battle ever to be on TV. From the outset the three-judge court made it obvious what their decision would be. Time's Bob Joffe read his plea, explaining that there was too much stockholder confusion for the Time directors to risk a vote. The justices let him present his argument. When Paramount lawyers tried to argue their side, they barely got in a word, interrupted by a skeptical barrage of questions from the justices. "How many times," crusty Justice G. T. ("Get Tough") Moore asked with unconcealed exasperation at the Paramount argument, "does this court have to speak on this question?"

After two hours, the justices adjourned at noon. By 2 P.M. they returned with their unanimous ruling: "We find no error of law by the Court of Chancery. We further find the facts as found by the Chancellor to be fully supported by the record. Therefore we affirm the decision."

Again the Timeincers had gathered in that thirty-fourth-floor War Room, their eyes fixed on the TV screen. But at the exact moment the verdict was pronounced, CNN's sound went dead. What they saw at first but could not hear was the Paramount lawyers shaking hands with each other. "Jesus," said one of the Time group, "maybe we lost."

Confusion, disbelief and some snapping at each other filled the room, until the sound came back and they knew the real verdict. Another cheer—then it became all work. By 4 P.M., Paramount withdrew its offer. At 5:01, a thoroughly prepared Time completed its $70-a-share buy of 100 million Warner shares, 59 percent of the company, by taking on $8.3 billion in debt. The remaining $6 billion for Warner shareholders would come in the next step, the so-called back end. Whether it would be all cash or various forms of stock ("paper") or a mixture of the two would be decided sometime later— heatedly, it turned out.

Levin promptly instructed the Time Inc. receptionist to begin answering the phone, "Time Warner."

BEFORE THE MERGER could be formally completed on January 10, 1990, both companies needed to work out a formula for the remaining billions that would go to Warner stockholders in the back end of the deal. Time's bankers, led by Wasserstein, Perella, persuaded Time to buy *all* Warner shares for borrowed cash, even though Ross had the right to insist on only half in cash. "Wasserella" argued that taking on even more debt was good for the company, the fashionable '80s view that high leverage led to a high stock price.

But Ross insisted on a two-step transaction to avoid such a large debt burden. The second step in the payout would be made up of $6 billion in various kinds of preferred stock. After what one participant called a "knockdown battle," Ross got his way. "How do you change Steve's mind?" someone asked. "In his zone of interest," replied a Time executive, "you don't." Ross, says Levin, "has more experience and facility with capital structures than any single person at Time, Nick included, so he was probably entitled to more regard in that area."

One Warner advocate put it differently: "Steve started to think and act like the leader of the combined enterprise, not as a representative of Warner. In my experience, I've never been in a situation where a boss was saying don't give us that much cash because we'll bankrupt the company. The Time group was so wrong. If you look at the company now trying to deal with the debt that it has, it would have been a disaster. The company would be in Chapter 11 today."

THE CHANCERY COURT HEARINGS had produced bales of documents and depositions, including questions about Steve Ross's past.

"Cover-up" is a harsh term, meaning that someone deliberately hid what was known to be damaging or critical information that should have been revealed. There is no evidence that the Time executives *covered up* Ross's or Warner's past record. They simply avoided serious inquiry into it. As a result, by their own account, they chose not to inform their board, their employees or the public about those events of which they themselves had no detailed knowledge. As it happened, they were abetted, in at least one surprising incident, by their law firm Cravath, Swaine & Moore.

In commercial litigation, lawyers often ask that the record be sealed—to be kept "confidential" or "restricted" in its distribution. Judges seldom permanently grant the request, except to remove "proprietary" information which would give competitors valuable commercial knowledge. In the idiom of the law, such omissions are called "redacting" parts of a court record (or "editing," in its Latin origin). Time and Warner lawyers repeatedly requested that large chunks of the record be redacted.

When the New York *Times* sent a brief demanding the record be opened, the lawyers decided not to fight, knowing they would almost surely lose. Of the entire 10,000-page record of depositions from Time and Warner executives, the judges ordered only *two* pages redacted or sealed (both contained inconsequential financial and valuation data, which got out anyway).

But when this reporter requested and bought copies from Cravath of the depositions given by Time and Warner executives, whole sections had been removed. The missing pages had common characteristics. All reference to Ross's Westchester Theatre, Atari, SEC and franchising experiences, plus loose talk about the Mafia, were missing. When the fact that the depositions were incomplete was pointed out to Cravath's Bob Joffe, he readily acknowledged that a "mistake" had been made and offered corrected copies (without charge). The second set that Cravath sent still had expurgated pages on those subjects. A third effort produced the full depositions, which this reporter had already acquired from the court.

How does Joffe explain the same "mistake" happening twice? "I really didn't know the details of Steve Ross's affairs," says Joffe. "I knew that the other side was trying to paint Ross as unfit in the deposition questions. By the time we had gotten through the Chancery Court, there must have been three or four different versions of each deposition. The paralegals sent you the wrong set—one of the earlier versions. What was expurgated didn't prove anything or add to the weight of the argument. To suggest that the pages that were left out were part of a cover-up, I really think is offbase."

Since the expurgated passages could be found elsewhere, Joffe's explanation appears plausible. But plausible or not, at many points in the testimony an effort was obviously made to keep Ross's past out of the record. In providing documents, law firms are not supposed to make the mistake of withholding such information. In a courtroom it can be grounds for contempt of court or a mistrial. This reporter's request was not a trial, only a request for public information. "We were very pressed," says Joffe, "the confidentiality order was a nightmare." Cravath's top man Sam Butler adds that "it had to be a paralegal's mistake. Bob called me and said, 'I really screwed up.'"

THE NARROWLY FOCUSED VICTORY for Time in Delaware brought into wide-angle view a debate as fundamental to the governing of business as interpretations of the American Constitution are to the governing of the U.S.

There were two questions, one easily answered, the second blurry. The first was Who owns public companies? Undeniably, the stockholders do. The second was Who controls public companies? Is it the stockholder owners or their representatives, the board of directors and management? In government, when those interests clash—

the power of the people versus the power of the government—the Supreme Court ultimately decides. In business, since most large companies are "Delaware corporations," the final arbiter is the Delaware Chancery Court. Chancellor Allen's decision brought moans of protest that he had wrested the power of the people (the stockholders) from their rightful hands and turned it over to self-interested, greedy executives and arrogant directors.

Not individuals directly, but a herd of financial institutions—pension funds, insurance companies, mutual funds, et al.—own between 60 percent and 70 percent of the stock in American public corporations. They insist that their rightful role in the capitalist enterprise system is to force managements and boards to give them—the owners—the biggest possible return on their investment. The financial institutions that invest on behalf of pension funds, individuals and trusts say they have more than that right. They have a legal *duty* to get the most for their investors' money. The law calls it "fiduciary duty," defined in *Fortune* by investment banker Peter Róna, head of the Schroder Bank & Trust:

> The hell with profits, return on assets, productivity—what matters is profits of shareholders, share prices. Management's duty is not to enhance the value of the resources employed, but to enhance shareholder value. This doctrine requires the board to subordinate the conflicting duty to everybody else—bondholders, labor, research and development, the environment, and sadly, the nation. That's why in less than two decades we have lost our ability to compete.

But if a company like Paramount was willing to pay $200 or more for the Time shareholders' stock, worth much less in the market, why shouldn't the shareholders be allowed the vote on whether to take their profit or not? They took the risk when they invested, shouldn't they be entitled to take their reward? The Delaware court's answer was sometimes they should and sometimes they shouldn't.

In the Paramount-Time case, Allen invoked a concept known as "the business judgment rule." It meant that 1) if a management and board could demonstrate a thoughtful business plan that offered reasonable hope of increasing the future value of the company beyond a raider's instant premium price, and 2) if the company could demonstrate that its plan was not merely intended to enrich the management or enable them to hold on to their jobs, then they had a right to pursue their long-term goal. Time had that right in this case, Allen ruled, whether the stockholders agreed or not. "It was," said one disparager of his decision, "a father knows best" attitude. "You kids, you shareholders don't know what's good for you."

In fact, Allen had decided, as most judges try to do, only the case before him. He had made no new fundamental law. Each future similar case would have to be decided on its own merits.

Whichever way one leaned, by the time Time and Warner came together the whole system that had made the Time Warner deal possible was in an uproar.

Massive mergers, tender offers, debt financing, LBO's, growth by takeover, expansions followed by meltdowns, suddenly went out of fashion. The Time Warner creation would be recorded in the history books not only as the biggest media combination ever, but as the last such highly leveraged deal of its kind in the booming '80s. It was completed exactly twenty-nine days before new federal banking guidelines slammed the door on banks lending to companies with too much debt. (RJR Nabisco and Time Warner were two companies with the biggest highly leveraged bank loans.)

Fresh to the new game, the leaders of Time Warner overnight heard a mounting national chorus of gloom, doom and foreboding about debt, junk bonds and corporate behavior in the '80s. The period had been at once a glittering and barren decade, full of transient Masters of the Universe and bonfires of vanities. When the financial journalist Robert Lenzner asked a prominent retired investment banker if he might see the banker's letters for a possible biography, the reply was "What letters? All I have is confirmation slips." Howard Stein, chairman of the Dreyfus Corporation, knew what he meant. "This new god—the maximization of shareholder value," said Stein, "I don't know how we can get it to end until it's run its course. You don't get rid of a god until the god crashes."

And crash it did, just as Ross and Munro signed the formal wedding papers. Standard & Poor's and Moody's, the two official rating agencies, had already reclassified the new Time Warner bonds. It was a new experience for top-rated Time. "It's official: Time Warner Inc. is a 'junk bond' company," the *Wall Street Journal* reported. The new Time Warner stock was headed for a low ($66), close to one-third of its pumped-up-by-Paramount high ($182). The timing of the merger couldn't have been worse.

. . .

SIGNS OF AN APOCALYPTIC transformation of the financial climate were everywhere.

Bruce Wasserstein, Time's principal financial adviser, who urged his clients to "dare to be great," saw many of his deals plunge into disrepair, bankruptcy or misery. Most notable was Robert Campeau's $7 billion acquisition of Allied/Federated department stores (Abraham & Straus, Bloomingdale's, Bullock's, Burdine's, Filene's, Foley's, I. Magnin, Lazarus, Rich's). After paying investment banking fees of $350 million for helping him borrow money to take over the stores, Campeau quickly went into bankruptcy. As was the case with Time, Federated's directors had never met Campeau, who, they might have discovered, had a history of manic depression and visibly erratic behavior for most of his adult business life. "The idea," said Wasserstein, in a familiar refrain, "was to get the deal done." (Wasserstein egged Campeau on with the help of Cravath lawyer Allen Finkelson, the same senior duo that had advised Time.)

Donald Trump, who bought the Eastern Airlines shuttle, in part with his gains from speculating in Time stock, had to hock it to its tail fins in order to cover his mounting debts. Eastern itself later folded its historic wings altogether, admitting it had trimmed on safety maintenance to pay its debts. Trump was in such financial trouble that he was forced to sell and further mortgage his properties, get rid of his personal airplanes, his yacht and was put on a living allowance by the same lenders who had bankrolled his whirling excesses. On Trump's financial and marital troubles, columnist William Safire chortled, "Donald Trump, the nation's most celebrated deal artist, is working on a leveraged throwout of his wife, who betrayed his trust by turning 40."

Not only had a string of criminal scandals rocked the investment world, but the apostle of junk bonds, Michael Milken, was indicted and then sentenced to ten years in jail for fraud and stock manipulation. Among scores of deals that Milken bragged about, before they went sour, was newspaper entrepreneur Ralph Ingersoll II's freewheeling acquisitions and expansion. Ingersoll had to abandon his leveraged new empire, which later filed for bankruptcy. Ingersoll himself moved to Europe, where he set himself up for new deals in England. Another ironic sign of the new times was seeing the same banking houses that had fueled the '80s investment fires turn right around and stoke up another high-fee business—disinvestment strategy. "De-leveraging," they called it, in another new accommodating term.

In the months before Milken went to jail, he said, "I am a great admirer of Steve Ross. He's one of the twenty best chief executives in the country. Steve's biggest challenge for Time Warner is managing their debt correctly." Ross returned the compliment (Arthur Liman was one of Milken's leading lawyers *too*). In a letter to Milken's sentencing judge, Ross wrote, "Michael has been not just a financial and strategic adviser but, more important, a close friend whose social philosophy about the obligations of corporations to the community are parallel to my own. He is being falsely blamed for virtually every ill in our society."

One substantial estimate was that by the end of 1989, more than 70 percent of the earnings of U.S. companies went to paying interest on their debt. The biggest symbol of the changing times was Drexel Burnham, the major investment bank where Milken was the hyperstar. It was forced to declare bankruptcy, adding outrage to the shock by paying its princes multimillion-dollar bonuses on their way out the door. "To me it was very simple," said one money manager. "The Drexel era, the junk-bond era, the leveraged buy-out era is over."

To *Fortune* writer Louis Kraar, "The '80s were over when Drexel filed for bankruptcy and the Trumps filed for divorce."

"NOT MANY PEOPLE KNEW," says Jerry Levin, "that it was going to be the tail end of the period where leverage was good and a lot of leverage was very good. That was the advice we were getting."

More than five hundred Warner employee-stockholders and retirees were happily banking their $677 million in new cash riches and many were getting new stock options. With the bottom falling out of Time Warner stock, one senior Time executive said, "I find this very frustrating. I don't like getting in the elevator with someone from Time when they have their life savings there and the stock is under $100. It bothers the hell out of me. And the letters we get, you had a $200 offer and now the stock is at $100. I find that a very unfortunate set of circumstances. You feel a responsibility for your shareholders and mostly your employees. But we know we're just living through a period. We also know that one of the skills of this combined management—and Steve is particularly gifted at this— what we'll call any future recapitalization of the company—will be more inventive than any other company could possibly do."

Nicholas dealt with the morale problem by reassurances that in the long run Time's employee-stockholders would benefit far more than if they had cashed out. "It is better for the Time shareholders," he said, "because it has much more upside under this deal than they had under the original. But there's more risk. Some members of the board who haven't been business people have a hard time because of their own experiences, which is not dealing with reality. The next four or five years are going to have enormous opportunities for us. Yes, I want to have CNN. There are a number of trophy Tiffany things that fit into our global image of ourselves. I want to run away from the pack—our company is so clearly the leader, the most influential, the most profitable, the most respected. A few more pieces are missing. We know what we want to do. That's what strategy is all about. There are Nervous Nellies around. But we're confident." The hope fell on skeptical ears.

The financial world and business press didn't share his confidence. "It's amazing," wrote one investment banker, "the Time Warner executives appear to be the only ones not concerned with their debt. Only a few months ago buy recommendations spewed across Wall Street. Now the pendulum has swung in the other direction, and the stock is viewed with the disdain normally accorded to a skunk walking into a church social." A financial columnist wrote, "The market, which has developed a severe allergy to highly leveraged companies, is treating the world's largest media conglomerate as a leper."

The Time Warner executives were concerned all right but at first there was not much they could do about it. Nicholas explained why. "In this market, selling any kind of assets you don't get what they're worth. First of all, we're not going to sell magazines. Cable assets, the banks won't lend a traditional loan on real value right now. I'm not going to take the haircut. Minority partners right now are not going to pay what the assets are worth. We've got great cash flow, great management, but no way am I going to make a short-term stupid move. Liquidity will return to the financial markets as surely as the groundhog is going to come up. Right now there are certain things—the Pacific rim, Europe. There will be windows of opportunity that we will jump through. Why is the only cheer we seem to be getting from Wall Street the Bronx cheer?"

A different cheer came from one expectable quarter. With the stock hovering around the miserable high $60s, Mike Dingman, chairman of the board's finance committee, who was having trouble keeping his own overleveraged Henley Group going, predicted, "Time Warner is positioned. They've got years because they're running a good company. It's going to be one of those turnarounds in history that just surprises the hell out of people."

THE ORIGINAL MERGER, BEFORE Paramount upset it, had been debt-free. When it had to be changed to a cash transaction, Time's investment bankers convinced the board—and amazingly even said they would convince Wall Street—that highly leveraged companies would be better off in Wall Street's evaluation than companies with little or no debt. Even as Nicholas trumpeted to anyone who would listen the virtues of the new deal over the old, no one believed him. Not even Munro and Ross.

"I'll never forget after we did the deal," recalls Munro, "we were all in Nick's office and he was trying to convince us what a good deal this was. I said, Nick—there's some gallows humor in this—look me in the eye and tell me that this is wonderful. Nick laughed and I laughed. No one in their right mind can say that the final deal was better than the original one. This is called trying to make chicken salad out of chicken shit. No one wanted this debt but we tried to put the best face on it we could." Ross, who has been nervous about debt all his business life, agreed. "Our debt is not the way we planned it originally. Davis made us change our deal. We like our original concept."

Ross, Nicholas and Levin took some comfort in their financing and their projections for their future cash flow, with no longer an urgent need to address themselves to quarterly earnings results. "I feel liberated," said Nicholas, adding, as if to insist on his credibility, "I really do."

Much of the debt was with banks at a fixed favorable rate of 9.4 percent, they said, one point below the prime rate at the time. From their operations, Time Warner expected to take in about $2.3 billion, with annual interest payments of about $1.4 billion. Anticipated capital expenses were about $500 million, leaving between $400 and $500 million, not nearly enough to cover mandated depreciation and amortization charges, resulting in huge losses in their financial reports using traditional accounting.

So in order to divert attention from the losses and focus on happier numbers, the company made a radical alteration in its quarterly and annual financial reporting. Instead of bragging about earnings (after interest payments on the debt and the other charges, there were only multimillion-dollar losses), Time Warner became the first major company to get the SEC's okay to use a new tongue-twisting acronym "EBITDA" (earnings before interest, taxes, depreciation and amortization), essentially meaning cash flow. The second company to use the acronym was the leveraged buy-out magicians KKR (Kohlberg Kravis Roberts).

EBITDA wasn't even among the 30,000 terms and definitions listed in the 1991 edition of the authoritative *Dictionary of Finance and Investment Terms* (co-authored by Jordon Elliot Goodman, Time Warner's own *Money* "senior finance and investment reporter"). Using the smallest, agate type, Time Warner explained in a footnote to the first annual report why EBITDA was the new scoreboard: "The fundamental operating performance of acquired business is obscured by the [traditional] accounting requirement. Therefore EBITDA is presented to reflect operating income."

Time Warner's new quarterly and annual reports opened with gains in EBITDA. Losses were reported in later paragraphs. The financial press wasn't buying, no matter how hard the company was selling. Headlines and news leads everywhere in the press still emphasized losses, not EBITDA.

The Sunday New York *Times* business section greeted the first new quarterly reporting with the headline "Time Warner Takes It on the Chin." Even Time Warner's own *Fortune* didn't include the new term in its corporate rankings. More painfully, the magazine had to move its parent Time Warner to the "Five Largest Losses" list of companies.

Wasserstein's and the other investment bankers' promises to educate Wall Street about EBITDA did not work. "The financial press," explained Levin, "is trained to report actual historical earnings. So it doesn't make any difference what we write in our releases, they go by the book." The new financial reports, says one top Time Warner executive, "are not consumer-friendly documents. That's because of the confusing accounting rules. The Street understands it. But for the average person it's terribly confusing." It was also confusing to the daily press, which ran more Time Warner items in their "Corrections" boxes than other companies requested.

Ross dismissed the debt with a salesman's flourish. In an effort to dispel worries about Time Warner's debt, he repeatedly gave interviewers a unique non sequitur. "If you take our debt of $10 billion, and you drop a zero, that would be a billion. But we have about $2.3 billion in cash flow. If you dropped a zero there, that would be $230 million. All of a sudden people would be saying this company has only $1 billion in debt and $230 million in cash flow. What a great ratio and what a great company. They won't have any problem paying it off!" A zero here, two zeros there—"It's all relative," says Ross.

THE TWO BOARDS MET together for the first time on August 17, 1989. Twenty-four Time Warner directors, with supporting troops, crowded into the Time boardroom (craftsmen later replaced the table with a larger $100,000 cherrywood and elm burl model). Name placards were at each place. On the table were glass bowls of hard candies and Nicholas's favorite munchies, M&M's, altogether different from the provender at Warner meetings, where smoked salmon, bagels, sliced delicatessen meats and cookies were the usual fare.

Munro presided because it was agreed that, despite his other virtues, "Steve couldn't run a disciplined meeting," a Time director explains. At least two of the directors had more than finance on their minds. Time's Ed Finkelstein and Warner's Beverly Sills, old friends both heftily overweight, sat alongside each other whispering about their rigorous liquid diets. (It worked for Finkelstein, who lost more than fifty-five pounds; Sills was a recidivist.) "Ed practically slapped my hand," says Sills, "when I reached for the M&M's. His own diet was making him edgy. Ed was doodling and he's not a doodler. We fantasized about what we would each have for our first real meal."

Despite the nitty-gritty financing details, the meeting had the air of a celebratory outing. John Opel, the Time-side director and former chairman of IBM, who as someone present said, "couldn't tell a joke if he was reading it off a Teleprompter," urged caution. "Remember," said Opel, "it's not over until the fat lady sings." Diva Sills, the only female on the board, noisily cleared her throat, and the room broke up in laughter. Three meetings later, on speakerphones, in separate sessions and together, they reached agreement on Ross's back-end formula.

Then they scheduled a quick honeymoon sojourn for late October 1989 to get to know each other and their companies better. It was to be at Time's favorite pondering place in the sun, the Lyford Cay Club in the Bahamas.

part 3
TIME WARNER INC.

chapter 14

Together
at Last

O N THE WESTERN TIP of the Bahamas' New Providence
Island rests the Lyford Cay Club, encircled by a half mile of
beautiful small beaches.

The palatial centerpiece of the spread, its Georgian clubhouse, is
surrounded by an eighteen-hole golf course, twelve tennis courts, an
outsized swimming pool, croquet grounds, outdoor barbecue pits,
and a sport fishing fleet at the nearby Lyford Cay marina. The em-
erald grass lawns are planted with blooming red, yellow and blue
ixora, bougainvillea and palm trees.

Inside the pink clubhouse are meeting and dining rooms, indoor
and outdoor patio bars served by Bahamian waiters and stewards.
Each of its fifty rooms and eight cottages has a terrace overlooking
the turquoise sea. Many of the club's members, closets stocked with
the lime-green and tomato-red slacks of their northern golf clubs,
own elaborate second or third homes within golf-cart distance of the
clubhouse.

Before the main force of Time Warner honeymooners arrived,
there was a more intimate Time family gathering. A small band
(twenty-six in all) of Time's magazine editors, publishers and other
Time Inc. brass met at Lyford for two days to wrestle over editorial
matters—and money. When Nicholas told them the merger and debt
would cause no new belt tightening for the magazines, he was confronted with disbelief. One publisher boldly objected to all the ma-
larkey and said, "Hey Nick, why don't you tell it like it is. We'll
have a much easier time believing you. We know our budgets will
be under pressure." Nicholas replied that he couldn't say that because

it wasn't true. "That was pure bullshit—part of the company line," comments a senior editorial executive.

There was also some "reeducation" on the "new game" of cash-flow valuation of the company as opposed to net income accounting, a new concept to the Timeincers. McManus reassured his apprehensive editorial generals that they could get closer to their publishing partners without, say, the risk of the porcupines who huddled together against the winter chill, finding it warmer but more painful the closer they got.

Two weeks after the magazine meeting, waves of planes from the Time Warner air force carried more than seventy top executives and directors of the newly married companies to the island. The club's facilities were too small for the honeymoon sessions. Time conference arrangers fanned out and rented private houses around the club, hiring staffs to run them and stocking them with food and drink.

In charge of the program were Time's Levin and Warner's executive vice president Bob Morgado. "We wanted," says Levin, "to expose everyone to all the businesses in a way that was neither all glitz nor a shouting contest—a sense of Time Warner, not the old Time Inc. or the old Warner companies. Bringing together the two lifestyles was tough. You could certainly see the distinctions."

The "distinctions" were on view as soon as the two groups came together at the first-night dinner, all wearing identification nametags except Ross. Many of the uncertain Warner crowd, at Lyford for the first time, showed up in dark suits and ties. The supposedly buttoned-down Time bunch, on turf familiar to them, were tieless, informally dressed in sports shirts or at most blazers. Munro one night was in faded blue jeans with no belt and a yellow T-shirt. True, says Gil Rogin, a McManus deputy, "some of the Warner people didn't wear the kind of resort and golf clothes that we wear. They're not golfers. Lyford is a Time Inc. place."

At the opening session Levin, who had been supplied with the joke, quipped, "This is like a meeting of the National Conference of Christians and Jews." The line got only nervous giggles.

INITIAL WORRIES ASIDE, THE three-day encounter was a love-in. By the time it ended, it was hard to tell who was more impressed, Time with their new Warner friends, or Warner with theirs from Time. But different they were.

"We were as impressed as hell with the Warner people," said one

Time editor, echoing a widespread sentiment. "Our informal take was that their top guys looked better than our guys." At one dinner, *Time*'s Paris bureau chief, Christopher Redman, who flew over to tell the group about the European Community, sat with Warner's music impresario, Ahmet Ertegun. Redman tried to get Ertegun to tell him about the music business. Ertegun, the soigné son of the World War II Turkish ambassador to the U.S., insisted on hearing about the EC.

The daytime presentations swung from the jazzy special reels of Warner's new movies, matched only by Time's HBO reel, to a somber lecture by Jason McManus on what church and state was all about. *Life* managing editor Jim Gaines spoke about "magazine magic." Wide-screen video displayed analyses of "Cable Penetration of the U.S." and "TV Households." Warner speakers took the audience on knowledgeable tours of the arcane but intriguing record business; others spoke of Warner's international experience, every bit as interesting and impressive as *Fortune* managing editor Marshall Loeb's adding up of the American economy.

"These sons of bitches," said one Time journalist, "really knew what they were talking about, not just average corporate executives." Another said to a colleague, "I met people I'd never met before. It's just a very different world. I never realized what I was missing at Time Inc. And I liked it."

Time's editorial director, Dick Stolley, after speaking on how magazines make a difference in the world, "was very impressed with the Warner guys. They really knew their business. They seemed to have a sense of what creativity is all about. They did have to deal with creative people—probably more difficult people than we do. The most refreshing thing is that they weren't like us. They make a decision like that, snap. They talk plain. They have car phones and are never out of touch. They bring an atmosphere that's the kind of change we need. Time had such hardening of the arteries that we just couldn't go on this way."

Time corporate editor Gil Rogin found it a homecoming. "I had a very idiosyncratic, personal reaction. I rarely think of myself in Jewish terms, but when I went down there and met the Warner guys, I felt like I had come home. These are the kind of guys I'd known in Vegas and Miami Beach. I didn't know them, but I knew them all. And I felt a tremendous warmth. I liked them, I understood them. I knew what kind of people they were. Jerry Levin spoke on a high, almost lyrical intellectual level. Bob Daly, the head of the Warner studio, said some things that were pure Hollywood. Jerry's an intellectual and Daly is not. But Jerry doesn't characterize our company and Daly doesn't characterize his."

Homeward bound, Warner director Beverly Sills came away from the Lyford gathering with a revised view of the two cultures. They were not so different after all. "Time people feel that the movie and record business is flashy and glitzy and it is. It deals with celebrities. But celebrity makes the cover of *Time* and *People*. *Sports Illustrated* doesn't deal with statesmen of the world—nor does their bathing suit issue. I think the primary difference is that at Time the talent is part of the organization. In Warner's businesses, we're more of a go-between for talent. I'll never lay eyes on Madonna or any of those people. With the Time people, you can know and see them."

So far so good—no, excellent.

The wedding meats were barely cool when not just other Warner executives but Steve Ross himself began to make a new and refreshing impression on Time pessimists. "One of the things about the initial reaction to Steve Ross," says *Time* managing editor Henry Muller, "is something we have nothing to be proud of. We don't like anybody outside the family who's really not one of us."

From an assessment of Ross darkly clouded by suspicions, many of the Time skeptics began to see a brighter side. As they got closer to him, they thought they found a different Ross from the one they had vaguely heard about. "The more we saw of him," said one *Time* executive journalist, "the more we liked him." A *Sports Illustrated* editor agreed. "I respect Nicholas's competence," he said, "but there's an intangible element in Ross—the entrepreneur, the corporate founder—that's really impressive."

Ross accomplished the turnaround first with a dazzling new deal; then with his own charming presence; and finally as the result of a hard-edged account of the merger in the *New Yorker* magazine, which impressed Timeincers by displaying Ross's negotiating and entrepreneurial superiority.

IN THE MOVIE BUSINESS, ahead of any other, money does more than talk. It makes people walk—away from their most beloved mentors, no matter what their past declarations of undying loyalty.

At Warner, the brightly burning candles of the moment were two producer partners. One was Jon Peters, who told a reporter, "In

Hollywood it's all just the size of your dick that counts," to which movie producer-director Mike Nichols rejoined, "Tell him that nobody likes a whiner." The other was somewhat tamer Peter Guber. Within the span of eighteen months, the self-described "karmic brothers" had produced two of Hollywood's biggest hits—*Rain Man* and *Batman,* not to say some flops, including a disastrous rendition of *The Bonfire of the Vanities.*

Guber, with his ponytail hairdo, and Peters, with his madman antics, were hot. And a rising sun was invisibly focusing its rays on them. As part of the foreign invasion of Hollywood, late in 1989 Japan's Sony, after buying CBS's huge record company, also bought Columbia Pictures. Sony's CBS record chief, Walter Yetnikoff, the unchallenged champion in the use of four-letter words, wanted Guber and Peters for his new Japanese bosses. But the two had binding five-year exclusive contracts with Warner.

Yetnikoff, emerging from a Minnesota drug and alcohol rehab retreat, secretly set out to woo them away from Warner. He had gigantic bucks, an offer to Guber and Peters worth more than a billion dollars, and a rapist's determination. It was a new Yetnikoff, one of his friends told a reporter. "Walter went into the clinic like a wreck and came out like the Dalai Lama." Yetnikoff agreed, with a slight amendment. "Now I commune with my higher power, connect spiritually with my inner self, then I go out and try to fuck people." But he had yet to come up against the likes of Steve Ross.

"We were shocked, infuriated," says Ross about the Guber-Peters defection. "We helped build their organization. No one had the decency, the courtesy to contact us." Ross, who likes to describe all major business decisions with a homily or anecdote, recalled the moment of his epiphany. "One night I couldn't sleep, so I got up and looked at the contract that Guber and Peters had made with Columbia. I realized they had not indemnified Sony, that in fact Sony had indemnified them. It hit me. We could take Sony to the cleaners on this because Sony had the money."

Take them to the cleaners he did. He traded the ungrateful pair to Sony for the right to recapture the Warner Studio lot, the rights to the *Batman* sequels, plus a big distribution share in Columbia's record, videotape and television programming businesses—in all, concessions estimated to be worth $500 or $600 million. From top to bottom, his new Time partners, as well as the whole entertainment world, were dazzled by his dealmaking verve. At the Time Warner board meeting, where Ross explained the settlement, he got a buoyant round of applause. HBO's boss, Michael Fuchs, attending the meeting as an observer, cracked, "Have we any other producers who want to break their contracts?"

"We've been distracted," said Ross nonchalantly, "first by Paramount and now something called Sony. But when we get distracted, it's never been anything small."

ROSS IMPRESSED THE TIME people with more than his negotiating skills. In several meetings with inquiring editors and writers, he was equally compelling.

When he was invited to have lunch with Time's managing editors, their editorial director Dick Stolley remembers: "He started talking, in an extremely genial, self-effacing way about the usual stuff we'd all heard before. Then there was a pause and I said, 'I understand you really wanted us to ask you anything. Okay, give us your version of the Westchester Premier Theatre case.' Without a blink he went through it in a logical and impressive manner. He made the point about how little money was involved. He felt he had been badly served by subordinates. We didn't have to ask any questions. He anticipated questions and said that on advice of counsel he declined to appear before the grand jury. Looking back, he said he obviously trusted some people he shouldn't have. He seemed benign about the whole thing. We were all very impressed by the way he dealt with what was obviously very difficult. We asked about other bad periods in his life. And he said, well, clearly Atari. He talked a little bit about Atari, but said we came back from that. And he does this without any braggadocio. When he left, we talked about why we were all so taken with him. His character was the one thing that came across to us more than anything else in this two-hour lunch. Regardless of what he may have done or not have done in the past, under what kind of pressures, how attentive he may have been or whatever, we were dealing at this stage of his life with an ethical man. No question, we were all impressed."

When he didn't appear in person, Ross made his presence felt in other ways. A correspondent was asked to brief a group of Warner executives on Panama. After she returned to her office, she was startled and delighted to get a "lovely" note from Ross, with whom she'd spent ten minutes, accompanied by a lavish bunch of flowers. The scrappy business writers of *Time,* asking no one's permission, made a date to interview Ross. They too received thank-you notes addressed to each of them by first names. "Just a note to tell you how much I enjoyed our meeting. Your questions were inciteful [a typo for insightful] and very well thought out. I hope you will be able to meet on a more frequent basis and I look forward to seeing you again."

Time employees whose names, faces and work were invisible to Ross were complimented by similar first-name notes and bouquets for tasks they had routinely done in the past without getting any flowering huzzahs. Visitors to his office reported back that when they left, Ross never failed to show them to the elevator *himself*. Admire a bottle of wine at his table, and don't be surprised if he sends you a case. One correspondent who barely knew Ross was surprised when he got a thank-you note signed "Love, Steve," after the reporter did a turn for the company.

"Steve Ross had a checkered reputation," said the general manager of one Time magazine, "not the kind associated with Time Inc." But after Ross came to a middle management meeting attended by close to two hundred Time people, "he seemed like a very friendly guy. I think he won people over by mingling afterwards and talking to them. He was wearing his *Batman* pin. One of the Time managers asked, 'Where can I get one of those?' And Ross said, 'We're sold out but you can have mine.' We expected a slick Hollywood type, but he's not that at all. People do admire a successful manager and he certainly is that."

The view was not unanimous. There were still anti-Ross hardliners and yearners for the good old days. What better place to find them than at a lunch meeting of the Time-Life Alumni Society. The president of the group introduced Ross by saying that their foremost concern was "whether a co-CEO like Steve Ross might eat our guys for breakfast. That's why we're happy, Steve, to have you for lunch." Ross was quick with a rejoinder, "Dick, Nick and Jerry already had me for dinner."

His informal and almost diffident remarks got mixed reviews, covering the full spectrum from reassuring to awful. Most were affirmative: "Look what Ross has done, from very modest beginnings to this huge complex. He made a good impression personally." "I felt reassured. He's not as bad as the ogre image painted of him." "I think people were taken by surprise because they expected to see the devil incarnate up there." "He came across as a very warm person. I felt like giving him a hug.'' Or the contrary: ''He's a master on the subject of the bottom line,'' ''a snake oil salesman,'' ''the smartest con man I've ever met.'' One old-Timer had a lofty if confining analogy, an antiquarian giveaway. ''Why did Time Inc. need to expand? The gardens at Versailles never added more land. They just kept planting the same flowers and it gets more visitors than ever.''

JOURNALISTS, NO MATTER WHERE they work, have a need akin to children. They always look above and around them for their ''protector.'' To journalists, the need has a special meaning, not just job security or the kinds of benefits that unions or contracts codify. They look for the person in their organization who will stand up for their independence, brook no special favors from outsiders and will make sure that they have the financial backing to pursue what they consider to be their Holy Grail.

At Time, the protection was deified in church and state, an abstraction getting more elusive day by day. ''McManus got rolled over in all this,'' one Time journalist said sadly. ''Many of us think he's proved himself a complete corporate lackey,'' another said. As a result, they were not looking—where they might be expected to— toward their editor-in-chief for their protection. ''In defense of Jason,'' one of his managing editors explains, ''he knew the climate he had walked into in which the editor-in-chief is a pain in the ass. Jason didn't have the authority and freedom his predecessors did.''

As for Munro, said another, ''There is an affection for Dick as a human being but not as our leader, and he's leaving anyway.'' Nicholas seemed both smart and tough enough to them, raised in the Time tradition, as well as someone who had taken the trouble to cultivate the journalists. Levin, by far the most appealing to them, was judged not to be powerfully enough placed in Time Warner to make the difference. So at first Nicholas seemed to be their man, although some of the senior editorial staff were uncertain. ''I'm not sure Nick can be counted on to protect anyone,'' said one doubter, ''except himself.''

It was Ross who began to win their confidence, many Timeincers said. The beguiling impression he made face-to-face, what they heard—and Ross said—his hands-off style of managing creative people, his generosity of wallet and spirit, all began to win them over. It was a combination they liked. Then along came a long account in print of how the Time Warner deal was done, written by Connie Bruck, an incisive journalist who had sharpened her skills on the *American Lawyer* before she became the business writer for the *New Yorker*.

Her *New Yorker* article on Time Warner ("Deal of the Year") ran 25,000 words. Munro was worried when he was mistakenly told that the magazine would devote an entire issue to the story—like the issue on the Hiroshima apocalypse forty-five years earlier. In the story, Bruck made plain that she found Warner had taken Time, no matter what anyone said. She made short shrift of Nicholas, disparaged Munro, dismantled the church-state edifice, and above all emphasized how Ross had outwitted, outgunned and hoodwinked the Time patsies. Time executives already felt they had been pummeled and battered by the "competition" press. When the *New Yorker* story came out, they were indignant.

"The Connie Bruck thing," agonized Nicholas, "really pisses me off. I came away from it with a bitter taste."

After she had interviewed him, Nicholas confidently reported to colleagues, "I told her what the real story was." Upon hearing that, one of Nicholas's friends says he thought to himself, "Oh, my God—if she's smart . . ." Another added, "Nick can sometimes be his own worst enemy, especially when he's being interviewed by a journalist."

Munro was in despair, having been assigned by Bruck a villain's role for undermining editorial authority. One editor who admired the article, which later won the National Magazine Award for Reporting, nonetheless moaned that "Bruck never met a Warner executive she didn't like and never met many from Time Inc. she did."

McManus convened a managing editors' lunch for the express purpose, announced in advance, of discussing what to do about the *New Yorker*. "The general feeling in the room," says one of the editors present, "was that we take a lot of punches and we don't punch back enough. There was some discussion about either writing a letter—of course the *New Yorker* doesn't publish letters—or a letter to the New York *Times*, or something publicly to refute that article. Something needed to be done in the building to let the staff know that Nicholas was not going to roll over and let Ross push him around, some PR campaigning to lift staff morale."

One managing editor at the table remembers hearing the point, gently made, that "although Time Inc. was murdered and Ross looked like a genius, the article did succeed in helping to explain why the independence of the magazines was so important, even if it made Nicholas and Munro, and Jason too, look like stooges." There were others present who also looked on the bright side. "Sure Time took a hit in the piece," one of those present said, "but it was a relief to know what a great boss we'd have in Steve Ross. The piece cast him as a person who takes creative people seriously without too much interference, spending money because that's a better way of making money than saving it."

To most of the Time staff below the top executive level—editorial and business—the *New Yorker* article had an authentic resonance. "Everybody on *Fortune*," said one of its editors, "thought the Bruck piece was right on the button. Marshall [Loeb, *Fortune*'s managing editor] said it was a piece of crap. But then Marshall does tend to hyperbole." A *Time* editor observed, "There was a sneaking admiration for Ross as a very smooth operator who had taken our guys' pants off."

Another found that "Gradually there was a dawning that Ross and the Warner people are extremely impressive. Ross more so than anyone we had. The Guber-Peters thing, Ross's sense of leadership, then the Bruck piece, swung us around." One managing editor reflected, "I've heard people say they looked to Nick for their protection. I'm surprised they haven't said Steve Ross—one of these days they will." That day seemed to be arriving. "There was a suspension of disbelief," an older Time hand concluded, "we wanted Ross to make it and then we'd all be doing all right." A younger Time editor on the rise put it even more directly. "It looks like Steve is the one making the bold decisions. So we'd better hope he's on our side and get to like him."

WITH ROSS'S REPUTATION RISING inside, Time Warner's kept plummeting outside. "It's going to take some time," said Levin, "till it's recognized some of the things going on here." That time was agonizingly slow in coming.

To Wall Street, which had done a faithless about-face from the glorious guidon of leverage, Time Warner's debt was like an order to retreat. Many analysts and brokers started putting the stock on their "hate list," in a market where debt was suddenly a dirty word and earnings were again valued more than assets. Time Warner executives complained it was a short-term view, that the company had a wonderful base of "properties." Few investors were convinced, instead found Time Warner "perhaps the most visible example of the carnage in leveraged stocks." Painfully, the stock went down, down, down, opening at the beginning of 1990 to a brief high of $124, then dropping to only $66 a share and rising by the end of the year to $85, much less than the price of Time Inc. stock alone before the combined company with all its new assets was formed. Wasserstein's predicted 1990 range went from a cautious low of $133 to a pipe dream of $188.

"The only thing that will make the stock go up," one analyst said, "is a financial event, a major asset sale at a price that blows everyone away." But that was not to be. First Boston's investment banking analysts had seen a ray of hope in the company's creative energy, not in its balance sheet alone. It spotted two new projects. The first, "*Entertainment Weekly*," said First Boston's research analysts, "is an exciting new venture." And the second, the " 'Comedy Channel,' also demonstrates the company's willingness to invest in new vehicles within its operating segments." Time Warner's stock was a "buy," the report said.

Condé Nast, Hearst and Murdoch all had come out with hot new magazines. Not Time. In the sixteen years since *People* first appeared in 1974, Time had not launched a single successful new magazine. But by the first months of 1990 it was ready to try again. Time Warner's magazine chairman, Reg Brack, announced, "We have a clear and new idea for a magazine. It has been rigorously tested and received enthusiastic response from consumers and advertisers alike."

Entertainment Weekly, which had indeed been planned for five years and expensively tested for two, was to be a voguish guide and feature weekly on movies, books, video and music. Its editor called it a "browsable" handbook for "What do we do tonight?" The weekly was designed to give its readers the ultimate hip, swinging tour of the glamorous entertainment landscape. Its promotion motto said it all: "Kick Back. Chill Out. Hang Loose. Have Fun" (the theme words of a later Smirnoff vodka ad).

Except for the way the magazine looked, there was nothing low-rent about it. The *Wall Street Journal* called it "the most expensive and ambitious debut in the magazine industry's history," a $50 million launch with another $100 million exposure before it could get profitable. But for Time Warner, as the company's executives pointed out, it was a pittance compared to the movie and entertainment business, where in a single gulp a flop movie could cost more. (The *average* total investment in a single movie was $40 to $50 million.) The new weekly had an additional purpose. "This," said editor-in-chief McManus, "should be a major boost to all magazine employees, and a message to the outside world."

Some message. When it came out in February 1990, it was another high-visibility embarrassment, a bewildering hash of rapper graphics, with a miscellany of "gleeful chomps" of criticism, surrounded by multicolored guides to nowhere. Reluctant subscribers were wooed with four free copies, "welcome" gift boxes of microwave popcorn, coupons for records and videos. None of it helped much. It was so badly panned by advertisers and readers that Reg Brack, the publishing boss, had to be talked out of killing it altogether. The premier magazine company in the world, after five years of considering and planning, two years of testing, had produced an abomination. "Who was minding the store?" asked one experienced magazine editor.

Within four months, the new magazine was such a failure that it had to be relaunched. Its managing editor, the originator of the idea, resigned. Advertisers were advised in a blaring promotion headline to forget the infant *EW*. "It's NEW—from those wonderful folks who brought you" the old *EW*. Time's house organ *FYI* said the changes were made to "help the new magazine climb out of the primordial post-launch soup and up the publishing ladder." McManus forthrightly explained, "We felt we had to make changes quite quickly. The magazine was hard to read, not very user-friendly, and cluttered."

Without a doubt, the new *EW* was better but still not good enough to assure its place on the American scene. It did nothing for Time Warner's reputation, even though Ross predicted "it was going to be a smash," with such possibilities for synergy as "advertising flow-through to video cassettes and cable." *EW*'s start-up costs and losses pulled down Time's entire profitable magazine division. But for the moment Time Warner was sticking with it, reminding itself faint-heartedly of Condé Nast's *Vanity Fair,* rising from initial disaster to flourishing success, when its new editor-in-chief, Tina Brown, transformed it. Even Time's own *Sports Illustrated* took ten years before it became successful. But that was under Luce, who answered to no one. No publisher before or since had primed such a money-losing pump for so long.

. . .

IN THE SAME PERIOD, Time Warner started its new cable Comedy Channel, a rapid-fire selection of jokes, promotional clips from funny films and stand-up comics. It would take an even larger investment, with a potential of $500 million in annual returns. "HBO is completing its comedy manifest destiny," HBO chairman Michael Fuchs said. "It's the best concept we've had in ten years. Funny is money."

Money it cost; funny it wasn't—and it started out to be the worst, not the best, idea HBO had in ten years. Fuchs himself, Time's only movie mogul, has a gift for straight talk and tart humor. He gave his early programs a rating "of two on a scale of ten." *Newsday* evoked the spirit of the enterprise by describing its producer and his goals. "Its creative boss is Eddie Gorodetsky, wearing one earring, a tattoo, three-day-old stubble, Harley-Davidson T-shirt. With his growly voice, he looks like Hell's Angels. 'I'm trying to do something where the Comedy Channel will look like a TV station in the '50s, the feeling of cameras bumping into each other. It won't be as retro as the road show of 'Grease,' but it will have that feeling as opposed to a windowless environment with good-looking people who don't really have anything to say."

Not only was it another flop, but it faced nasty competition from Viacom's new Ha! comedy channel. Viacom, which also owned the Movie Channel, Showtime and MTV, had already slapped HBO with a vengeful $2.3 billion antitrust suit, requiring so far the disclosure of 15 million pages of documents from both sides. Viacom charged that HBO was unfairly competing by using strong-arm selling practices. In the annals of law, there has rarely been such a pot-and-kettle lawsuit. Three senior Viacom executives all had moved over from similar positions at HBO, where they created the system they were now attacking.

But the need for survival overcame their bitter name-calling. Comedy Channel and Viacom's Ha! gritted their teeth and combined into The Comedy Network, later renaming it Comedy Central, without calling off their antitrust lawsuit. If they couldn't make it apart, maybe they could together. It was one of their funnier riffs on a cynical old joke: "With enemies like you, we need friends like you."

PUBLICLY, STEVE ROSS ALLOWS not the slightest hint that he may be discouraged. Congenital optimism is his mien. The negative miasma hanging over Time Warner to him was "jealousy by people who want to see us fail."

With his customary show of bravura leadership, he told his executives, "Don't let the debt scare you. Make your decisions as though there were zero debt. If you let the debt affect you, we're all dead." He backed up his words with action. In rapid fire, Time Warner bought warrants for $18 million in a near-bankrupt cellular phone company; announced opening a chain of movie theaters in the Soviet Union, a stake in a European TV business channel and a Swiss TV company, an Australian record club and the start-up of a group of retail stores.

When Time Warner bought a 20 percent interest in the junk-bonded Six Flags theme amusement parks (later upped to 50 percent), where Warner cartoon characters could be featured players, the company's hype was in full flower. Forget Disney. Time Warner described the nearly bankrupt parks as the "largest *regional* theme park company in the world," the "second largest in the country in *physical* size." Without emphasizing the qualifiers, the description sounded like Groucho Marx's billing of his brother Harpo in a circus freak show "as the smallest giant in the world or the biggest midget."

Ross also starred at a dinner negotiation for the much larger acquisition of Lane Publishing, which Time had long wanted to buy. For $225 million ($80 million cash, $145 million in preferred stock) Time Warner acquired Lane's *Sunset* (circulation 1.4 million), the successful old "Magazine of the West," whose arteries had been hardening and its owners aging. Along with the magazine, once an outlet for stories by Jack London and Sinclair Lewis, came a line of books and a small film operation. Time put a New York publishing executive in charge, hired a new editor, cut the staff by 20 percent, set out to redesign the magazine and accepted liquor advertising in its pages for the first time.

Sunset's guiding leader would not be Time's editor-in-chief. "No church-and-state," Levin flatly confirmed. "That's right," says McManus, "those were the conditions of my office negotiated by my predecessors." Nevertheless, the announcement said that, like others Time had bought, the magazine would be an "integral part of the Time Inc. Magazine Company with a preeminent franchise in the country's wealthiest, fastest growing market—the 13-state American West."

The new investments involved still more borrowed money. That startled some, including one banker who said, "They still behave as an investment-grade company." Financial writer Bob Lenzner also thought it odd. "You wouldn't know they had a debt of billions from their actions," he wrote. But all of the ventures were small news compared to the high visibility of the next step. It ignited Ross's first uproar on the Time Warner board, filled his Time partners with doubts and brought a barrage of unsavory headlines around the world. This time it wasn't more borrowing that raised eyebrows. It was the man with whom Ross and Warner Bros. chose to try to make the deal.

IN ITS LONG HISTORY, the movie and entertainment business has been scarred—mostly from behind the scenes—by more than its share of hoods, crooks, frauds, loudmouths and con men. But out front it would be hard to find someone whose personal and financial record was more checkered than Giancarlo Parretti, the new demi-mogul who showed up in full regalia on the Hollywood scene in the spring of 1990. Parretti's aspirations and biography, unaltered, could provide the script for an inexpensive *Godfather IV*. Or—as it turned out—for a deal with Time Warner.

At times, Parretti looks and acts as if he could play the role of a stocky Godfather himself with a little makeup and direction. His eyes are often hidden behind dark aviator glasses, and a doubling chin complements his swelling paunch. In his mouth he clenches fat Cuban cigars, which he bragged to a reporter were Castro's favorite brand "that must be rolled against the thighs of beautiful girls no older than fourteen." He claimed to be worth more than a billion dollars, but nobody, including the SEC, could figure out where the money came from—or if he really had it. Repeatedly he announced multimillion-dollar new movie deals, which quickly fell through.

Parretti's rise in business was engulfed in dark clouds. He was said to have been a waiter in a Sicilian hotel owned by the local political boss, who was reported to have been indicted for embezzlement and then had the misfortune to be gunned down by Mafia enemies. Un-challenged accounts had the wounded patron fleeing Palermo and leaving his hotel chain and soccer team in Parretti's hands. Future Parretti backers and patrons were said to be involved in such affairs as the biggest insider trading scandal in France, the unsolved mystery of a dead body hanging from London's Waterloo Bridge, and in advising Libya's terrorist tyrant Muammar Qaddafi.

Parretti, like many a wayward rust bucket at sea, carries Liberian papers. His corporate headquarters was a room in Luxembourg, an international tax haven where the stock of one of his holding companies was delisted after he failed to provide the required financial information. "He's like a bar of soap in the water," the head of the Luxembourg exchange told a reporter. "Every time you try to get a grip, he slips through your fingers." Parretti did most of his American business out of three standard symbols of movie moguldom: a Gulfstream jet, a Rolls-Royce and a Beverly Hills mansion.

Three times he had been slapped in jail by the Italian police, for bank fraud, forgery and extortion. After being locked up, he managed to beat each rap. Spain also issued a warrant for his arrest in a money-smuggling scheme. When he showed up at Time Warner, he had just been convicted by a Naples court for bankruptcy fraud and sentenced to more than three years in prison. He was appealing the verdict again in a higher court after he lost his first appeal.

He also claimed to be a "good friend of Steve Ross," although Warner people said Ross barely knew him. It was the one instance where Parretti himself could have been misled. Ross had managed a $2 million contribution from Parretti, which was actually paid, for the Museum of Broadcasting, founded by Ross's former stepfather-in-law William Paley. Parretti made the grant presumably to improve his "image" in America.

For Time Warner, Parretti had a typically intricate proposition. Parretti with a partner was a part owner of France's Pathé Cinema and Cannon Films. From that base, he made a shaky $1.3 billion bid to buy Hollywood's hard-up MGM/United Artists, complete with its rich library of old films. But he had a problem. He was short of cash—as usual—so Time Warner agreed to recommend Parretti to its bankers for a $650 million loan, with the MGM/UA film library as collateral. For this favor in helping Parretti buy the American company Time Warner would get the distribution rights to the library and an option to buy 20 percent of the company. If Parretti defaulted on the loan, the film rights would go to Time Warner.

The deal was so complicated that it left even aficionados of Ross's skills reeling. *Variety,* wise in the ways of Hollywood dealmaking, led off its page-one story: "No one can quite figure out the deal. And few as yet can sort out its implications." On Wall Street it was described as "one of the strangest deals ever seen." *Business Week* headed its coverage of the transaction, "DOES STEVE ROSS

KNOW WHO HE'S DEALING WITH?" London's *Economist* commented, "Parretti seems a strange corporate bedfellow—particularly for the East Coast establishment types that run *Time* magazine." Standard & Poor's bond raters took one look at the proposed Parretti contract and put Time Warner on its "credit watch list." Not mentioned was that Ross repeatedly deplored foreign ownership of American film companies.

GIVEN PARRETTI'S RECORD, TIME Warner took the precaution of again hiring Kroll, the investigative agency, to compile a dossier on Parretti. Kroll found the published charges to be on the mark and more.

But Ross told his doubting Time directors that they "were not getting in bed with Parretti." It was just a distribution deal in which they had everything to gain and nothing to lose. If Parretti defaulted on the loan, the film library was worth far more than the $650 million. On the other hand, if Parretti pulled off his buy-out of MGM/UA, Time Warner still had a rich package of revenue from the film and video distribution rights. There were lots of questions from directors but most swallowed hard and agreed with director Mike Dingman, who said, "It was an example of taking a chance in a new environment, looking at it very pragmatically." Another approving director, who had come from the Time-side, put it more bluntly. "The Parretti deal is really designed to steal the library from him—a typically ingenious Ross maneuver."

The heist was not that easy. After Ross got the approval he wanted from the board, two new Parretti stink bombs exploded. Most of the board had not known about Parretti's most recent bankruptcy fraud conviction in Naples until they read about it in the press when his Time Warner deal was announced. Even more embarrassing, Parretti gave interviews suggesting he had more than money as his motive. First he told the Hollywood correspondent of Italy's big Communist newspaper *L'Unità* that the Jewish media were out to get him. "The fact is that the Jews don't like the idea that I represent the first Catholic communications network. There doesn't exist a single media holding company in the world that isn't in the hands of Jews. Pathé is the first entertainment and editorial company in the world which is not Jewish."

Next day he tried to explain himself with that old turkey that some of his best friends were Jews. His remarks, he said, had "nothing to

do with Jews in general," only those attacking him. Ross was more
"outraged" that a Communist newspaper could be used as a source
than by the Parretti quotes. But it didn't help when it turned out
that Parretti had hit the same theme on an Italian TV interview
show. "All the big movie companies have never been anything but
American and Jewish. What I am trying to do is to create, for the
first time, a company that is neither American nor Jewish."

Time Warner flacks said, "Mr. Parretti has never exhibited any
bias or bigotry in his dealings with us." Parretti claimed he was a
friend of such eminences as Israel's former Prime Minister Shimon
Peres. One of his French partners, the schlock filmmaker Israeli-
born Yoram Globus, told another reporter, "He's not a racist. He's
not an anti-Semite. But people won't give him a chance. Why? Because he comes from the street." Still another supporter pointed out
that Parretti's rough edges came from his peasant background and
that his strongest suit was that "he loved people."

THE UPROAR AND AWFUL publicity were enough to call two
special emergency telephone meetings of the Time Warner board.
"We had approved it," said Munro, "but because of all the stuff
that came up about Parretti, we had to have other telephonic board
meetings to make sure the directors were still comfortable with this
character. Several of our directors said that's how business gets done
in Italy. They're always being investigated."

Beverly Sills spoke with the voice of experience. "I said at the
board meeting that the man is a scoundrel with an unsavory past.
We all agreed. But Steve said the risk was all MGM's. Once it cleared
that hurdle, essentially we were on easy street. I said I sang over
there for years and it's a different kind of world. I felt from my
experience they should be aware that contracts were somewhat different for Italian businessmen."

Hank Luce remembered from another era that his "father once
refused to buy the Blue Radio Network because it had the gossip
monger Walter Winchell as a feature. He couldn't stomach the idea
of having Winchell as one of his properties." Munro knew the deal
would "feed the skeptics who'll say that the old Time Inc. never
would have done that. I don't think that's correct—but I dunno.
We're in the entertainment business. It's a good business deal, not
illegal or unethical. We would have done it long before Steve Ross.
It's one of those little issues that gets blown out of proportion."

For Nicholas, "This was a close call for us. But it's a hell of a deal if we close. No matter what happens, it's a good deal." And Levin adds, "I consider myself to be very sensitive because our good name is our basic asset. But this transaction was structured with great care. I'm not happy about Parretti but I voted for the deal. It is a distribution deal with a potential for gaining control of the library."

Not yet. Another discovery was too much for Time Warner to ignore. When the company's executives reexamined their deal with Parretti, they saw that he was up to his old tricks. He was, in the most precise sense of the epithet, double-dealing. For MGM/UA, Time Warner complained, Parretti had used exactly the same rights contract, simply crossing out "Time Warner" and inserting "MGM/ UA." Instead of walking Parretti to the bank for a loan, Time Warner filed a $100 million suit charging that Parretti was trying to sell the identical distribution rights twice. Parretti promptly retaliated, upping the ante fivefold by doing a volte-face and suing Time Warner for a tidy $500 million, charging "breach of contract, fraud and libel."

It was not quite the end of an affair. Parretti was having so much trouble raising the money to buy MGM/UA that he sold his interest in his French movie company, got $250 million from Ted Turner for MGM/UA's film-TV rights and settled his lawsuit with Time Warner by yielding, for $125 million, the rights for home video distribution of its films. The rights both to Time Warner and to Turner were conditional on Parretti's completing his acquisition.

Then after a cliff-hanging series of maneuvers, Parretti finally did manage to buy a stripped-down, renamed MGM-Pathe. Within months, the beleaguered company's payroll checks were bouncing, including a six-figure payment to Dustin Hoffman and missed fees to Sylvester Stallone and Sean Connery. His new Hollywood prize was so broke it couldn't afford to release the movies it had completed. Within six months, Parretti was on the edge of bankruptcy, and his brief moment in the Hollywood klieg lights ended when his creditors forced him to resign. Back in Naples, the Court of Causation was still considering the second appeal of his prison sentence.

One Time lawyer, not involved in the Parretti negotiations, looked back on the whole affair and reflected: "I'm not surprised, because Time was never a hard-nosed company. It's behaved like a bunch of gentlemen used to dealing with people of their word."

• • •

RIGHT IN THE MIDST of the effort to control the collateral dam-
age to its reputation from the Parretti imbroglio, Time Warner lit-
erally had the book thrown at it.

The book episode was more damaging to the new Time Warner
for the widespread suspicions it aroused than for what turned out to
be the facts. The book was *Connections: American Business and the
Mob*. Its publisher was Time's own Little, Brown, a wholly owned
Boston subsidiary of Time Warner. The co-authors were two Time
alumni. The writer Roy Rowan had been for forty-two years a highly
respected and warmly admired *Time, Life* and *Fortune* correspondent, editor and writer, president of the Time-Life Alumni Society.
In his retirement, Rowan was still contributing to the magazines,
including an article in *Fortune* on the "Top Fifty Mafia Bosses," as
well as doing such tasks as writing the company's annual report and
editing its house magazine *Inside Timeinc*. His co-author was Sandy
Smith, an ex-Time-Life investigative reporter, who had done much
of *Time*'s breakthrough reporting on Watergate and a number of
other exposés in his twenty years working for *Life* and *Time*. Smith
was especially proud that Time had prevailed after his digging pro-
voked as many as a dozen separate libel complaints.

Two years before the Time Warner merger, Rowan and Smith had
signed a contract with Little, Brown for a book, in part expanding
on *Time* and *Fortune* articles, linking Mafia figures with such businessmen as former labor secretary Ray Donovan and New Jersey's
Schiavone Construction Company. It was Rowan's third book contract with Little, Brown. The writers received an $80,000 advance
payment, $80,000 more due on the completion of an acceptable
manuscript. All went well. The manuscript was finished on time,
editorial revisions were made, footnotes added, and it was sent out
for final copy editing.

The book jacket was designed and reproduced by the time the
book was announced in the May 1989 Little, Brown catalogue for
October publication (price: $18.45). The catalogue touted it in a full-
page blurb as "The first book about organized crime—the Mob—
that sets out to detail its connections with legitimate business in the
United States." It was to have "national advertising and promotion."
Only the standard legal review, which usually takes two or three
weeks, awaited completion before the book was to go to press.

· · ·

AFTER AN UNUSUALLY LONG four-month delay, Little, Brown's libel lawyer sent Rowan and Smith a list of a hundred questions that needed answering or backup to pass legal muster.

Smith, who did most of the reporting for the book, within a month sent back his 125-page point-by-point response to the queries. Most of the lawyer's worries concerned four chapters on the mob connections of the Schiavone Construction Company and what was said to be an FBI cover-up.

Schiavone and its gang were no strangers to Time. The year before, Time made its first major settlement in a libel suit over information it felt was correct. The concession was made after a round of court battles over a story in *Time* about Schiavone, reported by Sandy Smith. Time executives said that the "reporting issues" raised by Smith's work for the story "were not challenged," although privately they were uneasy about defending one slip-up. They decided to settle the suit to avoid the long public exposure and expense of what McManus called a "media extravaganza" of the kind that had so wounded the magazine in the Ariel Sharon suit, which they had finally "won" on First Amendment grounds.

The original Schiavone settlement outraged Smith. By then retired, he blew a loud whistle in the press, revealing the secret $500,000 settlement paid to Schiavone. He also accused his Time bosses of being a bunch of corporate "poltroons," charging they had caved in to hoods, undermined their reporters and seriously violated for the first time the long-standing Time policy of not settling libel suits when it felt it was right. Time executives began to regard Smith, a vintage member of the hard-driving investigative reporter breed, as a "loose cannon."

Little, Brown felt sure that the Rowan-Smith book would bring on similar threats of libel litigation backed by the deep pockets of Schiavone. The publishers said it was a "no-win situation." While they had worked with Rowan in the past, they had less confidence in Smith, who they regarded as querulous and hot-tempered. So they cancelled the planned legal review meeting that normally brings authors and lawyers together to iron out disputes. Instead, on June 8, 1989, two days after Paramount upset the original Time Warner merger plans, Little, Brown dispatched a cold letter to Rowan and Smith: "Counsel has advised us that we should not publish your work" because in their "judgment it contains libelous material."

The letter was signed by the book's editor, Roger Donald, a friend of Rowan's and previously an enthusiastic advocate for publishing the book. The letter declared a fait accompli, offering no meeting, discussion or appeal. That was it. The authors would not get their second payment of $80,000 and could keep all of their first, unless they sold the manuscript elsewhere. Howard Kaminsky, once a top book editor at Warner, Random House and currently president of William Morrow, remarked, "In twenty-three years of publishing, I had never known of a book that was copy edited, advertised in the catalogue and then withdrawn. It's almost unheard of—and very strange, even suspicious."

ALTHOUGH NEITHER ROSS NOR Warner was mentioned in the book, Rowan and Smith concluded that the last-minute rejection was connected to the impending Time Warner merger. At worst they suspected interference from Warner. At best, they guessed Time had lost its nerve because it didn't want a lawsuit on the subject of crooks and legitimate business in the midst of the already clouded merger negotiations.

Their literary agent, John Hawkins, sent off a letter to Little, Brown saying, "You owe my clients $80,000. They delivered the manuscript in July; you edited and they delivered a revised manuscript in October." Little, Brown's answer was "We do not intend to pay the second portion of the advance." Escalating, this time Rowan and Smith's lawyer demanded payment or "face legal recourse." When that too failed, their lawyer sent a second letter that was plainly an invitation for further negotiations. For openers, he asked $1.5 million. "This figure," he wrote, "is solely for the purpose of settlement, which included the remainder of the advance, uncollected royalties, the value of the book, opportunities lost and other damages."

Hastily, meetings were called in New York. No one wanted to hurt Roy Rowan, regarded with affection and respect throughout the Time & Life Building. For his part, Rowan said, "I don't want to go around sowing seeds of dissent." But the New York executives felt the decision had already been made in Boston by the president of Little, Brown, Kevin Dolan, without consulting anyone in New York. With a lawsuit threatened, no one in charge wanted to reverse the decision, even though almost everyone in New York would have preferred seeking a quiet settlement. "Settle this damn thing" was a widespread opinion in the upper reaches of Time's editorial high command.

At that point, the dispute was still internal. Then suddenly the whole media world was told about it. On the same day in the business section of the New York *Times,* two unrelated stories appeared. One reported Steve Ross's "outrage" at the published charges against Parretti. The other on the front page was a big layout whose headlines said, "Organized-Crime Book in Time Warner Dispute/ Killed Book Haunting Time Warner." The story's lead sentence described "a book that addresses subjects of acute sensitivity to Time." In the layout were pictures of Rowan and McManus, plus a circumstantially sinister chronological chart. The chart connected the Time Warner merger's steps by date and event with the history of the book and its rejection. Time's Jason McManus fired off a heated private letter complaining to the New York *Times* executive editor. Other Time executives firmly told anyone who would listen that there was absolutely no connection between the killing of the book and Ross or the Warner deal.

But no one, most painfully the journalists at Time itself and its outposts, believed them. Where was the editor-in-chief? was their cry. "I'm not responsible for books," McManus protested, "and there was less going on than meets the eye. I couldn't personally reverse the decision. I wanted to get it settled." True enough, but it was a meek effort, even though the editor-in-chief's charter provides that McManus has the "responsibility to express concern if activities of Time seem to be in conflict with editorial policies of the company's publications and standards of ethics." The book was widely assumed to be just such a conflict, casting doubt on the company's traditional editorial independence.

Columnists, alumni and reporters all over the country saw it just that way. Tendentious stories and analysis appeared with such headlines as "Corporate Culture Stifles a Book" and "Fear and Loathing in the Land of Luce."

At one paranoid point, Time executives suspected that Democratic nabob and lawyer Robert Strauss, working behind the scenes, had stirred up the whole embarrassment through a "Texas connection" with former Time director Arthur Temple. They theorized Strauss was seeking revenge for an unfavorable article *Fortune* had run about his son. In fact, Strauss, who is now U.S. ambassador to Moscow, had absolutely nothing to do with starting the fracas.

Within Time, the damaging publicity increased the movement to settle, though not to Nick Nicholas, who often angers too easily. He entered the fray late and was ready for combat. Heatedly, he exploded in his office one day. "The Little, Brown contract is bulletproof," he said. "I used to have very high regard for Rowan. I've lost it. Wait until the depositions come out. There's not going to be any goddamn settlement. I want to hear those guys under oath. I want each of our guys to line up and I want *them* to do that. It's bullshit. The only way our journalists will find that out is when they read the depositions in the lawsuit, even though this has perhaps been mishandled by some of our people."

Munro, predictably, had both a more conciliatory and more direct reaction. "That Rowan story in the *Times*—how can they run a story like that? Why Little, Brown handled it the way it did may be puzzling. But Jesus Christ, that's got nothing to do with the Mafia or Steve Ross. So we fucked up. We'll fuck up again. Maybe someone here should get his ass kicked. But to blow the whole thing out of proportion and to say that somehow we were manipulating it, I have never been so outraged. No one here has ever heard of that goddamn book. I never heard of it, Nick never did—and Steve, shit, Steve has never read a book."

In a prepared speech to a large group of magazine editors, Ross explained his innocence in more elegant terms. "There isn't a single instance in the history of Warner when I interfered—or directed someone else to interfere—with the writing of a book."

AFTER A FEW MONTHS of negotiations, Time belatedly did make a financial settlement with Rowan and Smith for a secret amount (under $500,000). The threat of a lawsuit by the authors was dropped. Little, Brown's president, Kevin Dolan, at fifty-three, took early retirement after twenty-seven years at Time Inc., to "spend more time with my family and improve my golf handicap."

From every indication and deep inquiry, the book was killed because Little, Brown feared "a real risk of litigation" with Schiavone. Whether big publishers should hold back just because of the "risk" of a libel suit was a different, debatable and dicier question.

In the end, there were no visible or even probative signs of any connection between the book and the Warner merger. The company had been presumed guilty until proved innocent. "We acknowledge," said Rowan and Smith in their settlement statement, "that Little,

Brown alone made this decision and made it in good faith, even if we disagree with it."

Everyone at Time, including Nicholas, again befriended Rowan, who came back to free-lance for Time's magazines. *Connections: American Business and the Mob* was never bought by another publisher.

Despite the publicly amicable outcome and the bum rap for malevolence instead of ineptitude in the handling of the book, the sum of the public exposure and suspicions could not have been worse for Time Warner, especially in the middle of its Parretti dealings. The Parretti affair raised the question of how far Time Warner would overlook personal standards of behavior for the sake of a business deal it liked. The unpublished book episode created the specter— even though it was circumstantial and unwarranted—of Time's link with Warner's compromising its editorial integrity.

"The Rowan-Smith book absolutely did produce the worst possible results for us," affirms Levin. "Why is our press so bad?" he asks aloud. "It's obviously disturbing. We take a holier-than-thou attitude about journalistic integrity, so we are being held to a high standard. It does get intense. Everybody is checking on us and observing us very closely, which is valid since we are the press. In the last year we have lost some of the old Time Inc. luster. It's going to take quite some time to get it back. Once the old Time Inc. didn't do certain things. The things that people see are the easiest to focus on, like Steve's bad history. Steve is not a schlock person. I don't believe in karma like that. But we've got a lot of bad aura. The real substance of Time Warner will eventually emerge. And I don't just mean in terms of good financial performance."

Ross describes the twelve-month aftermath of the original merger in fewer words: "Things kept us from getting together and really moving on a full scale. It was an unbelievable year."

HOW BEST SYNOPSIZE THE "unbelievable year"? Time Warner thought it found a way, with the publication of its first joint annual report. It was meant to startle—and it did. "Bored by Annual Reports?" asked the New York *Times*. Try this one, "Wall Street meets MTV. There's never been an annual report like it—the first statement by the entertainment and communications giant, a clue of how the company sees itself."

How did it? The cover was a psychedelic chartreuse fantasy with the word "WHY?" screaming out, inscrutably surrounded by six Day-Glo colored drawings of a bald head, a green outstretched hand, a pair of cracked lips, an eyeball lidded in blue under a lavender eyebrow, a disembodied ear and, topping them all, half a globe exposing only the African continent. Inside was a collection of what its designer called multicolored fluorescent "factoids," as baffling as the new EBITDA accounting methods used to report the company's financial results. Art directors judged it either the "best" annual report of the year or the "worst." No in-betweens. "It was an attempt to try to get noticed" was Levin's jejune explanation.

The dean of American graphics, Ivan Chermayeff, approved. "You don't need to read a word," he said. There were those who thought the purpose of good design was to make reading easier, not to replace it. Speaking of reading, once the spinal cord of Time Inc., what was reading's place in Time Warner?

chapter 15

Vital Organs:
The Magazines

"Print is dead.

"*An odd and curious conclusion to reach about Time Inc.,
Henry Luce's splendid magazine company. Yet there it was
in so many, uh, words, in a report presented to management in June,
1988 by a task force of senior operating executives.*"

Print dead? The verdict of an old-fogy naysayer? A snooty, pessimistic opponent of the merger? From one of the many jealous competitors whom Time Warner executives blamed for their negative press? Not at all. The statement was homegrown. It was the lead sentence in the first draft of an article on the Time Warner merger destined for Time's own *Fortune*.

Editors chucked this death sentence for print. As published, the article began, "Around six o'clock in the evening on June 6 . . ." After other revisions, it became a tamer and not especially revealing account of the merger. Published five months after the deal was concluded (two months before the *New Yorker*'s eviscerating treatment), it was *Fortune*'s longest piece in years. The writer was not a graying Time sentimentalist but a talented thirty-five-year-old member of *Fortune*'s board of editors, Bill Saporito, best known at the magazine for his bruising account of the earlier RJR Nabisco fiasco.

Saporito's first-draft lead, like many a reaching writer's, was an overstatement, a sensational attention grabber, written more for editing down or out than for using. It shouldn't have and it didn't appear in *Fortune*'s final story. But in three melodramatic words it put squarely the question on everyone's mind: What was to be the fate of Time Inc. journalism in the new company?

The keystone of every claim for the uniqueness of the Time Warner

merger was the preservation of the "Time culture." No one argued
that the company's core was Time's HBO, cable or mail-order books.
Nor was it Warner's glittering array of entertainment properties.
Advocates of the merger said it was Time's magazines that made the
vital difference.

Chancellor Allen's decision in favor of Time against Paramount
leaned heavily on his view that "the mission of the firm is not seen
by those involved as wholly economic. Time's traditional business
[is] the publication of magazines, most notably *Time* magazine."
Time director Matina Horner said, "The sale of Time would have
seemed inconceivable to me, if only because of the place of *Time*
magazine in this country."

Nicholas, who had not directly worked on the magazines but had
grown up professionally in their aura, expressed conviction about
their importance in the new company. "Anyone who didn't treat and
manage the magazine business of Time Inc. as we have learned to
do would undermine it. A national resource would be lost and the
stockholders would suffer dramatically as a result."

Jerry Levin puts it most emphatically: "*Time* is part of our genes.
The symbolism. The first name on the company. Whatever dimin-
ishing influence it has on this electronic world, it's still the thing with
the most impact on our print side. We need to make it clear, if we
haven't already, that unlike the collapsing of the news business at
the networks, Time Warner is irrevocably committed to maintaining
a news-gathering organization."

But the declarations of fealty to print were not accepted. Many
critics instantly began to make the mistake of attributing any woe in
Time Warner's Magazine Company to the merger. In reality the
most stubborn problems were apparent long before Warner ever
came along.

AMONG TIME'S SIX MAGAZINES in the late '80s, once the three
youngest of them sprouted to success and editorial identity, they
rarely had to look back.

Sports Illustrated, the best, elevated reporting on sports to a new
level of exploration, verve and interest; *People,* the most profitable
magazine in the world ($130 million in 1990 on only a $30 million
editorial budget), was celebrity popcorn (fifty-one Princess Di covers,
thirty-seven Elizabeth Taylors, eighteen Madonnas), said to be an
example of a "legitimate company appealing to our lowest instincts";

and *Money,* how-to-make-it-and-keep-it, was the most service-oriented and utilitarian of the three. All had small setbacks one year or another, but their growth was steady, their focus clear, their readers and advertisers committed. Year after year, their editors and publishers needed only to tinker with, not transform, them. The older titles, *Time, Fortune* and *Life,* were different. By 1986, all three looked into a clouded mirror.

Life, reborn as a monthly, was hopeless. It not only lost money but was guilty of a worse sin. Its content rarely made any difference. Waves of new editors and publishers never cured it. All kinds of new alternatives were explored: converting it back again to a weekly, transforming its outlook, even the misguided notion of perhaps combining it in some form with *Time.* All were earnestly discussed, dummied and then postponed. Late 1991 projections for even a revised *Life* showed it losing as much as $50 million in a single year. "We in the building know what *Life* is," says its senior editor at large Roger Rosenblatt, "but to the world used to compartmentalizing magazines, *Life* is a mysterious entity."

For the moment, Time couldn't bear to bury it again, "because it's the name on our building," one executive said. Perhaps he forgot that the weekly *Life,* which in its glory days had more readers and earned more than all Time Inc.'s other magazines combined, had been "suspended" in 1972, while it was the biggest revenue producer, as well as the biggest money loser.

Fortune, as a fortnightly, was marginally profitable, but its future budgets showed a steady decline in profits—intolerable for a magazine whose subject was the management of the enterprise system. Business news, no longer a journalistic backwater, had become a topic of broad interest, often covered by knowledgeable, enterprising reporters and editors. Luce could not say of his writers and reporters, as he once did, "Everything about business which does not actively offend them bores them." *Business Week, Forbes* and especially the daily *Wall Street Journal,* as well as expanded coverage in other big dailies, were assaulting *Fortune*'s pioneering and preeminent place as the quality publication of American executive life.

Marshall Loeb, successful and self-assured, was brought in as managing editor in 1986 to turn *Fortune* around. A *Time* and *Money* alumnus, Loeb with a task force of insiders felt that as a fortnightly *Fortune* needed to be sprightlier and closer to the news, no longer able to afford the luxury of its monthly depth or its past reputation as the most formidable and authoritative. It had become one of three magazines in its field, not *the* one.

Driven by news, executive lifestyles and advice ("The CEO's Second Wife," "Will You Be Able to Retire?" "How to Marry a Billionette"), eye-catching graphics and an ear tuned to reader-response telephone polls, Loeb enlivened it and brought it back to health but never to its uniqueness. He became a corporate hero and an impressive public spokesman, even though his editorial peers often gagged at his glibness. "I'm totally consistent," says Loeb, "about always wanting *Fortune* to be a weekly. I'd like to make it the *Sports Illustrated* of business," he says, as aging and departing *Fortune* intellectuals groan.

Not all the old *Fortune* hands minded. Hedley Donovan, the keeper of what was known as "the old *Fortune* mystique," could be least expected to approve. But shortly before he died in 1990, Donovan, seventy-six, pronounced his judgment. "*Fortune,* my child, doesn't have too much taste these days in graphics or style but has quite a lot of news and imagination. I miss those old, long pieces but I find some very good things in *Fortune.* They're not especially gracefully told or beautifully illustrated, but I think the magazine is good."

TIME, THE FLAGSHIP MAGAZINE of the company, which like the departed weekly *Life,* brought in and cost more money than any of the others, was a deeper and more intractable problem.

Page for page, it was the most expensive of the lot, with an editorial budget of between $70 and $75 million a year. Hardly for that reason alone did it get the most attention from the company and the world around it.

Under Luce, *Time* never strayed far from "The Weekly Newsmagazine" charter of its logotype. "People were dependent on us," says Tom Griffith, one of Luce's most senior retired editors. "Ours used to be the only place where you would find some things you wanted to know. Luce thought it a Calvinistic duty to be well informed." Until Luce "retired" in 1964, *Time*'s anonymous institutional voice, full of dogmatism, outraged many, including many on its staff, but the magazine never went unnoticed. It was an American fixture, necessary reading for the high and mighty, a habit for millions of others. To be on its cover was a signal honor. Who would be its "Man of the Year" was a national guessing game.

But the climate around newsweeklies had radically changed. TV became the nation's biggest source for daily national and international news. Newspapers went national, doing more of what the newsweeklies alone once did, summarizing and analyzing what people had already seen on TV. What was left to explain and display was sopped up by Sunday newspapers, fattening, expanding and providing more of the newsmagazines' fare. Specialized periodicals— "niche magazines" in the jargon of the trade—appealing to *special* audiences, were making it harder for weeklies that were supposed to appeal to *every* literate audience. And in the '80s, the affluent, who were the core of the newsmagazines' readers, were attracted not just by video and entertainment but by recreation and other busyness that cut into the hours left for reading. People in their thirties barely read *Time* at all; the average age of its subscribers was forty-nine in 1990. Even for *Time* zealots, "I rarely read *Time* or *Newsweek* the way I once did" became a familiar refrain.

WHILE THE EDITORS RECOGNIZED the change and tried to adjust, the problem for *Time* showed up at first most painfully in its accounting department.

Time's U.S. circulation in the mid-'80s was flat and mushy, its advertisers, drifting into TV and other new print outlets, were harder to entice. Worse still, to maintain its inflated U.S. circulation guarantee to advertisers (4.6 million), *Time*'s publishers went berserk with short-term discount subscriptions, spiced by such "premiums" as free electronics, telephones, radios, digital clocks, watches, cameras, calculators, as cheap as the junk mail and cable-TV ads that offered them. (*U.S. News & World Report* discovered that the 300,000 pens it gave away, embedded with tiny digital clocks, had instructions in Chinese. *Sports Illustrated* offered telephones shaped like sneakers.) "They all were buying their readers and selling their advertisers," it was said.

The gimcracks were addictive. To try to get people to resubscribe, churning a second premium was often necessary. At the end of the first premium fling in the late '80s, *Time* finally suffered the public embarrassment of having to cut back its circulation for the first time ever, first by 300,000, then by another 300,000, to 4 million.

Before he left as editor-in-chief in 1987, Henry Grunwald had warned, "We'll have to stop selling magazines by offering telephones and radios. This practice is pernicious [and] the whole notion of creating magazines primarily for advertisers is repugnant and ultimately self-defeating." *Time* confronted another reality, he added. While it remained the number-one newsmagazine, "*Newsweek* moved from being a second-rate imitator to a very strong challenger."

Anguish about *Time*'s future was nothing new. For more than ten years, Time's businessmen, in periodic fits, had pounded their heads about *Time*. Not about how the magazine was doing, which they always said was okay, but how it would profit in the future. Their projections down the road for the 1980s and into the 1990s showed either stagnation for *Time* in the U.S. at best, or more likely decline. Even though their dire predictions had not come true, the tocsin they sounded in 1987 was louder and harsher than it had been before. It also came from, and was heard by, a brand-new crew at the top.

Within twelve months in 1986–87, each of the three key executives who governed both *Time*'s editorial content and its business had just moved into his job. The magazine had a new editor-in-chief, managing editor and a new publishing boss with new subalterns for the whole Time Inc. magazine group. In short order, the publishers nailed a manifesto on the *Time* editorial church door.

THE LEADER OF THE MOVEMENT for change was Reginald K. Brack, Jr., fifty-four, who announces on his stationery, lest there be any doubt, his resounding title, "Chairman, President and Chief Executive Officer" of "Time Warner Publishing." His no-nonsense manner reinforced his heresies on the irrelevance of church and state. "Apart from advertiser influence, I don't believe there is any necessity for it. Where it becomes really problematic is in doing what's necessary to satisfy our customers."

From his marketing perspective, Brack thought that guesswork editorial instincts were an archeological relic. "The marketplace," he says, "should dictate what a magazine should be. Editors are doing the best job they can, more based on their desires than on any real understanding of why people read the magazine. Very few editors are attuned to readers' interests."

Kansas-born, raised in Dallas, off to college in Virginia (Washington and Lee, '59), Reg Brack is a thirty-year Time veteran who says of himself, "Basically I'm a marketing person." He is fond of such terms as "reader responsive, user-friendly magazines," "restructuring," "crucible of the marketplace." His conversation is bracketed by the perpendicular pronoun. "The magazines," recalls Brack, "had too many cooks in the soup until I came along—or I should say Nick Nicholas and I." One of his publishing credos, Brack says, is "Fix it or fold it." Brack describes Time's magazines and books as "basically software."

As the most dominating publishing chief Time Inc. has ever had, Brack has one priority. He stated it succinctly in a speech to other magazine publishers when he delivered his "Ten Commandments of Magazine Publishing." His First Commandment: "Increase Thy Profit Margin." Brack is faithful to his testament. When the magazine publishers under him ask what their financial targets should be for the year, Brack proudly says, "I won't tell them. Because whatever it is, it's too high for them and too low for me."

Brack was a *Time* ad salesman, ad director and the publisher of *Discover,* which was sold, not fixed or folded. Try as he does to seem affable, he presents such a dour visage that he cannot shake the old office joke, "The only way to get a smile on Reg's face is to turn him upside down." A colleague introducing him before a speech noted that "Reg started out when he was in college thinking of going to medical school. He gave up on that because he couldn't stand the sight of blood then. He seems to have gotten over it since."

Brack's own few Time corporate bosses found him a harder charger than they might have liked, as much as they valued his effectiveness as a bottom-line businessman. "For years he was mistreated because he wasn't one of the club of Eastern guys," one says. Another adds, "He's probably as good an executive as you'll ever meet, but he's not going to endear himself to a lot of people. He delivers the profit projections we want. With Reg, you know you can go home and he'll turn the lights out properly. You'll have to find out whether there's a soul there."

Brack's answer to his pit bull reputation: "Patience is not one of my strong virtues. So that given my positions, I often come off as brusque, uninterested, insensitive. But I pride myself on my tremendous degree of fairness. We have always been talked about as a people company. Frankly a lot of that was bullshit. We were one of the coldest, most ruthless companies in the world. If you were sick or had a problem, we were great. But cronyism was rampant. To get ahead in publishing with some of my predecessors, you'd better have been a good golfing buddy of your boss. My standard is performance. Yes it's tough. But it's fair."

• • •

THE TURNING POINT in Brack's career came at Time-Life Books, once enormously successful but in the red by the time he arrived in 1982. (To save on costs, its headquarters had been moved to Virginia.)

He reorganized the book operation, cut its staff, swiftly bringing it back from dismal losses to nice profits. One of the reasons given for the turnaround, explains a Time executive, was that Brack succeeded in "melding church and state." Brack heartily agrees that taking over the editorial church and attacking a business logjam were the reasons for his success at Time-Life Books. He overwhelmed editorial piety and quality control with his marketing and management bulldozer.

His regime launched nine new series, including one series on unidentified flying objects, mysterious creatures, cosmic connections, psychic voyages and other hokum. The financially successful series was titled "Mysteries of the Unknown" and was advertised with a screaming come-on, "Read This Book!" He is proudest of "the first series I launched on my watch, the 'Vietnam Experience,' at a time this country thought it didn't want to hear about Vietnam. I made the gut judgment standing in front of the Vietnam Memorial wall that this was a subject whose time had come."

After he was made CEO of the magazine group in 1986, at first his new editorial partners on the magazines agreed that more attention to business was long overdue. "In 1987 I restructured the magazine company," says Brack, in another of his many first-person declarations. Brack's new editorial partner at the top of all the magazines was editor-in-chief Jason McManus; *Time*'s new editorial chief was its new managing editor, Henry Muller. For *Time* magazine, a fresh trio for the onrushing '90s.

THE FRESHEST WAS TIME'S new managing editor, Henry Muller, forty, promoted in 1987 from chief of correspondents of the Time-Life News Service. "I admired Muller," says Grunwald, who appointed him, "but if you look at the past, he had shockingly short experience for that job." It was less shocking and short than different. His predecessors had waited in training as editors for years in New York long before they were anointed.

Muller's was a unique jump in *Time*'s history, during which correspondents in the field were a freewheeling corps apart, frequently at bruising odds with editors in the home office. It was a tension Luce himself had contrived, with the chief of correspondents reporting directly to him, to keep both editors and reporters, he said, "on their toes." Henry Muller ended the era of editors and writers on one side, correspondents on the other. He brought in three other correspondents as his top *Time* deputies. Although Henry Muller is popular and respected by his staff, many *Time* writers and editors resentfully said his first appointments were "the revenge of the News Service."

Muller was born of French-Swiss and German parents. When he was six his family moved from Switzerland to San Francisco and became U.S. citizens. They sent him to public and parochial schools, shipping him off briefly to the aristocratic Swiss boarding school Le Rosey so he wouldn't lose his French. Muller was a grammar school, high school and college (Stanford, '68) editor. He did a tour in the Peace Corps teaching in remote sections of Ethiopia before joining Time as a reporter for its house organ, *FYI*. In rapid moves, he became a *Time* correspondent in Ottawa, chief in the Vancouver, Brussels and Paris bureaus, returning to New York as a writer, briefly an editor, and chief of correspondents.

Of those who say, "He's very Swiss," Muller, trilingual in English, German and French, says with a smile, "They must mean I'm focused, organized and efficient—I don't mind that." His right-hand man, chief of correspondents John Stacks, who replaced Muller in that role, says don't be fooled. "Henry is Swiss but he was raised in California with a kind of antiauthoritarian, 'fuck 'em, nobody-tells-me-what to-do' attitude. It's invisible because of the correctness and politesse he has from his Swiss gene pool."

Muller had no specific editorial instructions from the top and didn't need any. From the day he moved into the managing editor's office, Muller says he knew "something different had to be done. I looked at the research. *Time* was an American institution, sure, but it didn't seem as relevant or as necessary to the kind of people we thought always read *Time*. A great magazine—but too many people felt they didn't need to read it. It was 'good for other people.' It needed a clearer place in American society again. My fear was that in the '80s it was going in a direction that ceased to matter." *Time,* agrees one of its promoters, "was an icon, but we needed to show that it was a living icon."

Well-established publications on a plateau of success but needing

change hesitate to do it radically. If they transform themselves overnight, they run the risk of losing the faithful without attracting the
new.

"My hope," says Muller, "was that we could make those changes
progressively without anyone noticing." So he started in concert, he
thought, with his publishing partners. Muller was more than a little
surprised when, without warning him, *Time* was savaged at a publishers' meeting in 1987, where it was predicted that unless something
happened fast, in the U.S. the magazine was headed within four
years from 10 percent profit (fluctuating above and below $50 million
a year) to zero. "They really wanted," says Muller, "a big bang."

In October of 1988, *Time* readers got it, a redesign, sprinkled with
graphics, boxes, charts and a jazzy "People" page. But it was not,
as he said, "Muller Lite." The first new issues included, among other
heavyweight pieces, a long interview with highbrow writer Susan
Sontag and a staff-written dense essay on "Myth and Memory."

IN PLACE OF TRADITIONAL "group journalism," Muller
opened the magazine to an eclectic chorus of staff and contract writers even more prominently by-lined than before.

As much as 25 percent of the weekly began coming directly from
correspondents and New York–based writers roaming the scenes
they wrote about. Well-known and high-priced journalists were
hired: political reporter Michael Kramer and Watergate's Carl Bern-
stein. Disparate outside essayists were put on contract: conservative
Charles Krauthammer, liberal Michael Kinsley. Muller didn't want
the magazine to seem "either polemical or opinionated, but I wanted
our contributors to have a point of view." There were dangers, says
recently appointed assistant managing editor Walter Isaacson. "Having no voice. Having too many voices. Having too rigid a voice. We
didn't want a collection of yo-yo liberals or hard-line conservatives.
We tried to be provocative and have opinions without being predictably on the left or the right."

The magazine moved away from its Washington beltway orientation, tried to plumb what was on people's minds, not just what the
news of the past week had been. The trademark *Time* cover more
than ever before avoided conventional news. The cover was more
often a topic (the environment) or an idea (ethics) than a person.
Rather than being driven by events when there wasn't compelling

news, the magazine concentrated on national problems and trends. *Time* put on its cover "Should Drugs Be Legal?"; "Do We Care About Our Kids?"; "Guns Kill"; "The Right to Die"; "Twenty-something: The Next Generation."

The magazine ran more trend and trendy covers and stories, devoting less space to minor news by compressing it into shorter items. Many of its critics thought that *Time* had gone "soft," abandoning its purpose of explaining to its readers what was happening and why in the whole country and the world. But *Time* still covered important weekly events worldwide and went full tilt for continuing big news like the end of the Cold War, the liberation of Eastern Europe, the war in the Gulf, the "second Russian Revolution" or, on a different plane, such popular Topic A's as Kitty Kelley's gossipy biography of Nancy Reagan (*Time*'s cover line: "Is She THAT Bad?").

Muller, says one of his top aides, "was changing the magazine by doing it rather than conceptualizing or defining it." The trouble, in part, was that *Newsweek* had started doing the same thing even earlier and often just as well or better. *Time* claimed it had more breadth and far greater resources of its own. *Newsweek* countered that it was quicker, less rigid, "feistier," more "with it." When pressed, editors of both magazines admitted they were both in the same new game. Only the "quality of the execution" week-to-week marked the real difference. Neither readers nor advertisers found *Time* the compelling standout it once had been.

More subscribers still chose *Time*. But the gap in size and distinction was closing. *Newsweek* reached 3.1 million guaranteed circulation; *Time* had been forced to reduce itself to 4 million. *Newsweek* more fiercely than ever competed with *Time* for ads, as did a resurgent *U.S. News*. Media buyers care less about a magazine's content than they do about the numbers they can count: demographics, cost-per-thousand, newsstand sales, pass-along readers. But financially, *Time*, whose ad rates were higher, had profits ranging from $47 to $53 million, still far outgunning *Newsweek*'s $15 to $30 million.

MULLER'S CHANGES CONFUSED AS many *Time* loyalists as they pleased, especially those whose journalistic roots were planted in the past. "*Time* is now a smorgasbord," said one old-*Timer*—"not a coherent expectation. It's good but it's no longer unique." Another complained, "At Burning Tree, where the whole Washington establishment plays golf, I used to be asked, 'Who's on the cover of *Time* this week?' Now they ask me, 'How's *Time* doing?' "

Newsweeklies were constantly branded an "endangered species" in the evolutionary print cycle, reminding some of such extinct national weeklies as *Life,* the *Saturday Evening Post, Look* and *Collier's.* "The old-fashioned magazine that tries to be many things to many readers is the one that virtually all studies tell us is in trouble," wrote Washington *Post* critic Jonathan Yardley, whose company owns *Newsweek.*

The trouble was exacerbated in 1990–91 by a recession that produced the worst media advertising drought in years. Early in 1991, Brack and his staff hit the alarm button again. The magazine's lower circulation guarantee of 4 million brought less ad revenue, which made its costs out of line and rising. This time the publishers set off a clang, overloading the circuits of the grapevine that connects every editorial office of the magazine.

The businessmen peered into the future and again found it bleaker than ever. The six expanding international editions of *Time* were growing (circulation 1.4 million, compared to *Newsweek*'s 840,000), showing promise but slowing profits. By most reckonings, *Time* in the U.S. had reached the limit of its readership. "Mature" is the euphemism. "Stagnant properties," Steve Ross had once described the magazines to a *Time* correspondent, before the merger.

At the current revenue and cost projections, *Time* publishers' computers showed a steady profit slide to oblivion. The solution was to keep, at less expense, the subscribers they already had, get new ones more easily and increase newsstand sales, rarely more than 5 percent of any newsmagazine's total. "They've run out of games to play on the business side," said an editorial executive. "So therefore they're thrown back as they never have been before on the importance of the editorial product. They're saying either make it better or make it different." Reasonable enough.

It was a familiar complaint but it was pounded home this round, in the eroding days of the business-editorial separation, by publishers with a bludgeon. Although Brack's troops frequently expressed private scorn for him, some of them in dealing with the editors went beyond the gospel according to Brack. Editor Muller was harangued, his editing and his shaping of *Time* disparaged. "It was obvious," said one top editor, expressing an editorial view heard widely, "that the business guys thought we were a bunch of nerds, policymakers, putting out a pseudo-intellectual magazine about world affairs full of what they call 'homework.' "

The publishers never said how they thought it should be fixed, but the implication was clear. "Your kind of news magazine is a dying breed. They wanted us to 'dumb it down,' " one editor charged. "They liked the profits of *People* more than the purposes of *Time*," said another. A top Brack lieutenant told an interviewer that magazine "survivors will be mostly personality, lifestyle, fashion and entertainment." *Time* editors were repelled by the implied message. They also felt it was a certain road to failure and hazardous commercially. "Our answer," said one of them, "is to increase the editorial quality of the magazine in order to increase demand for it instead of doing something stupid."

Publishers at Time rarely moved against editors with such unrestrained clout or specific gravity. They griped aloud about the editors. *Time*'s publisher, Robert Miller, with a shrug of his shoulders, said that if *Time*'s managing editor, Henry Muller, couldn't do better, too bad, he should get out. In the past, built-in tensions between publishers and editors had been worked out more as a collaboration than a brawl. No matter how hot either group was in private, they had remained respectful of each other even though their roles were different. "This may be the new era of Reg Brack," says one *Time* editor, "but he is not our father and never will be."

ARE THE EDITORS PRIMA donnas, unwilling to soil their hands in the countinghouse?

Ralph Graves, a former Time editorial director and last managing editor of the weekly *Life*, has a view which most Time editors today willingly accept. "As an editor," said Graves when he retired in the early '80s, "I wouldn't want any publisher telling me what stories to run or not to run. But there are very few figures in the world as boring and as arrogant as Time Inc. editors declaring their holy independence from the crass commercial influence of the publishing side."

Few doubted that *Time* was heading downward, not just because of the ad recession, but editorially against forces competing for people's attention. Confusing suggestions for change came from all sides: consultants, alumni, editors and publishers from Time's other magazines and most consequentially from an inside task force McManus had convened to search for a solution. Predictably, the task force report said the magazine should be "reader driven." McManus in a memo directed *Time*'s managing editor Muller to follow the group's recommendations. For the first time the changes envisioned for *Time* were at least as responsive to the pushing by its publishers as to the pulling by its editors.

Editor-in-chief McManus was known to feel, whatever he said to the contrary in public or to cheer on his staff, that *Time* magazine wasn't working. He heard the critics, scrutinized the readership surveys conducted by the publishers and was alarmed. In the past, *Time* editors rarely followed or even deigned to expose themselves to such weekly studies. But whether the surveys were accurate or not, the fact that McManus seemed to believe them meant more changes for *Time,* more searching for the formula that would make it work.

McManus lacked his own clear idea of what he wanted the newsmagazine to be when he ran *Time* as managing editor. He had not done much more than carry on where his predecessor Ray Cave left off. He was not much clearer now. Muller, in an effort to finesse conflicting demands, accepted the need for big changes but also seemed unable to define a new outlook for the magazine that he could fight for. "Henry is a process freak," says one of his editors, "not really sure what his vision for the magazine is." No one, including McManus and Muller, affirms a senior editorial executive, "seems very strong on the 'vision thing.' "

A young *Time* writer says earnestly, "We're people who never knew Henry Luce, but we've all been handed down the stories of Time Inc. in the old days. We, the younger staffers, can live with *Time* being the prestige label of a media empire. But we want the reason for that prestige still intact."

THE MOMENTARY SHOW OF force in 1991 by *Time* business generals was not unique in Time Inc.'s history. With Luce, it was never powerful for long because he owned the place and indisputably commanded both publishing and editorial armies. His two successors, Donovan and Grunwald, by dint of their personal strength and the success of the tradition, maintained their editorial autonomy. In harder times, McManus displayed no such strength. "If Jason were stronger," said one of Brack's publishers, "Reg would back down."

A more indulgent view comes from another executive who has watched Brack and McManus closely. "If we had an editor-in-chief who was stronger and a CEO of the publishing side who was brighter in certain respects—and they knew how to work together—that would be terrific. We don't have it. I'm not sure you ever have it. So it means that you work with it."

McManus says he feels not a bit threatened by Brack. "It's a difficult time for magazines," he explains, "and Reg brings me in his immense financial base. He and I talk privately a lot and he's very open-minded." Others view it differently. "Jason," says one Time editor, "is embarrassing to see in any meeting where Reg Brack is present. Reg is tough, articulate. I can't stand him, but there's a certain authority about him."

Brack's success or failure is reckoned by his own bosses, who live down the street in the Time Warner Building. One Time journalist pungently describes Brack's problem running the least profitable of Time Warner's big operations. "He's in a tight spot. The magazine business sucks these days. Brack's core magazines are not going to produce the revenue that he told the Time Warner bigwigs they would. Meanwhile he's got all these other big swinging dicks running Warner music, records, cable films and Lorimar TV—and he's kind of sucking wind with his contribution to the bottom line. He's also really burned up that he's not on the Time Warner board the way Jason is."

MCMANUS LIKES TO RECALL, not wholly in jest, that when he became editor-in-chief in 1987, Dick Munro, Time Inc.'s CEO, told him, "The journalists work for you. You work for God. Everybody else around here works for me. And if any of them don't understand that, just let me know." Steve Ross is aware of the old theology. In a speech to a large news media group, he said, "There's a tradition at Time Warner called church and state. Under it the editor-in-chief is responsible for protecting the independence of our editorial voice. Jason McManus is our Pope."

Ross should have said "Bishop." Even before the Time Warner merger, the system, the personalities and the environment had begun to change. With cable and video growing, the magazines had been put under the rubric of the Time Inc. Magazine Company, wholly owned by Time Inc. In the new scheme, the editor-in-chief, while still a member of the parent board of directors, was to work "in close consultation with the CEO of the Magazine Company," Reg Brack, no longer with the chairman of Time Inc., certainly not with the co-

chairman of Time Warner. It turned out to be more than an organization chart formality—much more, given the personalities involved.

Most senior editorial executives at *Time* are apprehensive about
the future. "What I worry about most," says one of them, "is a
combination of circumstances where the reader demand for *Time*
falls off. If our numbers get weak, we'll be a charity case within
Time Warner. That's where editorial integrity disappears. If we are
strong as a magazine, strong financially, a 10 percent profit is acceptable. Five percent is a real problem, but if we can stay somewhere
around eight, then nobody is going to have to subsidize us." In 1990,
Time's U.S. profit was $46 million, 10.5 percent of its $425 million
revenue. But with the recession still not over, in the first six months
of 1991, *Time*'s ad pages fell by 21 percent. Revenue was dropping
and costs were still rising.

The pressure on *Time* came more directly from Brack and his
troops in the Time & Life Building than it did from what is now
called "75 Rock," the center of Time Warner power. There, both
Levin and Nicholas still say, with a fervor that suggests they mean
it, and with public affirmation by Ross, that *Time*'s value to the
company is greater than the size of its profits. "I don't even want to
discuss with what losses I would continue publishing *Time*," says
Nicholas heatedly, "but I would. I don't care about its percentage
rate of return. That's not what I use to measure its success." Levin
concurs. "*Time* magazine is still the most powerful core symbol for
the entire company. It has very little to do with profit and loss
percentages." *Time*'s Muller believes them. "I think Time Warner
is a company where you can impress those bosses at 75 Rock with
something other than the bottom line. You also have to deliver the
bottom line. But it's not the only thing they look at."

WHEN THE DEAL WAS first announced, the biggest worries were
not about *Time* alone. Under the new Time Warner banner, there
was deep concern over whether all magazines could retain their editorial independence; and with the overhanging debt, whether the
magazines would get financial backing they needed from their new
parent company.

At first more than one skeptic asked the obvious: Wouldn't Time
magazines run into conflicts reviewing Warner movies—or Warner
records, books and TV programs? Even Time journalists seized the

question. "When Jason came down alone to talk to the bureau," says Washington bureau chief Stanley Cloud, "it was probably the correspondents' fault, but they spent most of their time arguing about the silly question of reviewing Warner movies."

The issue was trivial and should have been easy to dismiss. Time's magazines had for years been trashing HBO movies; Little, Brown's books got bad as well as good reviews; and the magazines gleefully needled or competed with each other at every opportunity. But the atmosphere of suspicion over the merger was so strong that some doubters persisted, arguing that that was the old way under Time Inc. Synergy would be the Time Warner theory; internal rivalry had been a lively and healthy Time practice. Critical irreverence toward Warner's entertainment, they predicted, would not be tolerated in Time Warner. On that limited score, they were wrong.

Entertainment Weekly, People, and *Sports Illustrated,* the "soft news" trio, have been as rough on Warner's stars, pop entertainment and sports celebrities as any other magazine. Who was more critical of Warner's biggest flop, *The Bonfire of the Vanities*? Warner's sequel to *Gone With the Wind,* one of the most expensively promoted books ever, was greeted before it came out by *Entertainment Weekly* with a variation on the Rhett Butler line "Frankly, my dear, no one gives a damn." When it was published, *Time*'s review was titled, "Frankly It's Not Worth a Damn." After a series of flops, the Warner-backed, -distributed and -ballyhooed 1991 movie *Robin Hood* was treated by *Time* with a dismissive "Naah, merits only a ho-hum."

On such matters, self-consciousness was often outweighed by the stubborn effort of Time's editors and writers to demonstrate their independence by poking their parents in the eye more than most other magazines do. If anything, Time's magazines were at least as critical of Warner *products*—as opposed to Time Warner the *company*—as they were of other companies' products.

Nor did the magazines avoid many subjects where it was not imperative to single out Time Warner. The company's executives were not overjoyed with *Time* articles on cable-TV regulation or on the nuisance of junk mail; both strayed from the Time Warner lobbying line. The stories ran unaltered. Neither did these executives cheer over a *Time* business story, "You're Leveraged? How Gauche! How Gauche!" or an essay titled "CEOs: No Pain, Just Gain."

Fortune articles deplored the corporate "borrowing binge," rapped managers of the '80s (who "paid too much attention to financial strategy, mergers and LBOs, not to creativity"), criticized corporate reporting ("most proxies obfuscate—the SEC should demand better"), took apart and hounded Time Warner's investment banker Bruce Wasserstein, questioned whether "directors earn their keep."

None of these pieces, all disparaging practices applying to Time Warner, had a self-conscious taint. *Fortune*'s sacrosanct lists ranking business winners and losers, caused Time Warner executives nervous sweats but produced no fiddling with computer printouts or juggling categories. Time Warner was fourth on the 1991 list of biggest *Fortune* 500 service companies but was also named as one of the worst "money losers" in the two years before; and a dreary 162nd on the list of the "most admired" companies in the U.S., next to the last in the publishing group.

FAR TOUGHER TO DEAL with, especially for *Time* and *Fortune,* was a more intricate problem.

The new company—as was the merger process itself—was so much in the financial news and had so many interests that the editors, writers and reporters kept running into themselves as they did their work. Both by self-consciousness and concerns from the editor-in-chief's office, it was hard to treat Time Warner's activities and problems as they would those of any other large company. The best evidence is that they try, but neither their bosses nor the editors always succeed. They have failed most conspicuously on the biggest stories involving Time Warner as a company, e.g., the merger itself, and goofs in financial maneuvering or management, which got big and damaging attention in other media.

The problem was exemplified in a comprehensive August 1991 *Fortune* retrospective titled "The Deal Decade: Verdict on the 80s." It sharply criticized leveraged excesses deal by deal, with the names and numbers of the dealmakers. But it skipped one of the highest profile deals of them all, the Time Warner merger, mentioned in only one indirect and barely visible chart notation.

When the time came to publish *Fortune*'s 1991 annual executive pay list, there was a gasp, two weeks' delay and a rush for "second opinions" on Ross's and Nicholas's rewards packages. After some heavy pushing and hauling, dealing with complaints from 75 Rock, finally the published article showed Ross to be the highest paid executive in all of American public corporate life ($39.1 million in 1990), 1,363 percent above the norm. (*Forbes,* using different methods, showed Ross on its cover with $79 million for the year, which actually included part of his 1989 payout that it had already reported.) Nicholas turned up in the *Fortune* reckoning for 1990 with $7.4 million in salary, bonus, deferred compensation and weighted options, 176 percent above the model and sixth from the top in executive pay.

The tough compensation story, which should have been a sign of *Fortune*'s corporate incorruptibility, was turned into an embarrassment for *Fortune* and Time Warner. The author, Graef Crystal, described by *Fortune* as "America's foremost compensation expert," was a regular contributor. After his article "How Much CEOs Really Make" appeared in June 1991, he announced that he would no longer be writing for *Fortune*.

In a letter to *Fortune*'s editors, Crystal wrote that he had "nothing but good things to say" about *Fortune*'s editors: "If there is integrity in journalism, yours are the brightest flames." But the process of getting the piece into print had not been easy. Also, he had received an "acrimonious," insulting letter from Time Warner's vice president for corporate compensation, Donald Guerette. "The *Fortune* piece," explains Crystal, "was like giving birth to a beautiful baby boy, but dying during labor. I don't want to have another baby with them."

The *Wall Street Journal* ran a top-of-the-page headline, "Writer Quits Fortune, Citing Meddling by Time Warner." The resignation incident, reported across the country by the Associated Press, left the damaging and widespread impression that the magazine had taken a dive, which it had not, to protect Ross and Nicholas from exposure of their massive rewards. In fact, the magazine had finally resisted the argument it got from its own company, the kind it often encounters when it reports on other business stories where sources differ with *Fortune*'s views.

And there were even worse embarrassments to come later in the year.

Editor-in-chief Jason McManus seemed conscious of the impression of weakness he was conveying. Under stress from his own editors, from Brack and his troops, as well as 75 Rock, McManus said in mid-1991 that he was changing some of his basic management practices.

"I've gotten tougher with all the editors. We went through this period because of all the scrutiny. And we found too much withdrawal from the three of us up here [McManus himself, editorial director Stolley and corporate editor Rogin]. We had to explain editing changes if the editors of the magazines had any sensitivity. But I said we have to go back to being grownups. The editors are going to get instructions from here. Some people are not going to like them. We're just going to have to say—the way Hedley Donovan and Henry Grunwald did—not only did the editor-in-chief order it, but you don't necessarily need an explanation. I think we went too far in the independence. And among the three of us there was a sense that things were a little out of control."

Control in what direction? More and more the magazines seemed to follow their readers rather than their uncertain leaders, who offered few resolute editorial compass headings. Focus groups, surveys, test mailings, can all be helpful as indicators of what may *not* be appealing. But they give few reliable clues as to what *will* be. For years avoiding such statistical editorial reckonings—except to impress advertisers—was a formula for success at Time's magazines. No longer.

MOST OF THE ENERGY for starting new publishing ventures and creating new magazines continued to be directed to the past or to the outside, just before as well as after the merger.

Struggling *Entertainment Weekly* was conceived and readied for print long before the Warner merger. New magazines were called "special issues," "line extensions" or "spinoffs," like *Sports Illustrated Classic*, or the two-year-old *Sports Illustrated for Kids*, the exploration of a similar edition of *Time*, or trying to change monthly *Life* to a weekly. None was really new; all were new versions of successful old ones. *Fortune*, in the wake of Time Warner's cry of "globalism," had published small Italian and French editions with foreign partners. But globalism or no, it killed the unsuccessful French edition, later dropped the Italian, and indefinitely postponed a planned Spanish edition.

The only wholly created new magazine since the merger was a jointly owned experiment, *Martha Stewart's Living*, a hyperactive magazine for modern homemakers. Its first test issue featured daunting self-help articles on "How to Repair Your Chandeliers," which seemed to require an artisan's tool chest and a glass cutter's finesse; printing your own multicolored Christmas paper; copper-coating leaves from the garden for decorations instead of burning them; and—from cover to last page—sixteen pictures of the eponymous editor. Stewart's magazine, wrote the New York *Times*'s publishing reporter, is "full of features on little girls in organdy dresses hunting Easter eggs in topiary gardens; wild mushrooms piroshki served on embossed antique china plates, and the pleasures of washing and ironing vintage linens."

After two test issues (circulation 350,000), the company liked Stewart so much that it signed her to a ten-year contract for what it billed, in the ever-proliferating Time Warner hype, as a "multimedia" extravaganza. "We used the idea of a wheel in building this concept," a publisher explained. "In the center is Martha and the Time Warner management. The spokes of the wheel are magazines, television, videos, trade books and ancillary products, like annual cookbooks or gardening books." In the here and now, the magazine was brought out as a bimonthly in July 1991. Its contents were slightly less exotic and frenetic, its circulation set at 250,000, and while there was a picture of Martha Stewart on the cover again, there were *only* eight others of her inside. She also got a weekly spot on NBC's *Today* show.

AFTER TWO YEARS as part of Time Warner, what was the Time Inc. Magazine Company's scorecard? Contrary to most predictions, except for coverage of their own parent company, the magazines were neither hurt nor helped by the merger itself.

In hard times for most magazines, mostly the same people at Time Inc. were doing what they had done before, moving in the same directions. There was even an opinion that they might be in more trouble if they were not in a company twice their old size. Ross himself was uninvolved and hands-off. Even his strongest suit, his ability to encourage with his largess and optimism, was curtailed. In a misreading of what church and state was all about, his Time advisers told him to stay as much as he could out of the Time & Life Building and away from its journalists.

Time's magazines were still suffering a hangover from their late-'80s hypermarketing orientation, some trying bleary-eyed to find their way in a new media environment. They were also being squeezed harder financially than ever before. But the strain came as much from Reg Brack's ambitions, preoccupations and the national recession as it did from the Time Warner debt with its voracious need for "cash flow."

One predicted possible benefit of the merger never materialized.

Some editors tried to look on the potential bright side. They had speculated that with the magazines now a smaller segment of the giant company, there would be more money available for them, even if they suffered in down years of the national economy. After all, as everyone had agreed, the magazines—specifically *Time*—were so symbolically important to Time Warner. It was not to be. One grouser remembered way back to the Warner board meeting approving the merger when it was explained that Time's magazines didn't have great growth prospects but produced enough excess cash to "invest in operations that would allow a higher rate of return."

Indeed, other, more profitable divisions of Time Warner went their high-stepping ways, as did their executives and bosses. There were also multimillions for dozens of new deals, despite the debt. But like other media companies pressed by a recession, Time's home-grown magazines were not part of the fun. In the fall of 1991, Brack and McManus announced budget cuts of more than 10 percent across-the-board, along with deep staff reductions of more than 600 jobs for all the magazines.

At the September 1991 board meeting, where magazine staffers showed up in force to protest the layoffs, Nicholas said firmly and ominously that "we are undergoing the painful but necessary work of reducing costs. This process isn't going to end. It's now part of the way we do business." Then, distancing himself from bad news, which he often does, Nicholas added, "Remember they're [Brack and McManus] the ones who made this decision."

Time, whose budget had not been increased in the three years past, was especially hard hit by a 14 percent reduction. Close to fifty editorial staffers were cut, nineteen out of its seventy-five correspondents, eight writers and twelve reporter-researchers, along with ad staff. Offices were closed and some "laptop bureaus" created where correspondents would work from their homes. The editors and publishers were just as happy not to be ready until after the cuts had been swallowed for the unveiling later of what they described as the "most radical redesign in *Time*'s history." The new design still had to be tested on focus groups and by other media and marketing research. One editor said it would be "the first reinventing after 1923, when *Time* started, of the newsmagazine concept."

McManus and the company wanted what even he called the "restructuring" of *Time* to be accepted as editorially motivated, not an economy measure. The message might have been more convincing if first the "new" *Time* had been agreed upon and then the cuts made, based on what the redesigned magazine required. "The new *Time*," said one of its hopeful editors deeply involved in the redesign, "will not be a cheapo." Managing editor Muller described it: "We've decided to see if there's a clearer, more accessible way to organize the entire magazine than the section-by-section format that has been the essence of *Time* since Luce invented the newsmagazine. At this point it's just too early to say if this process will lead to the most important reinvention of the newsmagazine in seventy years or down a blind alley."

PERHAPS THE MOST BIZARRE and embarrassing hangovers from the days just before the merger were the contracts that all Time managing editors signed.

Before 1987, Timeincers did not have employment contracts except under the most special circumstances. Informal fairness supposedly was enough. But with mergers, acquisitions or possible takeovers in the air, more formal protection for executives was thought to be necessary. Time lawyers prepared a boilerplate draft of three-year contracts for senior managers, including one provision that said they could be fired or lose their payouts after leaving "for denigrating the Company at any time during employment or thereafter." Heads of divisions were invited to tailor the contracts to suit their special needs.

Editor-in-chief McManus decided that his managing editors should have stronger language, which surprisingly he made infinitely more restrictive, not less. In a clause crafted and devised by McManus himself, each managing editor, in exchange for a three-year contract, agreed to a muzzling provision that would make a CIA agent blanch before signing up with the agency. "I can't believe it," says one alumnus, shaking his head in wonderment. "For God's sake, Time Inc. is in the free speech business."

The McManus special clause provided that managing editors "will not *at any time* denigrate, ridicule or intentionally criticize the Company or any of its subsidiaries or Affiliates, or any other of their respective products, properties, employees, officers or directors, including without limitation, *by way of news interviews, or the expression of personal views, opinions or judgments to the news media*." (Italics added.) Time's managing editors and McManus himself signed contracts with those words in them (only the managing editor of *Entertainment Weekly,* Jeff Jarvis, later refused).

Legally, if anyone wanted to enforce the contract, managing editors could thereafter be fired for running a negative review of a Time Warner book or movie, or speaking critically to a reporter about anyone or any aspect of the huge enterprise (e.g., "What did you think of Warner's involvement with Two Live Crew? or the heavy-metal group Guns N' Roses?"). And after leaving the company, if they violated the restriction by speaking freely, their contractual payouts could be cut off. Ironically, it was Steve Ross, at the final Warner board meeting before the merger, who objected to the clause. The minutes of the meeting reveal that "Mr. Ross questioned the advisability of such a clause. He suggested that they have this clause deleted but the request was denied by Time." So Ross dropped the matter even though Warnerites had no such clause in their contracts.

McManus chose to interpret the clause as applying only after the signer leaves. His lawyers corrected him in his presence, pointing out that legally it applied during employment as well as after, adding that it's obviously violated every day in print and in speech.

But why would journalists sign such a contract without at least pointing out that it was not advisable and surely would be embarrassing for a company in journalism? "I had no problems," says *Fortune* managing editor Marshall Loeb. "We got these terrific three-year provisions for the first time and I'm sure that clause was unintentional. Holy cow, they couldn't mean it!" *Time*'s Muller agrees. "The contract assures me that I'll get three years' pay if I'm fired. If they're willing to give me three years' pay, I didn't bother with the criticism clause."

And why would McManus, who acknowledges that he had "complete freedom" to draft the contracts, write the special restriction on senior journalists the way he did? "It's a very standard corporate practice," he says, without adding that where even milder restrictions are imposed in government or corporate America they are deplored and mocked by journalists as an infringement on free speech. "We would never apply such a clause," says McManus indignantly, "gagging people while they were employed. I thought it applied only after they leave. Given all the troubles we were going through in 1987–88, this seemed like a useful giveback."

Even after it was pointed out that no place in American journalism are there such gags—formally covering both before as well as after leaving ("after" was bad enough)—Time editorial contracts were not revised. Among the senior editorial executives, only McManus himself, who in November 1990 got a new five-year agreement, no longer has the restrictive clause in his contract. The managing editors' contracts are automatically renewable after three years. Their gag clause will not be removed, says one high editorial executive, "unless it becomes a public issue."

"McManus must be in personal agony," says an editor who works for him. "The hardest thing for him to know is that fellow journalists feel he let them down by not being a stronger force during the merger negotiations." An editor who has been a McManus friend for years thinks "Jason's principal job now is to convince the board, on which he sits, that they absolutely need *Time* magazine as the standard-bearer of the corporation whether it's a dazzling success or not." Another hopes for the best. "He hasn't been the good old Jason he was. But every editor-in-chief leaves a legacy. His should be defining and protecting the role of journalism in Time Warner. I hope he does that." McManus vows that he already has and certainly will in the future.

Chief of correspondents John Stacks, an outspoken member of *Time* managing editor Muller's quartet of top editors, outlines what he thinks the future may hold. Time Warner's position should be, he says, that "*Time* is something important to the corporation. We will try to make as much money out of it as possible. But we're not going to take it downscale in order to make more money out of it and let it fail that way. If it's going to fail because the world has changed to a point where it can't succeed, then let's ride the son of a bitch as long as it goes and go out with our heads up saying we did a goddamn good job. What's that—fifteen, twenty years maybe? But for anyone to blink now is ridiculous."

THE SCENE WAS AN editors' lunch in the editor-in-chief's dining room on the forty-seventh floor of the Time & Life Building. The purpose of the lunch, convened right after the Time Warner merger, was to reassure the journalists about their future in the new media conglomerate.

To the amazement of the twenty-odd editors present, McManus began with a long and angry criticism of "how vindictive and unfair" the reporting on the merger had been. "It was acutely embarrassing to most of us," said one editor present. "For Chrissakes we're journalists ourselves, and sure, there was a lot of criticism in the press about the merger. But a lot of things were said and done that deserved criticism." Another recalled, "We were all kind of looking down, wishing, 'Oh God, let's hope he gets this out of his system.' "

Then McManus got to his main subject. In the new Time Warner, he said, the Time people have to be successful and strong. "If we're not in charge, *we* won't deserve to be." Up from Washington for the occasion, then bureau chief Strobe Talbot, with a gentle smile, interrupted. He invoked mockingly the folkloric joke about the Lone Ranger who told "his faithful Indian scout," Tonto, when the two were facing hostile Indians, "we" can defend ourselves. "Excuse me, white man," said Talbott to McManus. "What's this 'we' shit. If you mean by 'we' the journalists in this enterprise, you're the only journalist who had any part in this merger and the rest of us are along for the ride, dependent on the way you've represented us as journalists." McManus looked saddened and struck.

Then the lunch broke up. Another editor present remembers, "Somebody needed to say something like that. It really crystallized our situation. The whole session was a disaster. It just made the Jason problem worse." Talbot recalls that "Jason was extraordinarily gracious with me about letting the moment pass into history."

As a memento of the lunch, McManus, who is open to dissent and says of himself, "I'm unoffendable," was given a small pillow by his secretary, which he keeps in his office. On it is inscribed in needlepoint: "McManus whined for ten minutes over the unfairness of the coverage. Hey Jason: Kick back. Chill out. Hang loose. Have fun."

chapter 16

Gone With the Wind

MELDING TWO COMPANIES is rarely easy, even when they are identical or fraternal twins. Time and Warner were neither. "When companies merge," said a business psychologist, "things become vague and the ambiguity causes stress."

Some stress came from the unanswered question of what their leaders had done and would do to the old Time Inc. and the old Warner Communications. And, most critically, with what standards and goals they would now operate as one. What was the character, the spine, of the new company?

First, in Time Warner's coupling, the rulers of each corporate kingdom had to move together into one governing palace, along with their aides and attendants. They had to assign new responsibilities and titles; fix priorities; keep the cash flowing to match their more than $3 million-a-day interest commitment; by promoting Time Warner they had to try to make sure Wall Street oracles shared their optimism. "Time became, after Luce, about as democratic at the top as capitalism can be," says an executive who has been deeply involved with both companies. "At Warner, when Steve said we're going to march, you marched." Now both cadres had to re-form and march to the same drummer.

It was much more daunting than deciding what they should now call themselves. A contest held by Timeincers suggested "Twinks," "Twinkies," "Time Winkers" or "Twerps" (Time Warner Employees Realizing Personal Success). What to call the executives appeared easier. Inflated titles were passed out like gas-filled balloons at a parade. Everyone from platoon leader up was a chairman, a co- or a vice: "Chairman of Time Warner International," "Chairman of Time Warner Trade Publishing," "Chairman of Time Warner Libraries," "Chairman of Time Warner Enterprises," "Chairman of Warner Music Group" with two co-chairmen of Atlantic Records under him and under them a "Chairman of Atlantic Records, Los Angeles," "Chairman Warner Music International"—prides of chairmen. After the announcement of one new post, a top executive got four phone calls from managers saying, "I thought that was my job." Nicholas says their functions are clear enough. "Don't let the titles fool you."

In a bicoastal, cross-cultural anointing, Time's house organ reported on the *real* titles under the heading "Honorable Menschen": "Within the same two weeks, Nick Nicholas was given an American Jewish Committee Human Relations Award in Los Angeles and Steve Ross was named the Man of the Year by the Entertainment Division of the UJA-Federation in New York."

At the most mundane level, some of the Warner people were nervous. One woman from Warner who showed up at a meeting in the Time & Life Building told her friends, "I was so excited that it's the first time in my life I've ever worn a slip." The Time people, a trifle snobbish, got their own comeuppances. "The Warner folks were very open and friendly," said one of Time's corporate staff, "not as stiff or bureaucratic as some of ours. At Time it got so you needed a requisition form to get requisition forms, really. Things at Warner were done very differently. You could cut a check in ten minutes for $50,000. At Time you couldn't cut a check for $50 in ten days."

AT FIRST, THE JOINED companies ran separately rather than together. "Split governance," they called it.

Nicholas explained that he "was responsible for the old Time businesses, Steve for the old Warner businesses. And we shared cable. I also became co-CEO and I was still chief operating officer of the Time businesses, so I had my old job too." As a result of the Paramount raid, laments a Time Warner director, "Steve and Nick were really preoccupied with cleaning up the balance sheet. That's been unfortunate, because Nick hasn't had the time he should have to be co-CEO."

Both Ross and Nicholas spent close to half their time trying to reduce the debt by an intensive worldwide effort to find foreign investors and partners. The search was hard work, but made easier by four company-owned transoceanic Gulfstream jets. An ex–Warner executive remembered that in the mid-'80s "there was much clucking in the office because Steve took his first commercial flight in well over a decade—the Concorde back from Europe."

The Time & Life Building offices (1.7 million square feet), with ten times the space of Warner's, were turned over to publishing magazines and books. Brack was the executive superintendent working out of Luce's old office. The older Warner Communications Building (322,000 square feet), which once housed Esso Oil, was renamed the Time Warner Building and became corporate headquarters. It was only half a block away from the Time & Life Building and connected to it by the tunnels under Rockefeller Center. Proximity made the move easier. But for the Time bosses, at first it was a jarring experience. "Moving is always traumatic for me," says Nicholas, "a marking place in life."

On the executive twenty-ninth floor of their Time Warner headquarters, with Munro retired, the senior troika of Ross, Nicholas and Levin were installed along with their personal aides in a command post of hushed isolation. Alongside Ross's aerie, quarters were carved out for Nicholas and Levin, close to double the size of their old Time-Life offices and paneled in rich burnished cherrywood. The "forests of Brazil were denuded," joked one aide. Gone were the bookcases that once lined their Time-Life offices, offering more space for paintings from Warner's art collection, a huge DeKooning for Nicholas, a Hopper for Levin. Ross had two Childe Hassams. It looked like the handsomest new men's club in town, with its own haute cuisine French chef, pantry, gym and barbershop, which Ross visited almost daily for a comb and trim. It also was an aloof tower of power—too aloof.

Nicholas and Levin, accustomed to walking the halls and informally dropping in on their staffs, or being dropped in on, sat in protected solitude, walled off by guards and a battery of TV security screens. The headquarters suite, with its private elevator, suited Ross's style more than Nicholas's and Levin's. "Look at the bottom of Steve's shoes," says one old Warner wise guy. "He never walks. We used to say that he got carried across the street to '21.' " "I miss the walking around a lot," says Nicholas, "but I still have the phone." A Time executive looking over the new offices wondered, "It's hard to tell from these Warner-style offices who was acquiring whom."

. . .

SYNERGY—THE THEORY THAT one and one makes more than two—was the "synthesis" that Time Warner's annual report had said "would lift us to a position that neither could achieve alone." But it didn't do much lifting.

Under the headline "After Two Years of Time Warner's Marriage, Stockholders Are Still Hearing Promises, Promises," the *Wall Street Journal* in mid-1991 reported: "It's almost two years since Time joined with Warner Communications in one of the most ballyhooed mergers ever, and the combined company has yet to demonstrate that it is much more valuable than the two separate parts."

"I don't like the word 'synergy,' " Levin says. "I don't know what it means and it's a terrible word." Forget that the merger papers had described "the synergy that the combination is intended to achieve." Synthesis, synergy, vertical integration, whatever they now chose to call the advantages of togetherness, to bring the companies closer they needed to take another step. They took it in the spring of 1991, when Levin was named to the new post of chief operating officer for Time Warner.

It was intended as a signal establishing that Nicholas and Ross clearly would in tandem be the co–policy leaders and strategists, as well as freeing Nicholas to get better acquainted with the movie and record business. The Levin appointment was also designed to squelch the widespread impression that Ross was dominating while Nicholas was merely a financial officer and manager, instead of being on a par with Ross. Levin, one chart level below, was supposed to bridge the operating gap between the Time and Warner people and be the focal point for all the company's diverse managers. "We told the board we wanted Jerry to be chief operating officer," says Nicholas, "and at first they were very surprised. Then they saluted."

Many old-Timers, while admiring Levin's impressive talents, were also surprised, considering him an odd choice to run the complex new combined company. During the mid-'80s at Time, Nicholas remembered, "Jerry had some brilliant ideas but often with no foundation under them to make them happen." But he quickly reminds himself, "That's not even an issue anymore because he's terrific with people and he's much better at running things today. There was a period of estrangement between us, but that was a crazy time. The caricature of me is that I'm a great operator and a lousy dreamer.

The truth is I'm a hell of a dreamer and a damned good operator and so is he."

When it was pointed out to Levin that at Time he had been known as the best thinker in the company but not the greatest executive, he shrugged off the rap. "That was a political situation," he says with confident ease. "Levin," adds a member of the board, "just seems to get better and better. In the last couple of years he's proved that he's a very good all-around executive. That wasn't always true, which just shows you how people can grow and change."

In public, Ross said everyone was "fantastic," while Nicholas professed "seamless" partnership, which was hard to believe and, of course, wasn't true. But at first Nicholas accommodated to Ross's rambling dreams more than Ross embraced Nicholas's more structured, didactic habits. How does Ross adjust to not having his old imperial command? "He has to adjust," replies Nicholas. "He doesn't have to defer, he has to share. Steve will often say, 'I haven't talked to Nick on this one, but here's what I think.' "

Nicholas and Levin agreed that no one was equal to Ross's financial wizardry, salesmanship or schmoozing face-to-face across the negotiating table. But Ross knew that at times he was the wrong upfront deal maker, so occasionally he stayed in the background. "Steve understands that," says one aide who has watched them both in action. "Sometimes he stands back because he's a total opportunist in wanting the deal to work." At times, Nicholas, always viewed at Time as unmatched in financial skills, had trouble getting on with Ed Aboodi, who, although not formally a Warner executive, continued to function as Ross's and Time Warner's chief financial guru.

At board meetings where Ross presided, one Time Warner director noticed that "Steve can go on and on and you want to say to him, 'We've got the damned answer—enough!' But Steve and Nick are terribly careful—both of them. Nick, who can be very brusque and abrupt, handles the relationship very well. The board seems very comfortable with what it sees." Another director finds Ross's lengthy explanations useful in "educating us about the arcane aspects of show business." To the world outside, a Time Warner director says, "Ross is such a star that it's still kind of Nick who? But Nick always understood that, so it shouldn't come as a great shock to him."

WHEN TIME WARNER BEGAN pushing cash flow and not earnings as a way to measure performance, Nicholas had crowed, "I feel liberated, I really do." No longer, he thought, would the company suffer the tyranny of an inspection every quarter by Wall Street on how its earnings compared to the quarter before.

But he had badly miscalculated. Time Warner's executives were victims of a new and more bruising tyranny: their $11.5 billion debt with its draining interest. It remained a pall hanging over the company and its deflated stock. It was the downer in almost every news story, Wall Street analysts' reports, and even in casual conversations about the new company. "Debt-laden Time Warner" was the phrase of choice.

No matter how much Ross or Nicholas bragged about Time Warner's glorious future, its deals and dazzling technology, Wall Street wasn't listening. Although its stock had risen to almost twice its October 1990 low of $66, it was stuck at first in the $70-to-$90 range, then rose to highs in the low $120s in 1991, in expectation of a big capital infusion from a new foreign investor. Rumors resulted in such bulletins as "Time Warner is reportedly trying to raise cash and expand internationally through a joint venture with Toshiba." But even at its 1991 high of $125, with the Dow Jones average surging past a record 3,000, Time Warner stock was still far below its investment bankers' promised land. "We're going to have earnings much sooner than people think," Nicholas asserted vaguely.

Too few new investors were willing to pay the price of waiting. Earnings, not assets, were the indicators of success. "We can afford to have them wait," said Nicholas. "We have no problem meeting the debt. It only restricts our ability to invest in new things—and I mean big things. If I have a home worth $40 billion and a mortgage of $11 billion, would I be upset? Not at all. Particularly if I knew that I had the only house that was made of gold and it was irreplaceable. People are so damned shortsighted, a bunch of worry warts. We're not hunkering down here saying, 'Oh the debt, the debt, the debt.' "

If they weren't, others were.

Time Warner was plagued by public preoccupation with its debt, its losses, its unrelenting high executive living, while costs were being cut in other operations. As a distraction and to go on the offensive, Time Warner mounted an unintentionally revealing side show.

The top Time Warner bosses seized on what had been scheduled as a routine announcement by its cable subsidiary and converted it into a three-ring circus with Ross, Nicholas and Levin each in a ring.

Their hyped spiel would have made a circus barker blush. Their own cable executives had warned them not to overdo it. It is recorded here at some length less for its significance than for its hyperbole, which characterized every Time Warner pronouncement.

ON A COOL, CLEAR MARCH morning in 1991, close to seventy reporters and TV crews settled into the plush seats of the movie screening room on the eighth floor of the Time Warner Building. The gathering was billed as a "major development in cable TV technology," the kind of Roman candle into the supernova that Steve Ross relishes. It was his first formal press conference appearance since the Time Warner merger. Must be something big. What could be so important?

Nothing less, Ross, Nicholas and Levin announced, than "a complete revolution in the home, an important step toward fulfilling the vision that inspired the creation of Time Warner, an enterprise that is once again demonstrating why it is the most exciting and innovative media and entertainment company in the world."

Quite a burden to lay on what they were unveiling: a short fiberoptic link to existing TV cable. The result, they said, would make available 150 interactive cable channels instead of the existing 75 one-way channels they had built on some of their systems. But that was just the beginning. One day a laser-driven signal would be "compressed" to fill 600 to 1,200 TV channels, a topping of caviar with crème fraîche for couch potatoes.

The press handouts and speeches were euphoric. They heralded the "world's first dawn of the third age of television, interactivity, a cornucopia of choice equipped to handle dramatically extended pay-per-view, high-definition, wide-screen TV, voice interactivity and linkages with computers, fax machines and personal computer networks, a state-of-the-art video highway into the home, electronic banking, travel booking, medical diagnosis, voting" and, "most important," the ability "to teach students according to their individual abilities, interests and educational needs."

Never mind that in the Time Warner plan the hookups were supposed to reach by year's end only 4,000 to 5,000 subscribers (it turned out to be many fewer) in two sections of New York City's ethnically diverse borough of Queens, home to Archie Bunker, which had waited twenty years to get *any* kind of cable TV. Steve Ross conceded that "these scenarios and others may be a few years off, but with today's announcement they're no longer pie-in-the-sky, now they're signals in the wire just waiting to be unlocked." It was, said Ross, using his favorite word "fantastic, fantastic."

What programs and services were "waiting to be unlocked" for the 150 channels, not to say the predicted 600 to 1,200 channels? Jerry Levin provided the answer. "This is our *Field of Dreams*," said Levin. "When we build it, we know the programming will come," as in the actual movie line, "If you build it [the baseball field in your cornfield], they [the star players] will come."

In the next day's papers, there were pictures of Steve Ross himself, beaming in front of an arrow-laden chart, which could pass as the board for a game of Monopoly. Despite the fanfare, *Newsweek, Forbes, Barron's,* even *Time* and *Fortune,* let the momentous event pass without a word of coverage. *Business Week* ran two paragraphs under the headline "WHAT'S ON CHANNEL 1,428 TONIGHT?" Wall Streeters were likewise unmoved. Time Warner stock coolly held its ground at a bleak $109 a share. "The announcement," said Nicholas in a huff, "was not organized for the stock market. It was oriented to the legislators in Washington. I don't care about the stock market."

THERE WAS GOOD REASON for skepticism. Thirty years before, when cable TV was aborning, prophets had talked glowingly of the same "wired nation," with life-changing results, that Time Warner was touting today. It had not happened.

Ten years later, a Time task force joined the far-seeing optimists, pointing out that the new miracle TV coaxial cable "bears the relationship to a telephone line that a garden hose does to Niagara Falls," and could be used for "narrowcasting"—the same laundry list of programs and services that Time Warner was now announcing in 1991.

Ross, who always soars when he talks about high-tech communications, was in there pitching in the early '70s when he waxed enthusiastic to a puzzled group of security analysts about something called the "Frame-Grabber," a device which in theory could enable viewers to dial up whatever they wanted on their TV screen. His own staff was equally baffled, and jokingly called later Ross fantasies Steve's "frame-grabbers." In 1977, Ross took a chance on a real innovation. He launched another premature dream, QUBE in Columbus, Ohio, "the world's first interactive service," with a "110-

channel home terminal." Pioneering and inventive, but as Ross later agreed, "ahead of its time." Like most cable instant miracles, QUBE flopped and went out of business within three years.

Could it be that the moment had finally come to believe?

BUT WHERE WOULD THE appetite for all those channels and the billions in financing now come from?

"It's right to be skeptical," Levin said. "It may sound as if it's never going to happen. But when you can do things as we did on pay TV, where you get a $65 million box office for one prizefight [George Foreman v. Evander Holyfield] on mostly primitive systems, you can envision that we'll have enough revenues from movies and sports to build the new capability. We have a shot at it. For the first time there's really something behind the hyperbole." His HBO had been launched sixteen years before with the Joe Frazier–Muhammad Ali fight in the Philippines, billed as "The Thrilla from Manila."

Levin, Ross, Nicholas and others at Time Warner believe the development converts ho-hum TV sets into a video wonderland. "The company has plans to roll out the enhanced service to 6.5 million subscribers." The new technology, they say, is the central nervous system and future of their company. "The digital intersection of print and video," explains Levin, "is where this company is headed. It's just so clear."

And lest one think such an outlook lacks what Time once called its "mission," Levin hastily added, "You can't provide social idealism without making money." Steve Ross was obviously aware of that. He described to reporters at the multichannel press conference a goal that would not just be replacing video stores for renting movies. "The greatest role interactive TV will play," says Ross, "is in education." Off the cuff, Ross elaborated to the reporters:

"One of the ways you have to educate is to make it entertainment. If you don't make it entertaining, if you're unable to get the right equipment in the home to sell education, we will not be able to educate America. How do we do that? No one will buy education. What they will buy is entertainment and certain information. Through that you will get the right equipment into the home. If you can make education entertaining, they will tune in and they will interact. One form is perhaps a quiz game, where you could have people of all ages on many different channels simultaneously answering questions and competing against people on their block, people in their area, in their city, all simultaneously. The people in their state against the people in their country and against the people in their continent, against the world.

"They will learn after a while that in order to have a very good chance of winning this competition—and there will be many awards given—they will have to read. We will get back to the use of the written word. We will send them something in the mail and they will understand that they will have a better chance of winning the spelling bee. Or winning the math problems, or the history or the geography. We will do that for all ages."

Since Ross's educational theorizing was impromptu, mercifully not a word of it was reported.

MONTHS EARLIER, WARNER'S WUNDERKIND, Robert Pittman, who "has a new idea every second," says Ross, commissioned for Time Warner an expensive ($750,000) twenty-five-minute promotion video, expertly produced, displaying winsome kids of every nationality and race glued to their TV sets. Alas, what they were lapping up was a numbing collection of brain-dead TV that could bring a child-abuse protest from every P.T.A. in the country. Its content was so mindless and embarrassingly lowbrow that wiser heads prevailed. "It certainly did not describe the soul of Time Warner," said an annoyed Levin. "It was not shown internally. It was shown once to a potential investor and was never used again."

Then, what to make of the "soul of Time Warner" on display when it reintroduced later in July 1991 its failed Comedy Channel, renamed Comedy Central, the joint venture with Viacom's Ha!? Its "Grand Opening," live from Manhattan's Times Square, and distributed to cable systems across the country, was the most leering, scatological outpouring ever produced under the aegis of and bearing the Time name—and probably Warner as well. Its narrator-host on the roof of an office building screamed, "The smell of urine is wafting up from the streets, and the urge to spit here twenty-five stories above the city is almost unbearable." Then he introduced the pièce de résistance:

The "Love Goddess," a bimbo decked out in a gold lamé evening gown, squealing "Hello, pigs," as she slipped into a "Love Harness much like the one she has next to her bed at home." Then she wrapped her legs around a greased flagpole atop the building. Burly riggers hoisted her inch by inch up the pole, declaring her safe because, said one of them, "I always packed a safe rigging. I have a condom on right now." For safety, the riggers, the host assured, all "are wearing condoms." As the Love Goddess slowly slithered up the pole she trilled, "Oh honey, this feels good, baby. I'm glad you greased up this pole. This makes me hot, makes my hormones dance. This is more satisfying than being serviced by Big Foot. Oh look, I see a woman breast-feeding her baby. Oh no, that's Cher with her new boyfriend. I'm ready to go husband hunting. I like my men hot, packed and unloading everything," she screamed. "If you want to get off, I had multiples." Narrator: "We can see up your dress and that's pretty frightening too."

Cut to the promo for another feature: A wild-eyed comic, after some talk about diarrhea, describes "what this show is, opening the stalls of public restrooms" and surprising people.

New wave late-night adult humor? Midnight Blue? A Playboy Channel smutty reject? Not at all. Its airtime was 5:45 P.M. EDT, the prime-time viewing slot for children home from school. Not a single senior executive at Time Warner or its cable and programming divisions would admit to having seen or knowing anything about the "Grand Opening." But the president of the new Comedy Central channel, Robert Kreek, was in Times Square for the spectacle and later viewed the full tape. "It was a little bluer than we expected it to be," says Kreek, "but we do sell the channel across the country as PG [parental guidance advised]. We got no complaints."

A day earlier, Time Warner also unveiled another new cable channel: enterprising Steven Brill's *American Lawyer* Courtroom Television Network (Court TV), which broadcast actual criminal and civil trials and hearings from all over the country. With skilled commentators and anchors, the early programs showed considerable promise.

Former FCC chairman Newton N. Minow, the creator of the term the TV "wasteland," recently reassessed the modern fare available on TV and cable channels. "In 1961 I worried that my children would not benefit much from television. But in 1991 I worry that my grandchildren will actually be harmed by it. If television is to change, the men and women in television will have to make it a leading institution in American life rather than merely a reactive mirror of the lowest common denominator in the marketplace."

.   .   .

IT MAY BE UNDERSTANDABLE that Ross, Nicholas and Levin had little time to monitor what they were selling or to set minimum standards of taste for their managers to follow. The three were very busy with their tricontinental financial search, trying to do something about the more than $11 billion debt—the damn debt.

At first they hoped to turn the stock's temperature up by clever public relations. They had said that even with $227 million losses in 1990, the company could handle the interest payments on its debt from its cash flow. It would "grow out of its debt" by increasing that cash flow from $2.3 billion a year to $4 billion, without selling any assets or cutting costs. Very few people believed them. "The stock dropped," to the low $100s, one director guesses, "when the analysts had no faith in the ability to handle the debt and restore profitablity."

Ross thought such shortsightedness an aberration. "What's been surprising to me—although it shouldn't be because the stock market should never surprise me—although it constantly does, is the lack of understanding in the market of what we have. The market is totally irrational. Just one little hint of something that we may be doing on a subsidiary level, a partial deal, and all of a sudden the stock goes wild. It's crazy, because even if you reduce the debt, you're giving up part of your cash flow, so it's the same thing. No one ever gets by the debt to see the cash flow." He pauses and adds, "Maybe I'm just too close to it or not seeing something." If you asked Nicholas what he hoped to do about the debt, he even balked at the term. "Not the debt," he corrected, "the balance sheet."

With no one buying their story, they had to try a new game and do some broken-field running. In speeches, interviews and handouts from their press and investor relation agents, they raised a new expectation. "To reduce the debt," said Nicholas, "we're not selling or buying. We're partnering." Their objective, Ross would explain, was for "global *strategic* alliances in the tricontinental economy," selling minority interests to investors who brought products, facilities and compatibility as well as money to the table. Maybe Japan's giant Toshiba with its hardware and manufacturing or France's Canal Plus with its big stake in pay TV. But the price and stiff terms turned off big potential investors. Anyway, potential partners all knew that Time Warner needed to find $3 billion in cash by March 1993 to pay its short-term debt. Closer to that date, they reasoned, hard-pressed

Time Warner would not be so haughty and could be forced to settle on more advantageous terms.

Ross would not even consider one alternative. He thought it appalling that a U.S. media company would sell a *controlling* interest to foreigners even in one of its subsidiaries. "That stinks," he said, overlooking that he had tried to help the Italian flim-flam financier Giancarlo Parretti take over MGM in order for Time Warner to get rights to its film library.

"WE WANT TO DO something that's strategically different," Levin explained, "and as a by-product of that deal reduce the debt."

In one day, on the rumor that Toshiba might be buying into Time Warner, the company's stock jumped eight points, only to slump back again when nothing happened. Two months later, a similar rumor about other deals drove the stock up six points.

Time Warner did find foreign partners to invest in new movies, for joint cable ventures in Sweden and other countries; to build multi-screen theaters in Britain, France, Spain, Japan, Italy, Denmark, even the Soviet Union; for theme parks in Australia. But while all these deals and many others promised future returns, they were penny-ante stuff to Wall Street, which was waiting for *the* big debt-reduction deal. "There was a strong sense," said a member of the board, "that the company was not getting enough credit in the marketplace for all the things it was doing."

The pressure was so great that the company postponed its annual meeting from the traditional spring date without announcing a new time, hoping to be able to reveal the news of the big partnership that would cut the debt. "It's a kind of running joke inside the board," said another director, "but we know exactly how long we can wait." Outside, they gave a different reason for the delay, a lame excuse that their annual report was coming out in six languages—English, German, French, Italian, Japanese and Spanish. The multilingual translations, layouts and printing, they said, were so complex and took so long that they couldn't hold their stockholders meeting at the usual time. There was no word or acronym for EBITDA, Time Warner's new financial reporting system, in any other language. When the reports finally came out in July 1991, EBITDA appeared that way, with an explanation of the term and justification in English as well as the other five languages.

Nicholas disparaged questions about the annual meeting delay. "What is an annual meeting?" he asked. "That's not what governance is all about. If we could take all the money that goes into annual meetings in the U.S. and give it to the homeless, we'd all be better off." Some cynics wondered, recalling that after the disastrous 1984 Atari year, Ross held no stockholder meetings at all until the following year.

But the New York Stock Exchange requires that the stockholders formally be given something more than brief quarterly earnings reports and verbal promises. So Time Warner mailed out an odd bare-bones version of its required annual 10-K financial statement. It also filed separately with the SEC an addendum containing the disclosures normally included in the proxy statement issued before a meeting. In it was information about salaries and bonus plans for top executives. Neither stockholders nor the press got the report. If either group was aware the information existed, the report (known as a "Form 8") had to be requested to be seen. What did it show?

Again, it would take a compensation genius with a jeweler's loupe in his eye to estimate the value of every facet of the diamond-studded compensation gems for Time Warner's chiefs. And the executives and their spokespeople campaigned against every independent estimate. But as closely as could be figured out from their complex fifteen- and ten-year contracts, during 1990, Time Warner's first full year together:

- Nicholas, who could already have accumulated at least $16 million in Time stock and old options, got a raise and a $1.6 million bonus (total cash compensation, $2.4 million), new stock options worth $12 million in the period they were reported, and tax-deferred compensation for his retirement years equal to half his base salary. On top of everything else he was guaranteed a lifetime pension of more than $500,000 a year. Retired or fired, Nicholas and the others would be very rich men for life.

- Levin, who by then could have an estimated $10 million worth of Time stock and options, received a $1.3 million bonus, new options worth $9 million when they were reported, plus other benefits similar to Nicholas's.

- Editor-in-chief McManus, with a new five-year contract, in addition to his $1.3 million cash compensation and his holding of an estimated $7 million worth of stock and options, was awarded new options then worth $2.7 million.

- Ross, who had received almost $200 million in compensation on the heels of the merger, got 1.8 million new stock options at $150 a share. If the stock rose 50 points above that as it was supposed to, they would be worth $90 million more. At that price, Nicholas's new holdings alone would be worth $36 million, Levin's $27 million, McManus's $15 million. "If the stock went up that much," says Levin, "that would be terrific for all the shareholders. That's what incentive compensation is all about."

- Ross's 1.8 million option grant at $150 a share was the largest ever recorded that anyone could find in American corporate history. If Time Warner's stock price appreciated at only 10 percent a year (the average for U.S. companies), Ross's stock options alone would be worth close to $400 million at the end of the twelve-year period, with Nicholas, Levin, McManus and many other Time Warner executives profiting proportionately.

- Ross also had a heavenly wrinkle in his contract. The clause, not noticed before, provided that after Ross's death his heirs would be entitled not only to his $7.9 million in company life insurance, stock holdings, pension, deferred compensation, long-term bonus and other benefits. They would also continue to get for three years his full salary and bonuses, based on past performance, just as if he had continued working. It was known in the compensation trade as a "golden coffin." One pay expert told *Fortune*, "It's a pretty stiff penalty the CEO has to pay to collect the money."

- In his first retirement year as co-CEO, Munro, whose stock was worth an estimated $20 million or more, received $1.5 million in cash. With his $750,000 payment as an "adviser," his pension and deferred compensation, wholly apart from the income his huge capital will generate, he will have a guaranteed lifetime retirement income of more than $1 million a year. (Future $750,000 fees for the top executives when they become "advisers," plus additional "bonuses at the discretion of the board.")

- During their five-year advisory period at $750,000 a year, and any bonuses the board may decide on, the company can call on Munro, Ross or Nicholas, if at all, not more than forty hours a month.

Their average hourly pay if they were called on for the maximum amount of time, which is highly unlikely, would be $1,563.50 an hour.

■ Luce as a founder never paid himself or his partner Roy E. Larsen more than $97,000 a year ($360,000 in current dollars). Their wealth came from their huge holdings in Time Inc. stock. Luce, his family and foundations owned 22 percent of Time Inc. with millions in dividends; Larsen, 12 percent. Until the merger, Ross, also a founder, held stock in Warner and then Time Warner of less than, or a hair more than, 1 percent.

"It's obscene," says Munro, who contributes a major part of his time *pro bono* to worthy social causes. "I don't mean at Time Warner especially," he says. "As a liberal, I mean executive salaries in corporate America. They're outrageous. My salary at the end, although you lose it in the rounding, compared to some of the others, was still too much money. They'll all end up making a huge amount of money. I certainly don't begrudge them that at Time Warner. But executive salaries are outrageous everywhere." With his largely honorary title as chairman of the executive committee of the board, Munro lost at least one perk. His friends say that Ross hadn't telephoned him once since he retired as co-CEO more than a year before.

Peter Drucker, the dean of American business management theory, feels such payments demoralize all but the top executives. "Their bitterness underlies a great deal of turmoil and the willingness of people to jump ship. Then top management complains, 'Where has the loyalty gone?' " A compensation expert puts it more graphically: "Executives rewarded this way are like blind dogs in a sausage factory."

WHILE THEY DO NOT APPEAR in the public reports, there were pleasantries.

Time Warner's movie and record companies acquired luxurious chalets for their stars and executives in snowbird celebrity heaven Aspen, Colorado. In addition, alongside Warner's sunlit Acapulco retreat, on the other side of its tennis courts, Ross planned to build a twin to the Villa Eden, with more bedrooms and a gym. "I think Steve wants it so that Time people can see the way they should live and entertain," one guest remarked as she was being shown the three-acre site.

To replicate the villa and add a gym would be quite a job. "The Villa Eden has the most beautiful view I've ever seen outside of Hong Kong," says one world traveler who has been a guest there. "It's a superb, intimate small tropical hotel, with a staff of ten, any kind of tennis clothes and equipment you might wish to use and keep, TV sets in every one of its bedroom suites, where you can dial up almost any movie ever made, two TV dishes, one for cable the other for broadcast, a large screening room for movies in the 'playhouse,' telephones at your fingertips and a lighted pool as pretty as I've ever seen, bathed in stereo music. It's the Steve Ross way of keeping his satraps happy."

Nicholas and Levin thought the company might, instead of building, buy a handsome nearby eight-bedroom villa. Whether it is built or bought, "if it happens," says Nicholas, "it's no different from buying paper for magazines, film stock or advertising. If it can add to the profits of the bottom line of this company, we'll do it. I regard it as a very useful place. I went down on the plane there with some music people for a weekend and at least one brilliant idea came out of that three-day meeting that's going to make us a lot of money."

Some great ideas might also be water-born on the 158-foot motor yacht, the top-of-the-yards *Klementine,* with eight staterooms and a crew of fourteen. Time Warner regularly charters her for Ross and his guests at $122,500 a week (plus $40,000 in tips and miscellaneous) for cruising in the Mediterranean and Caribbean. Her tender is a sixty-mph Cigarette speedboat.

Ross now talks with relish and anticipation about the palazzo ninety miles outside of Rome he acquired in 1990. To convert its fourteenth-century decor into something more suitable for a modern pop Medici, Ross and his wife have bought up the services of craftsmen for miles around. "The place is in terrible shape," Ross says. "Courtney will have to redo it. She's a great interior designer—fantastic. She decorated the offices and Steven Spielberg's house close by ours in East Hampton. It's the most gorgeous house I've ever seen—brilliant."

But Courtney Ross may find scant time to work on the new Italian quarters. In October 1991, she embarked on a year-long tour around the world beginning in Tokyo, Kyoto and then emphasizing visits to mostly third world places such as Thailand, Indonesia, China, Egypt, the Middle East, possibly into Africa, ending up in South America with a stop in the Galápagos. The itinerary is still not firmly set. But the Ross's eight-year-old daughter and a chum will accompany her, along with tutors, security men, special guides flown in from the U.S., a photographer, a masseuse, and other helpers. Mom's principal objective in plotting the trip was to give the kids an early multicultural education. A Warner team has advanced the grand tour, booking presidential hotel suites and support lodgings, struggling with such conundrums as whether it is wise to fly a Gulfstream IV into Cambodia to visit the Angkor Wat temples. They are also casing suitable telex, telephone and fax facilities should Steve Ross himself choose to drop in along the way. "Clare Boothe Luce," said one old-Timer, "would have loved to travel that way." Ross himself says that when he was a kid "a trip to the Empire State Building or the Automat" would have been a grand tour. (A month later, the romp had to be interrupted when Ross fell ill again, with prostatic cancer, and his wife and daughter returned home.)

The former head of a Warner subsidiary finds the pay and perks essential to Ross. "Steve," he says, "tends to people's needs, both financially and emotionally. He's very generous with other people's money, with the planes, with perks, with gifts, the yachts, everything else—all paid for by the company. He loves the perks, has always lived like a man who has an infinite amount of money. He gives these things to his top employees and he anoints them in the most generous fashion in the history of American business."

The Harvard Business School's Abraham Zaleznik views such corporate rewards as a barrier rather than an aid:

> People who are well placed in the power structure enjoy a
> protected position. There are certain narcissistic gains from
> belonging to the organization and being in that power position.
> The people in the lower levels are very much excluded from
> the mythological structure that provides these narcissistic gains.
> The lower level people feel very much left out and are very
> vulnerable to depressive reactions.

David Wolper, who was a classmate of Ross's at Columbia Grammar School and whose movie and TV production company is owned by Warner, regularly visits the Acapulco villa aboard a Warner jet. He has a view from 30,000 feet up of what he considers Ross's best management tool. "The airplanes are a key part of Steve's and Warner's success. If I can travel on my business on the corporate jet and I get the same deal without that perk at Fox, why the hell would I go to Fox? A jet is the best perk in the history of business. The Acapulco house—those things are important. Many people don't understand the psychology of people in show business. Some of them make a lot of money. But a corporate jet is a little above what they want to spend.

"People in show business are independent people. They're actors, Clint Eastwood, Steven Spielberg, Barbra Streisand, Goldie Hawn and all of these people, they're just not going to get a corporate jet. Steve discovered the one perk you can give Madonna, not jewelry, limos or grand hotel suites. That's all peanuts. You can give her your corporate jet. That's a business thing that glues them to Time Warner. You have to be in the business to understand that. It's not a financial thing, it's a convenience thing. They may think all of this is ridiculous on Wall Street. But they just don't understand. The first thing those movie producers [Peter] Guber and [Jon] Peters did when they went to Columbia-Sony was to get a corporate jet. They found out the key to why they were at Warner."

The second thing Peters did at Columbia was to get eased out.

IN HIS SALAD DAYS at Warner, Steve Ross would often sit at home far into the night wrapped in his bathrobe, or on weekends around the telephone-littered pool in East Hampton, scribbling on pieces of paper, weaving the skeins of intricate deals. It was his favorite sport, at which he was considered by friends and associates to be the world champion. Next day, he would follow a pattern, described by a onetime Warner senior executive:

"His financial acumen was amazing. He'd come into the office and say, Let me do a deal. He would have pieces of paper that sometimes he'd worked on all night long. He always carried a little spiral notebook. He'd go through the deal with all its permutations and variations. Then he'd say, Do you get it? Do it for me. You mean *you* understood it! Every paper would then be ripped up. If you understood it, he'd say, *they* will understand it, so that's not the deal I'm going to go with." Another former Warner insider often had the same experience. "Steve would describe a deal to me for twenty-five minutes or so. Then he'd ask me if I understood it. I'd say sure. Of course I didn't, but what did it matter? He'd change it twenty times after that anyway."

In the aftermath of his scribblings that had produced the trium-phant merger with Time, two years later Ross announced on June 6, 1991, the second-biggest deal of his life. The date happened to be the second anniversary of Paramount's surprise bomb drop on the original merger. The explosion this time was just as big. It was the announcement everyone was waiting for, Time Warner's plan to reduce its hobbling billions in debt. The intricate $3 billion plan was first suggested by Merrill Lynch bankers but it was vintage Ross: Nobody understood it.

It was so ill-received that even Time Warner's own *Time* magazine could do little else but greet it in the lead paragraph: "Wall Street responded with boos. But an even more widespread reaction was a baffled 'Huh?' " It was an understatement. Coupled with a wave of new criticism over his awesome compensation and perk-rich exec-utive lifestyle, Ross received a thrashing from all sides.

Ross's announcement of Time Warner's "rights" offer was a dis-aster. "I did a particularly lousy job explaining it," says Ross. It was attacked on Wall Street so badly that Time Warner stock plunged by 20 percent to $87 a share. It was denounced by Time stockholders, who ganged up to take their complaints to court, and was objected to by the SEC, which was awash in protests. In the Time & Life Building, the uproar converted most new Ross admirers and incipient Ross-lovers from thinking of him as their leader into regarding him bitterly as their undoer.

Ten days before the five-hour emergency board meeting to ratify the rights deal, with "gunslinger" Mike Dingman as chairman of its finance committee, Nicholas told a reporter, "I really shouldn't tell you this, but it's so exciting. We just shook hands on something. We're the only company that could pull this off. It's a real barn burner. I've been nurturing this idea for a long time, or a version of it."

"BARN BURNER" IT WAS, only it came close to burning down the whole Time Warner edifice. "Suddenly it made us feel like char-acters in Warner Books' new sequel to *Gone With the Wind,*" said a manager on one of the magazines, expressing a sentiment felt throughout the entire Time & Life Building. "All our old plantations were crumbling—and so was Tara."

For a scheme of its size, it was unique. It offered all Time Warner stockholders the "rights" to buy six-tenths of a share of the 34.5

million new shares the company would issue. It was the biggest rights offering ever. What was more unusual, and even unique for an offering of its size, was that the price of each share wasn't fixed. Instead there was a "pool" with a sliding price. If 100 percent of the shares were bought, the price would be $105 a share. As the percentage of rights exercised dropped, so did the price, to a floor, if only 60 percent were subscribed, of $63 a share. Shareholders who didn't buy the rights would have their holdings "diluted," meaning that the value of their stake in the company would be reduced. Thus it was described as a "coercive" gamble at no fixed odds and no fixed price. If the issue was subscribed 100 percent, Time Warner would have $3.5 billion in new capital to pay down its looming 1993 bank debt; if it went only to 60 percent, the yield would be $2.1 billion.

The offering had other eyebrow-raising features. Not that anyone but a lawyer with an accountant at his elbow could understand them. The prospectus reported: "The conversion rates of the company's convertible exchangeable preferred stocks, and the number of shares covered by certain stock option prices thereunder, will be adjusted in accordance with the antidilution provisions thereof. See 'Pro Forma—Information—Notes 4 and 5 of Pro Forma Information.' " "Notes 4 and 5" were even more impenetrable. Translation: The biggest employee beneficiary of the plan would be Steve Ross himself, followed by Nicholas and Levin. They and other executives who had options (Ross had the most, 1.8 million) would have their options adjusted upward.

The investment bankers were also doing just fine. Although they were putting up no money and were at no risk, they would be paid $41 million at the low end, but if they succeeded in promoting the whole offering, they would make the highest such fee ever, $145 million just for acting as salesmen.

The *Wall Street Journal,* as well as virtually everyone else, slammed the plan. "After months of assuring Wall Street that it was close to raising new equity through a strategic alliance," the *Journal* said, "Time Warner instead asked its stockholders to ante up more cash." One financial observer not involved in the deal said, "It's incredible, first Ross sells his company to Time and cashes in exorbitantly for himself and the Warner stockholders. The Time stockholders didn't even get a chance to vote on whether they wanted to take $200 a share from Paramount instead. But he finds the cost to the new company, which he's running, so great that its stock is drowning in debt. So what does Ross do? He sells the company again to the stockholders so they can pay down the debt his deal created. To go along with that, you got to have a lot of confidence in the guy and in the long term—no, now it's the long, long term."

"Those bastards," said one former Time director who still held a large block of Time Warner stock, "screwed me twice. They're not going to do it again." Many another disgusted old Time stockholder—some large—vowed to get out as soon as possible. "I've finally decided," said one, "I want nothing more to do with those guys. I want to put the whole sorry heist behind me."

Headlines, stories and commentators from coast to coast and across the oceans dumped on the plan: the Chicago *Tribune*, "Stock Plan a Bust"; *Daily Variety*, "Time Stumbles"; Houston *Chronicle*, "Another Fiasco at Time Warner"; *Hollywood Reporter*, "Angry Investors Blitz Time Warner"; Los Angeles *Times*, "Ross and Time Warner Re-Fleecing"; Washington *Post*, "Time Warner's Depressing Plan"; Philadelphia *Inquirer*, "Unhappy with Time Warner"; *USA Today*, "Time Warner Investors 'Betrayed' by Rights Deal"; Boston *Globe*, "Time Warner Deal Smacks of Unfairness"; New York *Times*, "Amid Anger and Confusion Time Stock Declines Again"; and the London *Economist*, quite simply, "They Goofed."

Business Week, on its cover, delivered the coup de grâce. Under a stark "TIME WARNER" was a shifty-eyed picture of Steve Ross, his dewlaps bulging over his shirt collar. Alongside was the point-by-point cover legend: "SYNERGY? Not much. STRATEGIC ALLIANCES? Not yet. RIGHTS OFFERING? Not so fast. No wonder shareholders are mad."

"The board," says lawyer Arthur Liman, who helped explain the deal to them, "made as informed a decision as anyone could make, and in the circumstances it didn't work."

"The rights deal was our own Exxon *Valdez* oil spill," exclaimed a Time staffer.

Variety editorial director Peter Bart wrote, "Today Steve Ross's press is one notch below Saddam Hussein's."

AFTER MORE THAN A month of misery, Time Warner's executives and suckered board of directors, embarrassed, embattled and harried, were forced finally to give up on their too tricky rights offer, which they had unanimously approved. "Steve and the others had us convinced," said one down-in-the-dumps director, "that it was a good deal. There'll be hell to pay at the next board meeting in September." (Hardly. The lengthy September board meeting was almost entirely devoted to "strategic alliances.")

On July 14, 1991, they announced a simpler way of raising some of the cash they needed. The day was once again a second anniversary, but a happier one. It was exactly two years before that the Delaware Chancery Court had announced Time's victory over Paramount. (Could it be Levin's "thaumaturgy" at work?—evenly spaced "horrible" and "cheering" events.)

The new plan was a standard rights offering, albeit still the biggest of its kind ever. Time Warner offered its stockholders the right to buy the same 34.5 million shares, 37 percent of the company, but this time at the *fixed* price of $80 a share. For employees other than executive officers and directors who held stock outside company plans, Time Warner offered loans from $1,000 to $48,000 to exercise the rights to buy up to 600 shares (102 employees borrowed $1.7 million). The interest on the loans was 8 percent a year, principal payable in three years. The company also lent $70 million to an employee benefit plan that held 1.4 million shares in trust for employees. For stockholders who didn't want to exercise their rights to buy stock, there was a lively market in simply selling the rights, swinging between $4 and $10 per right.

This time Ross, Nicholas and Levin declined any special benefit in upgrading their own options. Though the new rights offer was widely accepted, it was considered penance and backing down for past sins.

The corporate self-consciousness was most evident in three of Time Warner's magazines. *Fortune* ran not a word about the brouhaha, even though it was one of the biggest business stories of the month. Managing editor Marshall Loeb explains limply that "the story never quite broke right for our closing schedules." *Time,* after acquitting itself well in the first rights uproar, covered the new plan with the kind of casual applause that many read as a promotion for the new offer. The *Time* treatment, said critics, was "evasive" and "dishonest." The story never once mentioned the name of Steve Ross, who was the centerpiece of everybody else's coverage.

Money touched it not at all, except outside its pages. Its editors were invited to produce a special issue of the company's house organ, *FYI,* which began: "Unless you were in Ulan Bator, you know about the initial Time Warner offering—the one that ignited protests among shareholders and prompted questions from the Securities and Exchange Commission." The guide to the bewildered employees ended with a good-humored tagline from a staffer at Warner's *Mad* comic magazine. "If we exercise the rights, do we get a sneaker phone?" "No way," answered *FYI*.

On August 5, as scheduled, the underwritten issue was a sellout. As expected, Time Warner stock had settled at $85 a share. The company got $2.76 billion in new capital, with $110 million or so collected by the investment bankers who underwrote the offering. Within weeks Time Warner stock fell again to the high $70s, below the $80 rights price.

The lead underwriter was Salomon Brothers chairman John Gutfreund, who, said a Merrill Lynch competitor, had the "big balls" to come in and take on the job with few questions asked. One month later Gutfreund was forced to resign as chairman of Salomon, after his huge old firm admitted illegal government security transactions. To the rescue as acting new Salomon chairman came Omaha's Warren Buffett, who had twice offered to repel the sharks encircling Time Inc. Salomon's behavior, said Buffett, was "what some people might call macho and others cavalier. I don't think the same thing would have happened in a monastery."

A swarm of gnats charging in lawsuits that Time Warner was in "violation of fiduciary duties" with its first rights offering were handily swatted down by the company agreeing to pay a pittance in fees to complaining stockholder lawyers—$2.5 million.

Although Time Warner reduced its debt from $11.5 billion to $8.9 billion, what it gained in dollars it lost in reputation, especially Ross. Just as the second offering was being completed, the rights offering was slammed again, with special new emphasis on Steve Ross. Most damaging was the *Wall Street Journal*'s front-page story by the paper's able media editor-reporter Laura Landro, with Randall Smith. They blew the whistle on some of Ross's little-advertised perks, the company's executive high living, and highlighted that Ross's expensive palship with the likes of Steven Spielberg, Clint Eastwood and Barbra Streisand hadn't "produced a hit movie for the company in years."

The headline on the story said, "After the Stock Debacle, Some Ask If Hubris Will Undo Time Warner and Chairman Ross."

chapter 17

A Question
of Values

I N HIS QUEST FOR just the right "strategic alliance," Steve
Ross always made it plain he was seeking more than investment
money.

The linkup had to be, he repeatedly said, with companies that
would enhance Time Warner's position in the expanding TV world.
Finally, in late October 1991, Time Warner announced its first major
alliance, a $1 billion investment, split equally between Japan's big
electronics manufacturer Toshiba and Japan's largest venture capital
trading firm C. Itoh, whose company slogan is "Nothing is impossible."

The typically complex deal looked more like financial engineering
than product synergy. But Wall Street liked it. Time Warner stock,
which had already risen in anticipation, went up more than 3 points
in a single day to $89 a share. Nicholas described the intricate deal
as a "potential home run." Ross said it underscored his credibility,
first by his having reduced the debt with the rights offering and now
making the first big international alliance, which he felt certain would
lead to others. A month later the stock dropped to the low 80s.

"We intend to dominate that marketplace worldwide," said Nicholas. "Our destiny is interactivity." To which Levin added, "We
need to transform this whole cable plumbing system into the most advanced multimedia computerized pipe system anyone has ever seen."

In a 1958 *Fortune* article titled "The Light That Failed," David
Sarnoff, RCA's inventor-founder-chairman, described his business.
"We're in the same position as a plumber laying pipes. We're not
responsible for what goes through the pipe."

The article commented:

The outcome could, however, very well be history repeating itself: the restraints imposed on television by its own commercial interests will simply result in the raising of a new empire, the competing one of pay TV, and the crowning of a new set of kings.

The Time Warner kings were already crowned, their throne rooms rebuilt and adorned, their pockets overflowing with tens and hundreds of millions in lucre as a result of making the deal. Each of their fortunes was to be multiplied many times over by long-term unbreachable contracts as bountiful as any in the American corporate kingdoms.

But Time Warner's top executives aspired to be much more than some of the most affluent plumbers in the world. Unlike Sarnoff's business, their passion and future was in providing what flowed through their electronic plumbing. They called the pipe-and-product combination by a mouthful, "synergy within vertical integration." Or in Ross's plainer words, "software and hardware under one roof." They were betting the company's future on it.

They frequently predicted that one day "five or six media companies would dominate the world." They had promised to make Time Warner not just one of the mega-media giants. They aspired to be Number One—in the "long term," as they always said. Meanwhile, in the here and now, with their damaged reputations to repair, they also had some conventional businesses to run and make grow.

Their music and movies were increasingly exportable to foreign markets. Their volatile movie business in the U.S. was different. It could be a smash one year (1989, the year of *Batman*) and sink the next (1990, the year of *Bonfires* and passing up the hit *Home Alone*). Millions of miles of cable and connections to consumers were a sitting asset whose growth depended on technologies down the road, although some of HBO's "made-for-TV" programs started attracting more viewers than the networks' offerings.

Ahead were unforeseeable wild-card competition and unpredictable government regulatory policies. The company hoped to shape them by hiring a former FCC chairman, Dennis R. Patrick, two of his FCC aides and a new corporate "image maker" who had worked in the White House. They also had on retainers an elegant pack of the most connected Washington lobbyists. And they brought back from the SEC to help with "overall strategy and business plans"

Time's former video lawyer, later general counsel, Philip R. Lochner, who had left after the merger to be an SEC commissioner.

But all that heavy artillery, along with Ross's suave, and Nicholas's growing, lobbying skills, could not guarantee the outcome they were seeking. The telephone companies, new technologies, new legislation or new FCC rules could change the whole TV revenue and ownership game. Nor was it certain that cable TV, or fiber optics, or whatever developed, would necessarily be dominated by cable giants treading in thousands of American communities.

Whether Time's publishing skills were significantly exportable across worldwide language and cultural borders was doubtful. At home, *Life* was crumbling, *Entertainment Weekly* was still struggling and *Time,* once the foundation of the whole company, was floundering in its search for a new identity. Many at Time Warner, as well as other places, predicted the steady decline of reading for information and news. Perhaps so, but if a company is devotedly in the publishing business, its task is to find ways to overcome that alarming illiteracy, not to foster it. So far Time Warner has not demonstrated—except in easy words of reassurance—that it is resolutely committed to that goal.

Weighing in Time Warner's favor is its size, "the biggest media company in the world." Size alone does not assure a rosy future, as the conglomerates of earlier times proved, and as IBM and GM are now discovering. Also in the '90s, such overextended global giants in the media as Murdoch, Hachette, the Maxwell empire and others were pulling back rather than expanding. But Time Warner says it has much more going for it than size.

"The future belongs to the people who have the most bets on the table and the best people," exclaims Nicholas, full of hubris and an enthusiasm echoing Ross's own. "This company today, and in the future, will have more money at risk, more innovative entrepreneurial things going. Nobody else has the combination of financial resources, people and market position we do. So we're going to put these bets out there and the odds favor us. We have huge resources."

Nicholas, Ross and Levin could be right. Between their hyperbolic cheerleading on one side and the show-us skeptics on the other lies uncertainty, with promises of intricate deals and overstated outcomes. "The worst case," said Nicholas when pressed, "is that what you get as a shareholder or an interested party is no worse than what existed before. It's very hard for me to see the downside. We could always screw it up as managers. But we're the same people. We would have screwed it up anyway."

"The merger," says a consultant who has advised both companies, "may turn out to be one of the most brilliant business moves in their history or the stupidest. No one can really tell."

A LOT DEPENDS ON the man the Time crowd barely knew when the two companies came together. After Ross's history is known, witnesses heard from, records examined, his strengths and weaknesses assessed, hours passed talking with him directly about his life and business, what judgment can be made about Steve Ross? "When you're all done," said one veteran Warner executive who was forced out, "you can't make mincemeat out of the guy, because he has amazing talent—and huge fatal flaws."

In Time's and Warner's first two years together, his flaws were as apparent as his talent. One serious recurring Ross flaw, to which his Time partners were hardly immune, was to blame every bump in the road on "bad public relations." Not so. Good public relations is getting proper credit for good work. No amount of hype, dodging or attempts at manipulation can make a company, its products or its executives look good if they aren't. Time Warner's early knocks were real problems, not just situations badly handled.

Nor did the Time Warner bosses seem to understand that influential big media companies are glass houses easy to peer into from the outside, as they should be. Chasing down "leaks" within Time Warner became an activity almost as fervent as it was in Nixon's White House—with about as little success.

Many a biographer or journalist has made the mistake of recording flaws and foibles without taking the measure of the subject's accomplishments. Ross's life is the stuff of a Warner Bros. melodrama. A lead character, of undeniable talents, rising from sports slacks salesman and funeral greeter to become the leader of the most visible media conglomerate in the world. By every account, he took over—and got extravagantly paid for doing so—Time Inc., a prestigious American institution founded by Ivy League WASPs, perpetuated by intellectuals, litterateurs and stylish businessmen, with the help of some cable pioneers. In the idiom of show business, which Ross knows best, his takeover was a world-class act, "major cream."

Did he consider the merger with Time Inc. the capstone of his career? "I hope not," Ross says, "I don't see it as an end." In language reminiscent of George Leigh Mallory's answer to the question of why he wanted to climb Mount Everest ("Because it is there") or Willie Sutton's explanation of why he robbed banks ("That's where the money is"), Ross describes his inhalation of Time:

"I just feel it was something that had to be done, a natural. When you look at it as a businessman, it was there and we did it. Other people describe it differently, but I guess one would have to say that this is the biggest in my life because it was a $14 billion deal. In 1962, when we put Kinney together, then in 1969, when we acquired Warner–Seven Arts, that was unique, all different turns of events. So you reflect back and you say, well, you started a company in 1962 that was acquired in 1989 for $14 billion. It's something that one will always certainly remember."

These days when Ross contemplates his fall from grace within the walls of the Time & Life building down the street, he says that "I'm in a world that I've never been in before and I can't get my hands around." Financially, Ross adds, "I do believe, not with malice aforethought, that the publishing people got screwed" and he wants to correct that. "We do have a morale problem. A pocketbook morale problem. I've never had an employee morale problem before."

By the terms of the "blood oath" he signed with his Time partners, Ross is due to step down as co–chief executive officer in 1994 on the eve of his sixty-seventh birthday, relinquishing the co–chief executive title to Nick Nicholas, who will be fifty-five and will continue as president and sole CEO. Ross will still remain as chairman for five years more, and as an "adviser" for five years more after that.

Since his heart attack ten years ago, Ross has been wracked by a number of medical problems, including prostatic cancer. If his health holds up, very few outside Time Warner—and few inside—had expected much to change in 1994. Ross never wanted to manage anyway and there is nothing in his pledge that prevents him from continuing to dominate the company. After the initial on-and-off negotiations with Toshiba and the rights offering fiasco, relations between Ross and Nicholas grew tenser than they had ever been. "We've had disagreements, it's fair to say," Ross concedes, "differences of opinion." "The purring honeymoon," said one observer of the two of them, "if it was ever really on, is over." Even Nicholas's succession is now not certain. "Theoretically," says an outspoken former Time director now on the Time Warner board, "Nick will inherit the job. But he won't if he doesn't earn it. That's never been firmly etched in granite." Two irreverent reporters who follow the company put it more brutally. "I give Nicholas two years," the first speculated. The second said, "Maybe three—then he's out and Jerry Levin is in."

NICHOLAS REMINDS A VISITOR, "You know, three years from now I'm going to be the sole CEO. Jerry [Levin] and I have to think through what that means and implies."

They had little reason to look back. From the moment they set foot in the offices of Time's growing cable and HBO operations in the '70s, Levin especially, then Nicholas and finally their boss Dick Munro, saw the future of the publishing company on a TV or movie screen. Not that they spurned Time Inc.'s bedrock magazine journalism that had put them where they were. But their sights gradually reset on what to them became the wave of Time's future. By merging with Warner, the three felt Time was finally riding that wave. "Television," said Munro, "is where the world is going whether one likes it or not."

"It's true," says Time's ex–general counsel Bill Guttman, who left the company four months before the merger agreement, "they did love the company, and its influence in the world," along with the atmosphere in the Time & Life Building. "You can be influential in two ways," says Guttman. "By your size. Or by your journalism. The latter was Time Inc.'s traditional way. But everyone agrees that Time's journalistic influence was waning compared to electronics. So how do you stay influential? They got bigger by adding more TV and its handmaiden, entertainment."

Old Time potentates like Andrew Heiskell and the late Hedley Donovan had wanted them to stay in print, create new magazines and pursue, with the same vigor their successors went after Warner, an amalgamation with a big newspaper company (e.g., Dow Jones, Times Mirror, Knight-Ridder). "It wouldn't have worked," says McManus, "because print is going to be in a lot of trouble. While it certainly has an assured future, it's never going to return to its halcyon days. There are going to be a lot fewer magazines. Only the sturdy and strong will survive. Newspapers today would not look like a very good decision—given their state and the state of the magazine business. Just try to imagine today where we'd be in today's economy if we were only in magazines. The more we get into this, the more we're going to need multimedia, certainly TV, to help keep our magazines healthy."

What then to do about *Time,* still referred to almost as catechism by Time Warnerites as the "flagship" of the company? An alumnus, sympathetic to the beleaguered editors' plight, suggests: "Go for an audience that really wants to know. Try to convince your business bosses that they should make a sharper distinction between those who can be made to care about information and those who don't give a damn—yes, limiting *Time* to those people. There are enough of them left. The New York *Times,* the Washington *Post* and others do that profitably without being stuffy, writing down or ignoring changes in taste and interests." It doesn't take the director of the British Press Council to remind Americans that "the public interest is not defined as what is interesting to the public."

FROM THEIR EARLIEST DAYS, Ross and Warner have had two primary business objectives: making money and having a good time doing it.

Time, never a reverent monastery, always had a third objective which almost seems quaint today: to add to the quality of knowledge people had about the world. Therein lies the real "cultural" differ-ence between Time and Warner, so mangled and ill-defined during all the merger talks. Whether that cultural gap can be bridged, with all three Time Inc. values intact, remained unanswered.

Years ago, Henry Luce framed the question with an affirmation. "Chiefly we are struggling to do a better job. If we do, we are likely to get bigger and more profitable in the process, but I suggest that was never exactly the main point about Time Inc. and is not likely to become so."

Perhaps not. But there are people in Time Warner who believe and act as if the purpose of business is only business. And there are others who believe that beating the financial system is less an ac-complishment than making a profit by producing valuable products of which you can be proud.

In *Moby-Dick,* Herman Melville observes, "Though man loves his fellow, yet man is a money-making animal which too interferes with his benevolence."

No one should ask that benevolence be the priority of Time Warner or of any other public company. What can be asked is that this new company, with its human and material assets, have a spine that is more than stocks, bonds, rights, deals and tightly rolled greenbacks. It was once said of the rancorous old newspaper and magazine publisher Frank Munsey that "he and his kind have about succeeded in transforming a once noble profession into an 8 percent security. May he rest in trust!" If that should ever become an appropriate epitaph for the Time Inc. executives and board members who merged their company into Warner, they will have sacrificed a heritage that they vowed to preserve.

ON THE THIRTY-FOURTH floor of the Time & Life Building, the company-commissioned portrait of Andrew Heiskell, who had been Time Inc.'s chairman for twenty years, has come down, donated to the New York Public Library, where he was the chairman for ten years. The portrait of the late Hedley Donovan, editor-in-chief after Luce for sixteen years, has been moved to a less conspicuous place and offered to his family, who may keep it or send it to the campus of the University of Minnesota, where he was an undergraduate for four years. Henry R. Luce's portrait still overlooks what has become the Time Warner boardroom thirteen floors above, where Steve Ross now presides. Rockefeller Center, which owns both the Time & Life and Time Warner buildings, has put the top two floors of the Time & Life Building up for rental by a new corporate tenant. If one is found, the Time Warner boardroom could move to the old Warner Building. Who could say it doesn't belong there?

And Happily Ever After . . . ?
A Postscript

STEVE ROSS, WRACKED BY pain, numbed by Percocet, was sitting in a straight-backed armchair in the dark, cavernous living room of his Park Avenue duplex. He was tieless, his hair disheveled, not coiffed the way it had been most days of his meticulously attired life. Over his knees, covering his slippered feet, was a camel-hair shawl.

It was on the eve of bleak November 1991. He had invited me to spend some more time with him to continue my interviews for this book—even though for the last week he had been lying in agony on his bed upstairs, strapped in traction for what he said was an ailing back. I had explained in advance that I didn't want to add to his discomfort, but Ross had insisted.

Unfailingly polite, he half struggled to rise from his chair as I walked in. While still standing, I mentioned again that the interview was unnecessary and that he should go back to bed. "No," he said, squirming, "this probably takes my mind off my back. Up there it's all I can think about. This is a welcome distraction. Make yourself comfortable on the couch."

Then he explained that years ago to cure a bad back he had had a disk removed. (He neglected to mention that he had undergone prostate surgery.) Now the back pain had returned. A butler appeared, surprisingly dressed in a double-breasted blue pinstripe suit like a gofer out of the *The Godfather*. He deposited a silver tray with coffee, grapes, cheeses and crackers alongside my tape recorder. Ross had long since become accustomed to its blinking red light during hours of past interviews.

As Ross eased his weight from one side of the chair to the other,

I began with a few easy questions. Then, for the first time, he acknowledged the palpable tension between him and Nicholas, which I had discovered from other sources. He said yes, there were "routine differences of opinion." Whenever I'd asked him in the past how they were getting on, Ross had dissembled, invoking his favorite adjectives, "It's really a fantastic relationship, wonderful." (Time's former chairman, Dick Munro, correctly observed, "When Steve doesn't say someone he works with is the most wonderful person in the world, you know there's trouble.")

I explained that my book on Time Warner was about to go to press and I was obliged to ask him one very harsh question. "Please be my guest," he said, another of his oft-repeated phrases. I asked hesitantly about a new and more credible revival of an old rumor, "that you have cancer. Is it true?" "No, without any equivocation," he replied with a half smile.

It was then Ross's turn to ask questions. I told him that the book, which he would be reading in galleys within the month, reported all the bumps, glitches and public embarrassments of the merger and its aftermath. A lot of people wouldn't come off very well—including him. "You and some others may never want to speak to me again," I said. "So long as it's factual," he said, "I'll have no complaints." But how was it rough on him?

"Well, you always describe yourself as a dreamer," I answered, "and a journalist has to try to separate dreams from reality." He took the warning in stride, did not ask for details and said, "If you wrote what you honestly believe, it's okay with me."

"TELL ME SOMETHING AS a friend," he said, making his customary assumption that anyone who was not a declared enemy had to be his "friend." He wanted to know about "church and state," the traditional Time Inc. division between editorial (church) and business (state). I told him what the book said. "You know," he said with a pleading frown, "I've never spoken to any editor directly or through a third or fourth party about any stories in the magazines."

I mentioned that people told me they thought he was getting bad advice to stay out of the Time & Life Building and not expose the editorial staffs to his unique form of cheerleading and generosity. "My gut kept telling me to spend more time in the Time & Life Building," he allowed, even though his aides had advised him against it. "So it's my fault." (Disarmingly, Ross always feigned to take the rap when there was bad news.)

Ross, who never saw a budget or salary that couldn't be increased, said he felt strongly that the editorial and publishing people in the Time & Life Building had been treated badly and were "being screwed" financially. "Turn off the tape and I'll tell you what I'm thinking about doing." Off the record, he outlined some financial initiatives he was considering to improve the "pocketbook morale" of the print side.

He sought more information on what the book said about the decline of his reputation and the sinking morale in the Time & Life Building. "Tell me and save me the cost of buying a copy of the book," he joked. Then, name by name, he wanted to know what was reported about the personalities and abilities of business and editorial people on the magazines. He listened with rapt attention. When he came to Jason McManus's deputy, the editorial director, Ross made his most affirmative personnel evaluation. "Dick Stolley, I really like him, he's terrific." (Stolley was retired a year later.)

But his strength was obviously waning. Without asking I rose to leave, escorting him to the winding stairway leading to his bedroom upstairs. He ascended painfully, clutching the handrail. Over his shoulder he said, "Thanks for distracting me." He allowed himself to be distracted once more—for a retrospective on Ross and the merger for the New York *Times Magazine*.

Two days before Thanksgiving, his lawyer and intimate friend Arthur Liman phoned. Liman sounded uncharacteristically distraught. "You're the first call I'm making—and I'm making a lot. We're announcing in half an hour that Steve is beginning treatment for prostatic cancer," Liman said, "but Steve wanted me personally to call you first. One of the things that has caused him an enormous amount of anguish is that when he talked to you he denied it. They misdiagnosed his problem for the last several weeks. It's a stunner for him, because he thought that the last thing in the world he would need is this treatment. The doctor I spoke to is very optimistic."

I asked Liman to tell Ross that he should not worry about misleading me, just take care of his health. Next day I sent Liman a memo:

> For my forthcoming book going to press next Friday, December 6, I need to know how dysfunctional or sick Steve is right

now and foreseeably, not to print it but to deal with discreetly and sensitively.

The fact pattern is: several years ago Steve had a prostatectomy at Johns Hopkins performed by the acknowledged leading authority on this procedure in the world. *Anyone* who has had prostate problems, not to say a prostatectomy, who develops back problems, is immediately examined for the most likely possibility, namely a spread of the cancer to the lower back and spine. A third-year medical student knows that, as Steve's excellent doctors certainly do.

Liman replied immediately that someone had obviously made a terrible mistake.

Ross was admitted to Manhattan's Memorial Sloan–Kettering Cancer Center to be treated for the cancer. He then divided his time between his East Hampton house and his Manhattan apartment, while undergoing a course of six debilitating and risky chemotherapy treatments, each separated by twenty-one days. Between treatments, he summoned up his energy to engage in his favorite activity, work.

Senior politicians now must give detailed reports about their health. The SEC makes no such demands of CEOs. Some Time Warner board members complained that they lacked crucial information about Ross.

Although Ross did not go to the office, he was frequently on the phone to associates and board members. His wife, along with his longtime assistant, Carmen Ferragano, relayed his messages and instructions. Levin who visited Ross, said he expected Ross back in the office by spring, from what his doctors were reporting.

But between treatments Ross found enough strength to help in one major transaction. It made the biggest front-page news on Time Warner since the merger itself.

ONE WEEK AFTER THIS book, *To the End of Time,* was published in late January 1991, Nick Nicholas, fifty-two, was brutally ousted as president and co-CEO of Time Warner. It happened even faster than those who had predicted it had guessed. It was a career-killing blow to him, the sudden end of a lifelong dream. But there was nothing he could do about it, even though when the two companies merged he thought he had an iron-clad contract, combined with an oath "signed in blood" from Steve Ross.

Both documents provided that Nicholas would be equal partners with Ross, to succeed him in 1994 as head of the multibillion-dollar company. In a secret struggle for power, with one day's notice, Nicholas was forced out by the company's twenty-three-member board of directors, with one dissenting vote. The board unanimously replaced him with his old Time rival, Jerry Levin.

Nicholas was in shock. I phoned him. Could we talk once more? His answer was polite but brisk. "Nope. Nothing. I've decided that whenever I tell whatever I have on my mind I know who I'm going to tell and it ain't going to be you." End of conversation.

His answer was chilling for good reason. The reporting in *To the End of Time* had forecast his downfall. It was based on accounts from colleagues of his abrasive executive style, his self-incriminating words, his early clashes with Ross. Why should he agree to talk to me?

But he did. Three hours later my phone rang. This time it was a hot, impulsive Nicholas. With little preface, he told me, "What's on my mind is that I know a lot, as you might surmise. Not only *why* what happened and *when* it did and the *way* it did, but I also know a lot of other things. What I'm going to do probably is eventually find someone to tell the story. I have a journalist in mind [Connie Bruck of *The New Yorker,* to whom he later gave interviews]. It certainly won't be you. I have kept my mouth shut at the moment for a lot of reasons. Nobody has asked me to, but I have decided as a matter of personal conviction not to get into a pissing contest with this great spin bullshit they're putting out. I'm not talking to anybody for now. The sleaziness of the whole thing! I don't want to be associated with it until it is clear how sleazy it is." Goodbye.

What was he talking about? In the headquarters Time Warner Building, and a half-block away in the Time & Life Building, as well as through the board's telephone grapevine, there were whispered reports tarring him. They said Nicholas was complaining behind the closed doors of the office he still occupied that there had been plots against him from the very beginning. He was saying that for all he knew Ross might all along have been in cahoots with Paramount's Martin Davis, whose unwanted hostile bid had forced Time to buy Warner for $14 billion, yielding Ross millions more than he would have in the original deal. ("Someone must be kidding," said Davis. "That theory would be sick.") There were additional reports that Nicholas was suggesting all kinds of other malign "conspiracies."

In fact, Time Warner insiders admitted there had been a conspiracy, but its makings were not of the kind he darkly hinted. Nicholas had done himself in. The coup was startling only for its swiftness.

As the date of Nicholas's ascension grew closer, the onetime financial whiz kid seemed to be racing to his goal, stopwatch and calculator in hand, knocking over every barrier. When there were disagreements with Ross and others Nicholas could get downright disagreeable and explosive. Even secretaries in the office and other staff couldn't stand the turmoil. If press handouts didn't award Nicholas enough credit, he bitched. Magazine articles that slighted him caused him to sulk. "Nick never had any self-awareness of the impression he makes on people. He just plunges ahead, brimming with overconfidence," said a lawyer close to him.

The tension was so great that Ross and Nicholas had stopped communicating months earlier.

WHEN ROSS HAD TO take leave of the office, intermediaries were confused by conflicting orders. Insiders said the ambitious Nicholas had begun behaving as General Alexander Haig had when he announced on network television after the assassination attempt on Reagan: "I am in control here." Many thought Nicholas—like Haig—was out of control.

But Nicholas's collisions with Ross were predestined almost from the day they came together in their temporary embrace. Consider a description of the two from a friend of both, a senior member of the Time Warner board:

Ross: "He's the 'Great Schmooze.' An enormously effective personal salesman. Enormous! I've watched him in all kinds of situations. He has a warmth about him and a disarming, self-deprecating manner that's almost hypnotic. Eighty-five percent of it is real. Of course, we all have a little phoniness in us and I'm not sure what Steve is really like when the doors are closed and he's by himself. But he has a wonderful style, is a good listener, very diplomatic, sensitive. Steve has a tendency to talk you to death. One of his strategies of carrying the day is to exhaust you. He will just talk to you until you give up. He is not combative, just tenacious. Even though he wouldn't scream and holler at you, he doesn't let go."

Nicholas: "Nick is very tightly wound, intense, sometimes too intense, sometimes almost obsessed with his viewpoint. Unfortunately, he can be awfully quick with people. He's a better talker than a listener, sometimes too confident, too cocky, too self-assured. He may be the CEO of the nineties, where you'd better be one tough son of a bitch and you'd better be willing to make tough decisions. Make them quick. He has all the smarts. I sometimes get a little concerned with his humanity. Nick has a lot of people who are very fond of him. And a lot don't like him. He does everything himself, so he hasn't got time to be really nice to people. He doesn't schmooze a helluva lot, which doesn't endear people. He's not as bad as he sometimes projects himself to be, but at times his ambition and his intensity get in his way."

"Nick can be very brusque and abrupt," another director had complained, adding, "there was bound to be trouble. Jerry just gets better and better. There's always been a dark side to Nick. He doesn't easily accept the fact that there are other bright people around."

Could there be an odder couple?

IN THEIR FIRST YEAR together, Ross and Nicholas had started their working relationship with the practiced finesse of a figure-skating pair in a media Olympics. Ross never needed to assert that he was boss. Everybody knew that. But Nicholas was betraying early signs of impatience and hubris. When they talked strategy, Nicholas was for more hunkering down, selling assets (cable and music) if need be. Ross was insisting on expanding by taking in new partners.

The tension rose when Ross once again tried to make good on his failed but widely publicized promise to find "strategic partners," to reduce the company's debt. When Toshiba and the Japanese trading company C. Itoh offered to invest more than a billion dollars if they could share in some of Time Warner's movie and cable profits, Nicholas balked. He didn't want to share promised future profits with partners. Ross wanted to go ahead. Nicholas stormed out, refusing even to attend the planning sessions. He isolated himself in his office, bitter at being overruled.

Ross calls himself a dreamer. He relied on his guru, the financial metaphysician Ed Aboodi, to translate his dreams into numbers. Levin, the businessman-philosopher, now provided the rationale. Nicholas, structured and didactic, was odd man out. His opposition to the Japanese deal stalled it for four months, possibly costing the company, *Time* reported, "an extra $100 million to $200 million" before it closed.

It was only one of their many collisions, a signal of a deeper fissure.

/AS KNOWN FOR his financial skills, not manage-
ity. He was a conservative player, wary of risks. At
warner, the whirlwind combination of Ross and Aboodi didn't
require much help from Nicholas, who found Aboodi's presence
especially galling. (Aboodi was neither an officer of the company
nor on the board.) More important than the disagreements they had
over what Ross calls, "you should forgive the expression, strategic
alliances," were their incompatible styles. After his ouster, Nicholas
said their basic differences were over "strategy." But it was much
more the personality clash than differences over issues that made
the co-CEO arrangement impossible.

At first Ross had tolerated the situation diplomatically, admiring
the soft-spoken, passionate skills of Jerry Levin over Nicholas's sulk-
ing shoulders. As one informed friend of both Nicholas and Levin
put it: "Nick is as opposite in outlook from Jerry as Thomas Hobbes
["The life of man is . . . nasty, brutish and short"] was from Socrates
["The life which is unexamined is not worth living"].

When Ross got sick, Nicholas became even more overbearing.
The reality of his running the company alone, possibly soon, rose
like an ugly dawn. If Ross indeed was not to come back, it seemed
inconceivable to many, including some old Time directors, that
Nicholas would be able to run the company. Levin could no longer
imagine playing Don Quixote in a kingdom ruled by Nicholas. And
"Steve," said another director, "was a real believer in what Jerry
could do for this company."

Levin later told groups of Timeincers that his wife had said to him
she had always been so proud of him when he worked for Time Inc.
But now that it was Time Warner she no longer felt that way. He
told the staff that over Christmas at his Vermont retreat, he had
read galleys of what he called this "provocative" book. Afterward,
he said he had taken a "walk in the woods" and decided Time Warner
had to be fixed.

Ross had come to the same conclusion. His wife, Courtney, who
had canceled her world tour to be at his bedside, complained to
Levin that Ross's health was not being helped by all the executive
tension. Levin visited Ross in his sprawling East Hampton house.
They both decided that Nicholas had to go.

•   •   •

ROSS, WHO REFUSED EVER to fire anyone himself, left most of the heavy work of persuading the board of directors to Levin and Liman. A majority of the befuddled, feckless directors who had come from the Time board were ignorant of the inner workings of the company and were easy to turn around. Dick Munro, who had promoted Nicholas and had been his leading backer for years, after listening to Levin reluctantly came to the conclusion that Nicholas had changed for the worse in his new role.

By the time Nicholas got word of opposition, it was too late. Don Perkins, chairman of the Time Warner board's governance and nominating committee, a onetime stalwart Nicholas advocate, called Nicholas in Vail, Colorado, where he was on a family skiing holiday. *Fortune* later reported that Perkins began, "Are you sitting down, Nick?" After he heard he was being forced out, the magazine said, "Nicholas was so shocked and saddened that when she saw him, his wife Lynn thought that a member of the family had died."

Nicholas was invited at the last minute to argue his case before the board. He checked his sources and found that any directors who might have been swayed would have been overwhelmingly outvoted by the board's solid wall of Warnerites and disaffected Timeincers. He chose to stay with his wife in their Vail bunker.

In theory, Ross presided over the emergency board meeting the next day. Although vice chairman Martin Payson (who has since been forced off the board and resigned from the company) ran the meeting, Ross was present on a speakerphone. The board, which met for only a little over an hour, was almost unanimous in its vote to dismiss Nicholas. (Only Henry Luce III, son of Time's co-founder, dissented, urging more due process.) Then, by an uncontested vote, the board installed Levin in Nicholas's place.

The board solemnly agreed, "in deference" to Nicholas's feeling and reputation to keep their mouths shut (which, of course, they failed to do), and gave as their official reason "strategic differences."

Nicholas wanted as his Elba, an office in the Time & Life Building. "No way," said a senior Time Warner executive. (Instead he was given a Fifth Avenue suite as part of his settlement.) In the hardball game of business politics, he had become a nonperson to Time Warner. His name was not mentioned in the company's next glossy annual report. The details of Nicholas's financial settlement were never announced or reported in the proxy statement. In purely financial terms, one option was written firmly into his contract. Nicholas could technically remain an employee of the company for the next twelve years, accumulating as much as $50 million or more including his stock options and annual bonuses—for doing nothing. (This was in addition to the estimated $16 million he was worth at the time of the merger.) He had only lost his job, not the financial and other rewards that went with it. Sensibly, he took the payout his contract guaranteed, with stock options, estimated to be worth $40 to $50 million (not the $15.7 million widely reported), in addition to a continuation of all his lavish benefit programs (including life and medical insurance.)

Ironically, in Time's quest throughout the second half of the '80s to seek an acquisition or new partnership with such companies as Gannett, Capital Cities/ABC, CBS and dozens of others, every potential deal *always* foundered on one irreducible condition: Nicholas had to be the CEO of the new company to carry on and represent the "Time Inc. tradition."

No Time executive or board member—except Levin—had realized until long after the deal was completed, that in the fine print of the complex merger agreement they had missed the point. Nicholas's contract was only a money agreement, not a guarantee of his succession.

NICHOLAS'S SUDDEN REMOVAL WAS greeted almost everywhere with cheers and the self-righteousness of hindsight. Wall Street applauded by jacking up the company's battered stock by close to ten points. From the Polo Lounge of the Beverly Hills Hotel to the tables down at Morton's, Hollywood wise guys happily danced on Nicholas's grave. An overconfident "suit" one of them called him, "an amateur strutting on our turf." (Cynically, they began speculating on how long Levin would last before one of their own was put in. "Levin is very smart," said one show-biz lawyer, "but not big enough to lead that company.")

No one clapped louder than the journalists and publishers in the Time & Life Building, headquarters for the company's magazine and book publishing, where Nicholas had honed his cost-cutting reputation. (Reducing costs "isn't going to end," he had announced in a menacing tone, "it's now part of the way we do business.") Not only had the magazines become a small wedge of profit in the whole showy entertainment-and-cable company, they were also orphaned and left leaderless, their staffs and budgets cut, their morale at an all-time low. The standard-bearing magazines had been charged with forfeiting their independence, ignoring the activities of their parent company, or running self-serving, censored coverage.

Worse, for the first time in their history they were being ruled by the bottom-line businessman Reg Brack, a self-described "marketing man" and a Nicholas protégé. Brack dominated the editor in chief, who had always been the most powerful publishing figure. That exalted pulpit was now occupied by the almost invisible Jason McManus, whose wavering leadership had earned little respect from his managing editors or their staffs.

The journalists felt liberated when they heard that Nicholas's replacement was Jerry Levin. At first glance, Levin may have seemed an unlikely editorial hero, since he had never worked as a reporter or editor a day in his life. Virtually unknown to the world outside and barely acquainted with most of the journalists at Time Inc., he nonetheless, knew every symbolic button to push.

One of Levin's early calls after the surprise announcement was on the venerated Andrew Heiskell, chairman of the "old Time Inc.," whose company-commissioned oil portrait had been taken down and whose retirement office had been withdrawn, both bruising moves urged by Nicholas. Levin arrived in Heiskell's tiny rental office to redress the heavy-handed ingratitudes, which had both become public knowledge in this book. It was too late to restore the portrait to its place of honor, since it had been donated to the New York Public Library (where he had also been chairman). Instead, Levin invited Heiskell to occupy a "nice office in the Time Warner Building." Heiskell agreeably declined the symbolic gesture. But overnight, board minutes and budgets, from which Heiskell had been cut off, began coming his way again.

Levin summoned the managing editors of the magazines to the *Time* magazine conference room, not the thirty-fourth executive floor, where they had become accustomed lately to being summoned to receive bad news. Next, floor by floor in rapid succession, he met with the editorial staffs of the magazines and book publishers. Addressing each group quietly, without notes or histrionics, he seemed, said one editor, more like "Dustin Hoffman, pulling on his ear, looking at the floor, than the programmed business guys we usually hear."

Levin barely mentioned Nicholas. Instead, the new company president wanted to discuss the future. It was a new era, Levin declared, or actually the reaffirmation of an old one. The magazines were the "heart and soul" of Time Warner and they had been badly treated since the merger, demoralized, forced to concern themselves too much with profit margins, budgets and rates of return. But cost-cutting and layoffs were not to be "a way of life" (as Nicholas had warned). "Those kinds of layoffs died last week," he pledged. He wanted Time Warnerites to bring more love to their work. "By love I don't mean eros but agape," he explained, spiritual not sexual love. "Whoever heard a CEO use the word 'agape'?" exclaimed an editor after a meeting.

In front of the managing editors, he obliquely chastised Jason McManus for not being visible enough. He told the stoical McManus he needed to represent the values of the company's journalism, to step forward more assertively and reconsider his "consensus" style of management. McManus hopped on the accelerating bandwagon. "I have a new assignment," he announced. "This is a new age. The real beginning of the merger. I find it immensely liberating. I hope you will too."

On the thirty-fourth floor, where Nicholas had once cracked his whip, a receptionist blurted out: "Thank you, you're making us all feel important again." Down the hall one of Nicholas's former subordinates chortled, "Ding-dong, the witch is dead." In an editorial office there was a more elegant but equally unsentimental epitaph: "The Iceman Goeth."

One longtime Nicholas friend and associate had a kinder, if cliché, verdict: "Nick knew the lyrics of Time Inc., but he never really understood the music."

WAS LEVIN TOO GOOD to be true? Were they being conned again, this time by a quiet cheerleader who read books and spoke their language?

None of the skeptical journalists seemed to think so. "If he was pandering," said one editor, "at least he knew who to pander to." When the *Time* bureau chiefs were assembled in Florida to get the new message, one of them asked, "Why should we believe him?" His boss replied, "Let's say seventy-five percent is true. Let's not look *this* gift horse in the mouth."

The gifts came tumbling out.

Most remarkably, *Time* and *Fortune* both ran stories about the uproar with all the energetic reporting and candor they could muster. When the Time Warner merger was first announced, Jason McManus had blotted his reputation by preventing *Time* from reporting the story at all. (Levin alone among the high command had opposed McManus's decision). Not this round. McManus didn't even see the stories about Nicholas before they were published.

COUP AT THE TOP shouted *Time*. "Officially," the magazine said, "Nicholas 'resigned.' In fact he was ousted in a coup conducted, he angrily told friends, in a banana-republic fashion." In a story headlined AFTER THE COUP AT TIME WARNER, *Fortune* sharply raised the question of why the "not-so-independent board" had again been so ignorant and uninformed about the problems in the Ross-Nicholas relationship. *Time* and *Fortune*'s stories were the most honest, critical coverage the magazines had ever been allowed to run about their parent company, "making up for past sins," one critic observed. ("And we even ran favorable reviews of your book in *Time, Fortune* and *People*," one senior executive proudly said to me.)

There were other, less visible, signs of the change. A series of uniquely harsh demands that the management had been making in the Newspaper Guild negotiations were immediately dropped. The exploration of new magazines as well as other publishing initiatives and expansions were stepped up. Levin, like a stump politician out on the campaign trail, even made it a point to talk to disaffected senior alumni, seeking their renewed support.

Working dummies of the "new, redesigned" *Time*, were also discreetly unveiled to more alumni. Privately, Levin worried about raising expectations too high. "But he couldn't have started out better," one senior editorial executive said, a sentiment echoed in the halls on every floor of the Time & Life Building and its outposts around the world. "It was like the Prague Spring with no Russian tanks even in sight," crowed an impressed alumnus.

Levin summarized the situation with optimism. "Steve and I have a common purpose for the company. And it's a higher obligation than simply making money." Did Levin really mean those lofty words? "You can be certain I do," he said. "My integrity is at stake."

FOR A CORPORATION, WHAT are those "higher obligations"? Certainly that its employees, top to bottom, go about their business in a way that creates pride, not shame, in their collegiality—an atmosphere more often radiating from the top than prescribed in a code of behavior. Equally important is that the company's products adhere to standards of quality and responsibility whatever its business—entertainment, publishing or selling widgets. "Our good name," Levin had said, echoing a familiar refrain, "is our basic asset." At Haverford College, he added, "My value system was indelibly established. A sense of integrity was mightily shaped."

On balance, few doubted that Levin and the "old Time Inc.," had believed its oft-repeated vow to operate the "enterprise in the public interest." Time's key winning argument in the Delaware courts had been the preservation of that "special culture." But throughout the merger negotiations and after, many questioned whether the new conglomerate could provide such a corporate character, a spine of shared values from which all its many parts took signals.

The new company announced proudly, "Time Warner is in the business of ideas." What kind of ideas? Let many flowers bloom, it seemed to suggest, even if some ugly weeds might sprout. On the Muzak of such a company "Anything Goes" could fill its corridors.

Its stock struggling to keep up with the rising Dow Jones Index, with strategic alliances hard to come by, the company was hitting none of the promised financial home runs. Although its cash flow was up and debt reduced, "Wall Street simply does not understand this stock," said Capital Resources' Gordon Crawford, the company's largest cheerleader and stockholder (11 percent).

If the business news about Time Warner was less than glowing, some of the conglomerate's products got as much attention as an erupting volcano. Unfortunately, and often unfairly, companies and people tend to be judged not by their best work but by their worst. There were too many of the latter to enhance the company's already battered reputation.

ONE OF THE WORST bummers came from the rapper Tracy Morrow, Ice-T. His latest album, distributed by a Time Warner subsidiary, was titled *Body Count*. In one of the songs in the album Ice-T raps a street kid's warning: "I've got my twelve-gauge sawed off. I' about to dust some pigs off . . . die pigs die." The chorus intoned: "Cop Killer, it's better than you and me. Cop killer, fuck police brutality! Cop killer, I know your family's grievin'. Fuck 'em! Tonight we get even." The album's promotional copies were delivered in miniature body bags. (Another number in the album was titled,

"Momma's Gotta Die Tonight," whose refrain was "Burn momma, burn bitch, burn, burn bitch.")

Coming out one month before the 1992 Los Angeles riots, the lyrics touched off a national uproar. Editorialists, law enforcement organizations, pension funds and Hollywood celebrities picketed and organized boycotts of all the company's products. (Hundreds of stores refused to sell the album.) Many heard the lyrics as an invitation to murder cops. Ice-T himself made matters worse by saying on national TV, "I think cops should feel threatened. I feel threatened. They should know that they can't take a life without retaliation."

In Ross's absence, Levin decided to go on the offensive by posing a highfalutin question: "Is it our responsibility to limit the views of artists, writers, journalists, musicians and film makers so they don't offend corporate executives or society at large?" Absolutely not, he answered. Time Warner believed in free speech and artistic integrity. " 'Cop Killer,' " he said, "wasn't written to advocate an assault by black street kids on the police. One-sided, violent and scatalogical, it's the artist's rap on how a street kid feels. We stand for creative freedom. We won't retreat in the face of threats of boycotts or political grandstanding." Then, as if carried away by his own cosmic rap, Levin concluded: "We believe that the future of our country—indeed, of the world—is contained in the commitment to truth and free expression, in the refusal to run away."

Entertainment mogul David Geffen, whose company was once owned by Warner and peddled some heavy heavy metal itself, including the riot-making group Guns N' Roses, weighed in with: "The question is about responsibility. Should someone make money by advocating the murder of a policeman? To say that this whole issue is not about profit is silly. It certainly is not about artistic freedom." At the company's five-hour annual meeting in Los Angeles, there was little time to pour out news of stock dividends and splits, the latest annual financial results or to explain Nicholas's ouster. Ice-T was the brew of choice. Actor Charlton Heston questioned, "If the song were entitled 'Fag Killer,' or if the lyrics went 'Die, die, die, Kike,' would you still sell it?" Another protester stood up and said, "In my opinion you've lost your moral compass. I'm not trying to remove it from the stores. It's not a First Amendment issue. But if you target people for killing, what makes you different from Goebbels?"

Instead of saying "Oops, we made a mistake, it won't happen again," Levin, who had called rap "the CNN of the streets," stuck to his elaborate, irrelevant free-speech argument. Kathleen M. Sullivan, a Harvard Law School professor who is a specialist on free speech, explained the prevalent view: Actions such as pulling the album from stores "are not rightly called censorship. They are exercises of editorial discretion, judgment, social responsibility, market forces or just plain taste."

From inside and outside the company, writers for Time's magazines, producers of its movies or editors of its books pointed out that all were always guided by standards of taste and impact without complaints that their Constitutional rights were being violated. No one was suggesting that Ice-T should not be allowed to say whatever he wanted. " 'Cop Killer,' " one critic remarked, "is Time Warner's *choice,* not its obligation."

The uproar was so loud and the company so embattled that after three weeks of heavy national TV and press coverage, editorials, pages of letters and op-ed commentary, and with very few supporting his position, the company was forced into an about-face. Ice-T and Time Warner did just what Levin said they would never do. They retreated. The company announced that Ice-T had asked that the album be pulled from the stores (330,000 copies had been sold). It was reissued without its most offensive song. Months later, Ice-T and Time Warner parted company altogether.

THE COMPANY WAS ALREADY in a defensive crouch after Warner Bros., its celebrated movie studio, financed and distributed Oliver Stone's pseudodocumentary, *JFK.* The sensational film mixed real news clips with fiction. It told a younger generation of Americans and millions abroad the grotesque and groundless story that the president had been assassinated as a result of a plot by the Lyndon Johnson government, the CIA and the military-industrial complex.

Studio executives explained that it was an example of allowing Stone complete "artistic integrity." It served the belated social purpose, they said, of "opening up" the files on the case, which had been pored over for years without producing a shred of evidence to support the movie's thesis. Another example, the company said, of not interfering with Stone's "creativity."

But the film was roundly denounced for enhancing and endorsing a discredited conspiracy theory. Journalists (including Time's editorial director), historians and others who lived through the assassination horror, cried "foul." Historical novelist, William Styron (*The Confessions of Nat Turner, Sophie's Choice*) disagreed. Artistic license, certainly, he said, "but fiction must still not violate the larger historical code. There are at least a dozen historical lies in the movie. You can't stretch facts and plausibility that far."

A third challenge came when Time Warner advanced $60 million to form a multimedia partnership with the megastar Madonna for music, movies, TV and HBO specials—and books. Her first book, *Sex,* at fifty dollars a pop, was hyped into a blizzard of newspaper headlines and TV coverage. The one million copy printing quickly hit the top of the best-seller lists even though hundreds of disparagers, including the company's own magazines, *Time* and *Entertainment Weekly,* described it as a "Sodom High yearbook," "soft porn," "raunchy, trashy, erotic fantasy," "S&M camp," "hype," "Madonna's masterpiece of media manipulation." One reviewer dubbed it, "Just another day at the orifice" for Madonna.

No one greeted the dissonant trio of Time Warner "vehicles" more harshly than the *Wall Street Journal* in a lead editorial headed "Schlock Shock": "Time Warner—distributor of Madonna, Ice-T and Prince—is our undisputed *schlockmeister* but they call it art. We now have a significant media presence in the U.S. that's wholly dependent on the flow of concocted outrage to keep themselves in business." *Business Week* and others joined in: "Time Warner's standards of taste [are] on trial again."

Bookstore shelves were barely emptied of the Madonna book when the fourth Time Warner vehicle came rolling along, headlights on high. One month after the Madonna uproar, Warner released on screens across the country Spike Lee's angry, Afrocentric film biography, *Malcolm X,* powerfully reincarnating the protean black nationalist leader of the 60s. Behind the opening titles was a burning American flag incinerating into a blazing "X" and the infamous videotape of Los Angeles police brutally clubbing Rodney King.

Malcolm X, which was creatively faithful to history, was no *JFK*. Critics, for the most part, quarreled more with Spike Lee's racist promotional tumult and the film's length (3 hours, 21 minutes), than with its messages or with the fact that it softened some of Malcom X's most incendiary catechisms on, for instance, women, Jews and blacks.

Even those who saw *Malcolm X* as a skillful, overdue expression of black pride, wondered about the serial assaults on minds and emotions emanating from Time Warner. What was the company doing? Where did it draw the line? Who in the company decides how much is too much? A senior Time Warner executive gave the short answer: "This company is a home—in certain cases—for provocateurs."

Jerry Levin attempted a more complete company credo: "Time Warner is a home for journalists and artists who have significant messages to tell. They do it with journalistic and artistic integrity. Time Warner will finance, support and disseminate their work. That's what the company is."

But were diversity and free speech a definition of the company's character?

When Levin had been asked three years earlier, as the wedding feast for Time Warner marriage was being prepared, what would be the personality and character of the new couple, he paused thoughtfully and answered: "It will take a while to define." From the record of Time Warner's early years, obviously that time had not yet come. To critics of the company's blurred focus, including members of its own board, Levin responds with his confident rationales. "When he takes a stand," says one former colleague, "Jerry mesmerizes himself."

IN EARLY SPRING 1991, the company had announced Steve Ross was responding so well to chemotherapy that his cancer was in remission. It would not be necessary for him to undergo the final two of the six treatments. He was expected, the company said, to be back in time to preside at the July annual meeting. Two months before the meeting, came a grimmer announcement. Ross required more treatment and would this time take "an indefinite leave."

As late as that summer, Arthur Liman was asked by a concerned, mutual friend, "How's Steve doing?" Liman and others close to Ross maintained the compassionate fiction that he was "fine." But the few friends who saw him knew otherwise. "I cried after what surely must have been my farewell visit," said one. Another added, "I wouldn't have recognized him. It would take an honest-to-God miracle for a remission at this late date." Ross fought valiantly. He sought treatment all over the United States, from hospitals in New York, Houston and finally Los Angeles, where he underwent hours of radical surgery.

In early December 1992, Liman read some Time Warner board members a doctor's letter saying Ross was doing fine and was expected back at work. On Wednesday, December 16, Levin sent a year-end memo to the worldwide Time Warner staff, which concluded, "I can tell you that his treatment is progressing, that he and his doctors are optimistic, and that he is eager to get back to work."

But it was all denial of grim reality.

Four days later, in Los Angeles on Sunday, December 20, Steve Ross, sixty-five, died. With friends from Time Warner and Hollywood, his family and others looking on, he was buried under a blanket of lavender roses in a cemetary close to his home on West End Road in East Hampton, Long Island.

Steven Spielberg, his close friend and neighbor, mourned, "It's like a cold draft running through my heart; I can't get warm. Knowing Steve, he's up there right now with his yellow pad and pencil figuring out how to plug the holes." Liman eulogized, "I only hope that you, dear God, have plenty of yellow pads and pencils, for if you do and can understand his math, Steve will show you how to make heaven a better place."

ROSS, THE DREAMER, DID not live long enough to see whether the new multimedia conglomerate he created could ever achieve the financial success it promised. Nor did Time Warner prove it could keep the other promises it made to "synergize," with pride, the entertainment, culture and information the company now embraced—the "biggest media and entertainment company in the world," as it repeatedly intoned.

In the first three years, Time Warner was still more a collection of parts that clashed as often as they helped each other. The company appeared to many more like the frenzied conglomerates of the '60s and '70s, which split apart instead of harmonizing; or the high-debt bingers of the '80s, of which the Time Warner merger was the last big high-flier.

The company had yet to demonstrate that, coupled in corporate wedlock, Time and Warner might live happily ever after.

JANUARY 1993

(Some parts of this chapter appeared in Vanity Fair and the New York Times.)

The Reader Should Know . . .

I SPENT TWENTY gratifying and exhilarating years at Time Inc. as a journalist and executive, even centrally involved in my final days there in the company's early forays into cable TV. Like so many who grew up professionally under Harry Luce, I was doubtful at first, as well as predictably concerned, when I heard of Time's plan to merge with Warner. Two weeks after the first merger announcement (months before the Paramount intervention), I decided to write this book.

At the outset I set a goal, which some may consider as impossible or unlikely as beginning life all over again by erasing the past. But I tried scraping out of my mind, both professionally and emotionally, any nostalgic rust and attempted to report the present—the new financial circumstances, technologies, different people and changing times. I decided to try, as much as I could, to tell and report this story through the voices and opinions of others.

A lot has been made of the "access" I had because of my "old-boy" status. Not so. For close to a year, my friends and acquaintances who were high executives or directors at Time and Warner froze me out, putting off a decision whether they would even talk to me. During this period I received no cooperation or corporate access whatsoever. Finally the top executives reluctantly decided they would be interviewed, telling their directors at a board meeting that there was no "policy" for or against cooperating with me—each executive and director would have to decide. In the end, there was no one I wanted to talk to whom I did not reach.

The biggest conflict of interest for a journalist is the unequal treatment that can come from friendships. I had many friends who were involved in this story when I started and even more when I finished. But *in print*, I make a stern effort to have no friends (or enemies), although, after my family, my friends are the biggest treasure in my life. There are other possible invisible conflicts of interest. The only cure I know for them, apart from avoiding the obviously egregious, is full disclosure. Herewith:

- I have had no formal connection with Time Inc. since 1975. The office I have occupied in the Time & Life Building was rented three years before the start of this book, as a base for my pro bono activities (primarily as chairman of Columbia University's Seminars on Media and Society). Although, as a member of the Time-Life Alumni Society, I have a laissez-passer to the Time Inc. floors in the building, I have never visited them uninvited since the start of this book.

- Upon signing a contract for the book, I bought one share of stock each in Time Inc., Warner and Chris-Craft so that I could view each company from the vantage point of a stockholder. Those stocks represent my entire holdings in any media-related company. (I never acquired a share of Paramount because the period of its intervention was too short).

- For three months in 1984, at the beginning of Rupert Murdoch's Warner takeover attempt, I acted as paid consultant to the law firm of Paul, Weiss, Rifkind, Wharton, & Garrison. (I doubt that I acquired or gave any information during that period which was confidential but nevertheless I drew on no part of that brief experience for this book.)

- For two years I was retained part-time as a public policy adviser, and occupied office space at an advertising agency which was later acquired and then quickly sold by Lorimar Television, now a division of Time Warner.

- My daughter Susan Emma Dockendorff, who is the public relations director of *Fortune*, and who offers me more personal gratifications, totally recused herself from my work on this book.

- Paramount Communications, which owns Simon & Schuster, my publisher, made no effort, despite its involvement in the merger, to influence, edit or skew my reporting and writing any more than people outside of Paramount did. Their executives were interviewed and reported without favor, as anyone should be able to tell from reading the book.

My thanks are as abundant as they are earnest:

I am especially grateful to those Time Warner executives, board members and staff who ultimately gave me hours of their time— my tape recorder rolling—answering my questions. To single out any one of them would be distorting, although it is obvious from those identified and quoted with whom I spent the most time. No matter how they feel about the outcome, I owe my first thanks to them. But there are dozens of others (out of the hundreds interviewed) who for the most understandable reasons would not allow themselves to be identified. The popular notion that unattributed sources are suspect can be naive. Candor and understanding often must be swapped for identification by name, especially when people are talking openly about their bosses—or even about their peers.

I am equally indebted to the unnamed people, a couple especially, who helped me and guided me, and to one anonymous editor in particular, who read the entire manuscript and proved, what I knew, that he is the best prematurely retired book editor around.

Without the assistance of named and unnamed present and former Time Inc. and Warner employees and directors, as well as the contribution of various lawyers, bankers and accountants, parts of this book would not have been possible.

Among the people who professionally helped me, I am most grateful to Stanley H. Brown, a journalist of integrity, wit and depth, who in the process became a valued friend. He is a former colleague from *Fortune* magazine. Later he wrote several books, briefly worked for Warner Communications and was on the staff of *Forbes*, as well as a contributor to a number of magazines. Several years ago he interviewed some former Warner employees for a book that he contemplated writing (with Robert Rolontz), which aborted.

Susan Biederman and Gordon McLeod, at the beginning and end of my labors, were extremely helpful in various aspects of the research. Barbara Widmayer, my indispensable office assistant, not only managed my office life with grace and efficiency but helped in the final preparation of the galleys, as well as at every other turn in this project.

My son, Michael Clurman, and his colleagues at Axiom Partners provided constant financial data, as well as guidance in the numerology of Wall Street. And my daughter Carol Clurman Duning, a

Washington journalist, urged me on, contributing two delicious grandchildren along the way.

My rightly renowned editor, Alice Mayhew, delivered shorthand bursts of suggestions, which exploded, when I reflected on them, into deeply experienced and thoughtful insights. She also provided encouragement, guidance and levity that were almost as resounding as her skillful text editing. Her two assistants, George Hodgman and Ari Hoogenboom, cheerfully saw me through the labyrinth of the book-publishing process, as did other capable and agreeable people at Simon & Schuster, including counselor Eric Rayman, art director Frank Metz, senior copy editor Marcia Peterson, Laurie Jewell, Eve Metz, Victoria Meyer, Adelle Stan, copy editor Greg Weber and others.

My literary lawyer-agent Mort Janklow auspiciously launched the project and has advised me throughout.

No one could have been more supportive, editorially helpful and accommodating in so many ways than my wife, once a Timeincer herself, to whom this book should be and is dedicated.

Marilyn Harris and Peter Costiglio of Time Warner's public relations staff were as gracious and helpful as they could be in climbing the company's walls to answer some of my queries.

My friends inside and outside of journalism have been a constant source of stimulation, encouragement and assistance that is impossible to assess but equally impossible not to mention.

Finally, I must point out that corporations—especially those in the business of communications—have no one to blame but themselves for the confusion and debate over their compensation arrangements and the reporting of other information to their shareholders and the public. These are purposely disclosed in fine print and complex legalese, replete with qualifying footnotes and remote references, so intricate as to obscure rather than reveal. To try to make the most responsible estimates of such matters, I have called on a number of legal, financial and compensation experts, none more valuably than Graef S. ("Bud") Crystal, formerly a contributor to *Fortune* and now to a variety of other publications. He is widely rated the leading executive compensation expert in the U.S. His most recent (October 1991) book *In Search of Excess: The Overcompensation of American Executives*, is a guide to the arcana of that field.

That old lesson from the Bible, "seek, and ye shall find," is one of the many joys of circumspect journalism, a constant process of stimulating learning and discovery. It has its converse these days, perhaps for many in business especially: "Hide and ye shall be found"—eventually.

DICK CLURMAN
NEW YORK
NOVEMBER 1991

Index

Westchester Premier Theatre case, 107–14, 117, 121, 126, 160, 171, 179, 181–85, 266
bankruptcy in, 110
financial brokers in, 108
Levin's views on, 183–84
Opel's ignorance of, 182–83, 185
Paramount's revival of, 229
see Armstrong Report
Westinghouse Cable, 78
Wharton, Clifton R., Jr., 88, 157, 160, 161, 179
Whitney, Betsey Cushing, 61
Whitney, John Hay (Jock), 61, 62
Who's Who in America, 54
Wilkes-Barre, Pa., 39
Williams, Edward Bennett, 111, 112, 113, 223

Wilmer, Cutler & Pickering, 243
Wilmington News-Journal, 241
Wilson, Don, 167
Wilson, Woodrow, 239
Winchell, Walter, 278
Wolper, David, 330–31
World War II, 56, 57
Wyman, Tom, 87–88

Xerox, 179, 180

Yardley, Jonathan, 298
Yetnikoff, Walter, 265

Zaleznik, Abraham, 330
Ziegfeld Theater, 198–99